SEX for SALE

A groundbreaking collection of essays on the sex industry, *Sex for Sale* contains original studies on sex work, its risks and benefits, and its political implications. The book covers areas not commonly researched, including gay and lesbian pornography, telephone sex workers, customers of prostitutes, male and female escorts who work independently, street prostitution, sex tourism, legal prostitution, and strip clubs that cater to women. The book also tracks various trends during the past decade, including the "mainstreaming" and growing acceptance of some types of sexual commerce and the growing criminalization of other types, such as sex trafficking. *Sex for Sale* offers a window into the lived experiences of sex workers as well as an analysis of the larger gender arrangements and political structures that shape the experiences of workers and their clients. The book greatly contributes to a growing research literature that documents the rich variation, nuances, and complexities in the exchange of sexual services, performances, and products. This book will change the way we understand sex work.

Ronald Weitzer is Professor of Sociology at George Washington University in Washington, DC. He has written extensively on the sex industry in the United States and abroad, and is currently writing a book on political conflicts over prostitution policies in selected nations. He is frequently contacted by the media for information and comment on issues regarding the sex industry.

Titles of Related Interest

SEX *for* SALE

PROSTITUTION, PORNOGRAPHY, AND THE SEX INDUSTRY

Second Edition

EDITED BY

RONALD WEITZER

Routledge
Taylor & Francis Group

NEW YORK AND LONDON

First published by
Routledge 2000

This edition published 2010
by Routledge
711 Third Avenue, New York, NY 10017

Simultaneously published in the UK
by Routledge
2 Park Square, Milton Park, Abingdon, Oxon OX14 4RN

Routledge is an imprint of the Taylor & Francis Group, an informa business

© 2000 Taylor & Francis
© 2010 Taylor & Francis

Typeset in Garamond Three and Akzidenz Grotesk by
Swales & Willis Ltd, Exeter, Devon

Library of Congress Cataloging-in-Publication Data
Sex for sale: prostitution, pornography, and the sex industry/Ronald Weitzer.—2nd ed.
    p. cm.
    Includes index.
    1. Prostitution.   2. Pornography.   3. Sex-oriented businesses.   I. Weitzer, Ronald
HQ115.S49 2009
306.74–dc22   2009005994

ISBN10: 0–415–99604–X (hbk)
ISBN10: 0–415–99605–8 (pbk)
ISBN10: 0–203–87280–0 (ebk)

ISBN13: 978–0–415–99604–4 (hbk)
ISBN13: 978–0–415–99605–1 (pbk)
ISBN13: 978–0–203–87280–2 (ebk)

CONTENTS

LIST OF TABLES AND FIGURES

FIGURES

TABLES

PREFACE

Like the first edition of *Sex for Sale*, this second edition breaks new ground by deepening our understanding of sex work and the sex industry. Some of the chapters are substantially revised and updated versions of chapters that appeared in the first edition, and the other chapters are entirely new to this volume. We present new data on the clients of prostitutes; a chronicle of recent trends in gay male pornography; an analysis of pornography made by and for women; chapters on telephone sex work and on the mainstream porn industry—studies that stand almost alone in research on these two topics; a comparison of strip clubs that cater to men and clubs that cater to women customers; an analysis of street prostitution in different locations in one city and a comparison of street and indoor prostitution in another city; an examination of similarities and differences between male and female escorts who work independently, with no ties to an agency or broker; an updated chapter on Nevada's legal brothels; an exploration of the "mainstreaming" of the sex industry, seen through the lens of the annual Adult Entertainment Expo in Las Vegas; a chapter on sex tourists and the workers who sell sex to them; and an examination of sex trafficking focusing on both the myths and realities of trafficking as well as public policies regarding this issue.

All of these chapters are based on carefully conducted empirical research and, taken together, they demonstrate the wide variety of sex for sale as well as differences in the structural arrangements and personal experiences of those involved in sexual commerce—the workers, customers, third parties, and businesses that differ tremendously from one context to another and make up a diverse, variegated sex industry.

The book would not have been possible without the hard work of the contributors, who graciously accommodated the demanding schedule I imposed on them and diligently addressed my suggestions regarding their chapters. I am delighted that these experts were willing to contribute to the book, helping to make this second edition as cutting edge and fascinating as the first edition.

SEX WORK:
PARADIGMS AND POLICIES

Ronald Weitzer

Sex work involves the exchange of sexual services, performances, or products for material compensation. It includes activities of direct physical contact between buyers and sellers (prostitution, lap dancing) as well as indirect sexual stimulation (pornography, stripping, telephone sex, live sex shows, erotic webcam performances). The sex industry refers to the workers, managers, owners, agencies, clubs, trade associations, and marketing involved in sexual commerce, both legal and illegal varieties.

OVERVIEW OF THE SEX INDUSTRY

Sex for sale is a lucrative growth industry. In 2006 alone, Americans spent $13.3 billion on X-rated magazines, videos and DVDs, live sex shows, strip clubs, adult cable shows, computer pornography, and commercial telephone sex.[1] Rentals and sales of X-rated films jumped from $75 million in 1985 to $957 million in 2006.[2] In just one decade, the number of X-rated films released annually more than doubled, from 5700 in 1995 to 13,588 in 2005.[3] There are around 3500 strip clubs in America, and the number has grown over the past two decades.[4] In addition to these indicators of legal commercial sex, an unknown amount is spent on prostitution.

A significant percentage of the population buys sexual services and products. In 2002, 34% of American men and 16% of women reported that

1

they had seen an X-rated video in just the past year.[5] As of 2000, 21% of the population had visited an Internet pornography site (32% of men, 11% of women).[6] The most recent figures on strip club attendance are from 1991, when 11% of the population said they had done so in the past year; fewer people (0.5%) had called a phone sex number in the past year.[7] And a significant percentage of American men have visited a prostitute. The General Social Survey reports figures on the number of men who said that they had ever paid for sex—between 15–18% in eight polls from 1991 to 2006 (in 2006, 4% said they had done so in the past year).[8] Remarkably similar figures are reported for Australia (16%) and the average within Europe (15%),[9] and 11% of British men say they have paid for sex with a prostitute.[10] Because prostitution is stigmatized, the real figures may be significantly higher. In some other societies, even more men say they have paid for sex. For example, in Spain 39% of men have done so during their lifetime, and in northeastern Thailand 43% of single men and 50% of married men had visited a prostitute.[11] An unusual question was included in a recent British survey: respondents were asked whether they would "consider having sex for money if the amount offered was enough": 18% of women said yes, as did 36% of men.[12]

A steady trend is toward the *privatization* of sexual services and products: porn has migrated from the movie house to the privacy of the viewer's house. Video, Internet, and cable TV pornography have exploded in popularity, almost totally replacing the adult theaters of decades past. The advent of the telephone sex industry and escort services also has contributed to the privatization of commercial sex. And the Internet has changed the landscape tremendously—providing a wealth of services, information, and connections for interested parties. Internet-facilitated sex work has grown as a sector of the market, while street prostitution has remained relatively stable over time, although it has declined in some areas.[13]

Despite its size, growth, and numerous customers, the sex industry is regarded by many citizens as a *deviant enterprise*: run by shady people and promoting immoral or perverted behavior. There has been some "main-streaming" of certain sectors of the sex industry (as documented in Chapter 12 by Lynn Comella), but it would be premature to conclude that sex for sale has now become normalized, as some claim. Polls show that 72% of Americans think that pornography is "an important moral issue for the country,"[14] and 61% believe that it leads to a "breakdown of morals."[15] The most recent poll (in March 2008) reported that fully half the population defined viewing porn as "sinful behavior."[16] And almost half the population thinks that pornography is "demeaning towards women" (one-quarter disagreed and the remainder were undecided).[17] When asked about the idea of "men spending an evening with a prostitute," 61% of Americans consider this morally wrong,[18] and two-thirds believe that prostitution can "never be justified," while 25% considered it "sometimes justified" and 4% "always justified."[19] (The term "justified" in this question is somewhat opaque, and we can only speculate as to what respondents have in mind when they say prostitution can "sometimes be justified.") Two-thirds of the British population believe that "paying for sex exploits women," and young people are even more likely to hold this opinion: 80% of those aged 18–24.[20]

Regarding public policies, most Americans favor either more controls or a total ban on certain types of commercial sex. More than three-quarters (77%) of the public think that we need "stricter laws" to control pornography in books and movies,[21] and half believe that pornography is "out of control and should be further restricted."[22] In 2006, two-fifths of Americans (39%) felt that pornography should be banned, and this figure has remained about the same for two decades (41% held this view in 1984).[23] A huge majority of women (70%) want porn outlawed today, compared to 30% of men.[24] Stripping and telephone sex work also carry substantial stigma. Almost half of the American public believes that strip clubs should be illegal, while an even higher number (76%) thought telephone numbers offering sex talk should be illegal.[25] Despite these personal opinions, people seem to think that the country is headed in the direction of increasing tolerance. There are no national polls on this question, but a 2002 survey of Alabama residents found that 73% believed that "society as a whole" sees stripping as an occupation for women to be "more acceptable today than ten years ago."[26] Many Alabama residents are dissatisfied with this trend, however. In the same poll, 54% felt that "stripping as an occupation is degrading or demeaning to the women," and only 24% thought that it was not, with the remainder undecided.

What we have, therefore, is a paradox: a lucrative industry that employs a significant number of workers and attracts many customers but is regarded by many people as deviant and in need of stricter control, if not banned outright. The sex industry continues to be stigmatized, even when it is legal.

COMPETING PARADIGMS

When I mentioned the topic of prostitution to a friend recently, he said, "How disgusting! How could anybody sell themselves?" A few weeks later an acquaintance told me that she thought prostitution was a "woman's choice, and can be empowering." These opposing views reflect larger cultural perceptions of prostitution, as well as much popular writing on the topic.

Many people are fascinated, entertained, or titillated by sex work; many others see it as degrading, immoral, sexist, or harmful; and yet others hold *all* these views. Indeed, some prominent people have simultaneously condemned and patronized the sex industry, and have been caught in hypocritical behavior:

■ Gov. Eliot Spitzer (D-NY) prosecuted prostitution rings when he served as the state's Attorney-General, but resigned the governorship in disgrace after it was revealed in March 2008 that he had spent $4300 on an escort employed by the exclusive Emperor's Club agency. Shortly thereafter, it was reported that he had also been a client of another escort agency, Wicked Models. Prosecutors later determined that Spitzer had paid for sex "on multiple occasions," yet they declined to press criminal charges against him.[27]

■ In 2007, Senator David Vitter (R-La) was linked to a Washington, DC, escort agency. He refused to relinquish his Senate seat, but nevertheless issued a public apology: "This was a very serious sin in my past for which I am, of course, completely responsible." He was also accused of repeatedly visiting a New Orleans brothel in the late 1990s, according to both the madam and one of the prostitutes. Vitter is well known for his conservative, "family values" positions.

■ In 2006, the president of the National Association of Evangelicals, Rev. Ted Haggard, resigned after revelations that he had frequently paid for sex with a male prostitute and had used methamphetamine with him. The Association claims to represent 30 million evangelical Christians in the United States.

■ In 1988, a prominent television evangelist, Rev. Jimmy Swaggart, resigned his church leadership after photos were released of him with a call girl in a New Orleans hotel (she later appeared on the cover of *Penthouse* magazine). He continued his television ministry. Three years later, when stopped by a police officer in California for a traffic violation, a prostitute in his car told the officer that Swaggart had propositioned her for sex.

■ In Britain, Anthony Lambton, the Under-Secretary for Defense, resigned in May 1973 after being photographed in bed with a call girl. A few days later, another Cabinet member and the leader of the House of Lords, George Jellicoe, resigned after confessing his own liaisons with call girls, what he called "casual affairs." Jellicoe had been in Parliament for 68 years, and he and Lambton were members of the Conservative Party.

■ Another member of the British Parliament, Mark Oaten, resigned in 2006 after it was reported that he had a year-long relationship with a male prostitute.

These are just a few of the many examples of public figures who have purchased sex illicitly. And, in addition to political and religious elites, the clients include officials in the criminal justice system, with police chiefs and prosecutors sometimes caught buying sex even as they are obligated to enforce the laws against prostitution.[28]

The poles of condemnation and normalization are reflected in two paradigms in the social sciences.[29] One of these, the *oppression paradigm*, holds that sex work is a quintessential expression of patriarchal gender relations and male domination. The most prominent advocates of this position go further, claiming that exploitation, subjugation, and violence against women are intrinsic to and ineradicable from sex work—transcending historical time period, national context, and type of sexual commerce.[30] These indictments apply equally to pornography, prostitution, stripping, and other commercial sex. The only solution is elimination of the entire sex industry, which is precisely the goal of those who adopt the oppression paradigm.

In addition to these essentialist claims, some writers make generalizations about specific aspects of sex work: that *most or all* sex workers were physically or sexually abused as children; entered the trade as adolescents, around 13–14 years of age; were tricked or forced into the trade by pimps or traffickers; use or are addicted to drugs; experience routine violence from customers; labor under abysmal working conditions; and desperately want to exit the sex trade.[31] These writers often use dramatic language to highlight the plight of workers ("sexual slavery," "prostituted women," "paid rape," "survivors"). "Prostituted" clearly indicates that prostitution is something done to women, not something that can be chosen, and "survivor" implies someone who has escaped a harrowing ordeal. Customers are labeled as "prostitute users," "batterers," and "sexual predators." As shown later, these labels are misnomers when applied to most customers and most sex workers.

Violating a core canon of scientific research, the oppression paradigm describes *only* the worst examples of sex work and then treats them as representative. Anecdotes are generalized and presented as conclusive evidence, sampling is selective, and counterevidence is routinely ignored. Such "research" cannot help but produce tainted findings and spurious conclusions, and this entire body of work has been severely criticized.[32] Unfortunately, the writings of oppression theorists are increasingly mirrored in media reports and in government policies in the United States and abroad.

A diametrically opposed perspective is the *empowerment paradigm*. The focus is on the ways in which sexual services qualify as work, involve human agency, and may be potentially validating or empowering for workers.[33] This paradigm holds that there is nothing inherent in sex work that would prevent it from being organized for mutual gain to all parties—just as in other economic transactions. In other words, coercion and other unseemly practices are not viewed as intrinsic aspects of sex work. Analysts who adopt this perspective tend to accent the routine aspects of sex work, often drawing parallels to kindred types of service work (physical therapy, massage, psychotherapy) or otherwise normalizing sex for sale. Eileen McLeod argues that prostitution is quite similar to other "women's work," and that both sex workers and other women "barter sex for goods," although the latter do so less conspicuously.[34] Writers who adopt the empowerment perspective also argue that the tenets of the oppression paradigm reflect the way in which *some* sex work manifests itself when it is *criminalized*. Much less is known about prostitution in legal, regulated systems. It is important, therefore, to avoid essentialist conclusions based on only one mode of production.

This kind of work may enhance a person's socioeconomic status and provide greater control over one's working conditions than many traditional jobs. It may have other benefits as well: "Many prostitutes emphasize that they engage in sex work not simply out of economic need but out of satisfaction with the control it gives them over their sexual interactions."[35] Some writers who adopt the empowerment paradigm go further and make bold claims that romanticize sex work. Shannon Bell describes her book, *Whore Carnival*, as "a recognition and commendation of the sexual and political power and knowledge of prostitutes," which sounds rather celebratory.

Both the oppression and empowerment perspectives are one-dimensional and essentialist. While exploitation and empowerment are certainly present in sex work, there is sufficient variation across time, place, and sector to demonstrate that sex work cannot be reduced to one or the other. An alternative perspective, what I call the *polymorphous paradigm*, holds that there is a constellation of occupational arrangements, power relations, and worker experiences. Unlike the other two perspectives, polymorphism is sensitive to complexities and to the structural conditions shaping the uneven distribution of agency, subordination, and workers' control.[36] Within academia, a growing number of scholars are researching various dimensions of the work, in different contexts, and their studies document *substantial variation* in how sex work is organized and experienced by workers, clients, and managers. Together, these studies undermine some deep-rooted myths about prostitution and present a challenge to those writers and activists who embrace monolithic paradigms. Victimization, exploitation, choice, job satisfaction, self-esteem, and other dimensions should be treated as *variables* (not constants) that differ between types of sex work, geographical locations, and other structural and organizational conditions. The chapters in *Sex for Sale* provide additional evidence in support of the polymorphous paradigm.

TYPES OF SEX WORK

A brief discussion of different types of sex work will illustrate the polymorphous approach.

Prostitution

Prostitutes vary tremendously in their reasons for entry, risk of violence, freedom to refuse clients and particular sex acts, dependence on and exploitation by third parties, experiences with the authorities, public visibility, number and type of clients, relationships with coworkers, and impact on the surrounding community. Table 1.1 presents a typology of prostitution. (Excluded from the table are borderline cases, such as lap dancing, "kept" women or men, geishas, etc.)

Before proceeding to a description of the different types of prostitution, it is important to note that individual workers may cross one or more categories. For instance, independent call girls may also accept regular or occasional appointments from an escort agency, and massage parlor or brothel workers sometimes moonlight by meeting customers in private and keeping the earnings for themselves. It is rare, however, for workers to experience substantial upward or downward mobility. As a general rule "the level at which the woman begins work in the prostitution world determines her general position in the occupation for much of her career as a prostitute. Changing levels requires contacts and a new set of work techniques and attitudes."[37] Occasionally, an upper or middle-tier worker whose life situation changes (e.g., because of aging, drug addiction) is no longer able to work in that stratum and gravitates to the street. But transitioning from street work to the escort or call girl echelon is quite rare, because most street workers lack the education and skill set required for upscale indoor work. Likewise, very few call girls and brothel workers have previously worked on the streets. If a move takes place, it is usually lateral and of limited mobility, such as from the streets to a down-market peep show or from a massage parlor to an escort agency or from an escort agency to independent work.

The most consequential division in Table 1.1 is that between street prostitution and the various indoor types. In street prostitution, the initial transaction occurs in a public place (a sidewalk, park, truck stop), while the

TABLE 1.1 CHARACTERISTICS OF TYPES OF PROSTITUTION

	BUSINESS LOCATION	PRICES CHARGED	EXPLOITATION BY THIRD PARTIES	RISK OF VIOLENT VICTIMIZATION	PUBLIC VISIBILITY	IMPACT ON COMMUNITY
CALL GIRL	Independent operator; private premises/hotels	High	Low to none	Low	None	None
ESCORT	Escort agency; private premises/hotels	High	Moderate	Low to moderate	Very low	None
BROTHEL WORKER	Brothel	Moderate	Moderate	Very low	Low	None, if discreet
MASSAGE PARLOR WORKER	Massage parlor	Moderate	Moderate	Very low	Low	Little, if discreet
BAR OR CASINO WORKER	Bar/casino contact; sex elsewhere	Low to moderate	Low to moderate	Low to moderate	Moderate	Equivalent to impact of bar/casino
STREETWALKER	Street contact; sex in cars, alleys, parks, etc.	Low	High	Very high	High	Adverse

Note: Table refers to female workers. The brothel and massage parlor workers depicted here do not include those who have been trafficked against their will or otherwise forced into prostitution, whose experiences differ from those who have entered this work consensually.
Exploitation by third parties means third party receipt of at least some of the profits.
Risk of violent victimization refers here to victimization of prostitute, not of customer.
Impact on community refers to effects on the surrounding neighborhood's quality of life.

sex act takes place in either a public or private setting (alley, park, vehicle, hotel, etc.). Many street prostitutes are runaways who end up in a new locale with no resources and little recourse but to engage in some kind of criminal activity—whether theft, drug dealing, or selling sex. Many street workers, both runaways and others, experience abysmal working conditions and are involved in "survival sex." They sell sex out of dire necessity or to support a drug habit. Many use addictive drugs; work and live in crime-ridden areas; are socially isolated and disconnected from support services; risk contracting and transmitting sexual diseases; are exploited and abused by pimps; and are vulnerable to being assaulted, robbed, raped, or killed on the streets. This is the population best characterized by the oppression paradigm. Other street prostitutes, especially those free of drugs and pimps, are in less desperate straits but still confront a range of occupational hazards. Judith Porter and Louis Bonilla's chapter in this volume (Chapter 7) offers a close look at street prostitution and documents differences between three prostitution zones in Philadelphia.

When most people think of prostitution, they are thinking of street prostitution, but off-street sexual transactions are just as important and, in many countries, far more common than street work even though we lack data on the exact numbers in each sphere. (In Thailand, for example, an estimated 0.7% of prostitutes work the streets, while the figures for the United States, Holland, and Britain are reportedly closer to 20%.)[38] We do know that ads for escort agencies and for independent call girls on the Internet are abundant and ever increasing.

Indoor prostitution takes place in brothels, massage parlors, bars, hotels, and private premises. Compared to street prostitutes, indoor workers are much less likely to have a background of childhood abuse (neglect, violence, incest), to enter sex work at a young age, to engage in risky behavior (e.g., to use addictive drugs and to engage in unprotected sex), and to be victimized by others. Off-street workers who have not been coerced into prostitution are much less likely to experience assault, robbery, and rape. A British study of 115 prostitutes who worked on the streets and 125 who worked in saunas or as call girls found that the street prostitutes were much more likely than the indoor workers to report that they had ever been robbed (37 vs. 10%), beaten (27 vs. 1%), slapped/punched/kicked (47 vs. 14%), raped (22 vs. 2%), threatened with a weapon (24 vs. 6%), or kidnapped (20 vs. 2%).[39] Other studies similarly find disparities in victimization between street and off-street workers, with some reporting high percentages of indoor providers who have never experienced violence on the job.[40] Although random sampling was not possible in these studies, the fact that they consistently document significant street–indoor differences lends credence to the general conclusion. In addition to differences in *ever* being victimized, street workers are more likely to experience *more frequent* and *more severe* victimization.

This does not mean that indoor work is risk free: structural conditions are a key predictor of vulnerability—conditions that include workers' immigration status, drug dependency, third-party involvement (as protectors vs. exploiters), etc. Moreover, indoor work in the Third World usually exists under harsher conditions than in developed countries, even when it is legal.[41] Having said that, there is no doubt that indoor settings are generally safer than the streets. Overall, "street workers are significantly more at risk of more violence and more serious violence than indoor workers."[42] Moreover, it appears that legal context makes a difference: that is, the safety of indoor work increases where prostitution is legal (see later).

Those who work collectively indoors—in brothels, massage parlors, saunas, clubs—have the advantage of the presence of gatekeepers and coworkers, who can intervene in the event of an unruly customer. Indoor venues often have some screening mechanisms, video surveillance, and alarm systems. Call girls and escorts are more vulnerable given their isolation when doing outcalls at hotels or clients' residences. But they also have a greater proportion of low-risk, regular clients (see Chapter 8, by Janet Lever and Deanne Dolnick) and they have their own methods of vetting potentially dangerous customers (though these methods are not foolproof). They share with other workers stories of bad clients who are then blacklisted, and they routinely check in by phone with the agency or a friend at a designated time before and after a visit. As one agency booker stated: "The girls call to check in when they first get to an appointment. We had code words, like 'Red Bull.' If I heard her say she needed a Red Bull, I'd try to distract the guy on the phone so she could get out of there."[43] The autobiography of former prostitute Dolores French describes her unique ways of alerting her agent (Sarah) that she was in danger in a man's hotel room:

> Sarah told me certain code names that were to be used for cops and crazies. . . . "Judy" meant a cop; "Phyllis" meant a crazy . . ... So I called Sarah and said: "Everything is fine here. By the way, has *Judy* been in the office lately? Well, if *Judy* comes by, tell her I'd like to meet her for coffee." [Sarah said] "Did he ask you to have sex?" "Oh yes, he's lots of fun." Any positive answer I gave meant yes, any negative answer . . . meant no. It was amazing how wonderfully this all worked. As soon as Sarah understood there was danger, she was on full alert . . . She knew I was in a bad situation, and she knew it was up to her to help get me out of it.[44]

Such providers learn ways of screening their clients before they meet as well. A study of independent call girls noted that they develop "a sensitivity to detecting potential danger in the caller's attitudes, manners, tone of voice, or nature of the conversation."[45]

It is not widely known that indoor and street prostitutes differ in the services they provide. Because street workers spend little time with customers, their social interaction is fleeting. As one street worker remarked, "Usually, they're not even interested in talking to you. What they want is quick sex."[46] Indoor interactions are typically longer, multifaceted, and more reciprocal. Diana Prince, who interviewed 75 call girls in California and 150 brothel workers in Nevada, found that most of them believed that "the average customer wants affection or love as well as sex."[47] Consequently, indoor workers are much more likely to counsel and befriend clients, and their encounters often include a semblance of romance, dating, friendship, or companionship—what has become known as a "girlfriend experience" and the counterpart "boyfriend experience" offered by male escorts (see Chapters 8 and 9). As one study of call girls discovered, "for many men, sex is the pretext for the visit, and the real need is emotional."[48] Indeed, escort agencies and independent call girls increasingly advertise their expertise in providing non-sexual benefits to clients. The Emperor's Club escort agency, for instance, billed itself (on its website) as offering an experience that would make life "more peaceful, balanced, beautiful, and meaningful." In a sense, the customer buys a kind of "relationship" with an escort rather than just sex. Some customers who become "regulars" have long-term relationships with providers and develop a real emotional connection, albeit one that is paid for.[49]

The nature of physical contact also differs, in the sense that it is more varied and more "romantic" than what a client and provider experience on the street. Indoor workers are more likely than street workers to be caressed, kissed, massaged, or hugged by, and to receive oral sex or manual stimulation from, a client (see Chapter 8).[50] Indeed, in at least some indoor venues, the workers *expect and request* such sensual and sexual behavior from clients as a routine part of the encounter.

Indoor workers tend to be more adjusted and satisfied with their work than street workers, and the former differ little from non-prostitutes in mental health and self-esteem. The stress and danger associated with street work contribute to psychological problems. By contrast, escorts and call girls tend to have the "financial, social, and emotional wherewithal to structure their work largely in ways that suited them and provided . . . the ability to main-tain healthy self-images."[51] Although call girls generally express greater job satisfaction than do those employed by third parties (brothels, massage parlors, escort agencies) and are subject to employer demands, the latter are nevertheless more satisfied than street workers. An Australian study found that half of call girls and brothel workers felt that their work was a "major source of satisfaction" in their lives, while seven out of 10 said they would "definitely choose" this work if they had it to do over again.[52] And a worker in one of Nevada's legal brothels remarked: "I've always been a sexual person. I enjoy doing it. I mean, the money's wonderful but, hey, I enjoy what I do for a living too. I love the people, it's safe, it's clean."[53] A majority of indoor workers in other studies similarly report that they enjoy the job, feel that their work has at least some positive effect on their lives, or believe that they provide a valuable service.[54]

Prince's comparative study of streetwalkers and call girls in California and legal brothel workers in Nevada found that almost all of the call girls (97%) reported an *increase* in self-esteem after they began working in prostitution, compared with 50% of the brothel workers but only 8% of the streetwalkers.[55] Similarly, a study of indoor prostitutes (most of whom worked in bars) in a Midwestern city in the United States found that three-fourths of them felt that their life had *improved* after entering prostitution (the remainder reported no change; none said it was worse than before); more than half said that they generally enjoy their work.[56]

Why would self-esteem be high or increase among those working in the upper echelons? Psychological well-being is associated with a range of structural factors, including education, income, control over working conditions, relations with third parties, and client base. Income is a major source of self-esteem among call girls. While middle range call girls earn $200–$500 an hour, top-tier workers charge between $1000–$6000 an hour (or a session) and they are also lavished with fringe benefits, such as expensive gifts and paid travel to meet clients.[57] Escort agency, brothel, and massage parlor employees make considerably less because a large share (30–50%) goes to the agency. Another reason for an increase in job satisfaction is revealed by indoor workers who describe "feeling 'sexy,' 'beautiful,' and 'powerful' only after they had begun to engage in sexual labor and were receiving consistent praise from their clients."[58] In other words, in addition to the material rewards of high-end sex work, positive reinforcement and other good experiences may help enhance workers' self-images.

At the same time, prostitutes of all types experience stigma from the wider society, as shown by opinion polls and by public condemnation during sex scandals involving public figures. This disapproval compels sex workers to engage in various normalization strategies, including: compartmentalizing their deviant work persona from their "real identity"; concealing their work from family and friends; distancing themselves from clients; using neutral or professional terms to describe their jobs ("working woman," "provider"); and viewing their work as a valuable service (providing pleasure or sex therapy, comforting lonely men, keeping marriages intact).

The studies reviewed here and by other scholars provide strong evidence contradicting some popular myths and the central tenets of the oppression paradigm.[59] While certain experiences are generic to prostitution (coping with stigma, managing client behavior, avoiding risks), the literature indicates that other work-related experiences, as well as the harms typically associated with prostitution, vary greatly. The prostitution market is *segmented* between the indoor and street sectors—marked by major differences in working conditions, risk of victimization, and job satisfaction and self-esteem.

Other Types of Sex Work

Some sex workers specialize in one type of work, but others transition between different sectors or work in two arenas simultaneously. Examples include strippers who meet clients outside the club for sex; porn stars who tour strip clubs where they are the "featured" entertainer and command much higher prices than local talent; dancers and porn stars, male and female, who advertise online for personal sexual encounters with their fans; and, as mentioned earlier, prostitutes who work in more than one venue.

The variation characteristic of prostitution is no less true in other types of sex work. Strip clubs and their dancers have been studied fairly thoroughly, largely because of easy access to the clubs.[60] One finding is that club structure and norms are a strong predictor of workers' job satisfaction and experiences with both customers and managers, with some clubs being highly exploitative and disempowering for dancers and others affording them substantial control over their working conditions. In other words, the social organization of a club shapes the degree to which workers are exploited by managers, DJs, bartenders, and bouncers, as well as the routine experiences they have with customers. One study distinguished three types of clubs—"hustle clubs" where dancers get little protection from management and have fairly stressful relations with other dancers (because of intense competition) and with customers (because managers instructed dancers to mislead and "hustle" the men to extract money from them); "social clubs" that resemble the sociability of neighborhood bars and are marked by supportive relationships between the workers and friendships with many of the patrons; and "show clubs" that are more upscale, highly regulated by management, where a premium is placed on putting on a "good show," and where dancers are taught to personify a "goddess" seeking adoration from and exercising power over male customers.[61]

Clubs vary in the amount of customer violations of dancers' personal boundaries (such as uninvited touching and kissing, pulling off clothes), insults, and rejection. Over time, the accumulation of such experiences can deflate one's self-esteem and result in job burnout.[62] On the positive side, many dancers find the work exciting, validating, empowering, and lucrative. Customers may lavish them with compliments, tips, and gifts, and dancers develop a genuine liking for at least some of their regulars.[63] In terms of empowerment, one study reported that dancers "derive a sense of satisfaction at the power they felt they had over men" including manipulating men's fantasies and the "thrill of the chase" in the pursuit of money when they engage in "strategic flirting" and perhaps lap dancing with individual audience members.[64] At the same time, and like other sex workers, dancers often attempt to normalize their work by trumpeting stripping's "therapeutic" and "educational" effects on the audience.[65]

Few studies compare male and female strip clubs, but those that do suggest that female audiences tend to be more aggressive toward male dancers than male audiences in female strip clubs,[66] and that female patrons attended clubs in groups as a bonding ritual or as part of a celebratory gathering, whereas male patrons are more likely to seek an individualized experience and are much more likely to be repeat customers.[67] It also appears that male strippers experience less stigma than their female counterparts.[68] Relations between customers and dancers in same-sex clubs have their own distinctive patterns, as indicated by a study of gay male clubs[69] and by Katherine Frank and Michelle Carnes (Chapter 5) in their analysis of clubs featuring African-American female dancers and customers, where the atmosphere is one not only of sexual performance but also cultural bonding between the black women involved. Of course, in both gay and straight clubs alike, power struggles over personal boundaries are evident.[70]

Much of the literature on pornography is psychological, confined to laboratory experiments in which (usually male) subjects are exposed to images and then tested to see if exposure affects their attitudes toward women. Most of these studies find that the key variable is violent content, not sexual content, in increasing the viewer's negative views of or aggressive disposition toward women. Nonviolent pornography, like other nonviolent images, either does not have such effects on viewers or has a weaker effect—depending on the study.[71] The main pitfall of such experimental studies is their problematic external validity—that is, whether the findings in a lab are meaningful and can be extrapolated to the real world. Laboratory experiments are highly artificial conditions within which to watch and react to pornography; they are radically different from the private settings where viewers typically view porn; and the experimental subjects are typically male college students who may be unrepresentative of the larger population of real-life porn consumers. In light of these serious problems, it is surprising that so many lab experiments on pornography have been conducted.

Parallel studies examine whether pornography has effects on the real-world treatment of women. Such research examines (1) whether places with high availability of pornography (magazines, adult theaters, video rentals) have higher rates of sex crime than places where pornography is less available or (2) whether increased availability over time in one state or nation increases rates of sexual offenses. A comprehensive review of the literature concluded that macro-level associations between pornography and sexual aggression were dubious:

- These studies are bedeviled by their inability to control for all potentially relevant influences on male behavior.
- Some studies find that an apparent correlation between pornography and sex crime disappears after other variables are included in the model.
- Other studies report that increased availability of pornography coincided with a *decline* in sexual offenses, precisely the opposite of what the oppression hypothesis predicts. And some countries with an abundance of porn, such as Japan, have low rates of victimization of women.[72]

Part of the explanation for these findings may be the fact that most pornography in videos and magazines is nonviolent, as documented in several content analyses.[73] One study found that the most sexually explicit or hardcore videos contained the least violence and the most reciprocal, egalitarian behavior between the actors.[74] If violence is rare in porn, it is unlikely to promote sexual violence: "In the absence of any actual element of coercion, viewers would not have any messages about sexual coercion to process and would not be expected to change any of their attitudes in this area."[75]

The abundance of narrow, statistical "effects" studies skews the literature in one direction. Few researchers have investigated the deeper meanings of pornography in the real world—to men and women, consumers and nonconsumers. The neglect of actual consumers (as opposed to lab subjects) is remarkable in light of the sweeping claims that are often made about pornography's impact on viewers. Still, a handful of studies have shown that both men and women decode and use sexually explicit materials in a wide variety of ways. Some women dislike the portrayal of women's bodies in porn and fear that men might compare them unfavorably to porn models,[76] whereas other women find pornography to be educational, entertaining, or stimulating.[77] Some women who have little familiarity with pornography nevertheless hold very negative views of it.[78] Likewise, men interpret porn in multiple ways: exposure reinforces callous or sexist views of women for some men, while others interpret it quite differently. A study of 150 men by David Loftus found that most of them experienced porn as being about fun, beauty, women's pleasure, and female assertiveness and power. They did not like depictions of domination or aggression against women on "the rare occasions they see it in pornography, and most haven't even seen any."[79] It is "important to male viewers that the women really do seem to be enjoying themselves, that they are utterly involved in the sex for their own pleasure too, and not just serving the interests of the male actors and onlookers."[80] They also recognized porn as a fantasy world quite different from the real world in terms of people's behavior and appearance.[81] Men with this orientation, who distinguish the fantasy world of porn from the real world, seem to contradict some popular assumptions about such men as well as laboratory studies that hypothesize a unilinear, stimulus–response pattern when one is exposed to pornography.

Surprisingly, in-depth research on the porn industry and its workers is almost nonexistent. This gap is partly filled by two unique chapters in this book, both of which go behind the scenes with ethnographic studies of actors and producers. Sharon Abbott (Chapter 2) interviewed male and female actors in heterosexual films, documenting both positive and negative aspects of their work experiences, their views of their work and their audiences, and how they manage stigma. Jill Bakehorn (Chapter 4) had inside access to another sector of the industry—pornography made by women for women. She finds that female producers are often motivated by loftier goals than their counterparts in the mainstream porn industry. Instead of just seeking to make money, many of these female artists are motivated by feminist objectives, sex worker activism, and a desire to create materials that are an alternative to conventional representations of heterosexual sexual relations. This sector of the industry is ignored by writers who view pornography as inherently objectifying and demeaning toward women, and Bakehorn shows how this genre challenges simplistic and monolithic characterizations of pornography.

Studies of male sex workers are growing, but much more research is needed.[82] These studies point to some important differences in the ways male and female sex workers experience their work, but few of these studies are truly comparative—examining male and female workers in the same work tier and asking them identical questions. Juline Koken, David Bimbi, and Jeffrey Parsons' study (Chapter 9) helps to fill this gap. Not only does it compare male and female workers but it also sheds additional light on the work experiences of independent escorts. Similarly, little is known about gay male pornography.[83] Joe Thomas (Chapter 3) examines how gay male video porn has changed over time. Thomas also draws contrasts between gay male and straight pornography, specifically the radically different meanings of porn in gay and straight cultures. Pornography holds a fair amount of *esteem* within the gay community, but carries substantial *stigma* in the straight world.

Finally, little is known about telephone sex agencies and their employees.[84] Kathleen Guidroz and Grant Rich (Chapter 6) show that telephone sex workers hold a mix of negative and positive impressions of their work. They are troubled by callers who appear to be misogynists or pedophiles but they also feel that the calls can be therapeutic, as in other lines of sex work. The operators believe that they educate male callers about female sexuality and that they help to deter those with perverse or violent tastes from acting on those fantasies; the workers see this as providing a valuable "community service."

POLICIES AND CONFLICTS

Strip Clubs and Pornography

Strip clubs and adult video stores are governed by local ordinances in America, which means that what is permitted varies from jurisdiction to jurisdiction and over time. Some places have ordinances restricting the location of such establishments, stipulating where videos can be displayed in a store, or regulating strippers' attire and contact with customers. Many cities and counties restrict sexually oriented businesses to nonresidential areas or prohibit them from being near schools, parks, churches, and residences.

Such curbs do not satisfy those who want such establishments totally banned. Local-level struggles occur periodically throughout the country. Tactics include picketing outside an adult business, lobbying municipal officials, petition drives, and videotaping customers entering clubs and stores. Such efforts can pay off in convincing local officials to impose stringent controls on adult entertainment venues. In addition to instrumental efforts to change policy, groups use symbolic tactics as well: an Indiana group, for example, recently erected a billboard with a red slash through a triple-X symbol next to a picture of a young woman. The caption read: "Someone's Daughter"—an attempt to personalize the threat posed by porn.[85]

It is often claimed that adult stores and strip clubs have negative "secondary effects" on surrounding communities, such as increased crime. This argument was used successfully in the 1990s in New York City to justify the closure of many establishments in the Times Square area. A detailed discussion of the evidence supporting or contradicting the alleged adverse secondary effects is not possible here, but research studies give little credence to this claim. In fact: "Those studies that are scientifically credible demonstrate either no negative secondary effects associated with adult businesses or a reversal of the presumed negative effect."[86] The most sophisticated study found that crime was much more prevalent in the immediate vicinity of bars and gas stations than in the area near strip clubs, partly because of the security measures (bouncers, video surveillance) implemented by strip clubs.[87]

Pornography is legal in America as long as it does not depict minors and is not obscene. The prevailing test of obscenity remains the Supreme Court's landmark 1973 *Miller v. California* decision, which held that local "community standards" are to govern definitions of what constitutes obscene materials. Local prosecutors decide whether to prosecute a producer or distributor for a particular sexually explicit film, magazine, or other work; if prosecuted, the item is presented to a jury that decides whether it is obscene. *Miller* stipulated that the obscenity test would be whether the average person in a community would find that the work appeals to "prurient interests," depicts sexual conduct in a "patently offensive way," and lacks literary, artistic, political, or scientific value.[88] The community standards rule means that a work that is considered obscene in one jurisdiction may not be deemed obscene in another place. The only national standard on obscenity is the blanket prohibition on producing, possessing, or distributing child pornography.

Antipornography campaigns have been launched at various points in American history, with mixed success. In the early 1980s, activists Andrea Dworkin and Catherine MacKinnon succeeded in getting the city councils of Minneapolis and Indianapolis to approve far reaching antiporn ordinances. The laws allowed any woman "as a woman acting against the subordination of women" to initiate a lawsuit or file a complaint against anyone involved the production, exhibition, sale, or distribution of pornography. The individual would not need to demonstrate direct harm to oneself or others from pornography; instead, the claimant could simply act on behalf of women. The ordinances defined pornography vaguely as "the sexually explicit subordination of women, graphically depicted."[89] To be actionable, the work would have to include one of nine features, including images of women "presented dehumanized as sexual objects," women "presented as whores by nature," or women "presented in scenarios of degradation."[90] The terms "dehumanized," "objects," "whores by nature," and "degradation" are extremely elastic, and some people see all pornography in these ways. In Minneapolis, the proposed ordinance was vetoed by the mayor but the Indianapolis ordinance became law only to be overturned in the courts on the grounds that it would prohibit a range of materials that were legal under *Miller*.[91]

These municipal campaigns were followed by the equally controversial 1986 national commission appointed by Attorney-General Edwin Meese. The commission distinguished itself with its politically stacked membership, unfair procedures, and neglect of evidence running counter to its agenda.[92] Almost all of the material presented in support of a government crackdown on porn was anecdotal, based on the testimony of self-described victims recruited to appear before the panel.[93] It was therefore no surprise that the commission concluded that exposure to pornography contributed to sex crimes and other abuses of women.

The Meese Commission marked a turning point in the government's approach to pornography and demonstrated how quickly official policy and enforcement practices can change in the field of sex work. The U.S. Justice Department formally accepted the commission's recommendations and produced a report outlining steps the department was taking to implement them.[94] With a new Obscenity Enforcement Unit and its "Project Postporn," the Justice Department assumed a leading role in the campaign against the industry. Drastic changes were envisioned, as the new unit proclaimed: "Only by removing whole businesses from society . . . will significant progress be made against the existing industry."[95] The unit used antiracketeering (RICO) forfeiture laws to close adult book and video stores and relied on the novel tactic of simultaneous, multidistrict prosecutions of pornography distributors in order to bankrupt and close these businesses. Under this innovative strategy, a company was charged with violations of federal criminal law in several states at the same time. The goal was to force a company out of business under the weight of logistical demands and legal costs incurred in fighting numerous court cases in various jurisdictions. The targets were not confined to child pornography or extreme porn (e.g., featuring bestiality or simulated rape scenes) but included mainstream porn as well.[96] Prosecutors in the obscenity unit typically included Utah as one of the jurisdictions for multiple prosecutions, because its archconservative climate virtually guaranteed a conviction.

Enforcement against the pornography industry increased dramatically after the publication of the Meese report.[97] Whereas only 100 individuals had been prosecuted for violations of obscenity statutes between 1978 and 1986, the number of indictments quadrupled between 1987 and 1991. A top official in the obscenity unit revealed, "From 1988 to 1995, we [the Justice Department] got 130 convictions, took in $25 million in fines and forfeiture, and convicted most of the kingpins of the pornography industry at least once."[98] Meanwhile, several federal courts denounced the multidistrict prosecution strategy as a form of harassment.

The Clinton administration discontinued the policy of multidistrict prosecutions,[99] and it changed the obscenity unit's focus toward child pornography, renaming it the Child Exploitation and Obscenity Unit (CEOS). But, in a return to the past, the second Bush administration launched a new effort against adult pornography. It expanded and allocated additional resources to CEOS.[100] The Washington office of CEOS includes a team of specialists assigned to the daily task of searching the Internet for pornography, tracing the producers, and pursing tips sent in by citizens.[101]

In May 2005, Attorney-General Alberto Gonzales created a new office, the Obscenity Prosecution Taskforce, dedicated solely to the investigation and prosecution of hardcore pornography distributors.[102] The taskforce's agents work with the 93 local U.S. attorneys to prosecute obscenity crimes under the federal statutes that ban the transfer of obscene materials through the mail, via computer services, or through any other means of interstate or foreign commerce.

Some leading officials from the Reagan years have been reappointed to the department's obscenity unit, including the head of the unit, Brent Ward. As U.S. Attorney in Utah during the Reagan administration, Ward vigorously prosecuted distributors of video pornography, attempted to impose greater controls on strip clubs, prosecuted a phone sex company, and closed Utah's two remaining adult theaters.[103] Another major figure is Bruce Taylor, who served in the Justice Department's obscenity unit in the Reagan years, was legal counsel for the nation's premier antipornography group (Citizens for Decency through Law, founded in 1956), and served as president of another antiporn group (the National Law Center for Children and Families). He is now the obscenity unit's senior legal counsel.[104] Since he has been such a major player in the antiporn crusade, both as Justice Department official during two administrations and as an activist, Taylor's views on pornography are especially noteworthy:

> I still believe that pornography has a bad effect on society and on families, and it's not a good thing for guys to look at. It's like the training manual for how guys get to be chauvinist jerks. I mean, you don't treat a woman well if you treat her like she's treated in a porn movie. It's not the kind of thing you want your boy to be looking at or that the guy who comes to date your daughter is looking at. You don't want your husband looking at it. You don't want your boyfriend looking at it. You don't really want your wife looking at it.[105]

Taylor has a rather expansive definition of obscenity, which may be much broader than what some community standards would define as obscene. For Taylor, all depictions of penetration are by definition obscene, which means that "just about everything on the Internet and almost everything in the video stores and everything in the adult bookstores is still prosecutable [as] illegal obscenity."[106]

The continuing debate over pornography illustrates the twin trends regarding the sex industry in America. As noted earlier in the chapter, there is evidence of a degree of normalization or mainstreaming of sexual commerce and its growing availability via the Internet. At the same time, this trend runs up against a countertrend fueled by some powerful forces inside and outside local and federal governments—forces intent on criminalizing and stigmatizing the sex industry. The notion of a fierce "sex war" remains as apt today as it was in the past, and these two trends are apparent both in the U.S. and internationally.

Prostitution: Decriminalization and Legalization

Prostitution is treated in a more uniform manner in the United States, with *criminalization* being the reigning policy. This means that solicitation to engage in an act of prostitution is illegal, except in certain counties in Nevada, where about 30 legal brothels exist. Other offenses include pimping, pandering, trafficking, operating a brothel, and running an agency that offers sexual services.

Approximately 80,000 arrests are made in the United States every year for violation of prostitution laws,[107] in addition to an unknown number of arrests of prostitutes under disorderly conduct or loitering statutes. Most arrests involve the street trade, although indoor workers are targeted in some cities. Regarding street prostitution, arrests have the effect of either (1) *containment* within a particular area, where prostitutes are occasionally subjected to the revolving door of arrest, fines, brief jail time, and release, or (2) *displacement* to another locale where the same revolving-door dynamic recurs. Containment is the norm throughout the United States; displacement requires sustained police crackdowns, which are rare. During crackdowns, workers may simply relocate to an adjoining police precinct where enforcement is lax or move across the city limits into another jurisdiction.

Full decriminalization would remove all criminal penalties and leave prostitution unregulated, albeit subject to conventional norms against nuisances, sex in public, or disorderly conduct. Under full decriminalization, street prostitution could exist on any street, so long as the workers and customers did not disturb the peace or violate other ordinances. *Partial decriminalization* would reduce but not eliminate penalties—the penalty might be a fine instead of incarceration or the charge may be reduced from a felony to a misdemeanor or violation. A third possibility is *de facto decriminalization*, which simply means that the existing law is not enforced, yet the offense remains in the penal code. Decriminalization may or may not be a precursor to legalization (government regulation).

Proposals for full decriminalization run up against a wall of public opposition. A 1983 poll found that only 7% of Americans thought that there should be "no laws against prostitution" and, in 1990, 22% felt that prostitution should be "left to the individual" and neither outlawed nor regulated by government.[108] American policymakers are almost universally opposed to the idea, making it a nonstarter in any serious discussion of policy alternatives. Advocates sometimes manage to get it placed on the public agenda, however. In 1994, the San Francisco Board of Supervisors created a Taskforce on Prostitution to explore alternatives to existing prostitution policy. After months of meetings, a majority of the members voted to recommend decriminalization,[109] but the board of supervisors rejected the idea. In 2008, a measure on the ballot in San Francisco stipulated that the police would discontinue enforcing all laws against prostitution; the measure was rejected by 58% of voters. A similar ballot measure in Berkeley, California, in 2004 called on police to give prostitution enforcement the "lowest priority." The measure was also defeated, with 64% voting against it.[110] Opposition was likely due to both measures' laissez-faire approach; people are more inclined to support some kind of regulation, just as they are with regard to some other vices. Still, it is noteworthy that 42% of San Franciscans voted for full decriminalization in 2008, suggesting that approval of this kind of policy shift remains a distinct possibility in the future, at least in this city.

Unlike decriminalization, *legalization* implies regulation of some kind: vetting and licensing business owners, registering workers, zoning street prostitution, mandatory medical exams, special business taxes, or officials' periodic site visits and inspections of legal establishments. A segment of the American public favors legalization (see Table 1.2), but only in Nevada do legal brothels exist, since 1971 (see Chapter 11). The 30 brothels are relegated to rural areas of the state and are prohibited in Las Vegas and Reno due largely to opposition from the gaming industry. A slight majority of the Nevada population supports this policy (52% in a 2002 poll felt that legal brothels should be retained), and the system is even more popular in counties with legal brothels. But this rural-only model is remote from the issue of prostitution in

TABLE 1.2   ATTITUDES TOWARD LEGALIZATION OF PROSTITUTION

UNITED STATES	AGREE (%)
Legalize prostitution (1991)[1]	40
Legalize prostitution (1996)[2]	26
Decriminalize prostitution, Berkeley, CA (2004)[3]	36
Decriminalize prostitution, San Francisco, CA (2008)[4]	42
Prostitution does not hurt Nevada's tourism industry (1988)[5]	71
Retain legal brothels, Nevada (2002)[6]	52

OTHER NATIONS	FAVOR LEGALIZATION (%)
Britain (1998)[7]	61
Britain (2006)[8]	65
Canada (1998)[9]	71
Czech Republic (1999)[10]	70
France (1995)[11]	68
Israel (2005)[12]	65
Netherlands (1997)[13]	73
New Zealand (2003)[14]	51
Portugal (2001)[15]	54
Western Australia (2000)[16]	71
Western Australia (2006)[17]	64

Sources: [1] Gallup poll, 1991, N = 1216. Legalize and regulate prostitution to "help reduce the spread of AIDS"; [2] Gallup poll, 1996, N = 1019 ("prostitution involving adults 18 years of age and older should be legal"); [3] November, 2004, ballot measure (Measure Q), instructing Berkeley police to treat enforcement of prostitution law as the "lowest priority"; [4] November 2008, ballot measure (Measure K), instructing San Francisco police to discontinue all prostitution arrests and defunding the city's john school; [5] Nevada poll, N = 1213, conducted November 1988 by the Center for Survey Research at the University of Nevada, Las Vegas. 22% thought that prostitution "hurts the state's tourism industry"; [6] Nevada poll, N = 600, *Law Vegas Review-Journal*, September 17, 2002; [7] ITV Poll, reported in *Agence France Presse*, November 16, 1998, N = 2000 ("legalizing and licensing brothels"); [8] IPSOS/MORI Poll, January 6–10, 2006, N = 1790 ("prostitution should be legalized"); [9] Compas Poll, Sun Media Newspapers, reported in *Edmonton Sun*, October 31, 1998, N = 1479 ("legal and tightly regulated" = 65%, "completely legal" = 6%; [10] IVVM poll, reported by Czech News Agency, National News Wire, April 26, 1999 ("legalizing prostitution"); [11] French poll reported in *Boston Globe*, January 22, 1995 ("legalized brothels"); [12] *Jerusalem Post*, July 19, 2005, N = 500 (legalization of prostitution and licensing of prostitutes); [13] Dutch poll cited in Brants (1998) ("legalization of brothels"); [14] *New Zealand Herald*, May 14, 2003, N = 500. "Don't know" responses removed from total (legal brothels); [15] Marketest poll of residents of Lisbon and Oporto, reported in *Financial Times* and *Diario de Noticias*, August 14, 2001 ("legal brothels"); [16] *Sunday Times* poll, March 26, 2000 (legalization of brothels); [17] Poll reported in *The West Australian*, February 15, 2006 (legalization of prostitution)

urban areas. Illegal prostitutes flourish in Las Vegas and Reno, despite the existence of legal brothels in adjacent counties. What is needed is an urban solution to an essentially urban phenomenon.

Since Nevada legalized brothels in 1971, no other state has seriously considered legalization. Legislators fear being branded as "condoning" prostitution and see no political advantages in any kind of liberalization. On those rare occasions when the idea has been floated, it has had a short life. As a Buffalo, New York, taskforce reasoned in 1999, "Since it is unlikely that city or state officials could ever be convinced to decriminalize or legalize prostitution in Buffalo, there is nothing to be gained by debating the merits of either."[111] This seems to put the cart before the horse, by preempting debate that might indeed result in new policy proposals. One exception to this cynical view occurred recently in Hawaii (discussed later).

American opinion contrasts with that of some other western nations. Recent polls, presented in Table 1.2, show that majorities in several European countries endorse legalization, either in the abstract or in the form of brothels. This is the case for approximately two-thirds of the British and French populations, and similar majorities in France believe that legal brothels would make it easier to control prostitution and that the change would not lead to an increase in the French sex trade.[112] A recent poll reported that 59% of the British public believed that "prostitution is a perfectly reasonable choice that women should be free to make"; this did not extend to family members, with 74% saying that it would be unacceptable for a female family member to work as a prostitute and 87% saying it would be unacceptable for a spouse or partner to pay a prostitute for sex.[113] Dutch views on prostitution are equally noteworthy: in a 1997 poll, 74% of the Dutch public regarded prostitution as an acceptable job and 73% favored the legalization of brothels,[114] and 2 years later, 78% said prostitution was a job like any other, so long as there was no coercion involved.[115] As a Dutch woman told me when asked about prostitution in Holland, "It doesn't even cross my mind that it should be illegal." This is not the typical view of the majority of Americans, who seem to take criminalization for granted.

Legalization raises several important questions. First, is it likely to lead to an increase in or proliferation of prostitution? The number of prostitutes is partly affected by demand, which might limit the growth of the sex trade, though it is possible that greater supply—especially under conditions of legality—might increase demand. Were legal prostitution limited to one or a few cities, it would undoubtedly attract an influx of workers into that locale. Were it more widespread, each locale would hold less attraction to outside workers, reducing the migration problem. The state may impose limits on the number of sex establishments or the number of workers, as illustrated in the Nevada case, and in New Zealand nationwide legalization in 2003 has not increased the number of prostitutes.[116] Prostitution has increased, however, in some Australian states after brothels were legalized.

Second, will prostitutes comply with the regulations? This is an extremely important question. Insofar as legalization includes stipulations as to who can and cannot engage in sex work, those ineligible (e.g., persons who are underage, HIV positive, or illegal immigrants) would be forced to operate illicitly in the shadows of the regulated system. In addition, every conceivable form of legalization would be rejected by at least some eligible prostitutes, who would see no benefits in abiding by the new restrictions (e.g., mandatory registration or health examinations) and would resent the infringement on their freedom. A possible exception would be the zoning of street prostitution into a suitable locale: away from residential areas but in places that are safe and unintimidating for prostitutes and customers alike. Some streetwalkers would reject this arrangement for personal reasons, while others would find it satisfactory (as evidenced in some European cities). Red-light districts in industrial zones would be shunned because such areas typically lack places of refuge and sustenance, such as restaurants, coffee shops, grocery stores, bars, parks, and cheap hotels—amenities required by most streetwalkers.[117] Even if a generally acceptable locale could be found, there is no guarantee that street prostitution could be confined to that area; possible market saturation in the designated zone is only one reason why some workers would be attracted to other locales. Moreover, while zoning presumably would remove street prostitution from residential areas, it would not necessarily remedy other problems associated with street work, such as violence and drug abuse. Indeed, such zones may simply reproduce these problems in a more concentrated manner. Although no U.S. jurisdiction has altered its prohibitionist policy toward street prostitution, some other countries have experimented with a more tolerant approach, including New Zealand and the Netherlands.

A Two-Track Prostitution Policy

If neither formal decriminalization nor legalization is a viable policy in the United States at present, is there any other alternative to blanket criminalization? Since prostitution manifests itself in fundamentally different ways on the street and in indoor venues, it may seem logical to treat the two differently. A *two-track policy* would (1) target resources exclusively toward the control of street prostitution and simultaneously (2) relax controls on indoor prostitution.[118]

Track One: Indoor Prostitution

Some jurisdictions in the United States, Britain, and some other nations have adopted an informal policy of de facto decriminalization of indoor prostitution—essentially ignoring escorts, brothels, and massage parlors unless a complaint is made, which is seldom.[119] Police in other areas, however, devote substantial time and resources to this side of the sex trade, where it accounts for as much as half the prostitution arrests.[120] Law enforcement policies can differ dramatically even between adjacent areas. In Riverside County in California, police have regularly arrested Internet sex workers and their clients in recent years, whereas next door in San Bernardino County, police focus instead on more serious crimes.[121] Efforts against indoor prostitution typically involve considerable planning, and large-scale operations can last several months, becoming rather costly affairs.

Seattle police recently launched an elaborate sting operation in which undercover female officers placed ads and photos on Craigslist and made appointments with men who responded to the ads; a total of 104 men were arrested after they appeared at an expensive condo rented by the police department and were observed discussing a price with the female vice cop.[122] In another case, a vice squad officer in Omaha, Nebraska, posing as a visiting businessman, arranged a date with an escort he met online, had a limo pick her up and take her to a hotel where they drank wine, only to end in an arrest. A taxpayers group accused the Omaha police of wasting resources in the operation. The group's president complained that the police "were not good stewards with the taxpayers' dollars in spending the resources that were spent to have her arrested on a misdemeanor charge."[123] An even more shocking practice takes place in Nashville, Tennessee, where police pay confidential informants to help arrest indoor prostitutes, which typically involve some physical or sexual contact between the informant and the worker. The informants are paid $100 per bust and are used because police policy prohibits officers from disrobing during an investigation,[124] but the district attorney argued that a recorded agreement on a price should be sufficient to make an arrest (as it is in most other jurisdictions) and added that it was "contradictory letting the confidential informant engage in the very act you're trying to stamp out." In response, the head of the vice unit defended the practice: "What's the greater good? It may be distasteful to some people, but it's better that we have those places shut down." In 2002–2004, a total of $120,000 was spent to foster such encounters, with informants receiving more than $70,000.[125]

Such operations are usually launched by local police, but the federal government sometimes initiates a crackdown and it has done so more frequently in recent years. In one case, federal agents raided more than 40 upscale escort agencies in 23 cities. The sting was the culmination of a 2-year undercover investigation, costing $2.5 million.[126] Why so costly? The attorney for the "DC Madam," Deborah Jeane Palfrey, describes how costs can skyrocket in major investigations of a massage parlor or escort agency:

> Her case most likely involved 10,000 to 15,000 billed hours of labor over a five-year period and cost taxpayers many millions of dollars. As an example of the resources deployed here, consider the fact that agents retrieved photographs of escorts as they mailed money orders to Jeane, going back ten years. Escorts were also trailed to their appointments, confronted, and asked to disclose the identities of their clients under the threat of prosecution. A spreadsheet of over 500 pages was compiled tracking these kinds of interactions.[127]

Under the two-track policy, these resources would be targeted toward street prostitution.

Crackdowns on indoor prostitution can have the unintended result of increasing the number of streetwalkers—thus exacerbating the most obtrusive side of the prostitution trade. Closures of massage parlors and other indoor venues have had precisely this effect in some cities, as a New Orleans vice officer observed: "Whenever we focus on indoor investigations, the street scene gets insane."[128] Massage parlors offering sex proliferated in the 1970s, declined in the 1980s, but more recently have grown along with increasing immigration from Asia and Latin America.[129] In some jurisdictions the police conduct ongoing surveillance on such establishments.

The success of a policy of nonenforcement toward indoor prostitution would require that it be implemented without fanfare. A public announcement that a city had decided to take a "hands off" approach to this variety of sex work might serve as a magnet drawing legions of indoor workers and clients into the locale. But in cities where it is not already standard practice, an unwritten policy of nonenforcement might be a sensible innovation. It would free up resources for the more pressing problems on the street, and might have the effect of pushing at least some streetwalkers indoors, as one official commission reasoned: "Keeping prostitutes off the streets may be aided by tolerating them off the streets."[130]

Does the two-track approach favor the higher class, indoor sector and unfairly target the lower echelon streetwalkers? Inherent in any two-track approach are disparate effects on actors associated with each track, and with respect to prostitution there are legitimate grounds for differential treatment: (1) certain other types of commercial enterprise and individual behavior (e.g., nudity, urination, being drunk and disorderly) are prohibited on the streets and (2) "this kind of policy may not be considered too inequitable if the costs inflicted on society by the street prostitutes are greater . . . than from those working in hotels" and other indoor venues.[131] The legal principle on which this proposal rests is that the criminal law should not interfere with the conduct of consenting adults, provided that this conduct does not threaten the legally protected interests of others. Whereas street prostitution is associated with a variety of harms to workers and to host communities, indoor prostitution is in accord with the harm-reduction principle.[132] As the San Francisco Committee on Crime flatly concluded, "continued criminalization of private, non-visible prostitution cannot be warranted by fear of associated crime, drug abuse, venereal disease, or protection of minors."[133] A Canadian commission agreed: "The concern with the law is not what takes place in private, but the public manifestation of prostitution."[134] And another Canadian task force determined that "the two objectives of harm reduction and violence prevention could most likely occur if prostitution was con-ducted indoors."[135] The policy implication is clear: "reassign police priorities to those types of prostitution that inflict the greatest costs," namely, street prostitution.[136]

Track Two: Restructuring Street Prostitution Control

One advantage of the two-track model is that resources previously devoted to the control of indoor prostitution can be transferred to where they are most needed: the street-level sex trade. Under this model, the central objective of the police and social service agencies would be to (1) protect workers from violence and (2) assist workers to leave the streets. Some British cities such as Liverpool and Manchester have experimented with this strategy, under a formal "multi-agency partnership" approach to street prostitution.[137] It is certainly not the norm in the United States, but the policy was adopted in 2008 in New York State with regard to minors caught soliciting on the street. Under the new law, persons under age 18 arrested for prostitution will be channeled into services and programs (including safe houses, counseling, vocational training, healthcare) instead of being charged with a crime and prosecuted.[138] The police still arrest the youths, which seems necessary in order to compel compliance, but those arrested are not stigmatized by prosecution in court and formal punishment. This policy could be extended to adult street prostitutes as well.

This population has special needs because of their manifold, adverse life experiences—including drug addiction, sexual trauma, emotional problems, social stigma, arrest records, and health problems.[139] In most American cities, resources are scarce for both the homeless and sex-trading populations. For the latter, the dominant approach is overwhelmingly coercive rather than rehabilitative, yet past experience abundantly shows the failure of narrowly punitive intervention. Without assistance from service providers and meaningful alternatives to prostitution there is little opportunity for a career change. In order to reduce the amount of street prostitution, there is a desperate need for a comprehensive program of temporary housing, job training, drug treatment, healthcare, counseling, education, and other services.

A few blue-ribbon panels have recommended changes consistent with the two-track model. Commissions in Atlanta and San Francisco advocated a dual approach for precisely the reasons just described.[140] A landmark Canadian commission argued that abating street prostitution would require legislation allowing prostitutes to work somewhere else, and it recommended permitting one or two prostitutes to work out of their own residence,[141] a proposal subsequently endorsed by another Canadian taskforce and by a British government commission.[142] Indoor work by one or two prostitutes was seen as preferable to work on the streets or in brothels since it gives the workers maximum autonomy and shields them against exploitation by pimps and other managers. The commission also recommended giving provincial authorities the option of legalizing small, nonresidential brothels, subject to appropriate controls. Government officials rejected the recommendations of all three commissions.

The state of Rhode Island is unique in its dual policy toward street and indoor prostitution. State law criminalizes loitering for the purpose of soliciting sex, but loitering occurs outdoors and indoor solicitation per se is not a crime. Police have busted massage parlors for employing workers lacking a massage license, but not for prostitution.[143] Bills recently presented in the state legislature to criminalize all prostitution have failed, as a result of lobbying by the ACLU. Rhode Island thus stands alone in the United States in its formal adoption of the two-track policy. Some other nations also embrace the two-track approach—decriminalizing brothels or escort agencies and retaining enforcement against street prostitution. The legislature in Western Australia passed a bill of this nature in 2008.[144]

In 2007, the Hawaii State Legislature considered a bill that would decriminalize the indoor track and zone street prostitution. The bill stipulates the following:

> A person commits the offense of prostitution if the person engages in, or agrees or offers to engage in, sexual conduct with another person for a fee in a public

place that is likely to be observed by others who would be affronted or alarmed. For purposes of this section, a "public place" means any street, sidewalk, bridge, alley or alleyway, plaza, driveway, parking lot, or transportation facility, or the doorways and entrance ways to any building that fronts on any of these places, or a motor vehicle in or on any such place except areas that are designated as exceptions to this section. . . . The legislature and counties shall designate areas within their jurisdiction as exempt from the penalty provisions. . . . Designated areas shall include portions of geographic areas that have a history of this offense. The designated areas may be described both by geographic boundaries and by time of day limitations.[145]

The first part of the bill decriminalizes indoor prostitution, and the second part limits street prostitution to certain areas. The latter therefore departs from the two-track policy because it does not provide resources to help street workers get off the streets. The bill was supported by the ACLU, but it failed to pass in the legislature. One of the sponsors of the bill, Rep. Bob Herkes, saw the bill as a strategic stepping stone: "It's one of those bills you do it for public dialogue instead of trying to get it passed," and the bill's advocates hope to gain support for a similar bill in the future.[146]

Cracking Down on Clients

A major shift in enforcement policy over the past 15 years has been the targeting of prostitutes' customers. Traditionally, the act of patronizing a prostitute was not a crime in the United States, but it is now criminalized in all 50 states. In most areas, however, law enforcement falls most heavily on the prostitute. In 2002, for example, only 9% of all prostitution-related arrests in Phoenix were of men, 12% in Boston, and 14% in Las Vegas.[147] However, some cities specifically target the customers. In 2002, men accounted for 61% of all prostitution-related arrests in Kansas City, 72% in Detroit, and 75% in San Francisco.[148]

Customers are targeted in different ways. Police decoys walk the streets and make arrests when they are solicited. Public humiliation is another common approach, and it can be used after an arrest, as an added sanction, or instead of an arrest. One common tactic is publishing the names of alleged clients in local newspapers or on television. Kansas City created "John TV"—a weekly cable TV show displaying the names, addresses, and pictures of men arrested for attempting to solicit a prostitute.[149] Kansas City activists also created a "hooker hotline," a recorded list of the names of persons arrested for soliciting a prostitute. The hotline received several hundred calls every month.

In New Haven, Connecticut, posters naming a "John of the Week" were stapled to trees and telephone polls in one prostitution stroll. Posters provided the name and address of men observed soliciting a prostitute, with the warning, "Johns! Stay out of our neighborhood or your name will be here next week."[150] In Miami, freeway billboards have been used to announce the names of convicted johns. Americans are divided on the idea of shaming johns in these ways. A 1995 poll found that 50% of the public endorsed punishing men convicted of soliciting prostitutes by placing their names and pictures in the news.[151] At least 280 American cities are using some kind of shaming tactic against johns.[152]

A second tactic is a novel form of rehabilitation—the "john school" for arrested customers. San Francisco launched its First Offenders Prostitution Program in 1995, and between 1995 and early 2008, more than 5700 men had attended the program.[153] As of 2008, 39 other cities in America (as well as cities in Canada and Britain) have created similar schools. The programs are a joint effort by the district attorney's office, the police department, the public health department, community leaders, and former prostitutes. The men avoid an arrest record and court appearance by paying a $1000 fee, attending the school, and not recidivating for 1 year after the arrest.

Every aspect of the 8-hour course is designed to *shame, educate*, and *deter* the men from future contact with prostitutes. The content and tone of the lectures are designed for maximum shock value. During my observations at the San Francisco school, the men were frequently asked how they would feel if their mothers, wives, or daughters were "prostituted," and why they were "using" and "violating" prostitutes by patronizing them. The audience was also exposed to a graphic slideshow on the dangers of sexually transmitted diseases, horror stories about the wretched lives of prostitutes and their oppression by pimps, and information about the harmful effects of street prostitution on the host neighborhoods. My review of responses to a questionnaire completed by the men at the end of the day found that many seem to experience "consciousness raising" about the negative aspects of street prostitution and pledge to never again contact a prostitute, but others expressed cynicism or resentment at getting caught, at having to take the class, at being "talked down to" by the lecturers, and being otherwise demeaned. Some men insisted that they were innocent victims of police entrapment.

The growing targeting of customers in the U.S. is part of a larger, international trend toward criminalizing clients. The focus of antiprostitution groups has increasingly been one of ending "the demand" for paid sex. In 1999, Sweden passed a law exclusively punishing the customers of prostitutes, based on the assumption that they are the root of all evil in the sex industry. Since then, some other nations have either adopted or are considering adopting the Swedish system.

Policy changes are often driven by activists who hold a narrow view of sex work. Over the past 30 years, prohibitionists and liberals have been locked in battle, two sides that have clashing views regarding prostitution, pornography, and other sex work, and over government policies in this sphere. Prohibitionists adopt the oppression paradigm described earlier in the chapter, and actively promote it when they lobby public officials or appear in the media. Conservative prohibitionists are disturbed by the danger sex work poses to the family and moral fabric of society. Feminist prohibitionists denounce all sex work as the ultimate expression of gender oppression, violence against women, or "sexual slavery." The other, liberal side argues that commercial sex services are legitimate or valuable occupations, that pornography is protected under the Constitution (the right to free speech), or that prohibition only drives the sex trade underground and exposes workers to greater harms. This side tends to favor legalization or decriminalization as policies best suited to harm reduction for prostitutes. These are fundamentally different paradigms, turning on different images of the workers involved: *sex objects* vs. *sex workers*, quintessential *victims* of male domination vs. *agents* who actively construct their work lives. These are not abstract debates. Quite the contrary. A sex war is raging in the public square in many nations around the world, reflected in growing media attention and political debates in Australia, Britain, South Africa, and the United States—to name just a few. Theoretical perspectives have real-world consequences insofar as they are used by policymakers as a basis for new laws or new enforcement tools. As indicated earlier, over the past decade, some nations, such as the United States, have embraced the oppression paradigm and increased penalties and enforcement against those involved in sex work. Some other nations have legalized prostitution and some of these states have explicitly embraced the polymorphous perspective by treating street and (all or certain types of) indoor prostitution quite differently.[154]

CONCLUSION

This book contributes to our knowledge of several aspects of sex work and the sex industry, including dimensions that have rarely been studied in the past. The book breaks new ground, but we need even more research on telephone sex work, off-street prostitutes, the porn industry generally and gay and lesbian pornography in particular, legal prostitution systems, the dynamics of law enforcement, and the social forces driving changes in law and public policy. We know little about contemporary brothels, massage parlors, escort agencies, transgender prostitutes, and call girls, and we need much more research on the men involved at all levels—customers, workers, managers, producers, owners. This world does not offer easy access to the outsider, which helps to account for the paucity of research in many key areas; but gaining access should be viewed as a challenge rather than an insuperable barrier.

NOTES

1. Top Ten Reviews provides the following figures (in billions) for 2006: Video Sales/Rentals $3.62, Internet $2.84, Cable/PPV/In-Room/Mobile/Phone Sex $2.19, Exotic Dance Clubs $2.00, Novelties $1.73, Magazines $.95. http://internet-filter-review.toptenreviews.com/internet-pornography-statistics.html, accessed June 19, 2008. The site reports that worldwide pornography revenue in 2006 was $97.1 billion.
2. Eric Schlosser, "The Business of Pornography," *U.S. News and World Report*, February 10, 1997; 2006 figure from Top Ten Reviews.
3. Top Ten Reviews.
4. William Sherman, "The Naked Truth about Strip Clubs," *New York Daily News*, July 8, 2007.
5. James Davis and Tom Smith, *General Social Survey: Cumulative Codebook*, Chicago: National Opinion Research Center, 2002.
6. Zogby International poll, 2000, N = 1031.
7. Gallup Organization, *Gallup Poll Monthly*, no. 313, October, 1991.
8. Davis and Smith, *General Social Survey*. Another major survey found that 16% of American men aged 18–59 reported that they had paid for sex at some time (Edward Laumann, John Gagnon, Robert Michael, and Stuart Michaels, *The Social Organization of Sexuality: Sexual Practices in the United States*, Chicago: University of Chicago Press, 1994).
9. Chris Rissel, "Experiences of Commercial Sex in a Representative Sample of Adults," *Australian and New Zealand Journal of Public Health* 27 (2003): 191–197.
10. Ipsos/MORI Poll, January 6–10, 2006, N = 1790, aged 16–64.
11. Rissel, "Experiences of Commercial Sex"; Eleanor Maticka-Tyndale, "Context and Patterns of Men's Commercial Sexual Partnerships in Northeastern Thailand," *Social Science and Medicine* 44 (1997): 199–213.
12. Ipsos/MORI Poll, January 6–10, 2006, N = 1790, aged 16–64.

13. Hillary Rhodes, "Prostitution Advances in a Wired World," *Associated Press*, March 11, 2008; Bruce Lambert, "As Prostitutes Turn to Craigslist, Law Takes Notice," *New York Times*, September 4, 2007.

14. Scripps Howard News Service/Ohio University poll, February 10, 2005, N = 1001.

15. Davis and Smith, *General Social Survey*, 1994.

16. Ellison Research poll, March 11, 2008, N = 1007. This was the view of 42% of men and 57% of women.

17. Harris Poll #76, September 20–26, 2004, N = 2555. This was the view of 38% of men and 57% of women.

18. *Time* magazine poll, conducted by Yankelovich/Skelly/White, July 26–31, 1977, N = 1044 registered voters.

19. Pew Forum on Religion and Public Life poll, October 2006, N = 739.

20. ICM Research, Sex and Exploitation Survey, January 2008, N = 1023. Women (68%) were slightly more likely to take this view than men (62%).

21. NBC News/*Wall Street Journal* poll, June 10–14, 1994, N = 1502.

22. Penn, Shoen, and Berland poll, sponsored by Democratic Leadership Council, July 23–27, 1997, N = 1009 registered voters.

23. General Social Survey, 2006 and 1984. The question asks respondents which policy is closest to their own view: "There should be laws against the distribution of pornography whatever the age." "There should be laws against the distribution of pornography to persons under 18." "There should be no laws against the distribution of pornography." The figures presented here are for the first option, a universal ban on distribution.

24. General Social Survey, 2006.

25. Gallup, *Gallup Poll Monthly*, 1991: 46% thought female strippers and 45% thought male strippers "should be illegal at bars or clubs."

26. Only 5% thought that stripping was less acceptable today than a decade ago. Institute for Social Research, University of Alabama, Capstone Poll, Tuscaloosa, Alabama, 2002, N = 484.

27. Danny Hakim and William Rashbaum, "No U.S. Charges against Spitzer for Prostitution," *New York Times*, November 7, 2008, p. A1.

28. "Fresno Deputy District Attorney Busted for Soliciting a Prostitute," Channel 47 News online, Fresno, California, accessed August 27, 2008; "Ex-Police Chief Charged in Pa. Prostitution Case," *Evening Sun* (Hanover, PA), August 27, 2008.

29. Part of this section of the chapter draws on two articles: Ronald Weitzer, "Prostitution: Facts and Fictions," *Contexts* 6 (Fall 2007): 28–33, and Ronald Weitzer, "Sociology of Sex Work," *Annual Review of Sociology* 35 (2009).

30. Kathleen Barry, *The Prostitution of Sexuality*, New York: New York University Press, 1995; Andrea Dworkin, *Pornography: Men Possessing Women*, New York: Putnam, 1981; Andrea Dworkin, *Life and Death*, New York: Free Press, 1997; Sheila Jeffreys, *The Idea of Prostitution*, North Melbourne, Australia: Spinifex, 1997; Catherine MacKinnon, *Feminism Unmodified*, Cambridge, MA: Harvard University Press, 1987; Catherine MacKinnon, *Toward a Feminist Theory of the State*, Cambridge, MA: Harvard University Press, 1989.

31. Melissa Farley, "Bad for the Body, Bad for the Heart: Prostitution Harms Women Even if Legalized or Decriminalized," *Violence Against Women* 10 (2004): 1087–1125; Janice Raymond, "Prostitution as Violence against Women," *Women's Studies International Forum* 21 (1998): 1–9.

32. Ine Vanwesenbeeck, "Another Decade of Social Scientific Work on Prostitution," *Annual Review of Sex Research* 12 (2001): 242–289; Ronald Weitzer, "Flawed Theory and Method in Studies of Prostitution," *Violence Against Women* 11 (2005): 934–949, and Ronald Weitzer, "Rehashing Tired Claims about Prostitution," *Violence Against Women* 11 (2005): 971–977.

33. Arlene Carmen and Howard Moody, *Working Women: The Subterranean World of Street Prostitution*, New York: Harper & Row, 1985; Frederique Delacoste and Priscilla Alexander, eds., *Sex Work: Writings by Women in the Sex Industry*, Pittsburgh: Cleis, 1987; Nadine Strossen, *Defending Pornography*, New York: Anchor, 1995; Wendy McElroy, *XXX: A Woman's Right to Pornography*, New York: St. Martin's, 1995; Wendy Chapkis, *Live Sex Acts: Women Performing Erotic Labor*, New York: Routledge, 1997.

34. Eileen McLeod, *Working Women: Prostitution Now*, London: Croom Helm, 1982, p. 28.

35. Noah Zatz, "Sex Work/Sex Act: Law, Labor, and Desire in Constructions of Prostitution," *Signs* 22 (1997): 277–308, at p. 291.

36. Julia O'Connell Davidson, *Power, Prostitution, and Freedom*, Ann Arbor, MI: University of Michigan Press, 1998.

37. Barbara Heyl, "Prostitution: An Extreme Case of Sex Stratification," in Freda Adler and Rita Simon, eds., *The Criminology of Deviant Women*, Boston: Houghton-Mifflin, 1979, p. 198.

38. Thomas Steinfatt, *Working at the Bar: Sex Work and Health Communication in Thailand*, Westport, CT: Ablex, 2002, p. 19.

39. Stephanie Church, Marion Henderson, Marina Barnard, and Graham Hart, "Violence by Clients towards Female Prostitutes in Different Work Settings," *British Medical Journal* 322 (2001): 524–526.

40. See the studies cited in Ronald Weitzer, "New Directions in Research on Prostitution," *Crime, Law, and Social Change* 43 (2005): 211–235.

41. See Patty Kelly, *Lydia's Open Door: Inside Mexico's Most Modern Brothel*, Berkeley: University of California Press, 2008; Prabha Kotiswaran, "Born unto Brothels: Toward a Legal Ethnography of Sex Work in an Indian Red-Light Area," *Law and Social Inquiry* 33 (2008): 579–629; Kemala Kempadoo, *Sexing the Caribbean: Gender, Race, and Sexual Labor*, New York: Routledge, 2004; Kamala Kempadoo, ed., *Sun, Sex, and Gold: Tourism and Sex Work in the Caribbean*, Lanham, MD: Rowman & Littlefield, 1999; Denise Brennan, *What's Love Got to Do with It? Transnational Desires and Sex Tourism in the Dominican Republic*, Durham, NC: Duke University Press, 2004.

42. Libby Plumridge and Gillian Abel, "A Segmented Sex Industry in New Zealand: Sexual and Personal Safety of Female Sex Workers," *Australian and New Zealand Journal of Public Health* 25 (2001): 78–83, at p. 83.

43. Quoted in Joanne Kimberlin, "Women for Hire: Behind Closed Doors in the Escort Industry," *The Virginia-Pilot*, May 18, 2008, p. A11.

44. Dolores French, *Working: My Life as A Prostitute*, New York: E.P. Dutton, 1988, pp. 152–153.

45. Roberta Perkins and Frances Lovejoy, *Call Girls: Private Sex Workers in Australia*, Crawley: University of Western Australia Press, 2007, p. 51.

46. Quoted in Elizabeth Bernstein, *Temporarily Yours: Intimacy, Authenticity, and the Commerce of Sex*, Chicago: University of Chicago Press, 2007, p. 46.

47. Diana Prince, *A Psychological Study of Prostitutes in California and Nevada*, doctoral dissertation, San Diego: U.S. International University, 1986, p. 490.

48. Ann Lucas, "The Work of Sex Work: Elite Prostitutes' Vocational Orientations and Experiences," *Deviant Behavior* 26 (2005): 513–546, at p. 531.

49. A similar phenomenon has been documented for bar workers who spend extended periods of time with their customers. A survey of Thailand's bar prostitutes found that more than 80% of them "had a relationship with a customer in which they had developed strong feelings for him." Steinfatt, *Working at the Bar*, p. 251.

50. Charlotte Woodward, Jane Fischer, Jake Najman, and Michael Dunne, *Selling Sex in Queensland*, Brisbane, Australia: Prostitution Licensing Authority, 2004.

51. Lucas, "The Work of Sex Work," p. 541.

52. Woodward, et al., *Selling Sex in Queensland*, p. 39.

53. Quoted in Mark Waite, "Prostitutes Dispute Trummell Charges," *Pahrump Valley Times*, October 5, 2007.
54. See the studies cited in Weitzer, "Sociology of Sex Work."
55. Prince, *A Psychological Study of Prostitutes*, p. 454.
56. John Decker, *Prostitution: Regulation and Control*, Littleton, CO: Rothman, 1979, pp. 166, 174.
57. Upscale work is featured in the CNBC documentary, "Dirty Money: The Business of High-End Prostitution," which first aired in November 2008 (CNBC Television network). See also Adam Goldman, "Scandal Gives Peek Inside Call-Girl Ring," *Associated Press*, March 12, 2008.
58. Bernstein, *Temporarily Yours*, p. 100.
59. Vanwesenbeeck, "Another Decade of Social Scientific Work on Prostitution."
60. See the literature reviews by Katherine Frank, "Thinking Critically about Strip Club Research," *Sexualities* 10 (2007): 501–517, and Mindy Bradley, "Stripping in the New Millennium," *Sociology Compass* 2 (2008): 503–518.
61. Mindy Bradley and Jeffrey Ulmer, "Social Worlds of Stripping," *Sociological Quarterly* 50 (2009): 29–60.
62. Bernadette Barton, "Dancing on the Mobius Strip: Challenging the Sex War Paradigm," *Gender and Society* 16 (2002): 585–602.
63. Katherine Frank, *G-Strings and Sympathy: Strip Club Regulars and Male Desire*, Durham, NC: Duke University Press, 2002.
64. Tina Deshotels and Craig Forsyth, "Strategic Flirting and the Emotional Tab of Exotic Dancing," *Deviant Behavior* 27 (2006): 223–241, at pp. 231–232.
65. William Thompson and Jackie Harred, "Topless Dancers: Managing Stigma in a Deviant Occupation," *Deviant Behavior* 13 (1992): 291–311; Marilyn Salutin, "Stripper Morality," *Transaction* 8 (1971): 12–22.
66. Beth Montemurro, "Strippers and Screamers," *Journal of Contemporary Ethnography* 30 (2001): 275–304; David Peterson and Paula Dressel, "Equal Time for Women: Notes on the Male Strip Show," *Urban Life* 11 (1982): 185–208.
67. Beth Montemurro, Colleen Bloom, and Kelly Madell, "Ladies Night Out: A Typology of Women Patrons of a Male Strip Club," *Deviant Behavior* 24 (2003): 333–352.
68. Thompson and Harred, "Topless Dancers"; William Thompson, Jackie Harred, and Barbara Burks, "Managing the Stigma of Topless Dancing: A Decade Later," *Deviant Behavior* 24 (2003): 551–570.
69. Joseph DeMarco, "Power and Control in Gay Strip Clubs," *Journal of Homosexuality* 53 (2007): 111–127.
70. Frank, "Thinking Critically"; DeMarco, "Power and Control."

71. Robert Bauserman, "Sexual Aggression and Pornography: A Review of Correlational Research," *Basic and Applied Social Psychology* 18 (1996): 405–427; Edward Donnerstein, Daniel Linz, and Steven Penrod, *The Question of Pornography: Research Findings and Policy Implications*, New York: Free Press, 1987.

72. Bauserman, "Sexual Aggression and Pornography"; see also Berl Kutchinsky, "Pornography and Rape: Theory and Practice? Evidence from Crime Data in Four Countries where Pornography is Easily Available," *International Journal of Law and Psychiatry* 14 (1991): 47–64; Milton Diamond and Ayako Uchiyama, "Pornography, Rape, and Sex Crime in Japan," *International Journal of Law and Psychiatry* 22 (1999): 1–22.

73. Joseph Scott and Steven Cuvelier, "Sexual Violence in Playboy Magazine: A Longitudinal Content Analysis," *Journal of Sex Research* 25 (1987): 534–539; Ted Palys, "Testing the Common Wisdom: The Social Content of Video Pornography," *Canadian Psychology* 27 (1986): 22–35; Joseph Scott and Steven Cuvelier, "Violence and Sexual Violence in Pornography," *Archives of Sexual Behavior* 22 (1993): 357–371.

74. Palys, "Testing the Common Wisdom."

75. Bauserman, "Sexual Aggression and Pornography," p. 424.

76. Petra Boynton, "'Is That Supposed to be Sexy?' Women Discuss Women in Top Shelf Magazines," *Journal of Community and Applied Social Psychology* 9 (1999): 91–105.

77. See the studies reviewed by Feona Attwood, "What Do People Do with Porn?" *Sexuality and Culture* 9 (2005): 65–86.

78. Glona Cowan, Cheryl Chase, and Geraldine Stahly, "Feminist and Fundamentalist Attitudes toward Pornography Control," *Psychology of Women Quarterly* 13 (1989): 97–112.

79. David Loftus, *Watching Sex: How Men Really Respond to Pornography*, New York: Thunder Mouth Press, 2002, p. xii. Most of the men in the sample were contacted via the Internet and thus may be unrepresentative of the larger population, but the findings are consistent with some other inquiries, e.g., Marty Klein, "Pornography: What Men See When They Watch," in Peter Lehman, ed., *Pornography: Film and Culture*, New Brunswick: Rutgers University Press, 2006.

80. Loftus, *Watching Sex*, p. 249.

81. Loftus, *Watching Sex*, p. 137–147.

82. Jan Browne and Victor Minichiello, "Research Directions in Male Sex Work," *Journal of Homosexuality* 31 (1996): 29–56; Donald West, *Male Prostitution*. Binghamton, NY: Haworth; 1993; Peter Aggleton, ed., *Men Who Sell Sex*, Philadelphia: Temple University Press, 1999.

83. Exceptions are David Duncan, "Trends in Gay Pornographic Magazines," *Social Science Research* 73 (1989): 95–98, and Carl Stychin, "Exploring the Limits: Feminism and the Legal Regulation of Gay Male Pornography," *Vermont Law Review* 16 (1992): 857–900.

84. An exception is Amy Flowers, *The Fantasy Factory: An Insider's View of the Phone Sex Industry*, Philadelphia: Pennsylvania State University Press, 1998.

85. Eddie Adams, "Indiana Group Targets Adult Businesses," Adult Video News Media Network, November 16, 2007.

86. Bryant Paul, Daniel Linz, and Bradley Shafer, "Government Regulation of Adult Businesses through Zoning and Anti-Nudity Ordinances: Debunking the Legal Myth of Negative Secondary Effects," *Community Law and Policy* 6 (2001): 355–391.

87. Daniel Linz, "An Examination of the Assumption that Adult Businesses are Associated with Crime in Surrounding Areas," *Law and Society Review* 38 (2004): 69–104. See also Daniel Linz, Bryant Paul, and Mike Yao, "Peep Show Establishments, Police Activity, Public Place, and Time: A Study of Secondary Effects in San Diego, California," *Journal of Sex Research* 43 (2006): 182–193.

88. *Miller v. California*, 413 U.S. 15 (1973).

89. Paul Brest and Ann Vandenberg, "Politics, Feminism, and the Constitution: The Anti-Pornography Movement in Minneapolis," *Stanford Law Review* 39 (1987): 607–661.

90. Lisa Duggan, Nan Hunter, and Carole Vance, "False Promises: Feminist Anti-Pornography Legislation," *New York Law School Law Review* 38 (1993): 133–163.

91. Brest and Vandenberg, "Politics, Feminism, and the Constitution."

92. Carole Vance, "The Meese Commission on the Road," *The Nation* (August 2, 1986): 65, 76–82; Larry Baron, "Immoral, Inviolate, or Inconclusive?" *Society* (July–August, 1987): 6–12.

93. Daniel Linz, Edward Donnerstein, and Steven Penrod, "The Findings and Recommendations of the Attorney General's Commission on Pornography," *American Psychologist* 42 (1987): 946–953.

94. U.S. Department of Justice, *Beyond the Pornography Commission: The Federal Response*, Washington, DC: GPO, 1988.

95. U.S. Department of Justice, *Beyond the Pornography Commission*, p. 31.

96. Jim McGee and Brian Duffy, *Main Justice*, New York: Simon & Schuster, 1996, pp. 282, 293.

97. Ted Gest, "The Drive to Make America Porn-Free," *U.S. News and World Report,* February 6, 1989; Jim McGee, "U.S. Crusade Against Pornography Tests the Limits of Fairness," *Washington Post,* January 11, 1993.

98. PBS interview with Bruce Taylor, Transcript, Frontline/Public Broadcasting Service, 2001.

99. My interview with official in Child Exploitation and Obscenity Unit, February 24, 1999.

100. Richard Schmidt, "U.S. Cracking Down on Porn," *Deseret News*, February 15, 2004; Barton Gellman, "Recruits Sought for Porn Squad," *Washington Post*, September 20, 2005; U.S. Department of Justice, "Obscenity Prosecution Task Force Established to Investigate, Prosecute Purveyors of Obscene Materials," Press Release. Washington, DC: Department of Justice, May 5, 2005.

101. Laura Sullivan, "Justice Department Sets Sights on Mainstream Porn," *Pittsburgh Post-Gazette*, April 11, 2004.

102. Dept. of Justice, "Obscenity Prosecution."

103. Robert Gehrke, "Nation's Porn Prosecutor Fronts War against Obscenity," *Salt Lake Tribune*, February 26, 2007.

104. Schmidt, "U.S. Cracking Down on Porn."

105. PBS interview with Taylor.

106. PBS interview with Taylor.

107. Bureau of Justice Statistics, *Sourcebook of Criminal Justice Statistics*, Washington, D.C.: U.S. Government Printing Office, annual.

108. Merit Audits and Surveys, Merit report, October 15–20, 1983, N = 1200; Louis Harris poll, January 11–February 11, 1990, N = 2254.

109. "The Task Force therefore recommends that the City stop enforcing and prosecuting prostitution crimes." San Francisco Task Force on Prostitution, *Final Report*, San Francisco Board of Supervisors, 1996, p. 6.

110. See Ronald Weitzer, "Why Prostitution Initiative Misses: Measure Q in Berkeley Fails on Three Counts," *San Francisco Chronicle*, September 26, 2004, p. E3.

111. Prostitution Task Force, *Workable Solutions to the Problem of Street Prostitution in Buffalo, New York*, Buffalo, October 1999.

112. "Poll: French Want Brothels Legalized," *Boston Globe*, January 22, 1995.

113. Ipsos/MORI Poll, June 11–12, 2008, N = 1012, aged 16 and over.

114. October 1997 poll, cited in Chrisje Brants, "The Fine Art of Regulated Tolerance: Prostitution in Amsterdam," *Journal of Law and Society* 25 (1998): 621–635.

115. Edgar Danter, "Green Light at Last for Dutch Red Light Districts," *Deutsche Presse-Agentur,* February 6, 1999, N = 2600.

116. Ministry of Justice, *Report of the Prostitution Law Review Committee on the Operation of the Prostitution Reform Act 2003*, Wellington, New Zealand: Ministry of Justice, 2008.

117. Bernard Cohen, *Deviant Street Networks: Prostitution in New York City*, Lexington, MA: Lexington Books, 1980.

118. The policy is described in more detail in Ronald Weitzer, "Prostitution Control in America: Rethinking Public Policy," *Crime, Law, and Social Change* 32 (1999): 83–102. My discussion of indoor prostitution is restricted to workers who entered the trade voluntarily, and does not pertain to those who have been coerced or deceived into selling sex. Law enforcement directed at the protection of such victims is obviously laudable.

119. On Britain, see Catherine Benson and Roger Matthews, "Police and Prostitution: Vice Squads in Britain," in Ronald Weitzer, ed., *Sex for Sale*, New York: Routledge, 2000.

120. See, for instance, the six-page investigative report on the policing of massage parlors in Louisville, Kentucky: Jim Adams and Jason Riley, "Louisville Takes Aim at Parlor Prostitution," *The Courier-Journal*, July 11, 2004. A study of 16 cities in the mid-1980s by Julie Pearl found that in three of them (Baltimore, Memphis, Milwaukee) indoor prostitution accounted for between one-quarter and one-third of their prostitution arrests and half of the arrests in Cleveland. Pearl data cited in Weitzer, "Prostitution Control in America," p. 90.

121. Jessica Logan, "Internet Replacing Streetwalking for Inland Prostitution," *The Press-Enterprise* (Riverside), January 1, 2008.

122. Sara Green, "Prostitution Sting Leads to 104 Arrests," *Seattle Times*, November 16, 2006.

123. Quoted in Mike Brunker, "Prostitution Thrives on the Net," *ZD Net News*, June 7, 1999.

124. In some other places, vice officers are allowed to undress prior to making an arrest. See Robert Crowe, "Officers Disrobe to Uncover Crime: HPD Changed its Policy to Crack Down on Spas Fronting for Prostitution," *Houston Chronicle*, January 24, 2005. And in some other places, vice cops are allowed to receive some sexual contact. Louisville, Kentucky is one example: see Jason Riley and Jim Adams, "Officers Have Sexual Contact with Suspects," and Jason Riley, "Undercover Methods Draw Ridicule, Praise," *The Courier-Journal*, July 11, 2004. In half of the massage parlor arrests, officers' reports mentioned that they had received fondling or oral sex from a worker. Similar practices have occurred in Phoenix and some other cities, but these are exceptional.

125. Ian Demsky, "Police Defend Prostitution Tactic: DA Says Encounters Using Informants Unnecessary," *The Tennessean*, February 2, 2005.

126. *San Francisco Chronicle*, April 6, 1990.

127. Montgomery Blair Sibley, interviewed by Katherine Frank, *Spread* magazine, Fall 2008, pp. 24–25.

128. Vice sergeant interviewed by Julie Pearl, May 1985; transcript cited in Weitzer, "Prostitution Control in America."

129. In many American cities and counties, parlors exist that are populated by one ethnic group exclusively. Many of these are Korean, Chinese, or Mexican in composition, and some cater exclusively to clients from the same ethnic background.

130. San Francisco Committee on Crime, *A Report on Non-Victim Crime in San Francisco, Part 2: Sexual Conduct, Gambling, Pornography*, Mayor's Office, 1971, p. 44.

131. Helen Reynolds, *The Economics of Prostitution*, Springfield: Charles Thomas, 1986, p. 194.

132. Michael Rekart, "Sex Work Harm Reduction," *The Lancet* (December 17, 2006): 2123–2134; Linda Cusick, "Widening the Harm Reduction Agenda: From Drug Use to Sex Work," *International Journal of Drug Policy* 17 (2006): 3–11.

133. San Francisco Committee, *Report on Non-Victim Crime*, p. 38.

134. Special Committee on Pornography and Prostitution, *Pornography and Prostitution in Canada*, Ottawa: Department of Justice, 1985, p. 515.

135. Federal/Provincial Territorial Working Group on Prostitution, *Report and Recommendations in Respect of Legislation, Policy, and Practices Concerning Prostitution-Related Activities*, Ottawa: Department of Justice, 1998, p. 35.

136. Reynolds, *Economics of Prostitution*, p. 192.

137. Marianne Hester and Nicole Westmarland, *Tackling Street Prostitution: Towards an Holistic Approach*, Home Office Research Study 279, London: Home Office, 2004; Jane Pitcher, "Support Services for Women Working in the Sex Industry," in Rosie Campbell and Maggie O'Neill, eds., *Sex Work Now*, Portland: Willan, 2006; Clarissa Penfold, Gillian Hunter, Rosie Campbell, and Leela Barham, "Tackling Client Violence in Female Street Prostitution: Inter-Agency Working between Outreach Agencies and the Police," *Policing and Society* 14 (2004): 365–379.

138. The Safe Harbor for Exploited Children Act, 2008, New York State.

139. Adele Weiner, "Understanding the Social Needs of Streetwalking Prostitutes," *Social Work* 41 (1996): 97–105.

140. Atlanta Task Force on Prostitution, *Findings and Recommendations*, Mayor's Office, Atlanta, GA, 1986; San Francisco Committee, *Report on Non-Victim Crime*.

141. Special Committee, *Pornography and Prostitution in Canada*.

142. Federal/Provincial Territorial Working Group, *Report and Recommendations*, p. 71; Home Office, *A Coordinated Prostitution Strategy*, London: Home Office, 2006. In England, it is already legal for a person to sell sex in her/his own home, and the Home Office recommended that it be legal for three people to work in the same residence.

143. Amanda Milkovits, "Legislators' Attempts to Quell Prostitution Stall," *Providence Journal*, May 28, 2005; Denise Dowling, "Last Call for Sin," *Rhode Island Monthly*, June 2007.

144. See Ronald Weitzer, "Legalizing Prostitution: Morality Politics in Western Australia," *British Journal of Criminology* 49 (2009): 88–105.

145. Hawaii State Legislature, House of Representatives, HB 982, "Prostitution," 2007, §3 and §6. The companion bill in the Senate was SB 706.

146. Herkes, quoted in Mark Niesse, "Prostitution Bill Gains Support," *The Star Bulletin*, February 13, 2007. The bill had 13 co-sponsors in the House, 1 in the Senate.

147. Thomas Hargrove, "Men Make Up One-Third of Prostitution Arrests," *Scripps Howard News Service*, February 17, 2005.

148. Hargrove, "Men Make Up."

149. Art Hubacher, "Every Picture Tells a Story: Is Kansas City's 'John TV' Constitutional?" *Kansas Law Review* 46 (1998): 551–591.

150. "Curbing Prostitution on Demand Side," *New York Times,* April 20, 1992: B8.

151. *Newsweek* poll, January 26–27, 1995, N = 753.

152. Jordan Schrader, "To Reduce Prostitution, Cities Try Shaming Clients," *USA Today*, August 29, 2008.

153. Miyoko Ohtake, "A School for Johns," *Newsweek*, July 24, 2008.

154. On trends in the United States, see Chapter 14, and Ronald Weitzer, "The Social Construction of Sex Trafficking," *Politics and Society* 35 (2007): 447–475. On Western Australia, see Weitzer, "Legalizing Prostitution."

PORNOGRAPHY

CHAPTER

2

MOTIVATIONS FOR PURSUING
A CAREER IN PORNOGRAPHY

Sharon A. Abbott

Many people choose careers based on what the job can provide for them. Benefits may include money, status and recognition, opportunities for career mobility, and social contacts. Some are drawn to jobs that provide a sense of freedom and independence, jobs in which they can forge their own paths, set their own hours, and be free from rigid demands of authority. Careers in the pornography industry offer several of the same benefits to workers as many other occupations. But despite these similarities, jobs in the porn industry have rarely been studied as *work*.

Instead, most research on pornography has focused on the effect and reception of pornographic materials after they have been produced and distributed. Numerous experimental studies have addressed such things as gender differences in arousal, the possible links between pornography and aggression and callous attitudes toward sexual violence, as well as pornography's potential influence on gender equality.[1] This research has treated pornography as a stimulus of behavior or attitudes but ignores other aspects of pornography. Similarly, feminists and legal scholars have engaged in theoretical debates on erotica and pornography,[2] but fail to examine pornography as an industry and career choice and thus limit a broader sociological understanding of the medium.

As a form of work, pornography requires participants to enter its stigmatized world and to then develop strategies to maintain involvement in the industry. The structure of the industry influences these motivations.

Heterosexual pornography production can be broadly divided into three categories: "professional," "pro-amateur," and "amateur." Professional companies are the largest and most organized, typically employing between 50 and 100 staff members for sales, marketing, distribution, promotion, and production scheduling. Each company releases more than 20 new videotapes a month featuring the most glamorous and popular talent in the industry. Budgets for professional features range from $50,000 to $150,000, averaging closer to the lower end. In contrast, amateur companies consist of a few individuals who perform a variety of tasks, including acting, directing, sales, and marketing. Budgets range from a few hundred to a few thousand dollars. Most commonly, amateur companies do not produce, but rather edit and market "homemade" materials that are sent in by interested participants. Pro-amateur or "gonzo" companies include small companies with large budgets, medium size companies with small budgets, and subsidiaries of professional companies. Budgets average between $15,000 and $25,000. Unlike the specialized employees of professional companies, the staff at pro-amateur companies perform many functions within the organization. Pro-amateur productions create a bridge between professional and "homemade" productions by offering products with high production quality, relatively low cost, and known performers.

This chapter investigates the work of actors and actresses in the production of pornography. I focus on the motivations for entering a porn career and maintaining subsequent involvement, and I describe the ways in which motives are influenced by two factors: actors' gender and the type of production companies with which they are affiliated.

RESEARCH METHODS

Data were collected in two primary sites of pornography production, Los Angeles and San Francisco, in 1996 and 1998. Access to the industry was gained through a former porn actress who retained high status in the industry and provided contacts to others, including someone who eventually became a key informant, a director involved in the industry for more than a decade. The informant facilitated access to industry events and introduced me to a number of actors and actresses. Other opportunities to make contacts arose in the course of my attendance at several organized events—including a dance, an industry awards show, and the Video Software Dealers' Association trade show. Field observations and informal interviews were conducted at these events.

In-depth interviews were conducted with participants involved in all facets of production, including producers, directors, company owners, magazine editors, agents, makeup artists, camera operators, and actresses and actors. Regarding the last group, who provide the core data for this chapter, I conducted in-depth interviews with 50 actors and actresses currently involved in the adult entertainment industry (31 actresses, 19 actors). Three-quarters of the interviewees were white, with the remainder being Asian, Latino, and African-American. Interviews typically lasted between 1 and 3 hours. Whenever possible, interviews were taped; half were tape-recorded and, for the other half, detailed, written notes were recorded. All participants knew my role as a social scientist and were assured confidentiality. Respondents' length of time in the industry ranged from 2 to 15 years, with an average of 4 to 5 years. As discussed later, this average was higher for actors than actresses. Most had acted in at least 50 videos, with the range being between 40 and 600 (typically corresponding to years in industry).

Initial respondents referred me to other people, and to give me a "full picture" of the industry, the key informant referred me to individuals whom he felt represented all aspects of the business. In addition, whenever possible, I sought out interviews with people I met in other situations who were not connected with the key informant. Both methods helped to increase diversity among the sample. Most of the interviews took place at the respondent's home or office. Interviews at offices provided an opportunity to observe various settings in the industry and to meet other participants.

I also conducted observations on six production sets. This provided a unique opportunity to both observe the pornography production process and to "hang out" with the participants and discuss many aspects of the industry during low-activity periods in production. Such conversations provided some additional rich data, allowed me to build rapport with the participants, and led to invitations to other events.

ENTERING THE WORLD OF PORN

Respondents were asked what jobs they held before working in pornography, and what jobs they would likely hold if they were no longer involved in adult entertainment. These questions often led to discussions about the benefits of pornography over jobs in the "straight" (not X-rated) industries. In addition, actors and actresses were asked a series of questions about their involvement with different companies, their status in the industry, and relationships with their peers. This information shed light on patterns of mobility and organizational culture. Porn actors and actresses are often referred to, and refer to themselves as, "talent." This term is used to differentiate their role from those who act in films that are not X-rated, while also providing a sense of legitimacy and normality to their occupations. "Talent" is less stigmatized than "porn star."

Individuals enter the porn industry for five main reasons, as now described.

Money

Popular beliefs maintain that the lure of "easy money" draws people, particularly the young, to the world of pornography. This belief is supported by trade and fan magazines that glamorize the industry by focusing on the lavish lifestyles of its members. While the industry cultivates the idea of porn as profitable, income varies greatly by individual. Furthermore, rather than "easy money," respondents reported that most of the work is tiring, boring, or physically exhausting.[3] Like prostitutes, a few make a great deal of money while most make a modest or meager living.

While money earned from appearing in pornography videos may seem high compared with many other jobs, annual incomes generated from porn alone typically approximate middle-class earnings. For example, respondents reported that at the "professional level," actresses receive between $300 and $1000 for an individual scene.[4] The fee is based on the actresses' popularity, experience, and audience appeal, as well as what the scene entails. Masturbation and "girl/girl" ("lesbian") scenes pay the least, while anal sex and "double penetrations"[5] generate the most money. The most common scene combines oral sex and penile–vaginal intercourse, and pays, on average, $500. Although the hourly pay is high, income is limited by the amount of work actresses are offered; this money must often stretch between extended periods of no work.

In addition, particularly at the "professional level," actresses must spend a major portion of their income on their appearance. Cosmetic surgeries, such as liposuction and breast augmentation, are the norm in the business, and must be paid for out of the actresses' earnings.[6] Appearances at industry parties and local "gentlemen's clubs" (erotic dancing) often require costumes, which consume a portion of earnings. While actors do not have these expenses, they do pay to support their images. Males are expected to look good and stay in shape, and are expected to have the status symbols associated with being a porn star (e.g., motorcycles and cars). Even the HIV testing, required every 30 days in order to work, must be paid for out of pocket.

Women earn more on average than their male coworkers.[7] Respondents in this study reported that male talent earn approximately 50% less than their female coworkers. Pornography, therefore, is one of the few occupations in which men experience pay inequity. Furthermore, while actors often have more individual scenes per video than do actresses (with the exception of the star), they only rarely appear on box covers (which provide high fees). Therefore, actors' earnings are typically lower for the entire project. Since men in the industry make disproportionately less than women, money alone is an unlikely motivation for actors.

Earnings also depend on the category of porn. While money is a motivating factor at the professional and pro-amateur level, participants in amateur productions are often paid little, if anything at all. Individuals who sell amateur tapes to a distributor are paid, on average, $150. The fee is paid to the individual who sells the tape, not the participants, whose pay is unknown. When videos are produced by amateur companies, talent earn between $50 and $150 per scene. In addition to paying relatively low wages, amateur companies do not have the same connections to such moneymaking opportunities as erotic dancing and modeling, common at pro-amateur and professional levels. Therefore, actors and actresses at the amateur level were far less likely than individuals at higher levels to cite money as a primary motivation.

At the pro-amateur and professional level, the effect of money may be a key factor in keeping members involved in the industry even after they decide to leave.[8] Accustomed to periods of time in which money is plentiful (albeit sporadic), actors and actresses have difficulty finding jobs that offer the (perceived) freedom and flexibility of porn work. This phenomenon is illustrated by the following exchange between a husband-and-wife acting team:

Tim A friend of mine knew the contacts for porn, and another friend of mine really pushed me into it, and once I tried it, I got hooked into it. I liked the lifestyle. And then I didn't like it. I went through a period where I didn't like it, and it was too late, because I was already in it, and I already changed my cost of living. And that's a mistake that porn actors and actresses make.

Keri They start off making $5000 a month in the beginning.

Tim They start off and bite off more than they can chew financially a month, and then you're stuck, because most of us can't turn around and go get a CEO job, because now we're in the $80,000 to $100,000 a year bracket. We are used to big houses and nice cars.

The inability to find jobs with similar benefits may keep participants involved in the industry. In addition, talent may begin to "live beyond their means," and the need to support their standard of living serves to keep them in their jobs.

Fame and Glamour

Many respondents report that "becoming known" is a greater motivating factor to enter the industry than money. This motivation is most common at the pro-amateur and professional levels, which have a large distribution of materials, and thus, more opportunities for recognition.[9] Porn stars I interviewed reported being photographed, applauded, and having their autographs requested. Fan clubs offer more opportunity for stars to be admired.

Fan magazines often portray the world of porn as glamorous, and the industry attempts to promote this image. At the pro-amateur and professional levels, the release of high-budget feature films and videos ("glamour pieces") are often accompanied by black-tie parties in highly visible settings (e.g., hotels or convention centers). One key component of these parties is the hordes of photographers from fan, trade, and entertainment magazines who serve as paparazzi for the industry. The mixing of glamorization and advertisement is best exemplified in a recent billboard erected over a busy street in Los Angeles featuring the top actresses of a large company. Other examples include the two domestic award shows each year hosted by the industry (a third is hosted abroad). Tickets to these black-tie affairs typically cost $100 apiece. While the focus of these ceremonies is often on high-budget features, amateur productions are also honored. The opportunity for "fame" is therefore available to participants at all levels.

Several actresses, actors, producers, and directors commented that the desire for fame was a desirable trait in talent because enthusiasm for their work increases as popularity and recognition grows. In contrast, if talent is only motivated by money, they are often left frustrated or bored. As one actor argued, "If you are doing it for the money, you won't last long." Production companies similarly assume that interest in money is evident to viewers and disrupts the fantasy that the talent really enjoys their work.

When contrasted with the "straight" (not X-rated) entertainment industry, porn offers a relatively quick and easy means to earn public recognition. Acting in the straight industry is typically characterized by few opportunities, high competition, and waiting for "luck" or "big breaks."[10] Straight actors and actresses often audition for hundreds of parts just to win a few. In contrast, someone aspiring to be a porn star, if attractive enough, can sign up with an agent and appear in a video within days. And fame tends to come quickly in pornography.

Fame and recognition are sought by both actresses and actors. Although actresses attract considerably more attention in adult publications, there are fewer actors overall in the industry, so they become familiar and easily recognized. But while this motivation is not determined by gender, the concept of "fame" varies between the sexes. For females, being famous includes not only being recognized and supported by the industry, but also being desired by viewers, which is much less true for male actors, since the viewers are largely heterosexual males.

Freedom and Independence

Research into the motivations of many other types of sex worker suggests that individuals often become involved in the industry because of their low socioeconomic status and restricted opportunities. For example, in their study of table dancers, Ronai and Ellis argue that women who work in gentlemen's clubs have fewer resources and opportunities than other women.[11] Other conventional explanations for why sex workers enter the trade include broken homes, poverty, sexual abuse, and few opportunities to make money legitimately.

By contrast, a number of my respondents reported that they turned to the adult industry because it offered them what they wanted in a job—namely, flexible hours, good money, and fun. It is not blocked opportunity but an understanding of the often inflexible and demanding nature of conventional work that motivates entry into pornography. Porn is appealing because it offers more flexibility and independence. Joanna, a native of France and an experienced actress, said:

> I just can't work in an office. I flip out—I get sick after 2 weeks. With this, I get to travel and have freedom. I got to come to the United States. I have enough money to take a vacation whenever I want. I just took 2 weeks off, although I am trying to save money.

Other respondents claimed that they were drawn to the ease of the work. As Kurt explained, "I might be on set from 8 A.M. to midnight, but I don't do a goddamn thing. They pay me to show up, read a book, flirt with girls, and fuck. As far as that goes, it's cake."

A sense of freedom and independence is supported by the structure of the industry itself. A few dozen actresses and two actors hold exclusive contracts with professional companies.[12] The contracts assure these individuals a number of features each year, as well as public appearances and modeling engagements. (While the contracts offer some stability, they also limit talent's exposure to other companies, and thus are often regarded with ambivalence.) Most talent, however, work as "freelancers" or under nonexclusive contracts, in which they guarantee a company a set number of days each month. Not being held to a contract allows talent to select jobs and projects that best fit their schedules, interests, and preferences. As Dane explained, not being under an exclusive contract can also increase overall earnings, because a person is free to work on more projects and spends less time on production sets:

> The reason I accepted a contract is because they are not keeping me exclusively. . . . I have a guarantee that's just about as big as a normal contract, but I can still work around, and my hours are less. I don't stick around for dialogue and bullshit, I just show up and ba-da-bing, I'm done, like, in 3 hours. In a contract where I am doing a feature, I sit around for 10, 12 hours. If you spread $500 over 12 hours, it's not as much as if you spread $500 over 3 hours. Logically, it makes a lot of sense to be nonexclusive.

Producers benefit from this freelance system as well by being able to select participants on a project-by-project basis. Only a few well-publicized stars are needed under exclusive contracts to promote the company.

While porn offers freedom and flexibility in comparison to most other jobs of equal pay, there are certain requirements for being regarded as professional and competent. In order to assure future projects, actresses and actors in all categories are expected to arrive on time, have all necessary paperwork available (identification and HIV test results),[13] be sober and cooperative, and be willing to stay overtime. Being labeled a "flake" is detrimental to a career, and includes everything from forgetting appointments, being uncooperative, and being unable to perform the requirements of the job (for men). Therefore, while the work is unconventional, some aspects of the job are typical to many industries.

Becoming a quasi-professional is possible only at the professional and pro-amateur level. The reasons for this are threefold. First, amateur productions specialize in "new," "different," and "never before seen" talent, leaving little possibility for repeat projects. Second, amateur productions attempt to capture "real" and "authentic" sex, and will not typically hire anyone with a "name" or with experience in the industry. Finally, because amateur productions pay so little (relatively) and are seldom linked to other money-making avenues (such as stripping), it is unlikely that someone could survive financially at this level.

Therefore, these participants are motivated by individual interest and opportunity, not a desire for flexible employment. This interest, however, is created by the freedom the industry offers. Many respondents reported that once they made the decision to enter the industry, the doors were open to them.

Opportunity and Sociability

At the amateur and pro-amateur levels, individuals typically find their way into the industry via friends, lovers, and coworkers. For example, amateur companies rely on actors and actresses to invite their friends to participate in a production. Agents are rarely involved with amateur productions because their fees would be too low, but "talent scouts" are used to refer reliable talent (scouts are typically paid $25 to $50). The opportunity to enter pornography therefore often comes from other participants. This avenue of entry applies to both women and men.

Once in the industry, it is easy to make connections that foster sustained contact with the business. On low-budget productions, for example, actresses and actors are often friends, and are brought onto a project specifically because of these relationships. On set, new relationships are formed, which in turn lead to additional projects. On professional sets, stars are given the opportunity to select their costars. Having these social ties is therefore critical for success. In addition, these relationships sustain interest and enthusiasm when other motivating factors, such as the lure of money, diminish.

As in many other careers in deviance, once in a subculture, friends and social networks typically become limited to individuals who are also part of the subgroup. Being part of a stigmatized group fosters these relationships. In the porn business, industry parties and less formalized social gatherings provide opportunities to socialize and network. Networking is as vital in porn production as it is in "straight" industries. These parties thus serve to make contacts, form alliances, and provide opportunities to "be seen."

In addition to opportunities via friends, lovers, and acquaintances, other sectors of the sex industry provide an avenue into the world of porn. For women, erotic dancing presents an opportunity to enter the porn industry. Dancers are often informed that they can make more money stripping if they appear in a few pornographic videos, and if a dancer has established a name for herself, she may be recruited by the porn industry. Based on her physical attractiveness and name recognition, a dancer may be offered both an exclusive contract and her pick of directors and co-talent.

If stripping can lead to porn, the reverse is true as well. It is rare for a big-name actress not to "dance" (strip) at least periodically. Dancing provides an opportunity to increase recognition and fan appeal, and thus, to make oneself more "profitable" to the industry. When an actress "headlines" (a featured appearance) at a dance club, the owners advertise that they have a porn star performing, which in turn draws larger crowds. Bigger crowds and increased interest results in higher tips for dancers and more business (and thus more profit) for the clubs. Therefore, actresses, club owners, and porn companies all stand to benefit from this symbiotic relationship.

Porn companies, particularly those offering semi-exclusive or exclusive contracts, often encourage actresses to dance in order to advertise the company. Larger companies retain booking agents for their dancers so that arrangements and pay negotiations are handled "in house." In addition, videotapes in which the dancer has performed are often made available for sale. When state laws prohibit such sales, "one-sheets," advertisements for videos with photographs taken on the set, are made available to the customers.

Increased recognition, however, can have negative effects on an actress's career. Porn companies are continually searching for "fresh" faces in order to appeal to both new and old viewers. Actresses who are "overexposed" in videos, magazine layouts, and dancing appearances are assumed to be unable to offer much appeal for viewers since their images become too familiar. Therefore, although publicity is mandatory for a profitable career, it is often a reason for limited company interest. The ingredients for a successful career are the very things that can end one.

Because magazine spreads and dancing opportunities are far more available for women than for men, actors are not vulnerable to overexposure, and as a result, their careers in porn commonly last twice as long as women's. As one actress explained:

> Girls have a shelf life of 9 months to 2 years, unless you are different. Like me, I am Asian, so it helps. Men stay forever. It is different for a man. If he can perform, he can stay in. There are guys that have been in the business 10 or 15 years.

Furthermore, as Levy[14] found in the "straight" film industry, popular successful actresses are younger on average than their male counterparts, suggesting the beauty norms held by both producers and audiences. In both the straight and adult industries, actors are able to age, while actresses are replaced by younger, newer talent.

Being Naughty and Having Sex

A number of my respondents reported that porn offered them a chance to snub the prevailing norms of acceptable sexuality. Few careers offer the same stigma as appearing on screen engaging in what most people consider a private act. While porn undoubtedly attracts exhibitionists, it is also a vehicle for people who wish to violate, challenge, and refute social norms. This phenomenon is particularly relevant for women, as the double standard offers more stringent norms for female sexual expression, whose violations carry additional sanctions. Male stars in many ways embody sexual norms that equate masculine sex with prowess, adventure, and detachment. A humorous comment by Dane evinced the link between male sexuality and porn: "[An actress] asked me if I had ever thought of being in the adult industry. I am an American male and I have seen porn—of course I have" thought of being in the industry.

One company in the study catered to and profited from this desire to be "naughty." The owner–director sought actresses and actors interested in being "bad." He believed that talent interested in money was rarely interested in sex, while those who desired fame were "used up" before they achieved it. Being "naughty" could easily be captured on film and would be appealing to viewers who want to see "real sex" (i.e., not acting). Interestingly, working for this producer offered actresses and actors an additional opportunity to be "naughty" since this particular company was marginal even within the industry (due to personnel, content matter, and geographical location).

In the course of violating social norms, porn offers the opportunity to have sex. Although it is widely assumed that the actresses are "acting" (at least to some degree), many respondents claimed that there was some sexual pleasure in their jobs. Being with "nice" and "gentle" guys was mentioned as increasing arousal. Several also reported that girl/girl scenes were more arousing or erotic because of the interpersonal dynamics between female participants. (They also claimed that girl/girl scenes were easier and faster, since they did not require waiting for erections.) While female arousal is often exaggerated or faked, it is undeniable that males are obtaining erections and ejaculating in front of the camera (typically constructed as "enjoying" sex). Even when filming softcore versions,[15] sexual activities are rarely simulated. Furthermore, most scenes end with external ejaculation as a means to suggest that the sex was real. Not surprisingly, most actors cited "getting laid" as a primary motivation for entering a porn career. Once in the industry, sustaining an interest in sex is critical for a successful career. Experiencing sexual problems (inability to maintain an erection or control ejaculation) is the fastest way to end an acting career. As one actor, Chuck, explained:

If you are the new guy, the first scene is usually no problem. If you have problems in the second scene, don't count on a third and fourth. At first it is fun because it is new. One day you realize it's work. Some guys can't continue.

A vested and sustained interest in "getting laid" is therefore a primary motivation for male actors in all three categories of pornography production.

Being part of the porn world offers sexual opportunities for interested participants off set as well. While many respondents reported that they were in monogamous relationships outside of work, single participants and those involved in swinging reported many opportunities for sex as a result of being involved in the industry. In addition to these opportunities, individuals involved in norm-violating subcultures are likely to hold nontraditional attitudes toward sex and sexuality, and thus be drawn to an arena in which they can exercise these interests. For example, because girl/girl sex is a staple of mainstream productions, actresses have ample opportunity to explore such relationships, which may carry over into private behavior. Nearly two-thirds of my female respondents self-identified as bisexual, although only half of them had had sex with women prior to entering the industry.

REMAINING IN PORNOGRAPHY

Actresses and actors can be divided into those who are forging a career in the adult entertainment industry and those who drift in and quickly out of the industry. Some who assumed it was a "one-time deal" may later decide that they want a career in the industry, while others, planning a long-term career, drop out early. Entrance into the industry, choices made to maintain involvement, and mobility within the industry are all affected by whether the goal is long-term or temporary involvement. Those who "drift" into the industry are more likely motivated by money, sex, desire for independence, and opportunity. Those who are attempting to achieve a long-term career are motivated by success and fame. Achieving and sustaining a successful career is dependent on many factors, including making profitable decisions, having connections, acting professionally, achieving a high status, and being seen. Each factor plays a part in maintaining involvement in the industry.

Making a Name

Just as the desire for fame and recognition motivates actors and actresses to enter the pornography industry, maintaining and increasing fame is a primary motivation for continuing a career in porn. This motive becomes stronger over time as initial fame develops into a respected reputation. In an industry that continually seeks new talent, maintaining fame is hard work. Strategic choices and fan support are crucial to retain one's position as a star. The perks for stardom, however, justify this work. Stars are paid considerably more per project (scenes and box covers), have more say in whom they will work with, spend less idle time on set, receive more recognition for their efforts, and are highly regarded within the industry.

Stars also receive considerably more attention from fans. Individual fan clubs, often maintained by managers, serve to announce local appearances and new releases. They also provide members with such things as personal messages, candid photographs, and trivia about the star. In addition, a well-known producer within the industry has formed a fan club which hosts its own award show and allows members to participate in industry gatherings. Fan clubs serve to make porn stars more accessible to the audience, a primary motivation for "intimacy at a distance."[16] More important, they offer advertisement and support for continued interest, both crucial for a successful career.

Building a fan base is supported by the industry. In an industry that thrives on offering "fresh" faces, actresses frequently appear in more videos during their first year in the industry than in any other year in their career. Generating fan appeal is assisted by the number of projects in which they appear. It is not uncommon for actresses to receive industry awards in their first year due in part to the sheer number of videos they appear in. Actors have a different experience. Because there is a small pool of male talent, their involvement continues as long as they do not experience any problems (usually sexual) on set. While actors do not typically have fan clubs, they achieve star status because of their longevity and recognition.

Fans occupy a peripheral position within the industry. Because most consumption of porn is anonymous, producers, directors, actors, and actresses rarely know who their audience is. Although the industry is dependent on fans for survival, many of the respondents reported a fairly negative image of the imagined viewer. Comments about viewers ranged from "lonely" and "hard-up" to "stupid" and "disgusting." Ironically, then, actresses and actors are motivated in part to receive recognition from a group they know little about and often disparage. In addition, they reported little pride in the products they produce.[17] Like most artifacts in the "sleaze industry," porn is disposable, mass produced, fungible, and easily forgotten. "Classics" such as *Deep Throat*, *Devil in Miss Jones*, and *Behind the Green Door* are rare, but are highly regarded and carry the promise of "getting your name known." The reward for appearing in more successful (and profitable) productions is fame, not money. Unlike the "straight" industry, actors and actresses are paid a flat fee for their performances, and receive no royalties for successful projects.

While striving for admiration from the "outside," actresses and actors are also motivated to be successful in the eyes of their peers. "Having what it takes" to succeed in porn is dependent on both internal and external approval and admiration. Conformity and peer pressure are as common in the adult entertainment industry as they are in most jobs. Although achieving status in the industry is critical for success (particularly in regard to securing work), it also provides a primary motivation for staying in the business. Building a reputation among peers and being famous in regard to fans were the most commonly cited motivations for maintaining a career in pornography.

Achieving high status serves multiple functions for both participants and organizations. The porn industry forms a closed community in which members rely on one another for both social activities and professional connections. As in other deviant careers, relationships take on a dual function because the deviant lifestyle limits interaction and sociability with "nondeviants." Furthermore, many respondents claimed that the industry was much like a family, albeit one full of competition and gossip. Achieving status within this group is dependent on many factors, including being well liked and/or respected, being recognized as competent, and achieving career longevity in the business. While networks and friendships are crucial for careers, they also offer support, social opportunities, and validation.

Career Strategies

Compared to many jobs, porn offers more freedom, independence, money, and sex. Once in the industry, many respondents reported that they were motivated to make a successful career of it. Some respondents commented that being involved in porn had hurt their chances of working in mainstream jobs, making them even more motivated to make porn work profitable. While most recognized that the career was short term, they engaged in strategies to prolong their involvement and to make their careers more lucrative.

For actresses, one means to achieving a career in pornography is to make themselves consistently desirable and available (at least visually) to the public. This includes erotic dancing, modeling, being photographed, granting interviews, responding to fan groups, appearing at award shows, and signing autographs at trade shows (such as the Video Software Dealers' Association and the Consumer Electronics Show). In addition, computer technology has led the pornography industry to offer fans interactive software, CD-ROM, and online chat sessions. A pornography career thus can extend beyond acting in videos.

For actors, a successful career is dependent almost exclusively on one's ability to perform sexually. There is little supplemental work an actor can do to boost his career beyond being dependable, consistent, and available.

Because there are few opportunities in related settings, some actors support their careers by holding other jobs in the industry. For example, one actor I interviewed also worked as an editor for a pro-amateur company. His goal was to use these skills to make a leap into the straight industry, although a number of respondents reported that this type of mobility is difficult due to the stigmatized nature of porn. Other actors advance within the industry to directing videos and working in other aspects of production. Although they often make less money than when acting, they achieve some degree of "professionalism" and prolong their careers by developing other skills.

In addition to building fan appeal or recognition, building a career requires making sensible choices and decisions throughout one's involvement in the industry. Working with the successful companies increases one's chances of being famous and developing a career. Regardless of the point of entry, to "make it" in porn, actors and actresses must quickly move up to professional companies. Those who are unable to break into the professional scene are unlikely to achieve fame. As previously discussed, while some recognition is afforded to those in amateur productions, there are simply not enough opportunities for exposure to achieve fame. Furthermore, working with reputable companies with high budgets (for both production and advertising) increases the chance of winning industry awards, which in turn offers fame and recognition.

A successful career is also dependent on having the right connections within the industry. For example, although several respondents claimed that talent agents were relatively useless in the industry, connecting to a reputable agent increases the possibility of a porn career. For example, two producers I interviewed reported that although virtually all of the actresses and actors are known to them beforehand, they continually pay an agent fee. In return, agents contact them first when "hot" talent enters the industry. This relationship is also advantageous to actresses and actors, who subsequently enter at the highest level possible. In addition, agents often provide opportunities for modeling, as they are connected with both pornography and adult magazine companies.

Beyond agents, decisions about who will work on a particular film are made by directors, producers, actresses, and occasionally actors. (Actresses are usually asked who they would like to work with on a particular production and are given the opportunity to reject possible actors. Actors were far less likely to be asked this question.) It is not uncommon for arrangements about future work to be made while on the set of another project. Furthermore, the directors refer reliable talent to other directors, and the participants request and refer each other for upcoming work. It is mandatory therefore to have high status and a good reputation within the industry. High status, however, is different from being well liked. Competition for desired projects and publicity further affect these social relationships. These relationships are enmeshed with the interpersonal politics of the culture. Most respondents reported that knowing and pleasing the right people, being in the "in crowd," and competing with adversaries are key components of the work. Since project opportunities often come via informal networks, being involved in the porn subculture is essential for continued involvement in the industry. Actresses and actors who remain peripheral to the culture and/or who are excluded from it are more likely to drift out of the pornography industry because of limited opportunities. Maintaining a career is therefore dependent on being involved in the porn subculture.[18]

Mobility and Commitment

Mobility in the industry is difficult to measure in its traditional sense, partly because of the organizational structure of the industry. For example, on entry, actors and actresses often move up from the amateur to the professional level. This is particularly true for actors who must prove themselves sexually in amateur productions before they are allowed to advance to pro-amateur and professional features. Because of the higher budgets, higher number of participants, and tight production schedules in professional features, directors need to be assured that there will be no unnecessary delays on the set because of sexual difficulties.

In contrast, some actresses enter at higher levels. Those who enter via modeling or dancing typically start at the pro-amateur level and, after proving their commercial value, are advanced to professional productions. Actresses who are considered exceptionally attractive and individuals with pre-established public recognition often start at the professional level. Once established in the professional scene, however, actors and actresses often appear in pro-amateur productions with no repercussions to their careers. Furthermore, because pro-amateur organizations are often owned by professional companies, this movement is supported by the industry.

Actresses who display little interest in moving up are often criticized by their coworkers and others as "fuck bunnies," "sluts," or "skags," and are seen as lacking ambition, skills, or knowledge.[19] This judgment is encouraged by the assumption that any pretty woman can make it in porn if she wants to. As unskilled laborers, the work of actresses is regarded as fairly easy, even in comparison with their male coworkers, who must "perform" to remain employed. In addition, because of higher pay and higher levels of publicity and fame, females reap more benefits in the industry. Therefore, those who cannot make it despite these advantages are assumed to be lacking personal ambition, with little consideration given to structural constraints.

Mobility is facilitated by longevity and commitment. "Sticking around" and "taking it seriously" are observable qualities, and are often translated into "having what it takes." Moving between pro-amateur and professional productions and working outside the porn industry are essential for a freelance career, suggesting the importance of horizontal rather than vertical mobility. The phenomenon of "working the circuit" is common in other industries where employers' commitment to employees is low and employees operate as independent contractors. In sum, those who wish to stay in the industry must display a continuous interest in forming networks, choosing the right projects, "looking good," being seen, and getting along with others.

CONCLUSION

Actors and actresses who are searching for quick money and/or sexual adventure quickly leave the industry once those goals are met, as do those who take one-time opportunities to act in porn videos. Those who remain must build a career for themselves in an industry that centers on the temporary. Motivations change with experience and are replaced with other goals. Of the motivations that are associated with entry into the industry, fame and recognition appear to be the most sustaining. In addition, although the construction of fame differs between actors and actresses, the desire for admiration and renown does not appear to be limited to women.

Initial motivations may be replaced by more substantial goals once talent is established in the industry. For example, although many respondents reported that "being naughty" was a primary motivation for entry, this goal is met in a relatively short time. It does not take many video appearances to establish one's rejection of traditional values. Over time, those interested in challenging mainstream societal values forge a career in which they receive approval for their actions and opportunities for recognition and exposure. Being "naughty" gives way to longer term career goals. Those motivated by sex quickly learn that they must be able to perform on command in order to remain in the industry. Having sex becomes work, and actors and actresses are motivated to remain in the industry because they are among those who can "do the job." The motivation for sex is replaced by the desire to keep the job.

The careers of porn actors and actresses share some similarities with other deviant careers. Participants often have a difficult time "going straight" (or leaving the business) after growing accustomed to the money associated with their work. In addition, being part of a stigmatized group reduces one's chances of achieving success in the "legitimate" world.

Finally, gender differences are also evident in other sectors of the sex industry. For example, research on male strippers suggests that males experience less social stigma than their female counterparts.[20] In the porn industry, male respondents felt less stigmatized, and had greater opportunities for certain kinds of career advancement within the industry (e.g., working as editors or directors). In addition, just as many female strippers have held previous jobs that required some display of their body (modeling, go-go dancing, topless waitressing), porn actresses were far more likely than their male counterparts to have had previous ties to the sex industry. A final comparison comes from a study comparing male, female, and transgender prostitutes.[21] The authors found that male and transgender prostitutes were more likely to report sexual enjoyment with clients than female prostitutes. Porn actors, similarly, were more likely than actresses to report sex as a motivation, and were more dependent on enjoying the sex in order to maintain their careers.

NOTES

1. Luis Garcia, Kathleen Brennan, Monica DeCalo, Rachel McGlennon, and Sandra Tait, "Sex Differences in Sexual Arousal to Different Erotic Stories," *Journal of Sex Research* 20 (1984): 391–402; Edward Donnerstein and Daniel Linz, "Mass Media Sexual Violence and Male Viewers: Current Theory and Research," *American Behavioral Science* 29 (1986): 601–618; Larry Baron, "Pornography and Gender Equality: An Empirical Analysis," *Journal of Sex Research* 27 (1990): 363–380.

2. Lisa Duggan and Nan Hunter, *Sex Wars: Sexual Dissent and Political Culture*, New York: Routledge, 1995; Nadine Strossen, *Defending Pornography: Free Speech, Sex, and the Fight for Women's Rights*, New York: Scribner, 1995.

3. Sharon A. Abbott, "Careers of Actors and Actresses in the Pornography Industry," Ph.D. dissertation, Department of Sociology, Indiana University, Bloomington, 1999.

4. Similar figures were reported in Chris Heath, "A Hard Man Is Good to Find," *Details* (September 1996): 96–291.

5. Double Penetrations or "DPs" refer to either two organs (usually penises) in a single orifice, such as an anus or vagina, or penetration of two organs

of a single individual (for example, one male penetrating a woman's anus, and another her vagina). The latter is more common.

6. Because they are typically freelance employees, they are not offered health insurance by the companies they work for. Even the few talent on contract are not offered health benefits. Protecting Adult Welfare, an industry action group, is attempting to organize a low-cost health insurance package for the industry.

7. Similar findings were reported in Susan Faludi, "The Money Shot," *New Yorker* (October 30, 1995): 64–87.

8. Phasing in and out of the industry is fairly common, particularly for actresses. The most common pattern reported by trade magazines is for actresses to become romantically involved with someone outside of the industry, and to drop out for the duration of the relationship.

9. Interestingly, *Adult Video News,* the industry's premier trade publication, reports that pro-amateur features have a higher sales and rental rate than professional features.

10. Emanuel Levy, "Social Attributes of American Movie Stars," *Media, Culture, and Society* 12 (1990): 247–267.

11. Carol Rambo Ronai and Carolyn Ellis, "Turn-Ons for Money: Interactional Strategies of the Table Dancer," *Journal of Contemporary Ethnography* 18 (1989): 271–298.

12. Interestingly, the likelihood of "being under contract" is not linked to years experience, as it might be with other industries. The reasons for this are twofold. First, actresses' status typically decreases with years in the industry, becoming less profitable and thus less desirable with time. Second, many experienced talent reported that contracts are often too restrictive and are not advantageous to a successful career.

13. Talent in the heterosexual porn industry are tested for HIV antibodies every 30 days, and must have their test results available on production sets.

14. Emanuel Levy, "Social Attributes of American Movie Stars."

15. Professional companies usually make both a hardcore and a softcore version of each video produced in order to reach multiple outlets, including cable, home video, international, and hotel markets. Softcore versions show no actual penetration and are restricted in allowable language.

16. Laura Leets, Gavin de Becker, and Howard Giles, "Fans: Exploring Expressed Motivations for Contacting Celebrities," *Journal of Language and Social Psychology* 14 (1995): 102–123.

17. Most respondents reported that they watch videos they appear in only for the "acting" (dialogue), not the sex. Interestingly, producers interviewed suggested that the audience fast-forwarded through the dialogue to get to the sex scenes.

18. While being involved in the subculture is beneficial to actresses and actors, it does have its negative aspects. For example, there is a great deal of gossip in the porn subculture, which can damage a career. Several male respondents reported that at some point in their career, another actor had accused them of being gay or of appearing in gay pornography. While homosexuality is generally used to insult someone's masculinity, in the porn world this gossip carries additional weight. Actors reported that female coworkers would often refuse to work with male talent "accused" of homosexuality out of fear of HIV infection.

19. Each of these insults carries implications about women's sexuality. In one regard, they may suggest that the woman in question was "too interested" in sex. Since sex is less commonly a primary motivation for female talent, it may suggest a double standard within the industry. However, these insults may also be linked to a more general phenomenon of insulting women by referring to their sexuality or genitalia. See Kathleen Preston and Kimberley Stanley, "'What's the Worst Thing . . .?' Gender-Directed Insults," *Sex Roles* 17 (1987): 209–219.

20. William Thompson and Jackie Harred, "Topless Dancers: Managing Stigma in a Deviant Occupation," *Deviant Behavior* 13 (1992): 291–311; Paula Dressel and David Petersen, "Becoming a Male Stripper: Recruitment, Socialization, and Ideological Development," *Work and Occupations* 9 (1982): 387–406; Paula Dressel and David Petersen, "Gender Roles, Sexuality, and the Male Strip Show: The Structuring of Sexual Opportunity," *Sociological Focus* 15 (1982): 151–162.

21. Martin Weinberg, Frances Shaver, and Colin Williams, "Gendered Prostitution in the San Francisco Tenderloin," *Archives of Sexual Behavior* 28 (1999): 503–521.

GAY MALE PORNOGRAPHY SINCE STONEWALL

Joe A. Thomas

Gay porn makes up a disproportionately large segment of the pornography market. Estimates of porn's total economic clout range from $8 to $10 billion annually, with gay porn making up 10 to 25%;[1] some industry insiders have even estimated as much as one-third to one-half of the adult industry is gay sales and rentals.[2] Gay porn, however, has generally been neglected in the fierce debate over pornography during the past four decades. Perhaps the fact that the debate has largely been driven by feminist claims about pornography's exploitation of women has led to gay pornography's neglect. Yet our understanding of pornography cannot be defined solely in heterosexual terms, and an analysis of gay pornography may help to expand our knowledge of pornography in general.

What distinguishes pornography from other types of expression is its primary goal of sexual stimulation. Richard Dyer has noted that the goal of the pornographic narrative itself is sexual climax;[3] there is a parallel between the activities depicted and the activities they are intended to inspire. Pornography, as opposed to other forms of sexual representation, is recognized by both its creators and its consumers as an instrument of sexual arousal. Such sexually explicit material has a long history, dating back to prehistoric images of stylized male and female deities and continuing through classical antiquity; but despite pornography's Greek etymology, its current classification as a media genre began during the 19th century. While the content of pornography has usually reflected the heterosexual orientation of the dominant culture, same-sex imagery and narratives have always played a role in the history of erotic expression. In the years since the landmark Stonewall protests of 1969, gay porn has developed into a significant force both in the pornography industry and in gay cultural life.

Understanding the history of gay porn in film and video is vital for understanding the gay video phenomenon of today. Many of its unique qualities (as well as those that it shares with straight porn) can be explained by tracing the stylistic and iconographic evolution of the gay porn film. In some respects, the development and growth of gay porn mirrors the political ascendancy of gays and lesbians. As the struggle for gay liberation expanded and gained a higher profile during the 1970s, so did the gay segment of the pornography industry. Similarly, the belated adoption of condom usage in gay films reflected the advent of AIDS in the 1980s. Gay porn also expressed changing gay cultural ideals of masculinity and beauty. Ultimately, because the sexual activity depicted in gay porn represented the basic difference that created the homosexual identity, gay porn's popularity can be seen as an affirmation of gay life and culture.

This chapter describes and analyzes the history, production, and content of gay male pornography in various motion picture media. It focuses particularly on video (including videocassettes, DVDs, and other media designed for home use), which has been the most popular and prominent pornographic medium for gays since the 1980s. From that time most print magazines have assumed a supporting role to video, commonly featuring layouts of video performers, or stills taken from videos.[4] The contemporary gay pornography industry thus centers on live-action features.

The chapter is based on an extensive review of the literature on gay pornography and analysis of a number of videos produced since the 1970s. Part of this chapter focuses on the historical development and stylistic evolution of the videos. It also examines the economics and culture of gay video, both in the industry and in gay life.

HISTORY

The history of gay male pornography in motion pictures falls into several overlapping periods. The pre-Stonewall era encompasses material through 1969. These were mostly stag films (short features designed for viewing at specialized arcades or at all-male "stag" parties) along with a sprinkling of underground films and a few short movies derived from "physique" pornography (the popular softcore male pinups from mid-century). Much of this early material is not "hardcore," lacking images of penetration. The film era dates from around 1970 through the early 1980s. During this period, traditional 16mm celluloid film dominated the industry, both in short "loops" in arcades and in theatrical features, and hardcore became common. The advent of home videocassette recorders during the early 1980s marked the beginning of the video era, which lasted until the millennium. After 2000, digital formats (DVD and on the Internet) came to dominate the industry, creating the digital era. While technical changes in medium seem largely to define this periodization, changes in content and context often accompanied them.

The earliest surviving filmed depictions of gay sex date back to the 1920s. Thomas Waugh's research showed that about 8% of surviving stag films from this early era contained some sort of gay content, usually bisexual.[5] During the 1960s, gay sex films were largely limited to softcore posing and wrestling movies made for home projection, along the same lines as the older stags. However, the number of sexually explicit films did increase in the decade; Thomas Waugh has documented about 100 explicit all-male stag films from the 1960s (in contrast to a handful from earlier years),[6] but most of these were amateurish at best.

Gay subjects did not, however, share in the surge of popular "sexploitation" films characteristic of the 1960s. Instead, while straight viewers were subjected to an onslaught of "nudie" and "nudie-cutie" films from prolific producers such as David Friedman, gay viewers found their own tastes reflected in relatively highbrow underground art films. Many of the prominent underground filmmakers in New York in the early 1960s were gay (Kenneth Anger and Andy Warhol), and their avant-garde works, while generally non-narrative, often contained suggestive or overtly homosexual content. Anger's *Scorpio Rising* (1963) was a dreamlike, impressionistic, homoerotic montage involving a motorcycle gang; Warhol's *My Hustler* (1965) told the story of two bitchy queens who fought over a handsome young prostitute. What made these rather esoteric art films appealing to a gay audience was their open representation of the eroticized male body presented within the relatively safe (for closeted gay viewers) context of avant-garde art. And according to Richard Dyer, the precedent of such avant-garde underground films often provided important formal and narrative models during the early days of gay porn in the 1970s.[7]

Developments in jurisprudence also contributed to the growth of gay pornography. John d'Emilio and Estelle Freedman described how a series of U.S. Supreme Court rulings between 1957 and 1967 helped to open the floodgates for increasingly explicit sex movies. The famous *Roth v. United States* case of 1957, which sustained the conviction of a bookdealer for selling pornography, paradoxically cracked open the door for more explicit materials by proclaiming that "sex and obscenity are not synonymous." By 1967, the infamous book *Fanny Hill* was found not to be obscene because it was not "*utterly* without redeeming social value."[8] Although these two court decisions laid the initial framework, the early 1970s' explosion in sex films was likely triggered by the Supreme Court victory of the Swedish film *I Am Curious (Yellow)* in 1969; a startling number of erotic film festivals followed.[9] A simultaneous growth in eroticism in mainstream media was exemplified by Hollywood productions such as *Midnight Cowboy*, which chronicled the story of a male prostitute; as Hollywood moved into new sexual territory, the sex film industry moved from cheap stags to more lavish and explicit productions.

The growing commercial exhibition of gay pornographic movies marked the beginning of the film era in gay porn. John Burger has traced commercial exhibition of hardcore gay sex films in cinemas to at least as early as 1968, when the Park Theater in Los Angeles began screening the features of pioneering filmmakers Pat Rocco (*Sex and the Single Gay*) and Bob Mizer (the creator of the famous Athletic Model Guild porn production company), along with avant-garde underground films.[10] Pornography became a widespread, popular phenomenon in the early 1970s, with the unexpected popularity of the hit movie *Deep Throat*. In a significant change from the earlier sexploitation movies, *Deep Throat* was reviewed by all the famous movie critics, and by the end of 1973, it was among the top 10 money-making films of the year.[11]

However, *Deep Throat*'s emergence as a hugely popular hardcore phenomenon actually followed the earlier example of the first widely distributed, hardcore gay release: *The Boys in the Sand*. While its potential audience was naturally smaller, it nevertheless grossed $800,000 shortly after opening in December 1971 in New York at the 55th Street Playhouse (with a production cost of only $8,000).[12] Directed by Wakefield Poole, it starred soon-to-be gay superstar Casey Donovan, also known as the professional actor and model Cal Culver. Vaguely episodic, the movie had a dreamlike quality that betrayed the influence of the earlier underground films of the 1960s.

The Boys in the Sand showed the enormous market potential of gay porn, and the production of gay porn films continued to expand during the 1970s. Companies such as Jaguar and P.M. Productions began producing a stream of hardcore features for release in a limited number of gay porn theaters. As the industry diversified, it also became increasingly commercialized. Gay porn lost its early formal references to art films and its occasional aspirations to being something more than "just pornography." In many ways it converged with straight pornography: both genres began to minimize narrative and aesthetic content in favor of increased explicitness.

In 1981 there were 20,000 adult bookstores and 800 sex cinemas in the United States.[13] However, the proliferation of home VCRs during the following decade made video pornography readily accessible, and video soon became the primary medium. As prices of home VCRs fell during the 1980s, the market became increasingly lucrative, and producers began shooting films directly on video, aimed at the growing market of home viewers. From 1979 to 1988, the number of Americans with VCRs rose from under 1% to almost 60%.[14] Simultaneously, porn theaters (both gay and straight) largely disappeared.

The pioneering early 1970s' gay porn films often used whatever models were available. Later in the decade, companies such as Colt produced a few silent shorts with especially handsome, beefy men (which became their specialty), but most of the decade's production suffered from man-on-the-street casting—a definite problem when representing sexual fantasies for an audience of gay men highly attuned to particular standards of physical beauty. In contrast to the everyman of average 1970s' films, or the bodybuilders of Colt, gay movies during the first half of the video era were dominated by exceptionally young performers, smooth and sleek. The performers' body hair was minimal, the "swimmer's build" predominated, and models' ages never seemed to exceed the early twenties. Youth was at a premium. Directors William Higgins and Matt Sterling set the standard for the new 1980s' gay porn model. Higgins's work, ranging from *Sailor in the Wild* in 1983 to *Big Guns* in 1987, epitomized this change from the gay porn of the 1970s. Higgins's films generally starred a cast of slightly built, smooth-skinned, youthful men with an occasional muscular, mature performer. Matt Sterling's work, such as 1984's *The Bigger The Better*, also starred boyish performers but with more emphasis on muscularity. The change to younger models was seen in print pornography as well: during the 1980s more than 90% of the oldest models appeared to be only in their teens or twenties; in the early 1970s almost half had appeared 30 or older.[15]

Videos of the 1980s also tightly defined actors' sexual roles as "tops" or "bottoms." The top was the insertor in anal sex, and the bottom was the recipient. The top might occasionally engage in a little oral sex with his partner, but that was not typical. John Summers' *Two Handfuls* was a good example, as Brian Maxon was serviced by three different men, but hardly lifted a finger himself until the final scene. One could usually predict what roles the performers would play only a few seconds into the scene. The top was usually the more muscular, tan, and athletic; he also had the bigger penis. Exclusive tops held a privileged position both within the industry and in the narrative of the video;[16] most of the major porn stars of the 1980s were exclusive tops.

CHANGES SINCE 1990

During the early 1990s, the industry began to change in certain respects. The performers no longer looked alike; the image of the Calvin Klein underwear ad was no longer the single canonical standard of beauty in gay pornography. Moreover, production values improved, especially editing. For instance, in productions from reputable studios, viewers were no longer subjected to a 6-minute, continuous close-up of anal sex. Lighting became more sophisticated; and following the lead of straight porn, exotic and more expensive locales began to appear.

The trend toward professional refinement in videos may have been due to Kristen Bjorn's arrival into porn production in the late 1980s. A former performer, Bjorn's work possessed an unusually distinctive, signature style. He was said to film everything himself, without a large crew, and to spend days or weeks shooting each feature[17] (when most of the industry considered a 2-day shoot an extravagance). His longer shooting schedule enabled him to create the illusion that his performers were multiorgasmic, sometimes climaxing as many as five times in one scene. Each film usually focused on an exotic locale with exotic men. Early works such as *Carnaval in Rio* (1989) and *Island Fever* (1989) were shot in Brazil; later videos moved to the beaches of Australia, the forests of Canada, and the newly accessible cities of central Europe. More often than in straight films, gay porn was usually racially segregated into all-black and (more commonly) all-white features. Bjorn broke decisively with this convention, mixing attractive men of various races and ethnicities, and especially multiracial performers.

Bjorn's high production values threw down the gauntlet for the rest of the industry and set a new, higher technical standard. As a former still photographer,[18] Bjorn carefully framed every scene, using props extensively. Combined with his carefully chosen sets and locations, his meticulous productions resulted in lush, visually striking videos that consistently have been among the most popular rentals reported by video outlets. Probably as a result of Bjorn's efforts, production values, especially photography and editing, improved immensely across the industry in the 1990s as the other high-end studios attempted to compete with him.

The 1990s also saw a continuing expansion of the market.[19] Increased diversity among the models and experimentation with new approaches contributed to this expansion. In most top-of-the-line productions (often from Catalina or Falcon), the actors were more professional and actually seemed to enjoy their work. They represented a much broader range of ages and body types than in the 1980s. Although young performers were still frequently seen, it was no longer uncommon to find performers in their thirties and even early forties. Realtor Cole Tucker began appearing in videos in 1996 at 43.[20] Body hair began to make a major reappearance with the success of models such as Zak Spears and Steve Regis.

In their performances many actors of the 1990s were sexually versatile, overturning the porn conventions of the 1980s. Superstars of the 1980s such as Jeff Stryker were nearly always tops; rarely did an actor change his role from one feature to another, and almost never in the same scene.[21] In the late 1990s, however, many videos from Falcon (then the largest producer of gay porn) as well as from most other companies contained at least one scene with mutual anal sex.

Similarly, sexual "types" in general were less pronounced in the 1990s videos. A big bruiser like Steve Regis surprisingly turned out to be primarily a bottom. The late bodybuilder Steve Fox usually bottomed as well, defying the 1980s' stereotypes of "bigger build on top." Even the straight "trade" tops of later years (such as Ty Fox and Ken Ryker) were active participants in sex, even giving oral sex to their partners before proceeding to their standard top roles in anal sex. In *Playing with Fire* (1996) Fox did everything except passive anal sex, including kissing; the same went for Ryker in *Matinee Idol* (1996). More tops in the 1990s actually seemed to be gay men as opposed to "gay for pay," that is, straight men in gay porn films. Brad Hunt or Aidan Shaw were never penetrated on camera, but performed their roles with relish, kissing, sucking, and doing everything else short of anal penetration.

Another 1990s' development was the increase in foreplay, kissing, and caressing. In the 1980s, performers dropped their drawers and went straight for the dicks. With some notable exceptions, 1980s' videos showed little kissing or affection. In the 1990s, by contrast, actors commonly kissed even before removing their clothes, and kissing frequently continued throughout the scene. Both Kristen Bjorn and Falcon Productions were notable in this regard. In fact, extensive kissing would seem to distinguish gay porn from straight porn, which has rarely included such romantic content.

Safer sex standards were also established in the industry during the 1990s. In 1988, condom usage began to appear in gay videos, but only sporadically.[22] However, because of growing AIDS activism, by the early 1990s most actors consistently used condoms in anal sex scenes (although not in oral sex). The gay adult industry was far ahead of heterosexual pornography in this regard. Only in 1998 did the straight industry begin to consider condom usage instead of relying on periodic HIV testing, and then only in response to several performers' seroconversions. Even today, condoms are not standard practice in straight porn.

Plot and acting have rarely played an important role in video pornography. However, increased production values sometimes included a greater emphasis on style. For example, *The Other Side of Aspen 3* (1995) contained an unusual scene that exemplified the new stylishness of gay videos. Two men had sex in a car in a scene filmed in near-darkness without bright lights or explicit close-ups. The realism of the dark, cramped quarters and quick, frantic copulation lent a stylish sense of voyeurism to the video. Similarly, the 1997 GEVA and GayVN Video of the Year awards went to *Naked Highway*, an on-the-road story that borrowed from sources as diverse as Jack Kerouac, *Thelma and Louise*, and *Easy Rider*. It used flashbacks, sophisticated camera angles, and stylized editing to create a video with a clear narrative and a distinctive esthetic.

What caused the changes in style and content in the latter half of the video era? I would argue that, in this case, art imitated life: changes in video porn reflected a changing gay identity. As the AIDS crisis brought together divergent parts of gay culture, the rise of queer radicalism brought a renewed openness to diversity and a recognition of the value of difference. One of the tenets of the late 1980s and early 1990s radical group Queer Nation was the recognition of diversity within the gay community. The increasing consciousness of diversity seemed to be reflected in the new range of ages, ethnicities, and physical types within porn in the 1990s.

A sort of mini-sexual revolution took place as well. During the late 1980s and 1990s, sex and sexual orientation were scrutinized from new perspectives by a diverse range of scholars. Camille Paglia's ideas about the sexualized nature of western culture[23] received extensive media attention. And the popular columnist Susie Bright launched a lively media campaign against sexual repression. In articles and books[24] she promoted the open enjoyment of pornography, sex toys, and kinky sex, and discouraged and ridiculed sexual stereotyping of any kind. Pat Califia issued collections of her own question-and-answer columns[25] in which she, a butch lesbian, forthrightly answered the technical and emotional sex questions of America's gay men. These popular authors were part of a new sexual liberation that celebrated diversity, openness, and sexual pleasure. This new attitude was reflected in the loosening of conventions in video porn.

Changes in the medium itself echoed the recent changes in content as the digital era got underway in the new century. Titan Men had experimented with offering an interactive CD-ROM with their 1998 VHS release *Redwood*. In the late 1990s, a new digital medium, the DVD, became available. During the opening years of the 2000s, the DVD medium, with its improved resolution, compact size, and computer compatibility quickly came to replace the videocassette as the medium of choice for home viewers. By 2005, many porn studios had ceased making videocassettes in favor of DVDs.

The Internet was already an important part of the gay porn world at the end of the video era; most studios maintained extensive websites, and many performers—especially those who also escorted—had home pages. During the digital era, increased online connection speeds and faster computer processors made the Internet an ever more desirable venue for pornography. By the end of the decade, the important studios had expanded their web presence—offering pictures, streaming video, and downloads—to the point that Falcon expected Internet revenues to exceed wholesale in 2007.[26] Entirely new studios also emerged with products that were exclusively available as subscription services on the web.[27]

The Internet was the perfect medium for the expansion of highly specialized porn appealing to "niche" markets. Longtime straight-porn performer Nina Hartley has maintained that the development of such niche market videos was the most dramatic new development in adult films of the 1990s.[28] Gay videos joined in the straight industry's boom in niche videos, which included such specialized genres as amateur, wrestling, transsexual, bondage, and others. For example, Altomar Productions created videos featuring men from their mid-forties up through their seventies. This company also produced a line of fetish videos focusing on uncircumcised men and foreskin.[29] The very popular amateur genre started as pornographic home movies on videotape. Their unflinching realism was the attraction, and they went from being "mom-and-pop" operations to having widespread professional distribution. Because these products appealed to small, specific audiences, access was a problem during the video era. However, the low overhead of porn websites relative to traditional studios, plus the ability to reach a much larger population because of virtually universal access to the Internet, made it easier and more profitable to create porn for extremely specialized tastes. While major studios continued to produce certain specialized products (leather, fisting), much of the niche market moved to the Internet in the 2000s.

In fact, the Internet soon became major competition to the established studios. A number of websites such as RandyBlue.com. ActiveDuty.com, and SeanCody.com built on the earlier development of amateur and "gonzo" porn (which broke down the "fourth wall" between the filmmaker and subject) and gave it broad-based appeal. The new websites took nonprofessionals and made them Internet stars. Performers were frequently billed as straight, and initially masturbation was the primary act depicted. Over time, these sites focused increasingly on hardcore action as they hired more gay performers—and as their straight performers discovered just how far they could go for the right price. Gonzo-style interviews with the performers often preceded the action. Some of the traditional studios produced DVDs along similar lines, but using better production values, even as the quality of the Internet-based porn improved (some even broadcasting in high definition). The result is that boundaries between amateur and professional have become so blurred that the content is sometimes indistinguishable.

Probably the most important (and most controversial) development in gay porn during the digital era has been the meteoric rise of another niche market to the status of a major force: "bareback" videos, in which no condoms are used. Condomless sex began to reappear occasionally in gay life during the late 1990s, after the development of new HIV medications made AIDS seem less serious to a small segment of the gay population, and as those already infected saw little reason to use condoms with each other. Bareback videos began to appear in 1997 when a new producer of amateur fetish porn, Dick Wadd, filmed *NYPD*, a fetish video that was only incidentally bareback.[30] Another company, Treasure Island Media, followed the subsequent year. In the early years of the digital era, bareback proliferated with many more companies arriving on the scene. Taking their cue from amateur and gonzo, bareback videos rarely had plots or elaborate sets, but instead focused on intense, highly physical sex. As the genre developed, bareback began to fetishize semen, showing ejaculations in the mouth and anus and "cum-swapping" (the transfer of semen from one person's mouth or anus to another's). In most cases the performers were assumed to be HIV positive, but in 2003 *Rolling Stone* published a controversial article about "bug chasers": men who consciously sought out seroconversion through unprotected sex.[31] Although later shown to have vastly exaggerated the numbers, the publicity further tainted the bareback industry as it became associated with the self-destructive philosophy of bug chasing.

During the mid-2000s, American companies were joined by an array of European bareback producers such as Eurocreme. These studios focused on slim, extremely youthful performers (in contrast to the older casts of U.S. bareback brands) and were produced in countries from Hungary to Sweden. Unlike their American counterparts, they relied on periodic testing for their performers, just as did most of the straight industry.

The popularity and growth of the bareback genre has created intense debate. Some viewers see any unprotected sex as a symbol of the AIDS epidemic as a whole, and find the videos repugnant. Others fear that these videos romanticize and encourage such practices in men's private lives. A documented case of transmission on a bareback set in England[32] has lent credence to the idea that in the European scene, young naive men are being coerced or cajoled into taking risks they do not really understand. Still others take a libertarian perspective and argue that any sex is a calculated risk, and that consenting adults should be able to make their own decisions about limits and responsibilities. The annual GayVN Awards for porn eliminated bareback videos for nomination beginning in 2004. Considering the ongoing popularity of bareback and the continuing menace of AIDS, this promises to be a long-term debate.

Stylistically, the proliferation of truly amateur porn on the Internet has also resulted in something of an ironic devolution for gay video. Sites such as XTube made it possible for anyone to share homemade porn. The short length and poor quality of these videos was reminiscent of the grainy, short loops of the pre-Stonewall and early film era. It remains to be seen if the gritty realism and endless variety of XTube and similar sites will actually replace studio porn.

THE GAY VIDEO INDUSTRY

Video pornography's explosion in popularity in the 1990s (with the production of 50–70 videos a month)[33] included the birth of a complex, interactive subculture of industry players and fans: an array of celebrity directors such as drag queen Chi Chi LaRue and John Rutherford (who has a college degree in film production); influential critics such as Mickey Skee, who has written a variety of books on the industry as well as a constant stream of reviews; a variety of industry magazines and websites; and a vast number of popular performers who made profitable appearances as featured strip acts in gay clubs. Some also worked as professional escorts (the commonly used euphemism for male prostitutes).

Among the many directors of the 1990s, Chi Chi LaRue (perhaps the heir apparent to the incomparable drag queen Divine) was a prolific director who worked for many of the major studios. Originally from Minnesota, LaRue appeared on the porn scene in the late 1980s and quickly rose to *auteur* status while amassing a prolific and respectable body of work. LaRue freely incorporated drag into his public persona, appearing with his considerable retinue of buff performers as the emcee during their club dates. LaRue gained remarkable influence as one of the few directors who consistently worked with a variety of the top gay porn production companies. Establishing his own production company in the early 2000s, during the first decade of the new millennium LaRue gradually purchased several other studios and became the ultimate gay porn magnate. In interviews, some performers have credited him with creating a new respect and consideration for actors on the set[34] that seems to have extended beyond his own productions. Not coincidentally, Chi Chi came on the scene in the late 1980s, as major changes were taking place in the industry.[35]

Gay print pornography focused on the stars of videos, but so did the rest of the gay media. Popular gay men's magazines such as *Genre* featured interviews with gay performers such as Ken Ryker.[36] Another popular gay magazine, *Out*, featured several articles on the porn industry,[37] as has its rival, *The Advocate*. Many local gay periodicals also ran video review columns during the 1990s, usually humorous and tongue in cheek. The gay porn industry even developed its own awards shows, which were reported on in the numerous industry magazines such as *Starz* and *Skinflicks*. The two most prominent among these shows were the *Gay Video Guide's* Gay Erotic Video Awards (GEVA, from 1992 to 1998) and the Gay Adult Video News Awards (GayVN, from 1986 to the present), sponsored by the adult film industry's primary professional publication, *Adult Video News*.[38] The GEVA prizes were chosen by video critics and a celebrity panel; the GayVN awards by an international panel of gay judges.[39] As a mark of its increasing prominence, the 2007 GayVN awards show was a spectacle held in the Castro Theater in San Francisco and hosted by comedian Kathy Griffin, and featured prominently on her reality TV show (see Figure 3.1).

Figure 3.1   The 2007 GayVN Awards Show, Emcee Kathy Griffin, performer Roman Heart, and director Chi Chi LaRue. Photo courtesy of Adult Video News.

Actors making the dance circuit in the nation's gay bars became an integral part of the gay porn industry—and a major boost to performers' incomes.[40] Go-go boys had been around for years, but in the late 1980s, following the lead of the popular Chippendale's dancers for women, roving troupes of muscular male dancers began making the circuits of America's gay bars. Most bars seemed to have dancers on the menu at least once a week by the early 1990s.[41] These dancing boys represented the same peak of physical perfection that one found in contemporaneous videos. In the 1990s, many gay porn performers used their video work primarily as a means to make a name for themselves to obtain work on the dance circuit in gay bars, where they could make much more money.[42]

Additional work was necessary because working in gay sex films did not pay a living wage. Pay varied tremendously depending on the popularity and experience of the performer and the company and kind of work they were expected to do. Performers generally were paid by the scene, the rate ranging from about $500 to $2500 a scene.[43] Tops usually were paid more than bottoms because, as in the straight porn industry, reliable erections were a scarce commodity. There were no fringe benefits such as medical insurance. Pay was among a variety of factors luring self-identified straight men into the industry (known as gay-for-pay);[44] men were paid much less in straight porn than in gay. However, the rise of exclusively web-based porn has upset the economic status quo. Rumors have circulated about exorbitant rates paid in order to keep prize performers exclusive to a particular site. Initially, few of these performers participated in traditional studio DVDs, but in 2009 a number of popular Internet stars such as Leo Giamani began working for major studios as well as websites.

Gay porn performers for traditional studios more frequently pursued careers or had jobs outside the industry than did straight porn performers. Porn often provided only supplemental income, and usually only for a few years.[45] Most performers had "day jobs," such as realtor, hotel clerk, personal trainer, financial consultant, or registered nurse.[46] In addition, prostitution was not uncommon as a means of supplementing a performer's income. Indeed, for many escorting was their primary source of income.[47] According to porn star Blue Blake, as an escort he made "more money than God."[48] In the 1990s, magazines such as *Unzipped* (national) and *Frontiers* (southern California) contained hundreds of ads for escorts, which often included pictures of the "product." During the digital era these ads moved online, where multiple venues existed for listing their services, as well as for customers to post reviews. Many ads made note that the advertiser was a "porn star" or "former porn star" or "Colt model." Thus the porn performances became an important means of building a market for escort services. Charging $250 an hour or more, this could be a much more profitable occupation than working in videos.

The gay porn industry had important parallels with and differences from straight porn. The two branches of the industry saw similar growth during the expansion of the market in the video era of the 1980s. Both gay and straight porn had a well-developed "star system" in which certain popular performers received higher salaries and better working conditions.[49] Both segments of the industry were also geographically centered in California, and often used the same sound stages. Some performers even crossed over between genres: straight male performers occasionally performed masturbation scenes in gay videos, and female performers such as Sharon Kane had frequent cameos or nonsexual acting roles. In straight videos, however, women were always the primary focus. Men were purely supporting characters. Another important difference was the lack of a gay market for "softcore," which deletes images of penetration. Many straight videos were released in two versions: a hardcore version for the home video market and a softcore version for adult cable television channels. Gay videos were scarce in the lucrative cable market, and only a few studios occasionally made softcore versions of major gay features.

One would think that a medium that flouted societal taboos about sexuality would itself be less subject to taboos. Instead, both gay and straight pornography was bound by unwritten rules of representation. Restrictive sexual roles (e.g., tops and bottoms, often determined by physical type) were only one aspect of pornography's strange dedication to tradition. The visible ejaculation, or "cum shot," was another necessity. Also typical: a third party who discovered a couple having sex would immediately join in. That such cliché tropes became something of a joke for both viewers and producers had little effect on their ongoing prevalence.

Consolidation and migration has taken place in the large gay porn studios during the digital era. In the film era, products were made in New York, San Francisco, and Los Angeles, but during the video era production was almost exclusively in Los Angeles (except for Falcon Studios in San Francisco). Two new studios that appeared during the 1990s, Titan and Raging Stallion, were also based there; All Worlds Video was in San Diego, and the rest were in Los Angeles. During the digital era the new bareback studios were based in San Francisco, and several Los Angeles companies moved there as well, such as Studio 2000 and Colt. In Los Angeles, Chi Chi LaRue gradually bought most of the remaining studios, establishing a southern California porn empire. By the end of the 2000s, the bulk of gay porn production was based in San Francisco.[50] Meanwhile, one maverick, Russian immigrant Michael Lucas, established a large company in New York. In some ways, the gay porn world has returned to its roots with three capitals.

However, during the digital era other major centers of porn production, both gay and straight, emerged in Europe and Latin America. In gay porn's early years, the only significant overseas product was made by Jean-Daniel Cadinot in France. Kristen Bjorn pioneered gay porn in Latin America and central Europe, and others soon followed. Most significant in Europe was Georges DuRoy and his Bel Ami studio in Slovakia and the Czech Republic, which soon became the brand of choice for youth-oriented viewers. Another center developed in Hungary, where the stable of performers was older and more muscular. During the digital era, dozens of directors and brands sprang up in Europe, and foreign directors from France and the U.S. also took advantage of the lower overhead and fresh faces available there. Brazil became the capital of the Latin American scene; only one major Brazilian producer distributed videos in the U.S. in the 1990s, but in the next decade numerous directors turned out an ever expanding stream of product. Between the explosion of Internet porn and the growth of overseas studios, gay porn is clearly a full participant in the new globalized economy.

PORN IN THE GAY COMMUNITY

Who watches gay porn videos? Statistical studies are scarce, but judging from its prominence in gay media and entertainment, viewership in the gay community appears to be quite high. Even in 1979, when print pornography was the main form of pornographic expression, one informal survey found that more than 50% of the 1038 gay male respondents said that they sometimes used pornography for sexual stimulation.[51] When *Frontiers* magazine held a survey of its readers in 1997, about one-quarter said they watched porn videos once a month, and about 15% viewed them once a week.[52] A 2004 study showed that gay men viewed pornographic videos and Internet porn at over twice the rate of heterosexual men.[53] Perhaps not surprisingly, heterosexual women sometimes confessed to enjoying gay porn, just as straight men enjoyed watching women have sex with each other. Much more surprising was the presence of a small but enthusiastic audience of lesbians. Falcon Studios' promotions director estimated in 2001 that 10% of their customers were female, and half of those were lesbians, for whom the attraction of gay porn ranged from its overall production quality to identification with the intensity of the sex portrayed.[54]

Porn has played an important role in the social and cultural life of gay America. As Bruce Whitehead put it: "Pornography is so ubiquitous in the gay community that I'm not sure you could escape it and still claim to be an active part of gay culture."[55] A major difference between gay and straight pornography was that gay porn was more thoroughly integrated into gay life, whereas straight porn was typically considered deviant and stigmatized by much of the mainstream heterosexual world (despite inroads made by popular performers such as Jenna Jameson). One gay porn industry insider wrote that straights were far more fascinated with his work than gays: "To gay men, the concept of screwing a stranger is not beyond the pale of everyday life."[56] Michael Warner has argued for the importance of a public culture of sex in gay society,[57] of which pornography is a major part. Porn has always held a more accepted, even exalted position in gay culture than in straight; as sexual outlaws, gays were less concerned about being called perverts. As Michael Bronski pointed out, straight culture generally considered pornography to be highly dangerous, and gay pornography doubly so.[58] In spite of the changes wrought by the sexual revolution, mainstream America remained highly discomfited by the open display of sexuality, even heterosexuality. What better way to assert a gay identity than by the open, casual acceptance and celebration of homophobically dreaded sex acts? The omnipresence of sexual imagery in gay media—even beyond pornography—has been explained as a way for gays to create a "positive definition" for themselves.[59] Charles Isherwood has written that porn came "out of the closet" in the late 1980s in conjunction with a politicization of the gay community that found a vehicle in groups such as ACT-UP; porn thus became a personal assertion of gay identity.[60] Heterosexual society's continued discomfort with sexuality in general and pornography in particular meant that gay men's casual acceptance of pornography provided another tool for thwarting the norms of the dominant culture. As a means of social communication, in some ways porn has supplanted the earlier tradition of the "camp" sensibility. Camp's arch appreciation for the marginal provided an oppressed subculture with a secret code of taste that helped to unite and identify closeted gay men. Porn, a marginalized genre, perhaps provided a more aggressive unifying force for a later generation—one that openly celebrated gay sexuality.[61]

In the gay community, video porn has become as common and quotidian as bar hopping. Or, as one writer put it: "That pornography is so accepted in the gay community that we are almost blasé about it, is a cliché."[62] Along Santa Monica Boulevard in West Hollywood, a predominantly gay neighborhood in Los Angeles, a large billboard was used at least twice in the 1990s to advertise newly released porn films: for *Idol in the Sky*, superstar Ryan Idol's last movie, and later for *Ryker's Revenge*, the comeback film for the popular early 1990s' star Ken Ryker. Porn star Tom Chase's image graced two billboard advertisements for an adult video store in the gay quarter of Houston in 1998. Such public ads are hard to imagine for a straight video outside the immediate vicinity of a porn store.

Gay videos have achieved an almost respectable position in gay life. The swapping of gay porn videos has become common, and rental outlets are no longer the sleazy adult stores and arcades that were the initial locus for pornography. During the 1990s, legitimate gay bookstores began to rent and sell porn videos alongside pride flags and *New York Times* bestsellers, and in the digital era, Netflix-style online rental businesses sprang up. Robert Hofler reported that porn stars have been seen regularly at disco openings and various public and private parties. Porn work could even provide an entry into influential gay social circles—ones available to those with the proper abs and pecs but without other credentials.[63] A number of popular documentary films about gay porn have been produced.[64] DVDs often feature "making-of" documentaries as part of the special features. Porn videos themselves have included an inordinate number of stories involving the industry itself: from *Giants* (1983) to *The Making of a Gay Video* (1995).[65]

Gay videos themselves sometimes actively demonstrated a connection between porn and gay life. In *Show Your Pride* (1997) scenes from an actual gay pride parade centered around the float of director Chi Chi LaRue, who was surrounded by hordes of scantily clad, muscular porn models dancing to the disco beat, much as they might during their frequent club performances. This montage played out against the sound of a plaintive voice wailing "Show your pride" to a repetitive disco tune. This scene, sandwiched in the middle of the video, segued abruptly to a massive orgy. This video illustrated the exalted position of porn stars in gay life through their prominent position on a float in a real pride parade; and through its quick jump cut from scenes of a cultural event to hardcore sex, it was also a metaphor for the casual ease with which many gay men approach pornography.

Despite its integration into gay life, gay porn has not been without its critics. Writers such as Michelangelo Signorile and Daniel Harris have vilified gay porn and its muscular bodies as presenting destructive and impossible models of beauty and sexuality.[66] However, research on responses to pornography has shown only a minor correlation of gay porn viewing with social physique anxiety and a drive for muscularity, and no connection to negative body image or other psychological problems.[67] Gay porn has also been subject to much of the same criticism applied to straight porn: that it is sexist, degrading, and violent. These arguments have depended largely on the assumption that pornography, per se, was demeaning and aggressive, and that in gay pornography one partner (the bottom) was inevitably subordinate, submissive, and "degraded," and was thus merely a stand-in for a woman. In this way (the argument goes) gay pornography merely reproduced hetero-sexual norms of violence and sexism.[68] Convincing arguments have been made against this position.[69] Gay men may easily identify with both performers in a sex scene; and the performers themselves do not always adhere to such rigid role identification. When performers slip easily between the roles of penetrator and penetrated, even within a single scene, the identification of the penetrated as subordinate and oppressed becomes purely syntactical and without rele-vance to social realities. While the straight porn industry has been criticized as exploitative of women, the lack of female performers in gay male porn argues against a simple extrapolation from straight to gay pornography. In fact, the pornographic depiction of a forbidden gay sexuality serves to subvert, rather than emulate, the highly gendered strictures of straight culture. Carl Stychin makes a strong argument for the liberatory potential of gay pornog-raphy, and he takes issue with the sweeping claims of the feminist critique of porn, which "when extended to gay porn, completely fail[s] to consider the basic differences and needs of a culturally and socially marginalized sexuality, and in fact mimics the traditional patriarchal views of sex and eroticism."[70]

The casual acceptance of pornography into gay life also creates something of a political conundrum: when right-wing religious extremists are continually defining gays primarily in terms of radical sexual practices (such as in the "documentary" *The Gay Agenda*), does the popularity and broad acceptance of pornography play into the hands of right-wing religious extremists? To some degree, it probably does; but this negative should be balanced with the positive value of having one's own sexual identity—rejected and stigmatized by the status quo—validated by seeing it played out in front of one's very eyes. Public displays of same-sex affection like those enjoyed by heterosexuals are dangerous and generally forbidden for gays. Whereas the mass media constantly and openly affirm heterosexual identity, gay pornog-raphy is one of the few venues for seeing gay sexuality presented in a positive light.

NOTES

My thanks to Butch Harris of Mannet.com, Harker Davis at AVN, and the contributors to the discussion forums at Atkol.com.

1. Jeffrey Escoffier, "Gay for Pay: Straight Men and the Making of Gay Pornography," *Qualitative Sociology* 26 (Winter 2003): 531–555, at p. 534. The high estimates of porn sales have been questioned recently;

a more conservative estimate is $1 billion; Brian Braiker, "Hard Times for the Porn Industry," *Newsweek* (February 7, 2007).

2. Mickey Skee, "Tricks of the Trade," *Frontiers* 16 (August 22, 1997): 43.

3. Richard Dyer, "Male Gay Porn: Coming to Terms," *Jump Cut* 30 (1985): 28.

4. One study showed that 57% of gay porn magazines in the 1980s featured scenes from videos. David Duncan, "Trends in Gay Pornographic Magazines: 1960–1984," *Social Science Research* 73 (1989): 97.

5. Thomas Waugh, "Homoerotic Representation in the Stag Film, 1920–1940: Imagining an Audience," *Wide Angle* 14 (April 1992): 4–19.

6. Thomas Waugh, *Hard to Imagine: Gay Male Eroticism in Photography and Film from Their Beginnings to Stonewall*, New York: Columbia University Press, 1996, p. 359.

7. Richard Dyer, *See It: Studies on Lesbian and Gay Film*, London and New York: Routledge, 1990, p. 171.

8. John D'Emilio and Estelle B. Freedman, *Intimate Matters: A History of Sexuality in America*, New York: Harper & Row, 1988, p. 287.

9. George Csicsery, ed., *The Sex Industry*, New York: New American Library, 1973, p. 197.

10. John R. Burger, *One-Handed Histories: The Eroto-Politics of Gay Male Video Pornography*, New York: Harrington Park Press, 1995, p. 14.

11. Kenneth Turan and Stephen F. Zito, *Sinema: American Pornographic Films and the People Who Make Them*, New York: Praeger, 1974, pp. ix, 141–143.

12. Turan and Zito, *Sinema,* p. 191.

13. Dennis Altman, *The Homosexualization of America*, Boston: Beacon Press, 1982, p. 88.

14. Frederick Lane III, *Obscene Profits: The Entrepreneurs of Pornography in the Cyber Age*, New York: Routledge, 2000, p. 33.

15. Duncan, "Trends in Gay Pornographic Magazines," p. 96.

16. Burger, *One-Handed Histories,* p. 25.

17. Jamoo, *The Films of Kristen Bjorn*. Laguna Hills, CA: Companion Press, 1997, pp. 22, 37; Dave Kinnick, *Sorry I Asked: Intimate Interviews with Gay Porn's Rank and File*, New York: Masquerade Books, 1993, p. 58.

18. Jamoo, *The Films of Kristen Bjorn*, pp. 17–19.

19. Marc Mann, "The 'Daddy' Genre in Gay Porn," paper presented at the World Pornography Conference, Los Angeles, 1998. Marc Mann is both a performer in "daddy" niche market videos and the proprietor of Video Horizons in Laguna Beach, California. He reports that the products featuring young eastern European men are his best sellers and renters.

20. Mickey Skee, *Bad Boys on Video: Interviews with Gay Adult Stars,* Laguna Hills, CA: Companion Press, 1998, pp. 206–216.

21. Burger, *One-Handed Histories,* p. 25.

22. Burger, *One Handed Histories,* pp. 27–28.

23. Camille Paglia, *Sexual Personae: Art and Decadence from Nefertiti to Emily Dickinson*, New York: Vintage, 1991.

24. Susie Bright, *Susie Bright's Sexual Reality: A Virtual Sex World Reader*, Pittsburgh: Cleis Press, 1992; Susie Bright, *Susie Bright's Sexwise*, Pittsburgh: Cleis Press, 1995; Susie Bright, *Susie Bright's Sexual State of the Union*, New York: Simon & Schuster, 1997.

25. Pat Califia, *The Advocate Adviser*, Boston: Alyson Publications, 1991.

26. Wyatt Buchanan, "Hub of All That's Hot," *San Francisco Chronicle* (February 23, 2007): E-1.

27. Lane, *Obscene Profits*, pp. 54–77, 121–48, describes the early history and rapid expansion of Internet porn.

28. Nina Hartley's comments were made at a panel discussion at the annual meeting of the Society for the Scientific Study of Sexuality, Los Angeles, November 13, 1998.

29. James Williams, "Gay Porn for a Specific Audience: Mature and Uncut Men," paper presented at the World Pornography Conference, Los Angeles, 1998. Williams is the owner of Altomar Productions.

30. Moore, Parker, "You Don't Know Dick," *Unzipped* (October 2001). http://www.unzipped.net/features/0103/U0103_features_wadd.asp, accessed October 9, 2008.

31. Gregory A. Freeman, "In Search of Death," *Rolling Stone* (February 6, 2003): 44–49.

32. Madeleine Holt, "HIV Scandal in Gay Porn Industry," BBC2 Television, March 4, 2008. http://news.bbc.co.uk/2/hi/programmes/newsnight/727 7000.stm, accessed 11 October 2008.

33. Douglas Sadownick, *Sex Between Men: An Intimate History of the Sex Lives of Gay Men Postwar to Present*, San Francisco: Harper & Row, 1996, p. 190.

34. Skee, *Bad Boys on Video,* pp. 173, 181, 193.

35. Chi Chi LaRue [Larry Paciotti] with John Erich, *Making It Big: Sex Stars, Porn Films, and Me*, Los Angeles: Alyson Books, 1997.

36. Hal Rubenstein, "Bye-Bye Barbie: Ken Ryker Comes Out (And We Don't Mean to Play)," *Genre* (October 1998): 38–41, 74–75.

37. David Groff, "Letter From New York: Fallen Idol," *Out* (June 1998): 43–50; Eric Gutierrez, "Porn Again: Life After Skin Flicks," *Out* (July 1997): 64–68, 105; Dan Levy, "Falcon Rising," *Out* (July 1996): 73–75, 106–107.

38. Awards for gay videos were initially presented along with straight at the annual AVN Awards starting in 1986. Producers started a separate show for gay awards in 1998, which is ongoing.

39. Skee, "Tricks of the Trade," p. 43.

40. Jeffrey Escoffier, "Porn Star/Stripper/Escort: Economic and Sexual Dynamics in a Sex Work Career," *Journal of Homosexuality* 53 (2007): 173–200, at pp. 190–192.

41. Some documentary evidence does support this assertion, in addition to the anecdotal evidence. For instance, in the free Texas gay weekly *This Week in Texas,* the issue of October 15–21, 1982, featured 61 bar ads, none of which mentioned male dancers. In the July 24–30, 1998 issue, almost half mentioned male dancers, although the total number of bar ads had diminished to 20.

42. In Ronnie Larsen's 1997 documentary film *Shooting Porn,* a number of performers explained that video rarely paid the bills, but rather established a reputation for them to build on as escorts and dancers.

43. Jeffrey Escoffier, "Porn Star/Stripper/Escort," p. 181; Gary Indiana, "Making X: A Day in the Life of Hollywood's Sex Factory," *Village Voice* 38 (August 24, 1993): 30; Minuk, "Sex, Guys, and Videotapes," p. 20; Skee, "Tricks of the Trade," p. 43.

44. Escoffier, "Gay for Pay," analyzes the extensive use of heterosexual men in gay porn.

45. Escoffier, "Porn Star/Stripper/Escort," p. 186.

46. "Working Stiffs," *Unzipped* 13 (October 1998): 13–27.

47. Scott Seomin, "Infomercial for a Hustler," *Icon* (July 1997): 14–16; Indiana, "Making X," p. 30.

48. Seomin, "Infomercial," p. 15. Blake echoed this sentiment in Ronnie Larsen's film *Making Porn.*

49. See Sharon Abbott's chapter in this volume.

50. The local newspapers have acknowledged San Francisco's new status as the capital of gay porn: see Buchanan, "Hub of All That's Hot."

51. James Spada, *The Spada Report: The Newest Survey of Gay Male Sexuality,* New York: New American Library, 1979, p. 135.

52. Austin Foxxe, "That Type of Guy," *Frontiers* 16 (August 22, 1997): 65–68.

53. Scott J. Duggan and Donald R. McCreary, "Body Image, Eating Disorders, and the Drive for Muscularity in Gay and Heterosexual Men: The Influence of Media Images," in Todd Morrison, ed., *Eclectic Views on Gay Male Pornography: Pornucopia,* Binghamton, NY: Harrington Park Press, 2004, pp. 51–52

54. Chelsey Johnson, "Dicks 'n' Dykes," *Out* (March 2001): 68–73.

55. Morrison, *Pornucopia*, p. 204.

56. Benjamin Scuglia, "Sex Pigs: Why Porn is Like Sausage, or The Truth is That—Behind the Scenes—Porn is Not Very Sexy," in Morrison, ed., *Pornucopia*, p. 187.

57. Michael Warner, *The Trouble with Normal: Sex, Politics, and the Ethics of Queer Life*, New York: Free Press, 1999, pp. 149–193.

58. Michael Bronski, *Culture Clash: The Making of Gay Sensibility*, Boston: South End Press, 1984, pp. 165–166.

59. Richard Dyer, "A Conversation About Pornography," in Simon Shepherd and Mick Wallis, eds., *Coming on Strong: Gay Politics and Culture*, London: Unwin Hyman, 1989, p. 210.

60. Charles Isherwood, *Wonder Bread and Ecstasy: The Life and Death of Joey Stefano*, Los Angeles: Alyson Publications, 1996, p. 62.

61. Joe A. Thomas, "Notes on the New Camp: Gay Pornographic Video," in James Elias, et al., eds., *Porn 101: Eroticism, Pornography, and the First Amendment*, Amherst, MA: Prometheus, 1999.

62. Bradley Moseley-Williams, "The Porn Boy Next Door," *Icon* (July 1997): 27.

63. Robert Hofler, "The Men of Koo Koo Roo," *Buzz* 9 (January 1998): 65.

64. Producer and director Ronnie Larsen has made a cottage industry creating dramas and documentaries about the gay porn industry. His play *Making Porn* opened in Los Angeles in 1994 and toured nationally. He followed up with a documentary film in 1997, *Shooting Porn*. German director Jochen Hick's 1998 film, *Sex/Life in LA,* and its sequel, *Cycles of Porn: Sex/Life in LA 2* from 2005 documented several socioeconomic levels of gay sex work in Los Angeles; they made the rounds of all the major gay film festivals.

65. Richard Dyer, "Idol Thoughts: Orgasm and Self-Reflexivity in Gay Porn," *Critical Quarterly* 36 (1994): 1–54. Dyer gives an extensive list of films about making porn films, as well as an extensive analysis of this trend.

66. Daniel Harris, *The Rise and Fall of Gay Culture*, New York: Hyperion, 1997, pp. 124–128; Michelangelo Signorile, *Life Outside—The Signorile Report on Gay Men: Sex, Drugs, Muscles, and the Passages of Life*, New York: HarperCollins, 1997, pp. 145–146. Harris excoriates contemporary porn and compares it unfavorably with pornography from the seventies. Signorile points out the elevated status of porn stars and their ideal physiques and connects it to gay men's use (abuse in Signorile's mind) of steroids and plastic surgery. They echo their condemnation in Hofler, "The Men of Koo Koo Roo," p. 78.

67. Duggan and McCreary, "Body Image," p. 53; Todd Morrison, Melanie Morrison, and Becky Bradley, "Correlates of Gay Men's Self-Reported Exposure to Pornography," *International Journal of Sexual Health* 19 (2007): 33–43.

68. John Stoltenberg, "Gays and the Propornography Movement: Having the Hots for Sex Discrimination," in Michael Kimmel, ed., *Men Confront Pornography*, New York: Meridian Books, 1991; Christopher Kendall, "Real Dominant, Real Fun: Gay Male Pornography and the Pursuit of Masculinity," *Saskatchewan Law Review* 57 (1993): 21–58; Christopher Kendall, *Gay Male Pornography: An Issue of Sex Discrimination*, Vancouver: UBC Press, 2004. Kendall makes unreasonable claims about the industry as a whole based on very limited examples of unusual sadomasochistic porn.

69. Thomas Waugh, "Men's Pornography: Gay vs. Straight," in Corey Creekmur and Alexander Doty, eds., *Out in Culture: Gay, Lesbian, and Queer Essays on Popular Culture*, Durham, NC: Duke University Press, 1995; Scott Tucker, "Radical Feminism and Gay Male Porn," in Michael Kimmel, ed., *Men Confront Pornography*, New York: Meridian, 1991.

70. Carl F. Stychin, "Exploring the Limits: Feminism and the Legal Regulation of Gay Male Pornography," *Vermont Law Review* 16 (1992): 859–900, at pp. 899–900.

WOMEN-MADE PORNOGRAPHY

Jill A. Bakehorn

Much of the research on pornography has focused on only a few of its aspects: its effects on attitudes and behaviors toward women,[1] other attitudinal changes linked to exposure,[2] and analyses of content.[3] In addition, some researchers have written ethnographies of pornographic stores[4] and others have analyzed antipornography movements.[5] Very little research has focused on other important aspects of pornography—such as the actors and creators, its meaning to consumers, and women's use of it.[6]

My research adds to this body of literature by studying women who make pornography and particularly those who make porn for a female audience. I examine the production of this type of pornography, how the women become involved in it, and how they view their involvement. While Sharon Abbott's study (Chapter 2 of this volume) examined actors' explanations for participation in the mainstream porn industry,[7] no research has examined women's participation in alternative pornography. Abbott reports that women become involved in mainstream pornography for both money and fame. I find very different motivations for women who make alternative pornography.

The chapter begins with a description of the genre of alternative pornography and describes my research methods. I then outline (1) the avenues by which women become involved in alternative pornography and (2) the motives and justifications that underpin their work. Because most of these women are not involved in mainstream pornography and would not consider working in that sector, the reasons for their participation are very different than for women involved in the mainstream industry. For most of the former, a sense of purpose or activism is important in both their decision to make pornography and in the types of pornography they make. I identify five main avenues of entry into the world of alternative pornography and then discuss the objectives or motivations for women's involvement in this sector of the industry.

THE GENRE OF WOMEN-MADE PORN

The world of women-made pornography is fragmented; it lacks a central location for production and is less established than the mainstream porn industry. This chapter does not provide an exhaustive analysis of women-made porn, but it does examine general patterns based on my research. The study focuses on visual pornography in two main formats: (1) film, including DVDs and streaming video on the Internet, and (2) pornographic websites, which include photo layouts, streaming video, message boards, blogs, and chat rooms. The imagery portrayed can be hardcore, softcore, or educational. Hardcore is typically defined as showing sexual intercourse—penetration or oral sex. Softcore images depict nude bodies but do not show explicit images of sex. Educational materials can be hardcore or softcore.

Over three-quarters of the women in my study have made DVD films. These range from hardcore features with a plot and characterization to all-sex "gonzo porn" to educational films. Over one-third of the women have made videos that are available for streaming or for downloading over the Internet, although this number has probably increased recently with the popularity of this method. In some cases, these videos are being sold both as DVDs and as streaming Internet content.

Nearly half of the women are involved with pornographic websites. The content and administration of these sites varies widely. Some feature hardcore videos, while others focus on softcore and/or hardcore photographs. Websites like Suicide Girls feature a large number of models and focus on softcore, pin-up style photos. Potential models submit photos of themselves to the website, and, if accepted, the woman will receive a one-time payment. In addition, models include a personal profile, maintain a blog, and chat with fans online. About 15% of the women in my study have worked for a site like Suicide Girls, although some are involved with hardcore sites. More than one-tenth of the women in my study have their own websites. These can be soft or hardcore, feature photos only or include video, be strictly solo or include partners who are often other women. Some women create their own sites, called "single girl websites." These sites feature one girl, who has total control over the content and makes money through membership subscriptions. Single girl sites are often very personal and will include a biography, blog or journal, chat rooms, live video feeds, and even essays on various social issues.

Over two-thirds of my interviewees make lesbian, bisexual, or transgender porn and over one-third have made heterosexual porn. These categories can overlap, with some people being involved in both lesbian and heterosexual genres. Nearly one-quarter of the women are involved in making BDSM (bondage, discipline/domination, and sado-masochism)/fetish pornography. A handful of my informants have connections to the mainstream porn industry; a few actors work in both mainstream and alternative pornography; and a few directors have deals with mainstream companies to produce alternative content.

RESEARCH METHODS

I worked on six different pornographic film production sites in San Francisco from May 2006 to April 2007, which totaled 21 production days. I was a production assistant on five of the sites, where my duties included helping the crew set up for the shoots, moving and setting up equipment, running errands, doing paperwork, collecting model identification documents/photographs required by law, and keeping track of the script. I also performed some technical work for which I had no prior experience: I was boom operator on a couple of sets; I assisted with lighting; and on one set, I shot behind-the-scenes footage for inclusion on the website and DVD. At the sixth production site, I was the first assistant director. My duties in this case included many of the same tasks I had performed as a production assistant with additional responsibilities: I ensured that all cast and crew arrived on set on time and received any important information; kept the production on schedule; and kept track of daily expenditures and managed the budget.[8] In addition to working on sets, I also attended three film premieres and two cast-and-crew parties. And finally, I examined films, company websites, press releases, and media reports to get a sense of the thematic content.

I started soliciting interviewees by identifying women-run porn companies on the Internet and subsequently used snowball sampling to generate new contacts. Many of my interviewees are women who worked at my field sites. I conducted 72 in-depth interviews with individuals who work in this sector of the porn industry. Almost all of them were women (N = 66); there were two men and four transgenders (female-to-male) in the sample. I interviewed 33 directors and producers, 37 actors (in films) and models (in photo shoots), 15 crew members (camera, lighting, etc), four distributors, three documentary filmmakers, and three staff (PR, editors). Many women move between roles or hold multiple roles simultaneously, and many directors are also actors or models. Some had started out as models and became directors and some are directors who also appear in the films they make. Some have made mainstream film pornography. Most are located outside of the San Fernando mainstream industry and are located in San Francisco and New York City. The sample is primarily white (81%); one-tenth were African-American and the rest were Asian, Latina, or mixed race. These numbers reflect the lack of women of color in alternative pornography, a problem cited by a number of interviewees.

Interviews took place via telephone or in person at a location chosen by the respondent—usually a coffee shop, their place of business, or their home. Interviews ranged from 45 minutes to more than 3 hours. I recorded and transcribed all interviews. Questions included: how they got into the pornography business, their prior work, why they are involved in pornography, the kinds of images they believe important to portray, why women-made porn is significant, whether they identify as feminist, and whether they view their work as activism. Each interview ended with a number of demographic questions. Some of the names used in this chapter are pseudonyms and others are either the person's real name or their stage name. The decision regarding the use of pseudonyms was made by the participants themselves. Some requested that I use their real name; others wanted their stage names used. If someone did not have a strong preference, she is identified by a pseudonym.

ENTRY INTO PORN

The paths that led the women in my study to participate in pornography are varied and complex. Below I identify five main factors that are important in beginning a career in this type of pornography: (1) a background in sex education; (2) an activist stance; (3) an artistic background; (4) previous involvement in sex work; and (5) a connection to porn through a friend or lover. These are not discrete categories: people rarely enter porn through a single avenue but usually via a combination of two or more. Training in sex education coupled with feminist sensibilities and a background in film-making, for example, may all be important paths of entry.

Background in Sex Education

Overall, nearly half of the women in my study have a background in sex education. A few received formal education in sexology, earning a master's or doctorate, while others had gone through training programs but did not receive a degree. Some of these women used their expertise to make their own films and many of their films have an overt educational message. Dorrie, for example, put her sex education politics into practice by making sex educational videos:

> At the time that I made my first video, it was a sex video on sex parties and safe sex issues for women, and the CDC didn't even admit that women could transmit HIV to other women . . . and this was back in the early eighties, they had all these guidelines about how to define a lesbian and it just didn't fit, it wasn't reality. And so there was no information basically for women-to-women transmission. So, from there I became a real activist in [issues regarding] predominantly lesbian but [also] bisexual women and the issues of safe sex and how STIs and STDs and HIV infect us. . . . There was no teaching and the only example of education was in porn. And it wasn't very good, it wasn't very helpful, it wasn't woman-dominated. It just wasn't the vision that I was looking for, so I created my own.

Many of those with a sex education background got their training, knowledge, and desire for education by working for a sex toy store. Such stores are typically run by women and provide training in sex education, including anatomy, sexual practices, safe sex, and the use of the products sold in the store. These stores often have a mission statement citing sex education as a primary goal. Employees interact with and provide information to customers who have questions, and many also run workshops. Examples of sex toy shops include large companies with multiple locations like *Good Vibrations* in the San Francisco Bay Area and *Babeland* with locations on the east and west coasts, as well as single stores typically run by one or two women. Oriana, a queer woman of color, received her training in sex education from one of these sex toy shops. She then went on to write, direct, and star in a hardcore, educational film made by and for queer women of color. She brought together women from various sex educational backgrounds:

> Everyone who signed on to be a part of this movie signed on not because there was some gigantic paycheck. . . . All of us were educators in our own way. Every single person who was a character in the film is someone who comes from a

background of either advocacy or health or having been sex workers themselves or being performance poets that talk about these issues. Every single one of us in that film are coming from a place of looking for a platform to get out there what we think the world needs to know.

Not all the women who had a sex education background decided to make educational videos; some took the hardcore feature route instead, but still tied their decisions to their sex ed background. Many of the women discussed the lack of formal sex education in this country and believed that pornography, while not overtly advertised as sex education, nonetheless serves this function for the public in lieu of information anywhere else. They reason that if pornography is teaching people about sex, people should be taught accurate, responsible information.

Activism

Many of the women were or are actively involved in a wide variety of activist pursuits. These include issues of women's health and reproduction, sex positivity, feminism, and identity politics (gender, sexuality, race), but also the environment and economic justice. For those with a sex education background, making pornography, especially porn that is overtly educational, is an extension of their activist work. It was sometimes difficult, however, to ascertain whether an activist stance was the primary factor leading to involvement in pornography, was a philosophy that women came to espouse after beginning the work, or was simply a narrative justifying the work. In any case, for most of the women, taking an activist stance on issues of gender, sexuality, and race are important aspects of the work they do outside of pornography. Within the world of alternative porn, women draw on activist or progressive ideologies to inform their work, set priorities, create mission statements, and devise marketing strategies. There are three main types of activism:

1. feminism
2. sex positivity
3. identity politics

While some women primarily identify as feminist, most of the women have broad activist goals that span the three categories.

Feminism

Most of the women I interviewed (85%) identify as feminist and their feminist activism carries over into their work in pornography. A number of women are involved in various feminist organizations, including nonprofits working in women's health and reproduction and women's art collectives. Others have not been involved in direct feminist organizing or activism; for them, feminism is an important identification and also an influence on their work. One woman who rarely attends demonstrations told me that she believes her films are "where I speak my politics." However, not all feel comfortable identifying their work as feminist. Some feel this label is too limiting and others see it as a marketing no-no, as one producer told me: "We actually don't externally do any marketing calling ourselves feminist because that would kill the video." Others feel that there were too many different kinds of feminism to use that term.

There are women who readily proclaim their work is feminist, however. Many are troubled by the rise of antiporn feminism and want to proclaim that women can be feminists and make pornography and that the work they produce is feminist. Some argue their work is feminist because women are in control of the content. Renee, who was formerly a model in feminist porn, a sex educator, and now is the porn buyer for a large sex toy shop, sees this as an important part of her feminist politics:

> I think having women in charge of what they're doing and their vision and having control over how they're portrayed or what they're doing is the biggest shift that I see happening right now. And being proud and enthusiastic and sort of reclaiming that energy [unlike] maybe in the past . . . [when] the porn world [was] profiting primarily off of exposure of women's bodies. And now a lot of women embracing that and speaking out about the positive aspects of that.

One woman, previously a director of lesbian pornography, who now distributes porn made by women, offered a definition of feminist pornography that was typical of the views of other informants:

> I've heard people say, well, it's where the women really cum. That's one way of putting it. In general feminist pornography is made with a female viewer in mind. The guys might get off on it but it's not made with them in mind and what they're going to want to look at. It's more made . . . with what women might want to look at. . . . [It] comes from a women's own personal experience, I think, with sex that gives her her vision. And she puts it on film hoping that

other women will appreciate her vision and be something that they can relate to or see themselves in or just get off on. [So] that they don't feel that when they watch it the women are being taken advantage of or that the women's feelings aren't important. The women can look and they can see that woman and she really is having an orgasm.

In a similar vein, Trixie told me: "So I guess that feminist porn to me is porn that doesn't lie about women. Porn that is honest about sexuality, about women's sexuality." Some frame the issue as one about choice. Tristan Taormino makes how-to and gonzo films and has a sex education background:

Feminism for me is about choice. And that choice extends to women having choices about what to do with their bodies, about their jobs and their careers, and about their lives on basically on every level: physical, emotional, spiritual, financial, all of that.

Others believe women can be empowered both by the experience of being in porn as well as watching porn. It is around these issues that feminism intersects with sex positivity.

Sex Positivity

Out of recognition of the multiplicity of ways people can experience their sexuality, women who make pornography often embrace the philosophy of sex positivity. "Sex positive" was originally conceived of as one type of sexuality among others in different cultures, along with "sex negative," "sex neutral," and "sex ambivalent."[9] Researchers use these types to understand the role of sexual repression and sexual permissiveness in different societies. Today, the term sex positive is used by a growing number of people who subscribe to the idea that as long as the activities are consensual, sexual practices are inherently healthy and sexual variation should be encouraged. The "sex-positive" movement is dedicated to providing sex education and advocates for the valorization of all sexual acts, particularly those that have been devalued in the past. In part, sex positivity arose during the feminist "sex wars" of the 1980s as a response to antipornography factions of feminism. Andrea Dworkin and Catherine MacKinnon, who were closely associated with antiporn feminism, fought for the censorship of pornography as a vehicle for curbing violence against women. So, for some, feminism represents "a system of sexual judgment" whereby women are constructed as victims and disempowered objects rather than sexual subjects.[10] Because of feminism's close ties to antipornography ideology, some activists within the sex-positive community do not align themselves with feminism. Others see the possibility of working within feminism to not only articulate women's sexual subjectivity, but also as a platform to fight for sex worker rights.

Sex-positive feminists see pornography as a vehicle to explore, expand, and enhance women's sexuality. A longtime director and producer of pornography explained sex-positive feminism:

> Sex is an important part of women's lives and it is still negated for a lot of women; women still aren't free to explore their sexuality like perhaps men are. So being a pro-sex feminist means I'm working toward and believe in women's rights to explore fully their sexuality with whatever means they have.

Pornography, then, is a way to give women access to sexual knowledge. Those with a sex education background almost universally identify as sex positive, and women-run sex toy shops build sex positivity into their mission statements. For some, sex positivity is a philosophy that sex is natural and positive, which made them open to being involved in pornography.

Identity Politics

Many women are activists or identify with particular communities and see pornography as a place where they can put their principles of gender, sexuality, race, and community into practice. Making films from the standpoint of being a woman is an important political statement. Allison made a video with a fellow film student that was marketed as "by women for women":

> I think the biggest difference is that it was women making this, not men. That's the fundamental difference, because we grew up as women, we've been gendered as women. So, we set out to make it for different reasons than mainstream men who are making it. We weren't necessarily trying to make a product, we were trying to make something that women would like.

Some of the women who make alternative pornography, particularly lesbian or queer porn, have a history of activism around LGBT issues including gay/straight alliances, sex education and outreach, ACT-UP and Queer Nation, and queer artist collectives. Some of the pioneers of lesbian pornography were on the front lines of feminist, lesbian political organizing in the 1970s and 1980s. For women like Nan Kinney and Deborah Sundahl, making pornography is directly linked to an activist agenda—changing the representations of lesbian sexuality. Nan Kinney, founder of *On Our Backs* magazine and owner of Fatale Media, had this to say:

> I felt lesbians' sex lives were being screwed over by the antiporn movement and the antisex lesbians. I personally dated and went out with women that wouldn't have certain kinds of sex because it was wrong. They wouldn't even do any kind of penetration because it was influenced by the male-dominated society, and we were identifying with males if we did that and being part of their culture. To be a true lesbian you didn't do that. And that just really upset me. I thought this is so screwed up, and I took it very personally. And I think the same with Deborah. I think our sexuality was really important to us and we found that sex is a source of power and creativity. And our way of expressing that was putting out *On Our Backs* and then the videos.

Along with portraying "real" women and "real" lesbians, some are also concerned with issues of race. Alex is a mixed-race Asian queer with fluid gender who does not feel represented in mainstream porn:

> Why I became involved in pornography—a lot of it's identity politics. As a queer woman of color, there's very few places that you see yourself out in the world or like a mirror of yourself. And one of the most abundant fields that a queer person can see themselves in [has] obviously been porn. . . . I find myself in that same kind of community and wanting to be a part of that dialogue, and so I step in on this pre-created foundation where porn really is important because of its social position in the representations in politics. And the majority of those representations are owned by affluent, white males, and they give representation to people who they are not. It's speaking on behalf of someone else. . . . [Women-made porn has] become this path to say, look, there's all these representations of what queers are, what queer women are, who these people are, and this is one I'm adding myself.

One final category of identity politics involves "alternative" communities or lifestyles. In the last few years there has been a proliferation of websites and DVDs that are considered "alt porn"—alternative pornography. Alt porn, as the name suggests, arose as an alternative to mainstream pornography, which was seen as inauthentic and, for many, something to which they could not relate. Situated near Hollywood, mainstream porn came to be seen as homogenized and mass produced. Whereas mainstream porn models are considered professional and interchangeable, alt porn sites tend to highlight the amateur status and diversity of the models. Alt porn is most popularly associated with subcultural groups like punks and Goths, where the models featured have brightly colored, dyed hair, tattoos, piercings, and other body modifications. Mainstream porn companies have taken notice of the success of these sites and have launched alt divisions. Vivid, one of the major mainstream porn companies, has now released 16 DVDs under its imprint, Vivid Alt, that focus on a punk, alternative skater aesthetic. Alt porn has expanded beyond punk music subcultures and there are now vegetarian and environmental porn websites that seek to educate and connect other like-minded people. Pixie, who has modeled for vegetarian and music-based porn sites, thinks alt porn is adding to the diversity of porn and expanding who can identify with it:

> Alternative is a way to group all the weirdos into one thing. . . . I mean we for the most part are going to look different than your average person. We're going to have a lot of tattoos or weird hair or piercings. And before this whole thing started that was hard to find. When you looked at porn it was *Playboy* style or *Penthouse* style. And it was very normal looking, airbrushed girls, not that they don't airbrush us [alt models], they do . . . but I think it's cool that there's porn out there for everyone.

Activism also takes place around issues of sex worker rights, racial justice, the environment, HIV, free speech, and domestic violence. While many of these issues are not directly related to pornography, they demonstrate a larger commitment to activism by the women in my study that often translates into viewing pornography as activism as well.

Art and Sex Work Backgrounds

Some women became involved in producing porn through art—as performance artists, filmmakers, painters, photographers, graphic designers, writers, and dancers. What connects these artists is their effort to explore sexuality through art, and in many cases, a sense of familiarity and comfortability with their bodies. Those with filmmaking backgrounds often used their artistic skills for activism and for publicizing their perspective. One African-American director told me: "I have to put an alternate voice out there, I have to. I don't see that I have a choice; the story is being told. So, you can either bitch and moan about it or you can tell your own story, which is what I'm choosing to do."

About one-third of the women found their way into porn through their involvement with other types of sex work. These were primarily peep shows, stripping, and dominatrix work, although a few were involved in escorting, phone sex, or massage parlors. Many of these women are also activists in sex worker rights groups or the queer community or involved in sex education. Most also expressed having a longstanding interest in sexuality, telling me they always wanted to engage in work that involved sexuality.

Network Influences

Over one-third were introduced to the porn world through friends or lovers— although for most this was not their exclusive route into the business. Most were already involved in sex education or activism and, through this work, made contacts in the porn world. The few women for whom networking was the exclusive route were crew members. Women who make porn used their film connections to find women to work for them, so some crew members did not set out specifically to work on porn, but through the filmmaker community took jobs making porn. While alternative porn may not have been their primary work objective, many discussed being supportive of the work, particularly as it relates to activism around gender and sexuality issues

About 50% of both actors/models and directors/producers have a background in sex education, as do one-quarter of crew members. Only four of the women with a background in sex education did not go on to make educational porn. Everyone else made at least one educational video. About 60% of both directors/producers and crew members have an artist/filmmaking background, while 40% of the actors/models do. Less than 20% of directors/producers have worked in the sex industry; 50% of actors/models have. A little over one-third of actors/models got into pornography through networking, while about 60% of the crew members had. As might be expected, actors/models and crew members were more likely to mention making money as a primary factor in entering pornography, although this was true for less than 20% of my sample. Four people mentioned getting into porn on a "whim"— they were all models and got their start posing for Internet photos. Nearly everyone (96%) had some kind of activist background or sensibility prior to entering the industry. These avenues of entry differ greatly from Abbott's findings regarding mainstream porn actors (Chapter 2), where money, fame, and sociability were the primary factors.

MOTIVATIONS

The women I interviewed have two main motivations for making pornography: to create pornography that is an alternative to the mainstream industry and that will be educational for viewers.

Alternatives to Mainstream Porn

Most of the women I interviewed are making films and websites outside the mainstream porn industry although a few have ties to the mainstream world. Being outside the mainstream is a primary identification and hallmark of their work—it is what sets them apart and is used in marketing materials. There are four primary ways in which the women saw their work as alternative pornography: they make "better" porn; it is made by women; it is created for women; and they are changing the industry.

Making "Better" Porn

While being careful not to align themselves with the antiporn feminists, many of the women are critical of the mainstream industry. For them, most of pornography's problems stem from the fact that men run the industry. Participants criticize the types of representation of women and of sexuality in general. In mainstream pornography, they argue, the focus is not on women's pleasure and women's orgasms. Instead, it is all about the "money shot" (the visible evidence of men's ejaculation), women often do not appear to be having a good time, and women are not in control of their images and therefore of their sexuality. They also object to the narrow standard of beauty portrayed in mainstream pornography. Finally, many believe that mainstream pornography gives inaccurate information about sex. Susan, prior to producing films, was a video reviewer for a large sex toy store and she helped to decide which videos the store would carry:

> I was watching up to 8 hours of pornographic videos everyday, trying to screen
> through what was out there and trying to pick what was good and what was bad.
> And it was like, wow, there's a lot of bad stuff out there. There's a lot of stuff
> that isn't being done, so we gotta do it.

My interviewees have problems with racial imagery as well, arguing that pornography perpetuates stereotypes about women. An Asian woman who was an actor in two videos produced by a large sex toy store discussed Asian stereotypes as one of the reasons she decided to work in pornography:

> I have a couple reasons why I do sex work. There are hardly any images of a foxy,
> big Asian chick with huge tits out there. There are almost no images that are at
> all empowering. We're usually . . . in rope bondage or we're wearing clothes
> from 100 years ago because of course all Asians have long, black hair that they

can let flowing down with the chopsticks in their head. They're wearing kimonos, they're looking delicate. It plays into the stereotype. And so I think it is a feminist act to be out there and have none of those things, and I'm Asian and I'm foxy.

In addition to wanting to correct problematic representations in mainstream pornography, many of the women feel that mainstream porn omits important issues and falsifies what it does portray. Nan describes her inspiration as coming from wanting to contest, and provide an alternative to, the "lesbian" images portrayed in mainstream pornography:

I want to portray images that the mainstream porn companies aren't portraying. And right next to that is lesbians having lesbian sex. Real lesbians having real lesbian sex. Authentic, explicit, sexy lesbians. I look at what mainstream porn is doing and I just don't want to do the same exact thing. And that's what we mean by alternative. . . . I would say, after the authentic part of it, I want to show lesbians having a good time having sex, enjoying it.

Making better porn thus translates into taking women's pleasure seriously, putting women's orgasms at the center, being mindful of gender and race, showing a diversity of bodies and sexualities, depicting fluid genders, using "real" people with real bodies, and creating something that audiences can identify with (see Figure 4.1).

Women-Made Porn

Calling their work "women-made" is the most basic and nearly universal claim to alternative status made by the women in my study. It is alternative because it is made by women—they consider this groundbreaking and radical in itself. Many said that women bring a different point of view to the work they do; they are contributing something different than the formulaic, overdone pornography fare. When I asked Christi, a staff person at a lesbian porn company why it is important that their films are made by women, she told me this:

Well first of all, it's another point of view when it comes to pornography because so much porn—or so-called lesbian porn, girl-girl porn—is produced by men. Then you don't have the point of view. . . . When you continually see things through a male point of view, through that male gaze, you're only seeing one side of the story. . . . I think women have something else to offer when they're behind the camera.

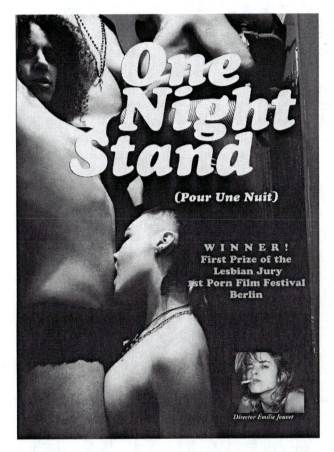

Making Porn for Women

Women typically describe their work as both "by women" and "for women." Most my interviewees see women as their audience: Their films are intended expressly for women's enjoyment. They held various notions of what a woman consumer would want in pornography, ranging from soft, story-driven porn to gonzo porn with no plot. As might be expected, the women draw from their own experiences and desires to craft something in which they think women will be interested. Those who had experience in sex education would have anecdotal evidence of what women were looking for based on their encounters with customers, and distributors get some feedback from customers. But overall there is no marketing mechanism in place to help them tap into a women's market. Many admit that men still comprise a large segment of the customers. But marketing it as something for women, or sometimes for couples, is a way to set themselves apart from the mainstream. Aki, who has appeared in three hardcore DVD features as well as Internet videos, talks about the director she works with:

> She wants to do porn for women, which hasn't been done, and I think that's an incredibly brave and heroic feat, and it's well-needed right now. It seems like an old debate about pornography and whether or not it's good for women, and it's really great to have especially a lesbian filmmaker of color take on that responsibility or that mission of actually making work that speaks to women and is for women even though it's a hot, hot film in general that men can get into. It's essentially for the women who are making it and the women who are watching it.

Thus, making porn "by women, for women" includes more than gender politics; women producers and directors also bring in sexuality and, to a lesser extent, race and ethnicity in an effort to represent their identities and communities.

Changing the Mainstream Industry

Some of the women also want to change the larger porn industry—to help bring about changes in both content and work organization. They hope more women will become involved in making porn, and that the mainstream companies will see that it is profitable and hire more women to be directors. Some talk about gaining recognition by winning Adult Video News awards and possibly being a catalyst for changes in imagery.[11] They also want to be role models for treating actors well. A desire to change the industry is part of the reason Tristan decided to work with a mainstream company to produce and distribute her movies:

> It's an incredibly powerful medium. And it's obviously a medium that continues to be debated among feminists and I'm a feminist. I love theory and debates just as much as the next Wesleyan graduate. But what interested me more was: What about the challenge of actually trying to make something different? What about engaging the beast? I like to call the mainstream adult industry "the beast". . . . Can I actually bring my voice and vision into the mix? Can I make a difference? Is it like a blip on the radar or can it actually have an impact? And I've always said that I don't love all porn; there's certainly plenty of porn that I dislike or that is not erotic or is offensive to me. But my answer to that is: I want to make porn that's different. I want to make the kind of porn that I want to see.

So some women try to change the industry by creating an alternative to the mainstream, while others try to change the industry from within.

Sex Education

Because so many of the women come from a sex education background, it's not surprising that education is one of the major motivations for making alternative pornography. Educational goals include making videos that highlight information about anatomy, sexual positions, and safer sex as well as depicting "healthy" sexuality. Many women discussed the lack of formal sex education in America and the function pornography serves in this regard. Carol Queen, a well-known sexologist, described pornography as representing a "classroom." She told me:

> People look at sex movies for information about sex and they don't always get very good information, partly because of the way that movies are made. The rushing, the not waiting for full arousal to happen, all of this canopy of things can make porn into pretty half-assed sex education. Some is much better than others. Some of the positions that you have to assume to get the camera angle [right] are not what most people would choose do at home.

Some films/websites are fundamentally about sex education: the education is an explicit and primary goal of the product. For the women making this material, education and activism are partly about providing people with accurate sexual information. One company produced a film that deals with safer sex for lesbians. On their website, the film is touted as "beautifully shot, scripted, and performed, [this film] will challenge negative attitudes toward safer sex for lesbians. . . . Safe Sex is Great Sex!" In this film women contemplate and debate the virtues of safe sex and provide arguments for safer sex practices, demonstrating these practices for the audience. This same company builds sex education ideals into all of their films. One of their directors explained the production process to me:

> The way we put it together is based on an educational outline. We have to also wrap in diversity, folks of different ethnicities and sexes. . . . So producing it you think, okay, we need a diverse group, we need folks that are exhibitionists, and we need to show sex that is hot, sexy, fun—but we have to have these marker points of putting on rubber gloves, using a dental dam, checking in with your partner, putting a condom on a dildo, using correct safe sex etiquette.

Carol Queen describes the power of providing information through explicit imagery in film:

> We know from some educational research that people retain more information if they see it or experience it than if they simply read it . . . . So one of the reasons to do explicit educational work in the first place is to help people really get it; seeing can be believing. I've always been exhibitionistic enough to feel that I could use my own body in that context to educate and to inform, and part of that is not seeing enough sex material out there compared to the amount that I would like to see available to the public.

A more implicit sex educational goal is utilized in other hardcore films: they are modeling healthy sexuality, exploring or advancing women's sexuality, and giving people new ideas to experiment with. Nina Hartley, a mainstream porn veteran of more than 650 films, makes how-to educational videos but believes her mainstream feature work is also educational. She told me:

> It was for me very important to get into the teaching aspect because that was always my goal and intention. Even my traditional videos are subtly and subversively teaching videos in terms of role modeling happy, positive, self-actuated behavior on the part of a female—which was more radical than one might think at the time.

Others stressed the importance of showing different genders, body types, and sexual activity in the hope both that women will benefit from seeing such diversity and to help break down the narrow standards of the mainstream industry.

CONCLUSION

Most of the women in my study approach their work as a form of activism. This activism can take the form of feminism, sex positivity, identity politics, or sex education. A background in activism or sex education are two of their main motivations for entering the pornography industry and these orientations were used in crafting their product. This activist sensibility translates into a desire to create pornography that is an alternative to the mainstream: their porn places women's pleasure at the center, pays attention to how gender and race are represented, involves products created by women and for women, and represents the diverse communities to which they belong. For some, the goal is to make fundamental changes to the mainstream porn industry that will benefit both actors and audiences. Very few cite money as their main motivation and a number of them stress that their work is a labor of love. While money and fame were the major motivating drives for mainstream porn actors in Sharon Abbott's study, this is not the case for women involved in alternative pornography.

This study bridges the perspectives of the pro-sex feminists and the antipornography feminists. The women in my study see porn as one way for women to take control of their sexuality. At the same time, they are very critical of the mainstream pornography industry and articulate many of the same critiques of that industry as antiporn feminists. My study demonstrates that pornography can be used as activism and also can also generate activism. On the one hand, many women use pornography as an activist enterprise with which to pursue larger goals (feminism, sex education), while, on the other hand, those who did not use pornography in this way nonetheless find themselves becoming more involved in activism as a result of their involvement in porn. More research needs to be done to assess the impact of women-made pornography on consumers and the pornography industry. But this study shows that sex work debates need to take into account the full range of activist work being done, because the motives and objectives of these activists demonstrate that pornography is richer and more varied than conventional, simplistic representations of the porn industry.

NOTES

1. Neil Malamuth and Edward Donnerstein, eds., *Pornography and Sexual Aggression*, Orlando, FL: Academic Press, 1984; Lynne Segal, "Does Pornography Cause Violence? The Search for Evidence," in P. Gibson and R. Gibson, eds., *Dirty Looks: Women, Pornography, Power*, London: BFI, 1993; Elizabeth Monk-Turner and H. Christine Purcell, "Sexual Violence in Pornography: How Prevalent Is It?," *Gender Issues* 17 (1999): 58–67; Vernon Padgett, Jo Ann Brislin-Slutz, and James Neal, "Pornography, Erotica, and Attitudes toward Women: The Effects of Repeated Exposure," *Journal of Sex Research* 26 (1989): 479–491; Gloria Cowan and Kerri Dunn, "What Themes in Pornography Lead to Perceptions of the Degradation of Women?," *Journal of Sex Research* 31 (1994): 11–21; Kimberly Davies, "Voluntary Exposure to Pornography and Men's Attitudes toward Feminism and Rape," *Journal of Sex Research* 34 (1997): 131–137.

2. Douglas Wallace and Gerald Wehmer, "Pornography and Attitude Change," *Journal of Sex Research* 7 (1971): 116–125; Elaine Hatfield, "Men's and Women's Reactions to Sexually Explicit Films," *Archives of Sexual Behavior* 7 (1978): 583–592; Kathryn Kelley and Donna Musialowski, "Repeated Exposure to Sexually Explicit Stimuli: Novelty, Sex, and Sexual Attitudes," *Archives of Sexual Behavior* 15 (1986): 487–498; Dolf Zillmann and Jennings Bryant, "Effects of Prolonged Consumption of Pornography on Family Values," *Journal of Family Issues* 9 (1988): 518–544; Daniel Linz, "Exposure to Sexually Explicit Materials and Attitudes toward Rape: A Comparison of Study Results," *Journal of Sex Research* 26 (1989): 50–84.

3. Don D. Smith, "The Social Content of Pornography," *Journal of Communication*, 26 (1976): 16–24; Gloria Cowan, Carole Lee, Daniella Levy, and Debra Snyder, "Dominance and Inequality in X-Rated Videocassettes," *Psychology of Women Quarterly* 12 (1988): 299–311; Gloria Cowan and Robin Campbell, "Racism and Sexism in Interracial Pornography: A Content Analysis," *Psychology of Women Quarterly* 18 (1994): 323–338; Jennifer Lynn Gossett and Sarah Byrne, "'Click Here': A Content Analysis of Internet Rape Sites," *Gender & Society* 16 (2002): 689–709.

4. Kenneth Perkins and James Skipper, "Gay Pornographic and Sex Paraphernalia Shops: An Ethnography of Expressive Work Settings," *Deviant Behavior* 2 (1981): 187–199; Richard Tewksbury, "Patrons of Porn: Research Notes on the Clientele of Adult Bookstores," *Deviant Behavior* 11 (1990): 259–271; Michael Carl Stein, *The Ethnography of an Adult Bookstore: Private Scenes, Public Spaces*, Lewiston, NY: Edwin Mellen Press, 1990.

5. Louis Zurcher, R. George Kirkpatrick, Robert Cushing, and Charles Bowman, "The Anti-Pornography Campaign: A Symbolic Crusade," *Social Problems* 19 (1971): 217–238; Louis Zurcher, R. George Kirkpatrick, Robert Cushing, and Charles Bowman, "Ad Hoc Antipornography Organizations and Their Active Members," *Journal of Social Issues* 29 (1973): 69–94; R George Kirkpatrick and Louis Zurcher, "Women against Pornography: Feminist Anti-Pornography Crusades in American Society," *International Journal of Sociology and Social Policy* 3 (1983): 1–30; Cecil Greek and William Thompson, "Antipornography Campaigns: Saving the Family in America and England," *International Journal of Politics, Culture, and Society* 5 (1992): 601–616; Andrea Friedman, "Sadists and Sissies: Anti-Pornography Campaigns in Cold War America," *Gender & History* 15 (2003): 201–227.

6. There is a recent trend toward more writing on the topic. See: Terralee Bensinger, "Lesbian Pornography: The Re/Making of (a) Community," *Discourse* 15 (1992): 69–93; Dana Collins, "Lesbian Pornographic Production: Creating Social/Cultural Space for Subverting Representations of Sexuality," *Berkeley Journal of Sociology* 43 (1998–1999): 31–62; Esther Sonnet, "Erotic Fiction by Women for Women: The Pleasures of Post-Feminist Heterosexuality," *Sexualities* 2 (1999): 167–187; Simon Hardy, "More Black Lace: Women, Eroticism, and Subjecthood," *Sexualities* 4 (2001): 435–453; Danielle DeVoss, "Women's Porn Sites: Spaces of Fissure and Eruption or 'I'm a Little Bit of Everything'," *Sexuality and Culture,* 6 (2002): 75–94; Clarissa Smith, "'They're Ordinary People, Not Aliens from the Planet Sex!': The Mundane Excitements of Pornography for Women," *Journal of Mundane Behavior* 3 (2002); James Beggan and Scott Allison, "Reflexivity in the Pornographic Films of Candida Royalle," *Sexualities* 6 (2003): 301–324; Karen Ciclitira, "Pornography, Women, and Feminism: Between Pleasure and Politics," *Sexualities* 7 (2004): 281–301; Z. Fareen Parvez, "The Labor of Pleasure: How Perceptions of Emotional Labor Impact Women's Enjoyment of Pornography," *Gender and Society* 20 (2006): 605–631.

7. See also Robert Stoller and I. S. Levine, *Coming Attractions: The Making of an X-Rated Video*, New Haven: Yale University Press, 1993.

8. I was not paid for my services on the sets. The directors and producers and I had an arrangement whereby I would have access to the sites for my research and in exchange would help with the productions. Everyone on the set, both cast and crew, was told that I was a researcher and everyone gave informed consent to be part of the research.

9. George Becker, "The Social Regulation of Sexuality: A Cross-Cultural Perspective," *Current Perspectives in Social Theory* 5 (1984): 45–69.

10. Gayle Rubin, "Thinking Sex: Notes for a Radical Theory of the Politics of Sexuality," in *American Feminist Thought at Century's End: A Reader*, L.S. Kauffman, ed., Cambridge, MA: Blackwell, 1993.

11. Adult Video News is an industry trade publication, and AVN hosts an annual banquet where they hand out awards to actors, directors, and films in various categories.

2

STRIPPING AND TELEPHONE SEX

GENDER AND SPACE IN STRIP CLUBS

Katherine Frank and Michelle Carnes

I like to dance, I like to feel like maybe for a moment in time, whoever is watching
is laughing, lusting, looking. . . . Whatever problem they're going through,
they're not thinking about it 'cause they're lookin' at what I'm doing.
　　　　　　　　　—*Oohzee, black performer at lesbian strip shows*
　　　　　　　　　　　　　　　　　(A Taste of Oohzee, 2007)

The academic literature on stripping and strip clubs has been steadily growing over the last two decades, often focusing on issues of exploitation or
empowerment with regard to the interaction between dancers and their
customers, but also taking up issues of deviance, regulation, authenticity,
performance, and working conditions.[1] In a recent article, Sheila Jeffreys
argues that much of the literature on stripping exemplifies a "decon-
textualized individualism"—through the focus on dancers' agency and
empowerment—that does not adequately incorporate broader systems of
gendered privilege.[2] Using media reports as her evidence, Jeffreys argues
that because of "their role in the growth of international capitalism and
organized crime, the masculinizing effects of club patronage on male buyers,
the subordination of hundreds of thousands of women in the clubs, and the
exclusion of women from equal opportunities in national and international
professional business networks," strip clubs are exploitative in and of
themselves and that the "harmful Western practice of stripping . . . signifies
inequality."[3]

Beyond the fact that "media reports" are not an adequate means of determining the potential "harm" involved in erotic labor, Jeffreys oversimplifies stripping. She writes: "Rather than empowering women, the strip club boom, as this article will contend, helps to compensate men for lost privileges."[4] By contrast, many feminist researchers emphasize the potential for the practice of stripping to *both* empower women and to compensate men or to reproduce existing systems of power and privilege.[5] Further, Jeffreys is not the first to suggest that the field be expanded beyond the gendered exchanges that take place onsite between sex workers and their customers.[6] Although her approach and conclusions are extremely different from Jeffreys, for example, Agustín notes that the frameworks commonly used to study sex work more generally are "fixed almost exclusively on the women who sell sex" (and, increasingly, the men who purchase it), thus ignoring "the great majority of phenomena that make up the sex industry." She suggests the adoption of a cultural studies approach that:

> [W]ould look at commercial sex in its widest sense, examining its intersections with art, ethics, consumption, family life, entertainment, sports, economics, urban space, sexuality, tourism and criminality, not omitting issues of race, class, gender, identity, and citizenship. An approach that considers commercial sex as culture would look for the everyday practices involved and try to reveal how our societies distinguish between activities considered normatively "social" and activities denounced as morally wrong. This means examining a range of activities that take in both commerce and sex.[7]

Considering Agustín's framework in the specific case of strip clubs, Frank suggests many other possible areas of inquiry for researchers, many of which still concern power and inequalities but might situate strip club transactions in a broader context and open up new realms of exploration.[8] Despite the academic interest in stripping, then, there are many aspects of this particular form of legal adult entertainment that are just beginning to be explored.

This chapter takes up that challenge, along with Weitzer's call to move beyond either the simple condemnation or romanticization of the sex industry.[9] We present a comparative look at the creation of strip club space for (primarily) heterosexually identified male customers and for black same-sex desiring women (hereafter, BSSDW).[10] In doing so, we take up issues of gender, race, privilege, and regulation as they emerge in this particular form of adult entertainment. We argue that the meaning and impact of stripping may be best understood by exploring the specific configurations of privilege impacting different types of entertainment sites and shaping the meaning of the transactions that unfold within them.

Strip clubs for heterosexually identified men are certainly the most ubiquitous venues in the contemporary United States, existing in small towns as well as urban areas. Their status as legal venues for adult entertainment is repeatedly challenged by local municipalities and they can be "lightning rods" for conflict over regulation,[11] yet strip clubs catering to straight men are still relatively mainstream. Women are occasionally seen as customers in strip clubs featuring female dancers, and a much smaller number of clubs featuring male dancers draw female crowds. In general, though, women do not exist as strip club customers in the same numbers as men; many events for women are actually weekly or monthly takeovers of strip clubs designed for men. Women may buy tickets to see the Chippendales or the Thunder Down Under for special occasions such as bachelorette parties; more rarely are they *regulars* at clubs featuring male exotic dancers (which often cater to gay men). Strip events for lesbian audiences are "the least visible in terms of a public street presence."[12] Events catering to BSSDW are even less visible—occurring weekly or monthly—and often in already marginalized areas of town (although Black Pride, which occurs each year in May, ushers in an increase in shows). Events take place nationwide, usually in urban spaces leased out for that purpose. Despite their relatively low profile, strip events for BSSDW are important to take into account when considering both the increasing importance of stripping as a form of entertainment and the ways that stripping is intertwined with other forms of consumption and other systems of meaning and privilege.

A COMPARATIVE APPROACH

Each of the authors conducted ethnographic research on stripping in the United States. Frank is an anthropologist and former exotic dancer who researched the motivations and experiences of male customers in five strip clubs in a southern city she calls Laurelton; in addition to her labor as a dancer and her analysis of her everyday interactions, she conducted multiple, in-depth interviews with 30 regular customers of those clubs.[13] Over the year and a half she spent in the field, she also interviewed other dancers, managers, DJs, and men who preferred other kinds of adult entertainment. Carnes worked as an exotic dancer in traditional strip clubs as well, but then pursued fieldwork at strip events catering to black female customers. She conducted interviews with 20 customers, dancers, and promoters and observed numerous strip events for BSSDW in the Washington, DC, area.[14]

Frank's research was conducted in five traditional clubs chosen to represent different positions on a hierarchy of "classiness" (ranging from the most prestigious clubs in the city to the lower tier "dive" bars) as well as on the types of service available within. Clubs were evaluated in terms of their reputations, dress codes, cover charges, food and liquor choices, club size and atmosphere, location, and predominant clientele. Each selected venue offered stage performances by the dancers, along with the opportunity for customers to purchase "private" table dances at their seats, on a raised platform or table, or while standing on the ground between the man's knees. Although a dancer could disrobe completely and place her hands on the customers' shoulders, other forms of bodily contact were prohibited (which distinguishes these clubs from others that allow more contact, such as lap dances). Dancers were also required to keep at least one foot of space between themselves and the customers during dances. Customers were not allowed to touch the dancers, or to touch or expose their own genitals. These rules were rarely openly transgressed, and when they were, the customer was usually asked to leave the clubs.[15] The erotic appeal of the men's visits, then, was not dependent on sexual release or physical contact.

The male interviewees ranged in age from 28 to 57. All identified as heterosexual and had at least some college education. Despite sometimes significant differences in income and occupation, all identified as somewhere in the middle class. Twenty-seven were white Americans, two were African-Americans, and one was a British citizen who frequently traveled to the United States on business.

Carnes' observations were drawn from three primary sites where BSSDW erotic events were held in Washington, DC—Cada Vez (a nightclub/restaurant), Wet (a gay nightclub that was used to host Soft 'N' Wet Afternoons), and Club Levels (a nightclub catering to black men and women). Both Cada Vez and Wet hosted black women's events during off hours (or days) when the club was not in use by more dominant groups. Events offered the opportunity to watch dancers on the stages as well as to interact more privately through personalized dances. Some events attracted a younger crowd, ranging from 21 to the early 40s, while others drew the over-40 crowd. The black female interviewees ranged in age from 22 to 81 and claimed a variety of sexual identities (dom, femme, boi, etc.). Customers ranged in professions from working class to pink collar, and came from Washington, DC, southern Maryland, or Northern Virginia.

These projects are detailed explorations of specific entertainment sites, the complexities of which cannot be replicated in a chapter of this length. Our analysis here, then, is necessarily limited in its aim and scope. What this chapter does illustrate, however, is that while the act of commercial stripping—removing one's clothes before an audience of paying customers— may have some similarities across demographic and context, there are also important particularities in practices and meanings that must be considered when drawing conclusions about stripping, and these variations challenge generalizations about such practices as intrinsically "harmful" or as signifying inequality, liberation, or anything else in a coherent, universal manner.

Most research on strip clubs focuses on a particular type of club—with female or male dancers—but rarely have scholars compared these different types of venue. The differences between male and female customers have been analyzed in a handful of studies.[16] One intriguing question is whether shows featuring male strippers for female audiences reinforce or invert gender stereotypes and power differentials. As Montemurro, Bloom, and Madell have noted, because "norms for sexual expression vary, the comparison of men and women in hyper-sexualized environments, like strip clubs, is telling with respect to the power and enactment of these norms in everyday life."[17] Their research, like similar research on male customers by other scholars, offers a typology of customers. They argue that men and women visit strip clubs for different reasons and that women use strip clubs "as an opportunity for social interaction and bonding with friends" more frequently than men did, although women were still interested in the voyeuristic elements of the show.[18] In this chapter, we move beyond the static typologies and explore in more depth how the creation of strip space and interactions reflects the unique cultural and historical positions of the customers, as well as how the specific needs of those customers shape the use and interpretation of strip events and clubs.

A Space of One's Own

We found that the motivations, experiences, and interpretations of their interactions in strip clubs of the primarily white, middle-aged, and middle-class men and the black, same-sex desiring women were strikingly similar in some respects, especially with regard to understandings of entertainment and leisure. Among the men, the most prevalent (and usually the first given) *spoken* motivation for visiting strip clubs was a desire to "relax." Strip clubs were perceived as relaxing, in part, because they provided an atmosphere different from both work and home and an opportunity for both personal and sexual acceptance from women. BSSDW also repeatedly described the events as creating a space to relax, interact with friends, escape from daily pressures, and gain personal and sexual acceptance. All the women interviewed expressed comfort in being able to unwind and get their minds off of their jobs, bills, or other stressors while viewing the performances.

In the sex industry—of which strip clubs are a significant segment—gendered sexual identities and desires, as well as privileges and experiences of race and class, explicitly intersect with consumer culture. Strip club visits are thus related to other aspects of everyday life—work, home, relationships, identities, and aspirations. Strip spaces designed for heterosexual men and for BSSDW fulfill different needs for the customers as well—needs that arise out of unique social and historical positionings— although both sets of customers also discussed some similar motivations and experiences. For the male regulars, the clubs provided a relative degree of "safety" as well as "excitement"—both as entertainment venues and in relation to their outside relationships with women—as well as the pleasure of a sexualized encounter without the pressure of physical performance. Discourses of class, race, and gender that underlie men's interpretations of their visits to strip clubs also informed the BSSDW experiences, although in different ways. Commercial stripping involves public erotic performances with personal and cultural meanings. For the BSSDW, strip events provide a sense of community— political and erotic—that helps them transcend everyday experiences of racism, sexism, and homophobia. In the next sections, these needs are discussed in more depth.

The Importance of Masculine Space

Strip clubs for men provide an atmosphere where men can engage in traditionally masculine activities and forms of consumption often frowned on in these other spheres—cigar smoking, drinking, and even being "rowdy," vulgar, or aggressive. Despite the fact that nudity eventually becomes commonplace to regulars, the clubs are still a place where many conventions are inverted; for example, women are undressed in a public space and tend to initiate sexualized interactions rather than the men, sometimes quite aggressively, and sexualized relationships are *openly* facilitated through economic exchange (rather than, as the customers pointed out, the many covert ways that this happens in everyday life).

For the male customers, for whom everyday relationships with women were often seen as a source of pressure and expectations, such inversions were experienced as relaxing. Many men described relations between the sexes in the U.S. as being "strained," "confused," or "tense." Over half the interviewees specifically appreciated having an escape from the rules of conduct and the social games involved when interacting with other women in other settings. Interactions with women in the workplace were also often felt to be constraining. One man pointed out that in the workplace he felt nervous about giving compliments to women for fear that they would accuse him of sexual harassment. Another said that club visits "let frustration out:" "With all of this sexual harassment stuff going around these days, men need somewhere to go where they can act like they want." In the clubs, another interviewee claimed, "everybody knows what the rules are." There are other spaces, then, where the men do not understand exactly what is going to "get them into trouble." Some men explicitly stated a desire to interact with women who were not "feminist," and who still wanted to relate to men in more "traditional" ways. Others said that men had to continually "be on guard" against offending women, experiencing and justifying their visits within a framework of confusion and frustration rather than simply one of privilege or domination. The rapid increase in the number of strip clubs across the U.S. in the mid-1980s, after all, coincided with an increase of women into the workforce and more attention paid to issues of sexual harassment, date rape, and criticism of the sex industry. While this is not a case of simple cause and effect, such developments certainly affect the ways that the men's visits to the clubs are spoken about and understood.

Men also sought personal and sexual acceptance through their interactions in the clubs. Dancers offered an opportunity to talk to women with whom they were not generally able to interact, for a number of reasons—a lack of attractiveness, age differences, class differences (in either direction), availability, and the women's willingness to interact outside of the clubs. Some men were also searching for acceptance of their sexual desires, telling dancers things they claimed they had never told their wives or lovers—usually specific fantasies or experiences they thought the other women in their lives would not understand or that had caused extreme negative reactions in the past, such as a desire to give or receive anal sex. Interactions purchased in strip clubs were also often felt to be "an ego boost" because they provided safe opportunities for interactions with women without the risk of rejection. Sexuality and sexual conquest, after all, can be experienced as humiliating and stressful for men as well as thrilling. Many sex workers joke about really being "therapists" and explicitly understand their jobs to be about boosting a man's ego by convincing him that he is desirable, masculine, and successful. One interviewee described his visits to a strip club during a failing marriage as "good for my ego to build me up, to make me feel like I was a man again." Thus customers were at times seeking a sense of escape from those aspects of the self that felt oppressive in other spheres—old age, ugliness or insecurity, a lack of social skills, or intimate failures. Men may seek to "maintain grandiose self-images" as part of their gender identity, images that gain a heightened importance in middle age.[19] Some men may not have experienced a sense of strength and influence in their everyday lives even during their younger years, yet think that they *should have*. For men who are willing and able to pay for it, the type of female attention available in a contemporary strip club can be notable.

Susan Bordo discusses male anxiety about female attractiveness and argues that "just as the beautiful bodies [in cultural representations] subject us women to (generally) unrealizable models of the kind of female we must *become* in order to be worthy of attention and love, they also subject men and boys to (generally) unrealizable models of the kind of female they must *win*—with equally destructive consequences."[20] Although most heterosexual boys settle for "inferior fixes," women who may be attractive but do not quite succeed in approximating the ideal, many men still "remain haunted by the beauties." Images of female perfection thus "not only shape perception, they also shape sexual desire," she argued, and "straight male sexuality is honed on the images, even fixated on them."[21] That some men perceive female beauty as being powerful, able to "invade male consciousness and arouse desire and then to reject that desire, leaving the man humiliated, shamed, frustrated," may lead some men to seek both solace and excitement in pornography or strip clubs.[22] In strip clubs, the "beauties" are there as a live fantasy—young, available, interested, and accepting. These customers were keenly aware of the fact that, in addition to male bonding, competition between men also often centered on the struggle to gain attention from women outside the clubs. Many welcomed the opportunity to avoid this competition. In strip clubs, Gary said, "the pressure's off. I have to be accepted."

Some of the talk about the relaxing aspects of strip clubs for men, then, must be understood as interconnected with the vulnerabilities of the body as well as the pleasures. An emphasis on male sexual performance remains high in the social context of changes in the expectations of intimate relationships (increasing expectations that intimate relationships will provide psychological support and gratification), in the reasons that individuals enter into relationships (for companionship rather than economic need or familial duty), the increasing importance of sexuality in consumer culture, and changes in the meanings of sexuality (such as a growing acceptance of the idea that sexuality will provide "ever-increasing rewards and personal meanings").[23] A no-contact strip club thus offers a certain protection from vulnerability that other arenas—including the bedroom at home—may not. In a strip club, a customer can fantasize about a sexual encounter with a woman, yet is not responsible for actually physically performing or providing pleasure to her. He is also prohibited from revealing his naked body to the dancers, which in itself can provide another form of refuge from judgment. Customers also sometimes want to be accepted as objects of desire, asking questions about how it felt to be a dancer, both on the job and in other settings, stating things like, "It must be nice to have everybody want you," "How does it feel to be perfect?" "Is it fun to be the one up on the pedestal?" or "I'd trade places with you if I could." The cross-identificatory wishes being expressed in such statements are rooted in complex fantasies of power, exposure, degradation, and idealization.[24]

Although more and more heterosexually identified women are visiting strip clubs featuring female dancers—with male partners, with business associates, and even with female friends—traditional strip clubs still generally create a masculinized space.[25] Female customers may be shunned by dancers, harassed by male customers, or chided by the DJ for not taking the stage. For same-sex desiring women, the harassment may be even more extreme, as their very presence can challenge the heteronormative assumptions on which the transactions are unfolding. The presence of female strippers alone, then, is not always enough to make such venues enticing for women who want to view the female body erotically.

The Importance of BSSDW Space

BSSDW events in Washington, DC, offer a range of experiences—erotically charged, choreographed dance performances, lap dances, live nude shower shows, and pole acrobatics. Strip shows catering to BSSDW provide an accepting space where sexual desires towards women are not only allowed but expected and valued and where black women have permission to be openly expressive about their desires, without fear of judgment, harassment, or even violence. Black women told stories of being approached by men at traditional strip clubs and being "hit on" or made to feel uncomfortable. For this reason, at Soft 'N' Wet Afternoons and other events, men were either denied entry or placed under obvious (if playful) surveillance by the audience and the emcee. Unless a man was known or announced as a personal guest (or his presence otherwise explained), the emcee always paid attention to male patrons through humor—such as suggesting he was gay or otherwise attempting to neutralize any threat the women might feel due to his presence. The emcee at these events—sometimes already a well-known community member or celebrity— also played an important role in allowing BSSDW to cast off the cloak of black female respectability through modeling openly desiring behavior. Alternatively speaking to performers, addressing the audience, and expressing her own delight for all to hear ("You've got me all wet up in here now! You'd betta watch out or I'm-a come get you!"), the emcee helps reduce tension and relax the women's inhibitions against experiencing and performing same-sex desire.

The needs of African-American women for safe and comfortable spaces must be contextualized historically as well, as they are connected up with discourses of race, class, gender, and sexuality. Racialized notions of the black female body as "hypersexual" were historically used to justify the sexual brutality inflicted on black women by white men under slavery. Black women have long sought to defend against accusations of promiscuity, immorality, and uncontrollable lustiness. Middle-class black women in particular have attempted to downplay expressions of sexual desire out of "racial obligation." In return, "the community gave them respect and recognition."[26] Among black working-class women, however, expressions of sexuality were also a vehicle for experiencing freedom and increased mobility after slavery, "one of the very few realms in which masses of African-American women could exercise some kind of autonomy: they could, at least, choose their sexual partners—and thus, they could distinguish their post-slavery status from their historical enslavement."[27] For a working-class black woman, choosing her own sexual partner was an act of liberation, albeit one for which black middle-class women judged them harshly. When the National Association of Colored Women formed in 1896, it charged middle-class black women with the task of going "among the lowly, illiterate and even the vicious, to whom they are bound by ties of race and sex . . . to reclaim them." Yet, as Angela Davis writes, "in the process of defending black women's moral integrity and sexual purity, sexual agency was almost entirely denied."[28]

Gender and sexuality not only impact understandings and expressions of desires but also opportunities for enacting those desires. Hammers notes that "struggles for legitimation have been in part about access to, and the claiming of, the public sphere."[29] And while men have long had access to venues providing sexual services and entertainment, "zones for sexual release, experimentation and casual sex geared towards women have never existed— at least, not on any scale comparable to that of men."[30] Male privileges are usually reproduced in queer sex zones, meaning that lesbians more rarely establish their own sexual enclaves in urban areas, instead making "parallel use of any gay male social space that tolerates their presence."[31] For same-sex desiring women, then, marginalization, stigmatization, and victimization results in an enhanced need to feel accepted and embraced before feeling fully sexually agentic. As such, the presence of other customers at the strip events has an intense significance, although for different reasons than it does for male customers. If a space is identified as a BSSDW erotic party but does not fill to capacity, women experience less of the safety of anonymity and belonging, of being among others "like me." Similarly, if promoters allow men to enter the space in order to cut their losses, the event may fail to produce the anticipated experience of acceptance and recognition. Rather than using tipping moments to stand out from the crowd in an affirmative way, as men do at their strip clubs, a woman in the same space is already standing out, by virtue of her gender—but without the control and choice to do so.

Petersen and Dressel argue that when women find a supportive environment for sexual expression such as a male strip club, they may exhibit aggressiveness in behavior similar to that displayed by men.[32] Other researchers point out that women may be even more aggressive than men when interacting with strippers. Liepe-Levinson found that female customers were permitted physical liberties that were often denied to men— "mutually aggressive hugs, kisses, body caresses, lap-sitting, and dirty dancing," in addition to touch or holding the "buttocks, chests and nipples of the male dancers," with the genital area being the only off-limits body part.[33] This was certainly the case at the events catering to BSSDW: female customers feel encouraged by the MC to engage in bawdy talk, "slapping asses," or otherwise physically interacting with the dancers in ways that were prohibited in more traditional strip clubs. At the same time, however, BSSDW often claimed that female customers are "more respectful" than male customers. BSSDW found that they could touch dancers more readily, particularly on the dancers' buttocks, because it was read as women appreciating each other's bodies, as a participatory act of desire rather than a show of masculine dominance or disrespect to the dancer. Dancers who performed for male and female audiences often reported a preference for dancing for women, saying that women appreciated them more than men.

Johari, a 26-year-old black lesbian in the Air Force who describes the erotic parties as "a space where I could just relax and be myself and just present myself the way I wanted," described her gender presentation as, "tomboyish, studdish, and dominant." She noted that strippers in traditional strip clubs may not be "turned on by that" and that her masculine gender presentation caused her to "not get as many looks" from dancers in those settings. Like traditional strip clubs, she recognized that BSSDW parties are "a business, so they [dancers] won't turn you down." However, she also felt that some dancers at the events "really like" black female customers who present in a masculine way, providing an atmosphere of acceptance that was important to her. Sociologist Mignon Moore points out that "the harshest, most critical language about black lesbians is reserved for women with a nonfeminine presentation of self," explaining that "the fear of stigmatization from one's own group members can be paralyzing, particularly when those whose opinions matter most, those to whom one feels closest, and those to whom one turns for support and protection from outsiders become one's harshest critics."[34] BSSDW parties invite and elicit expressions of sexual desire between women inclusive of the gender variance among them—a valuable and rare experience for black women whose gender presentation falls within a range of categories.

Johari explained that part of her enjoyment emerged from the opportunity to safely present herself in a more masculine way, pointing out the range of gender categories among black women beyond binary butch–femme dichotomies. She says, "in a woman-loving-women environment, there's a lot more roles. To an outsider who is not an insider, we're just imitating the traditional scene" of gender binaries, when in fact, there are a variety of gender categories recognized among black women. Moore identifies three of these categories:

[F]emmes, or feminine women . . . they wear dresses or skirts, form-fitting jeans, tops that are low cut or that show cleavage, makeup, jewelry and accessories such as a purse or high-heeled shoes that display a sense of femininity. . . . Gender-blender [is] a style related to but distinct from an androgynous presentation of self . . . they usually wear certain men's clothing like pants or shoes, combined with something less masculine like a form-fitting short or a little makeup. . . . [Transgressives] usually wear men's clothing and shoes and coordinate these outfits with heavy jewelry, belts with large, masculine buckles, and ties or suspenders for a more dressed-up look.[35]

Moore is careful to remind us that these gender categories are "limited to how they look physically" and are "not necessarily connected to any specific personality traits or ideologies about gender or gender display."[36] Moore also points out that individuals do not necessarily fit into one category exclusively.

Johari felt the same gender range was true among both the audience and performers at the parties. Whereas traditional strip clubs offered mostly feminine women as performers, BSSDW parties were more diverse:

I have gone to the Wet/The Edge—that's where I've seen the most shows. Most of the doms don't get completely naked. They wear a sports bra or something. They'll be dressed up with the tie for someone's birthday. I respect them for doing that. I've seen Ace the MC, she's one of the more infamous emcees in the DC area. I would consider her a dom . . . but she was doing the show and then came out in some feminine clothes and she started taking off stuff—and then she showed her crotch! . . . You never know when you're going to see a special show. In that space, people are allowed to express themselves how they want. For the most part, the audience responded well and that was really good to see. I think it's sexy, actually!

BSSDW parties thus provided opportunities for gender play, where supposedly discrete categories of gender presentation are multiplied, along with blurring lines of "who does what" and "to whom" based on gendered expectations of sexual desire and agency.

Another aspect of customer engagement in the BSSDW erotic parties is determining whether the female dancers are authentically "into" women or if their performance is "just an act." Having contact with customers while retaining a level of mystery is a balancing act that can make a dancer wildly successful, not just in terms of her image, tips, or payment for performance but also to increase audience demand at events where she performs as customers seek opportunities to interact with her and observe her responses— and perhaps get a glimpse into her "real" sexual identity. One audience member at Soft 'N' Wet repeatedly pointed out which of the black female dancers she thought was "gay," "straight," "bi," "with a boyfriend," or "with a girlfriend once but is single now." Whether or not she was correct in identifying dancers' personal sexual identities was not as notable as her feeling that such information was valuable and proof of her ability to gather "inside" information about performers, beyond the "act" that dancers perform and "ordinary" customers consume. A pattern of such information gathering, with a focus on a certain kind of authenticity, is also found in the male customers' interactions with female dancers, not just in terms of sexual identities but also with regard to "real names" and details about the dancers' lives. Audience members at BSSDW erotic events indulged in tales of having contact with dancers outside the club that led them to believe the dancer was same-sex identified and they also claimed to witness behavior pointing to the possibility of mutual attraction between them. Such storytelling added to a dancer's mystique, enhanced the teller's status and reinforced the space as a safe arena to speak openly about experiencing desire and being the object of desire among women of color.

EROTIC TENSIONS: SAFETY/DANGER, INDIVIDUALISM/COMMUNITY

For the male customers, strip clubs also derived some of their appeal from their ability to be both *safe* in a number of ways (when compared with the illegality of prostitution or the disruptiveness, risk, and vulnerability of a "real" affair) and *dangerous enough* to be exciting spaces. Interviewees discussed their experiences in the language of "adventure" in addition to "variety," "travel," "fun," and "escape." Some described themselves as "hunters" or "explorers." For many customers, especially those who preferred the lower tier clubs, the fact that visits to strip clubs often implied a journey into "bad areas" of town was exciting, a form of erotic slumming. Even in upscale clubs—which were not as often experienced as sinister spaces because of their many amenities and because a concerted effort was made to signify "classiness" rather than the potential of contamination—customers still fantasized about the dangerous, glamorous, and exciting individuals or the vice that might be encountered in them (despite their simultaneous lack of proof), such as rich New York gangsters laundering money or dealing cocaine, beautiful women who could lure a man into a private room and out of a month's worth of income, famous athletes buying oral sex from ex-*Playboy* bunnies, etc. The men's talk about danger and adventure was connected up with historical discourses about masculinity, travel, and encounters with various categories of "Others." Customers also discussed "adventure" in relation to sexual discovery—even without physical contact, they were getting to know someone in a sexualized situation, and engaging in a transgressive, mutual construction of fantasy. The interviewees identified with discourses that associated sexual conquest and desire with masculinity, freedom, and adventure and that made such practices meaningful as an expression of self, identity, and individuality.

Yet despite descriptions of strip clubs as places with "no rules" and as "outside the law," and although customers experience and express feelings of freedom, adventure, or excitement during their visits, the clubs have been tightly regulated. The city has usually delineated where such clubs can be located and what types of interactions can be found inside. Clubs also set additional rules for employees and customers, and most clubs have security guards in the parking lot and at least two or three floor managers to enforce those rules. Other kinds of behavior are policed by both the dancers and the other customers—such as proper etiquette in regard to watching table dances, tipping procedures, and customer-to-customer interactions. The men also control their own behavior—few bachelors *really* need their hands to be tied during a table dance, and even men who claim to be wild with testosterone are usually found sitting calmly in their chairs. Further, even men who claimed to be interested in purchasing some kind of actual sexual contact from the dancers were satisfied, over and over again, with *talking about it* and paying for table dances.

Many male regulars also explicitly claimed that strip clubs provided a safe space in which to be both married (or committed) and sexually aroused (or at least, interacting with other women in a sexualized setting). This is related to cultural ideas about heterosexuality, marriage, monogamy, and consumption. (The boundaries between different venues and services are less rigid in many other countries, with stripping more blurred with prostitution or with customers alternatively visiting venues that offer sexualized conversation, manual or oral release, or actual sex.)[37] For many of the American men studied, "looking" was the final limit with which they felt comfortable. At the same time, being able to look and express desire in a masculinized and eroticized environment enhanced feelings of independence, freedom, and self-identity.

Although BSSDW also derived feelings of freedom and excitement from their attendance at strip events, these experiences were enmeshed with different cultural discourses and personal meanings. Unlike white customers seeking the thrill of visiting a "seedy" part of town, black women visited spaces proximal to where they lived. As an event promoter explained:

> Back in the day, only a limited people wanted to rent their spots to gay people. . . . That's why we kept stayin' in that community down there in Southeast because that was designated as "our community." . . . No matter what club shut down and what club opened up, you'd still pretty much have the community because that's where the [black lesbian] community went anyway.

Both Cada Vez and Wet are located in traditionally black neighborhoods with low rents (compared to the rest of the city) and a broader reputation for being "dangerous" places to live or visit, particularly southeast Washington. At the same time, given that these were also neighborhoods known to the gay and lesbian community, these locations were experienced as welcoming and comfortable to these groups rather than dangerous or contaminating.

Further, although individual experiences of desire and performances of identity certainly played a part in the erotics of their attendance at strip events, for the BSSDW, these events were also wrapped up in understandings and experiences of community. In traditional strip clubs for men, male customers usually sit at their tables or line the stages as observers unless it is a special occasion such as a bachelor party and a guest is offered a chance to become part of the performance. While men may visit strip clubs in the pursuit of male bonding, or to instill feelings of camaraderie that might enhance business transactions, they do not usually describe experiences of emotional, political, or erotic "community" in relation to their visits. For BSSDW, however, feelings of belonging and community are important aspects of their visits, and promoters will criticize each other if their events seem to be too concerned with monetary motivations rather than benefiting the African-American women's community overall. Dancers themselves were judged harshly by audience members if they were perceived to only be participating for the financial benefits. Riley, an avid audience member at BSSDW events, explained: "There's a few performers [who] are not out there except to make money. If these people were willing to come out more, the gay community would be larger and we would have more events." Even when promoters or performers are making money, they're expected to put the larger community's need for spaces of freedom and acceptance above their personal financial gain. Certainly, male customers worried about being "hustled" by dancers who were more interested in money than genuine interactions. Yet these concerns were expressed at an individual level and tied up with discourses of commodification, masculinity, and sexuality rather than those of group participation or obligation.

There were several ways that BSSDW events in Washington enhanced feelings of community. For example, an evening might begin with pre-show audience dancing or group stepping (e.g., the Booty Call, the Electric Slide, or the Casper Slide). Group stepping helps mark the transition from the outside world into the welcoming, affirming party atmosphere at the parties. It allows black women to perform as a group and experience themselves as part of a moving entity, literally moving as one in dances rooted in shared history and meaning. Coming together for group stepping can promote black identity and pride and also often reinforce an enduring connection to heritage in Africa and a history in slavery, within which so many meanings around blackness emerged in the United States. Since group stepping is so often performed at other important black life rituals (weddings, funerals, sorority rushes), group stepping helps black women further develop a party space where an atmosphere of acceptance and belonging is crucial to the proceedings.

Events can also enhance feelings of community through the emphasis on "partying with a purpose," or offering opportunities for community health agencies to provide wellness and support information (e.g., support groups for black lesbians, free breast cancer screenings, smoking cessation kits). For BSSDW, a lack of health insurance coverage (unable to afford their own or through a partner) can impact their ability to have access to regular healthcare with a consistent health provider. In addition, many lesbians and women who partner with women may not have a health provider they trust and, therefore, to whom they can come out about their sexuality. When health providers administer inappropriate procedures (i.e., all female patients must undergo pregnancy testing as a matter of course) and medical background questions ("Are you on birth control?") based on heteronormative assumptions, women who partner with women cannot fully disclose their identities or behaviors and may believe the health provider is not aware of the health needs of women who partner with women. The Office on Women's Health in the U.S. Department of Health and Human Services holds that "past negative health care experiences can discourage a lesbian from seeking care in the future, including preventive and screening measures, which further jeopardizes her health."[38] As part of this emphasis on 'partying with a purpose,' the promoter of Soft 'N'

Wet allowed the Mautner Project, a national lesbian health organization, to set up a breast self-examination booth onsite. As a result, five women, including a dancer, found lumps but remain healthy thanks to the early detection.

Many medical health support service materials mimic the format of erotic party announcements, as organizations are aware that erotic imagery can help encourage both safer sex practices and healthier behavior more generally. Resources advertising free, local mammograms, HIV testing, lesbian support groups and other health-related services are often modeled after and co-mingled with clubcards or leaflets advertising upcoming events on one table for audiences to take with them before they leave.[39] Departing guests would often start at the top of the table and pick up one of everything in an effort to be fully informed about upcoming events, gathering support information alongside event announcements. Sometimes, organization volunteers would distribute cards and giveaway items personally (such as key chains, magnets, safer sex kits, stickers) to the audience or hand them out at the exit. With such little actual distance between medical health support services and erotic party announcements on the table, the boundaries between them blur. Being erotically engaged and connected with one's community becomes as critical and integral to one's overall health as an HIV test or blood pressure screening.

REGULATION

Despite their popularity and ubiquitousness, strip clubs are also a highly embattled form of entertainment, currently the subject of intense public scrutiny, debate, and regulation. The opposition to strip clubs is often fairly organized and groups such as the National Family Legal Foundation draw on discourses of public and private morality to bolster their attacks against such establishments.[40] Hanna notes that there are continuities between the stigmatization of exotic dance and way that many other popular dance forms— such as waltz, ragtime, flamenco, and tango—have been considered scandalous at times in their history. Condemnations and unfair regulations of exotic dance venues reflect a class bias: "Nudity can be seen in theaters (e.g., Mutations, Oh! Calcutta!) by wine-drinking quiche-eaters but not by beer drinking pretzel eaters."[41] The enactment and enforcement of regulations is also connected up with race and sexuality in somewhat complex ways, as we explore in this section.

Although exotic dance has minimal protections as a form of expressive conduct, there has been a tendency in the courts to allow local municipalities to enact restrictive zoning regulations based on claims that strip clubs pose public health risks, encourage prostitution, and lead to adverse secondary effects in areas where they are located—such as increased crime and decreased property values. Some conservatives have also suggested that strip clubs lead to increases in rape and domestic violence in the communities where they are located, despite a lack of evidence.[42] As zoning regulations are often designed and implemented to eradicate nude or topless dancing in communities[43] and tend to be based on fears of economic or moral blight rather than on solid research into whether or not the clubs cause social problems, they may have unintended or even humorous results. At times, regulations against particular sexual behaviors or adult entertainment venues in general may be deployed to speed the process of gentrification in particular neighborhoods. Four out of five of the clubs Frank studied have since closed their doors; although there are still numerous venues to watch female dancers in Laurelton, the locations of clubs shift for legal, economic, political, and cultural reasons. All three of the regular events Carnes studied have also since ceased to exist in their original venues, due to venue closure or gentrification which encroached on event privacy and affordability for both the promoters and the audiences.

In some ways, marginalized constituencies may fare worse than more mainstream ones when it comes to regulations. Visible red-light areas, and visible queer areas, may become easy targets for law enforcement. The shrinking of the "public world of queer sexuality," set off in part by anti-sex health regulations designed to eradicate commercial sex spaces (and especially those catering to gays and lesbians),[44] has continued into the new millennium. However, strip events for BSSDW have not disappeared altogether, instead migrating to suburban areas of Washington, DC (such as Prince George's County, Maryland). As they move into such areas, the invisibility factor that accompanies marginalization may offer additional protections. Because strip events for BSSDW lack an actual physical location, for example, they sometimes operated under the radar of enforcement agencies. An event for BSSDW such as Soft 'N' Wet may be thought of more as "a practice rather than a place," and thus is better able to "live beyond the law" and simply change locations to avoid being the target of zoning regulations.[45]

This ability to remain under the radar also results in different practices and behaviors at the events than one might see in more traditional strip clubs in the same city, as interactions between dancers and customers were less scrutinized by legal enforcement and by event staff. Women were not prevented from touching the dancers at BSSDW events and recognized that they "could do stuff that the guys would get in trouble for" not just because of how it was interpreted by the dancers but also because "no one was watching."

Thus, while events had a lack of visibility in and of themselves—due to taking place in spaces primarily designated for other constituencies and due to their periodic nature—participants also had a relative freedom from surveillance. Further, while the women may have also had a lack of visibility and self-recognition as desiring agents in the everyday world, in the space created during the events, it was precisely because of this fact that they could exercise freedoms towards the dancers that could have been read as disrespectful or degrading coming from a man.

CONCLUSION

Cultural expectations of gender as well as social inequalities and positionings affect people's opportunities, choices, and resulting satisfactions as well as the meanings of their leisure practices. Customers, consciously or not, are part of the scene in strip clubs or strip events, intricately involved in performances of identity, sexuality, and desire that generated meaning and pleasure out of their interactions. Engaging in sexualized or eroticized encounters with dancers in a public place, and in the presence of a live audience, was significant to the meanings of the experiences for both the heterosexual male customers and the BSSDW. For the men, such encounters could secure heterosexuality, at least temporarily or in fantasy, through a public performance of desire for a woman. Men could observe themselves desiring—literally, in the mirrored walls of the clubs, and figuratively, in the sense of self-reflection and fantasy. Further, the experience or performance of sexual desire could in turn serve as an affirmation of gender identity both to himself and to others (although sexual desire can feel different from or independent of gender, it can also serve to reinforce ideas of oneself as masculine or feminine). Public "consumption," whether it be of the attention of attractive women or the other commodities offered in the clubs, could also generate pleasurable experiences of self and identity (or conflicted ones). For the BSSDW, individual performances and experiences of desire at strip events are connected to understandings and experiences of being part of a political and erotic community, and contribute to an atmosphere of acceptance, belonging, and safety as well as one of libidinal abandon. Observing other women desiring women, and being observed oneself, is thus layered with meanings.

There are of course many aspects of strip club visits and their meanings to the participants that we have not been able to touch on in this chapter: complexities of the relational and psychological aspects; issues of authenticity and performance; the connections of stripping to the entertainment industry more broadly; discourses of classiness and respectability and their impact on the meaning of strip events and interactions to the customers; and more. Our aim here, however, was to begin drawing these comparisons between events for heterosexually identified men and for BSSDW to extend the analysis of stripping beyond simplistic generalizations about gendered power. We argue that while stripping—or other forms of adult entertainment—is implicated in the same structures of inequality as other forms of labor and leisure, there are also specificities in the meaning of its consumption that must be considered. Further, while a focus on gender is certainly appropriate when thinking about the organization and impact of commercial stripping, other axes of identity, experience, and inequality such as race, class, and sexuality must be taken into consideration if we are to truly understand the complex interconnections of power and pleasure that draw participants so consistently.

NOTES

Katherine Frank's research was supported by a fellowship from the Sexuality Research Fellowship Program of the Social Science Research Council, funded by the Ford Foundation.

1. See Katherine Frank, "Thinking Critically about Strip Club Research," *Sexualities* 10 (2007): 501–517.
2. Sheila Jeffeys, "Keeping Women Down and Out: The Strip Club Boom and the Reinforcement of Male Dominance," *Signs* 34 (2008): 151–173, at p. 170.
3. Jeffreys, "Keeping Women Down," p. 151.
4. Jeffreys, "Keeping Women Down," p. 151.
5. Bernadette Barton, *Stripped: Inside the Lives of Exotic Dancers*, New York: New York University Press, 2006; Katherine Frank, "The Production of Identity and the Negotiation of Intimacy in a Gentleman's Club," *Sexualities* 1 (1998): 175–202; Katherine Frank, *G-Strings and Sympathy: Strip Club Regulars and Male Desire*, Durham, NC: Duke University Press, 2002; Kari Lerum, "Twelve Step Feminism Makes Sex Workers Sick: How the State and the Recovery Movement Turn Radical Women into 'Useless Citizens'," in Barry Dank and Roberto Refinetti, eds., *Sex Work and Sex Workers*, New Brunswick: Transaction, 1999; Alexandra Murphy, "The Dialectical Gaze: Exploring the Subject–Object Tension in the Performances of Women Who Strip," *Journal of Contemporary Ethnography* 32 (2003): 305–335; Jennifer Wesely, "'Where am I Going to Stop?':

Exotic Dancing, Fluid Body Boundaries, and Effects on Identity," *Deviant Behavior* 24 (2003): 483–503.

6. Laura Agustin, "The Cultural Study of Commercial Sex," *Sexualites* 8 (2005): 621–634; Frank, *G-Strings and Sympathy*; Katherine Frank, "Thinking Critically about Strip Club Research," *Sexualities* 10 (2007): 501–517.

7. Agustin, "Cultural Study of Commercial Sex," p. 681.

8. Frank, "Thinking Critically about Strip Club Research."

9. Ronald Weitzer, "Why We Need More Research on Sex Work," in Ronald Weitzer, ed., *Sex for Sale: Prostitution, Pornography, and the Sex Industry*, New York: Routledge, 2000.

10. "Same-sex desiring" is used throughout the chapter to embrace a range of sexual identities, including "lesbian," "bisexual," "gay," and "dyke," all terms used by respondents to self-identify. Because the parties focus on same-sex desire, this term serves to encompass the spirit of the parties rather than attempting to define individual identities.

11. Judith Hanna, "Exotic Dance Adult Entertainment: A Guide for Planners and Policy Makers," *Journal of Planning Literature* 20 (2005): 116–134.

12. Katherine Liepe-Levinson, *Strip Show: Performances of Gender and Desire*, New York: Routledge, 2002, p. 36.

13. See Frank, *G-Strings and Sympathy*.

14. See Michelle Carnes, *Do It for Your Sistas: Black Same-Sex Desiring Women's Erotic Performance Parties in Washington, DC*, doctoral dissertation, American University, Department of Anthropology, 2009. The names of individuals quoted in the chapter are pseudonyms. Frank uses pseudonyms for the clubs and city in which she conducted fieldwork. Carnes identifies the club names and city in which she worked, as the historical specificities of that location form an important part of her analysis and the former original host clubs in her study are no longer in operation.

15. There were some ways that dancers and customers made contact that bordered on breaking the law or the club rules but were not reprimanded if the contact was consensual and quick. A dancer might lean in towards the customer during her table dance, for example, momentarily leaving less than 12 inches between them. She might touch his legs or shoulders during a dance, or let her hair graze his lap. Customers might sometimes be given a hug while the dancers were clothed, a thank you peck on the cheek after a tip or a dance, or be allowed to lay a hand on a dancer's leg while she sat next to him (again, clothed).

16. Paula Dressel and David Petersen, "Gender Roles, Sexuality, and the Male Strip Show: The Structuring of Sexual Opportunity," *Sociological Focus*, 15 (1982): 151–162; Maxine Margolis and Marigene Arnold, "Turning the Tables? Male Strippers and the Gender Hierarchy in America," in Barbara Miller, ed., *Sex and Gender Hierarchies*, Cambridge: Cambridge University Press, 1993; Beth Montemurro, "Strippers and Screamers," *Journal of Contemporary Ethnography* 30 (2001): 275–304; David Peterson and Paula Dressel, "Equal Time for Women: Notes on the Male Strip Show," *Urban Life* 11 (1982): 185–208.

17. Beth Montemurro, Colleen Bloom, and Kelly Madell, "Ladies Night Out: A Typology of Women Patrons of a Male Strip Club," *Deviant Behavior* 24 (2003): 333–352, at p. 335.

18. Montemurro, et al., "Ladies Night Out," p. 349.

19. Glenn Good and Nancy Sherrod, "Men's Resolution of Nonrelational Sex Across the Lifespan," in R. Levant and G. Brooks, eds., *Men and Sex: New Psychological Perspectives*, New York: John Wiley, 1997.

20. Susan Bordo, *The Male Body: A New Look at Men in Public and in Private*, New York: Farrar, Straus, & Giroux, 1999, p. 285.

21. Bordo, *The Male Body*, p. 287.

22. Bordo, *The Male Body*, p. 290.

23. Leonore Tiefer, *Sex Is Not A Natural Act and Other Essays*, Boulder: Westview, 1995, p. 153.

24. Frank, *G-Strings and Sympathy*.

25. Katherine Frank, "Just Trying to Relax: Masculinity, Masculinizing Practices, and Strip Club Regulars," *Journal of Sex Research* 40 (2003): 61–75.

26. Darlene Clark Hine, "Rape and the Inner Lives of Black Women in the Middle West: Preliminary Thoughts on the Culture of Dissemblance," *Signs* 14 (1989): 912–920, at p. 919.

27. Angela Davis, "Black Women and the Academy," in Jacqueline Bobo, Cynthia Hudley, and Claudine Michel, eds., *The Black Studies Reader*, New York: Routledge, 2004, at p. 93.

28. Davis, "Black Women and the Academy," p. 93.

29. Corie Hammers, "Bodies That Speak and the Promises of Queer: Looking to Two Lesbian/Queer Bathhouses for a Third Way," *Journal of Gender Studies* 17 (2008): 147–164, at p. 153.

30. Hammers, "Bodies That Speak," p. 157.

31. Pat Califia, *Public Sex: The Culture of Radical Sex*, Pittsburgh: Cleis Press, 1994, p. 208.

32. Petersen and Dressel, "Equal Time for Women."

33. Liepe-Levinson, *Strip Show*, p. 156.

34. Mignon Moore, "Lipstick or Timberlands? Meanings of Gender Presentation in Black Lesbian Communities," *Signs* 32 (2006): 113–139, at pp. 117–118.

35. Moore, "Lipstick or Timberlands," pp. 124–125.

36. Moore, "Lipstick or Timberlands," p. 124.

37. This blurring of the boundaries may also be the case in certain locales around the U.S. However, even in cities which offer full nudity and lap dancing, as in San Francisco, one can often also find profitable clubs offering table dancing or sexualized encounters without sexual contact and the possibility of release.

38. National Women's Health Information Center, "Lesbian Health Fact Sheet," U.S. Department of Health and Human Services, Office on Women's Health, 2005. http://www.womenshealth.gov/faq/lesbian-health.pdf.

39. "Clubcards" are postcard sized flyers, often full color and glossy with graphics, large fonts and photos of black women (sometimes the featured dancers) in suggestive poses, often wearing thongs and placing their buttocks in full and prominent view. Rarely does the word "lesbian" appear on clubcards; more likely are cues such as "women's parties," "girls' night out," "for the ladies only," "dom party," "for the femmes," alongside photos of two black women embracing or gazing into the camera together. On occasion, clubcards include a rainbow design or logo (most often, the promoter's organization).

40. Judith Hanna, "Undressing the First Amendment and Corsetting the Striptease Dancer," *The Drama Review* 42 (1998): 38–69.

41. Judith Hanna, "Toying with the Striptease Dancer and the First Amendment," in Stuart Reifel, ed., *Play and Culture Studies, Volume 2*, Stamford, CT: Ablex, 1999, p. 7.

42. Eric Snider, *Strip Club Politics*, Weekly Planet, 2003.

43. Tresa Baldas, "Prostitution Convictions Fought, Motion Claims 1st Amendment Protects Sex Talk," *Chicago Tribune*, July 24, 1998.

44. Wayne Hoffman, "Skipping the Life Fantastic: Coming of Age in the Sexual Devolution," in Dangerous Bedfellows, eds., *Policing Public Sex: Queer Politics and the Future of AIDS Activism*, Boston: South End Press, 1986, p. 339.

45. See Kendall Thomas, "Going Public: A Conversation with Lidell Jackson and Jocelyn Taylor," in Dangerous Bedfellows, eds., *Policing Public Sex: Queer Politics and the Future of AIDS Activism*, Boston: South End Press, 1996, p. 66.

COMMERCIAL TELEPHONE SEX: FANTASY AND REALITY

Kathleen Guidroz and Grant J. Rich

It has been more than 25 years since the first commercial telephone sex service—commonly known as "phone sex"—was introduced in the United States. Phone sex is ubiquitous—virtually all men's magazines, numerous newspapers, and the Internet[1] contain ads for this lucrative industry;[2] however, very little research has been done on the topic relative to other forms of sex work.[3] This chapter focuses on how phone sex operators view their work, how they manage sex calls, and how they attempt to create and maintain a positive identity while employed in a socially stigmatized occupation considered by many to be deviant and sexist.[4]

GENDERING THE TELEPHONE

When the telephone was invented, men staffed the first telephone systems; but by the end of the 1880s, almost all telephone operators were women. Since then, the telephone has remained a "gendered technology"; that is, it is "a site at which the meanings of gender are expressed and practiced."[5] Due to technological advances, the telephone is now a more private medium of communication,[6] which makes commercial phone sex possible.

The first commercial telephone sex became available in the early 1980s, when callers could have their credit cards billed through a company. There are now numerous ways for callers of telephone sex lines to pay for their phone sex, including 900 or 976 lines that allow per-minute billing, flat rate billing for a certain amount of calling time with an operator, and international call billing.[7] A growing number of phone sex services are now available throughout the world, some of which charge callers costly international phone rates.[8]

Telephone sex work can be conducted through companies in an office or by agency- or self-employed individuals working in their own homes. Some telephone sex companies have office space in which many women, and sometimes men impersonating women,[9] are sitting at desks with telephones or headsets in either one large room or in smaller closet sized rooms. Like most sex workers, phone sex operators have a work persona—a fake name and physical description—to protect their personal identity.

The majority of the calls requested by callers of phone sex lines include discussions of straight sex, lesbianism, rape, anal sex, adult baby/diaper lover (ABDL) or incest (including the operator playing the role of a mommy or "mother I love to fuck" (MILF) or "sister"), young girls and "barely legal," sadomasochism (S&M or BDSM), bestiality (e.g., animals), mutilation or dismemberment, transgenderism (e.g. "shemale"), and fetishism (such as cross-dressing or "force feminization").[10] Male callers can also make specific requests for a BBW ("big beautiful woman"), a "dominatrix" for S&M, or a GFE ("girlfriend experience" with some romance). A small number of calls are nonsexual. The telephone sex industry involves primarily heterosexual encounters and female operators; very few calls come from couples and even fewer are from women;[11] however, more recent phone sex lines advertised on the Internet are being marketed as lesbian or bisexual phone sex "*by* women *for* women."[12]

RESEARCH METHODS

The study is based on interviews with 12 female phone sex operators[13] employed by a company in an urban area of the United States, observations at the work site, and interviews with an additional six phone sex operators in other cities.[14] Interviews were conducted in both the respondent's home and at the work site.[15] Our questions focused on why and how respondents entered phone sex work, their experiences on the job, what they liked and disliked about the work, their views of the callers, and whether phone sex work had affected their personal lives. Most of the interviews were tape-recorded. Some respondents were interviewed more than once and some interviews were conducted over the phone, although the researchers had face-to-face contact with all respondents at least once. Our initial contacts were made through personal acquaintances, and snowball sampling provided referrals for interviews, which were conducted between 1996 and 1998.

The study uses qualitative methods for a number of reasons. First, since access to sex workers is limited (due to the stigmatized nature of the profession), a large sample of workers is not available. A large sample would have been necessary for quantitative analysis of the data. Second, little research has been done on phone sex work; thus there is a need for exploratory, qualitative investigation. Our study aims to give the workers a voice through in-depth interviews. Despite our modest sample of workers, the sparse existing literature on phone sex workers lends support to our basic findings.[16]

The main purpose of our study was to demystify the work of phone sex (which is often sensationalized by commentators) by viewing it through the lenses of the phone sex operators themselves.[17]

THE AGENCY: SEXY SMART GIRLS

The Sexy Smart Girls agency serves primarily male callers located throughout the country.[18] The agency advertises its services through men's sex magazines, and provides services via 800 and 900 numbers (for $3.99 a minute), and credit card, direct, and prepaid calls (for $1.99 a minute). An advertisement for the agency appearing in one of numerous pornography magazines features a young white woman holding a telephone in one hand and a book in the other. She is bare breasted and wearing a plaid skirt that is hiked up to reveal white lace panties. To fully communicate the phone sex operators' youth, sexiness, and intelligence, she is wearing lace socks, high heels, and glasses.

Approximately 40 workers are employed by Sexy Smart Girls. Most of the operators work part time, but several work up to 40 hours a week. Since most of the requests for phone sex calls come in at night, work shifts are typically between 11 P.M. and 5 A.M., when seven operators at a time work in the office, and one or two may work on a scheduled or on-call basis from their homes.

The agency rents a small suite in an otherwise drab office building near a part-residential and part-warehouse section of the city. Visits to the agency revealed a typical office space, with a main reception desk containing the "caller list" (a binder with an estimated 13,000 names), file cabinets, a water cooler, microwave, and the agency's policies and procedures for receiving and verifying callers' credit card numbers. The office contained none of the pornographic fliers and posters seen by Amy Flowers during her phone sex research.[19] The operators sit in small rooms with doors that may be closed but do not eliminate sound. One of the authors, for instance, heard Debbi speaking in a loud yet recognizable girlish voice, "Oh Daddy, I want your big cock inside my little pussy!" From the hallway outside the office, one could hear an operator screaming loudly while simulating an orgasm.

Similar to the phone sex company Flowers worked for,[20] security measures are stringent. The doors to the building and to the agency's office are kept locked at all times. Only employees are allowed into the office. Although the agency presents itself as a telemarketing company, most of the other occupants of the building know or suspect it is a phone sex company. Chrissy said:

Regardless of how quiet we try to be, they do know what we do. They are disrespectful to us. They leer; they jeer; they make comments. I don't even like going out of this office to go get something to drink.

Other workers had varying opinions about the office. Debbi liked the anonymity of the office location in addition to the structure of the office phone sex rooms:

I like the way the office is set up. I don't have to do my calls in front of anybody. I'm over by myself. Guys say, "I bet you're at a table with a bunch of girls with phones." And I reply, "You'd be able to hear them, for one." I also like the security of it. I talk to people in other services, and they're not like that. To me, that would be very scary. To have some guy show up who thinks I'm into being beaten into a bloody pulp and being raped by 20 different guys. It would scare me for someone like that to find me.

Like most office workers, the operators gave their office homey touches. They put up slogans and poems, recipes, and even humorous artwork depicting their least favorite caller at the time (e.g., a little voodoo doll in a suit with a huge phallus). These personal touches indicate that, to some extent, the workers attempted to humanize the office.

The Operators at Sexy Smart Girls

Our sample ranged in age from 21 to 45, although they presented themselves on the phone as being 20 to 23. Phone sex operators can be any race or ethnicity, age, gender, and have varying levels of education,[21] but all our interviewees were white. Our respondents' educations ranged from high school graduates to college graduates, but none thought she got her job due to her education.

Phone sex companies have difficulty recruiting and retaining employees. The women Flowers interviewed had worked at an average of three companies each.[22] Although our respondents reported fewer phone sex jobs, they had been employed in a fairly short-term capacity. In our sample, no operator had been working for the agency longer than 18 months.

Most of the workers had unconventional relationships outside work—not one was married, and several were divorced. Many had lovers who were either married or seeing multiple partners, and only one was engaged. Some were lesbian or bisexual. Given our data, it is difficult to determine whether the nature of the job precludes long-term monogamy or marriage or whether the job self-selects for candidates who preferred nonstandard romantic lives. As Mint put it:

> What's the guy gonna say, "Mom, Dad, let me introduce you to Mint. She's a phone sex worker, and we are going to get married"? My lover is a lawyer. What's he going to do, say to the [law firm] partners, "This is Mint. She's a phone sex worker, and we like to have phone sex from my office"? It's screwed up.

Since our sample was not random, it may not be typical of all phone sex operators. Additionally, the callers may not be typical. While data are scarce about the clients of prostitutes and other sex workers,[23] even less is known about phone sex callers—including their demographic characteristics and why they call phone sex services. Operators' descriptions of their callers' backgrounds may be inaccurate because the callers might lie about their occupations and marital status.

WORKING IN PHONE SEX

The women found the job via an advertisement in the newspaper or through a referral by a friend or acquaintance who already worked for the agency. Our data suggest that women seeking phone sex work share the following: (1) they need money, (2) they see phone sex as their most lucrative option, and (3) they feel reasonably sure they would be comfortable discussing sex over the telephone.[24] Several telephone sex operators described their motivation for entering the phone sex business because they thought it would be "fun" or "easy."

Elle had been working for over a year at the agency, and had no previous experience in the sex industry. She explained why she chose to work as a phone sex operator:

> I have a degree in social work. . . . I definitely wanted out of mental health. Surprisingly this isn't that far off from mental health, believe it or not. I thought,

"Wow, that's a lot of money." And I thought, "Who couldn't have sex on the phone?" I'd have to say initially it was the money that brought me in.

Similarly, Chrissy said:

I was going through a divorce. I had a real job because I do have a bachelor's degree, and I was burned out. So I quit that job . . . and I saw this ad in the paper. I thought, "Phone sex, ha ha. Oh my God, how funny. That would be really fun to do at night while I was looking for a better job."

Annette also indicated that a sense of the agency's normalcy and integrity was important to her. She added that the setting or environment was as important as the type of work when considering an agency:

I always thought that it would be such a hoot, so much fun to do; and I'll do domination calls. Then I saw it in the newspaper. . . . Here, all the women look like normal, wholesome-looking women. This boss weeds for this. I don't think many places weed out to try to get smarter, more wholesome, and normal women.

As a potential phone sex operator, each worker had to ask herself whether she would she be able to have phone sex with male callers, where the goal is the caller's orgasm. Heart remarked:

You have to be comfortable talking about sex. Obviously anyone with serious hang-ups wouldn't call for an interview—or they'd quit after the first weird call—which happens a lot. Some people just can't deal.

Job Socialization and Identity Construction

Conventional careers and phone sex work differ in the amount of formal training provided. Most phone sex operators receive very little training.[25] Why? There is an understanding that phone sex work self-selects operators who are comfortable discussing sexual topics and therefore will have a shorter learning curve; several operators were told during their initial interview that the work is "very easy."

When asked about taking her first call, and whether she received any training, Elle said she was able to consult her telephone sex agency's manual about how to fill out the required paperwork and how to set up a call. It included subjects the operators can and cannot say on the phone. Elle indicated that it did not go beyond these technical features of the job. She went on to describe how she actually learned to perform phone sex work:

> The [callers] teach you in a way. If you tell them it's your first time at phone sex they actually are more gentle with you. And there are all these guys who think it's really great to talk to "the new girl." It's almost like being a virgin again. You make lots of money the first couple of weeks. Everybody wants to try you out. . . . But no, there's no manual on how to do a good phone sex call.

The operators in our study were interviewed once by the employer and then immediately put to work. Almost all of the learning was on the job, and much of it was unsupervised; given that working hours were around the clock, many informants rarely saw the boss. Heart noted: "They just stick you by the phone and you talk. They probably give you an easy call. You just pick it up as you go, and you can talk to everyone else if you have questions." Another worker, Spice, commented: "You're on your own. . . . The manager was there for the first call—that's it."

Annette listened in on others' calls and learned from the other operators which words to use during a call. She said callers get turned off if operators use the word "penis" rather than "cock." To learn about possible scenarios callers would request, Annette also purchased pornography magazines to learn phrases like "come on my face" and then incorporate them into her phone sex repertoire.

Most of the job "training" is informal, and part of it includes talking with coworkers about working conditions, how to deal with problem callers, how work affected personal life, and future plans. In one spirited conversation, Spice gave Heart tips about the sexual preferences of certain callers, including methods to keep the caller on the phone for longer periods of time. Such professional exchanges are frequent at phone sex offices.[26]

Several respondents felt positive about the work even though they could not always disclose the nature of their work to everyone in their lives. For example, Gretchen said she loves her job although at first she was secretive because she did not want to embarrass her children. She is now open with her three daughters but not with her mother, who believes Gretchen is a telemarketer. Gretchen said:

> I never in my life thought I would really be happy being a phone sex operator, but I love my job. . . . My daughter has a lot of people in her office, and they wanted to know if there are any interesting stories. One day she had me come out to meet everybody. I felt like a celebrity.

Most of the workers we interviewed, however, did not envision phone sex work as a long-term career. Most had plans to return to college, obtain additional degrees, or move to another city and find work in "respectable" fields.[27] For example, Hannah planned to continue with phone sex work only while she was in college, while Debbi stated:

> Do I see myself as a phone sex operator for the rest of my life? No, I do not. When I started this job I was not looking for my career goals. Maybe I'll do it for the next year or 2 if I can't find something better.

Impression Management and Deviance Disavowal

According to sociologists, "occupants of degraded statuses find ingenious ways of enhancing their self-perceptions, and maintaining control of their work settings."[28] In his study of deviant subcultures, Becker notes that members of such cultures use techniques such as secrecy, isolation, and self-segregation to maintain a positive self-image and to protect themselves from legal and social sanctions.[29] Goffman describes the methods by which deviant people strive to conceal or manage their "discredited" and "spoiled" identities.[30]

Every worker reported being embarrassed at times by this work. They had various strategies for telling others about their work, such as selectively revealing details. Many used other occupations as a convenient cover for their work; the title of "telemarketer" was a common one. In fact, the agency manager would verify workers' cover stories. For instance, if a woman stopped working at the agency and wrote on her résumé that she was employed in "sales," the manager would verify this story.

Pepper noted that her brother, cousin, and close friends knew, but not acquaintances or the rest of her family. Elle noted that she can be open about her job with her boyfriend and other friends; however, she was "more honest with her credit card company" than she was with her family. Chrissy said that telling her family would "rock their world."

Concealing the nature of the work was often difficult. For instance, many workers did not want friends or family driving them to work. Even when concealment was not an issue, some women kept home and work entirely separate. Heart commented:

> When my car broke down I either didn't work or had to have a coworker pick me up. I could have taken calls at home but—even though she can't talk yet—I would have felt weird doing it with my daughter around.

Debbi feared that her identity would be revealed on a call. She explained: "What I like the least about my job is the fear that callers could identify me in some way. Once I got a call from a guy who dated one of my cousins. That was so weird." And Star noted: "When friends visit and want to see where I work, I flip out."

Workers are aware of the distinction between "home" and "work" and use this distinction to help define their identities. Thus while modern society and modern technology have created a situation that for many has blurred the distinction between home and work,[31] most phone sex operators maintain very separate home and work identities. Leading these "double lives" can be time consuming, stressful, and mentally exhausting. Spice, for instance, told her family she is employed in telephone sales at a place where she formerly worked. She reported worrying that she will slip and reveal the truth about her work in an unguarded moment, or that she will forget the details of her story and be caught in a lie. The guilt of lying takes its own toll. She sometimes "feels really bad about the whole thing—my family is proud that I have a steady job and a good income, but a lot of it is a lie."

One turning point is when the worker reveals her job to a new significant other. Star commented:

I don't do it at first—otherwise they either leave or get horny. I start the relationship and within a month or so, I feel trusting enough to open up about it. The guy usually asks a million questions and wants me to do it with him, which gets old fast.

Annette uses disclosure to test her dates:

If it's a man and you tell him you do phone sex, how they react is a good way to know whether or not you can go out with them. If they say, "Oh, give me a sample," then I think they're a pervert. I'm not gonna do it.

And Pepper noted:

They're fine with it at first, because they think it means I'll be loose in bed, but after a while some of them just think I'm low class—not marriage material. I've got to weed them out earlier.

Phone sex workers often feel degraded by persons who become aware of their work. When asked about the number one stereotype of phone sex operators, most respondents mentioned the notion that they are "sluts" in real life, willing to perform any sexual act with anybody. Several operators expressed contempt for callers who called the agency expecting the operators to act like "brainless bimbos" and were pleased when callers appreciated their intelligence or education.

One way of preserving their self-esteem is to distance themselves from women working in other sectors of the sex industry.[32] Heart commented:

> We're not like those streetwalkers—crawling down the street in the middle of night in the middle of winter. We work in an office. I never touch a cock. I can't get a single disease. I can't get attacked. I'm not a prostitute. I can sit here, read a magazine and just moan occasionally . . . and still get paid. I don't have to wash my hair or wear makeup; I can wear jeans; I can eat on the job. I can even work at home if I want.

Mint added: "I don't have sex. It's just pretend. I'm not like some escort girl, spreading my legs—this is more classy. Most of the job is just sitting around waiting for a call."

Another technique is for workers to professionalize their work. Gretchen, for example, indicated it is important to respond appropriately to the agency's "professional and executive callers" by assuring their anonymity and responding to their upscale tastes. Our respondents also capitalized on the agency's name, which offers "sexy smart girls," along with emphasizing the demanding nature of their work. Star said:

> The worker must be open minded, aware, and intelligent. And she must listen, listen, listen. A good phone sex worker finds something in common with the caller, even if it's small. She treats the caller like a person. She participates. It's 50% performance and 50% real.

Debbi emphasized that the work is not mindless:

> It's a lot harder than you think it is. People think that we get on the phone and we moan and grunt and make coming sounds. Some of these calls are very challenging. Really! And that wears on you emotionally. I've worked hard jobs, and I've done difficult things before and never gone home as tired as I do from this job because of the mental exhaustion some days. . . . Well, we do a lot more than they give us credit for.

In sum, our findings indicate that phone sex operators employ several strategies to maintain self-esteem, to protect themselves and their families from social censure, and to keep future career options available. Since being a phone sex worker is socially stigmatized, each respondent invoked elaborate impression management techniques to deal with this stigma. From renting apartments, to meeting new boyfriends or girlfriends, to applying for new jobs or to school, to fully disclosing the true nature of one's job, the workers soon realized that their work affects all aspects of their lives. Thus, workers maintained self-esteem by distancing themselves from socially undesirable "hands on" sex work and by embracing a socially desirable goal—namely, a stable, albeit challenging, job.

TRADEOFFS IN PHONE SEX WORK

Similar to workers in other areas of the sex industry, the operators experienced a combination of positive and negative experiences in their work at Sexy Smart Girls; consequently, many react with strategies for optimizing positive features of the work while minimizing negative ones.

On the positive side, worker self-esteem and job satisfaction were increased by the actions of certain callers. Spice reported with great pride that, on returning from a vacation, there were 42 messages waiting for her from callers who requested phone sex with her.

Workers also stressed the economic benefits of the job, and sometimes acted as if anyone not involved in phone sex was missing a grand economic opportunity. Not only was the income above minimum wage—$10 to $15 an hour[33]—but workers also received gifts from callers, which serve as additional self-esteem boosters.[34] Callers of the Sexy Smart Girls agency may send gifts to the workers through a post office box.[35] Workers also sell panties to callers, which usually bring $25 to $50 each. Heart said: "Sometimes I wear them before I send them, usually I don't. I tell them I get them at Victoria's Secret, but I just get them from Sears."

Sexual Enhancements

Several respondents said that working in the business had made them more knowledgeable about and comfortable with their sexuality, both in fantasy and in real life. Gretchen noted she became more tolerant of sexual expression in part because of her work as a phone sex operator. She said she was already open sexually in terms of her attitudes; however, she added, "This job has enhanced my awareness in the real world. In a lot of ways it's made me more tolerant." Gretchen also said:

My favorites are the cross dressers because I appreciate men who want to understand women better. I'm not put out by them wanting to wear silk panties. . . . We're often girlfriends and I take them shoe shopping. Sometimes they want to be with other men in their fantasies . . . though they may never have a gay experience in their life.

Heart commented on her own sexuality: "Sometimes I hear something from a caller that I've never tried before. It sounds cool. I ask the caller about it and then try it out with my real-life lover—sometimes my lover is like, 'Where did you learn that?' I just laugh."

Star added:

I used to be pretty shy. In my love life, I let the guy start everything. Now I'm in control. Some guys are even intimidated by me sexually. Phone sex opened me up—the worst thing that can happen is the guy hangs up. Big deal. I felt comfortable experimenting with new things in fantasy and then tried the things I liked in real life.

Mint also said:

Phone sex has made me more liberated. I got tied up by my boyfriend for the first time this weekend. It was great. I also want to try sex with another woman. I never would have thought about that before this job. Now I really want to experiment.

Bonding with Other Women

For some operators, their respect for women was enhanced because of the job. Chrissy, for example, "think[s] our society really fucks women over." Bonding with other women at work was frequently cited as the main reason they continue to work as phone sex operators. Hannah said she has extremely positive workplace relationships both with other phone sex operators as well as their female boss. She defines herself as a feminist and values the workplace environment. Hannah said:

The great thing about this particular job is that our boss is very understanding, unlike what I've heard about other places. She doesn't make us do any calls if we have a good reason that we don't want to do a call. . . . With this job, I think a lot of people want to be here because it's a pretty positive environment. So, even though it's the money that keeps me working here, it's a supportive, wonderful environment—like a sisterhood.

Several positive experiences were noted by the workers, including making a decent income, plus perks, gifts, and camaraderie. Several workers also stated that their attitudes towards sexuality—theirs and others—became more liberated as a result of the work.

Positive experiences with callers, however, were mentioned less frequently than negative experiences. Many workers reported that they lost respect for men as a result of the job. While workers reported with pride that doctors and lawyers call the line, they labeled a lot of callers "pathetic" and "losers." Spice said there were a lot of "pussy boys" and "whiners" who were passive and complainers. At the same time, she reported that many callers were "nice, sweet, sensitive guys who were lonely, desperate, or shy." Elle believed that men who turn to the sex industry for sexual gratification are usually "looking at porno magazines, looking at videos. It's amazing to me how much time and money and effort these guys spend on their penises."[36]

Challenging Heteronormativity

Women rarely called the agency, and when they did, workers' reactions differed significantly from their reactions to male callers. Generally, the work took place in a heteronormative environment, although a worker's own sexual orientation influenced whether she was comfortable taking calls from female callers. For example, Debbi said: "I'm not bisexual, so I tend to shy away from those. . . . And I did have a woman the first time the other day and I talked to her. It was a bit freaky. That's not my orientation." Annette said that when women call the agency as customers, most of the heterosexual operators do not want to take the call. She said: "We've gotten three or four calls from women. Another [operator] said, 'Oh my gosh, you have to do this call. It's a woman. No one else wants to do it.' I said, 'Whoa, a woman!'"

Annette's reactions toward female callers indicate a sense of ethics not always directed toward male callers. She said:

> They're very sweet calls—I like those calls. But if I had to have women calls all the time, then it'd be an upsetting job because these women are lonely, or I'm lying to this woman and I wouldn't want to do that.

In contrast to Annette, Olga said her female callers act "just like men," though Olga conceded that with calls from women she was "uncomfortable at first" but generally they are "nicer than your average guy calls."

In terms of phone sex calls from couples, which were as rare as the calls from women, respondents' reactions ranged from "funny" and "satisfying" to "usually a disaster." Several operators said they would solicit the other woman's consent to the fantasy before embarking on the call. Similar to the operators' reactions to women as sole callers, the operators expressed concern for a woman's wellbeing during couples' calls as well.

DEALING WITH DANGER: SYMBOLIC VIOLENCE

Sex workers experience some combination of real and symbolic violence in their work; and the disembodied nature of phone sex work does not prevent workers from experiencing psychological violence.[37] As in Flowers' study, callers with interests in rape fantasies, other violent sex, bestiality, and incest were common. The operators at this agency are provided a list of the types of call they can refuse, and they had much latitude in accepting or refusing them. Most of the respondents had negative feelings about these calls; however, there was variability in how workers responded to callers' requests for sexual violence.[38] Olga attempts to discourage callers from requesting distasteful fantasies, while Hannah simply refuses calls involving torture, mutilation, or children. Chrissy said:

> We don't have to do rape calls, incest calls, or animal calls. Rape calls bother me immensely. I cannot do them anymore. . . . I've had guys say, "I'm going to fuck your ass and you're a fucking whore and I'm gonna make your ass bleed." I don't do those calls.

In contrast, Gretchen said she rarely refuses callers, except those who request mutilation, torture, and murder, which she labeled "pathological." She does, however, accept rape calls and does not consider them to be pathological. Gretchen said she will also embellish the rape fantasies: "I'm very good at those. I give them what they want. I also throw in those extra details they might not have thought about." Regarding a particular caller who had been requesting dismemberment fantasies from several of the operators, Spice said:

> I hate "Mr. Mutilation." Wants to cut my head off. He's big into kidnapping, dungeons. He says it's not real and that he is just curious. I don't know. I hate it, but at least I figure if he is talking to me he is not out there really doing it.

Debbi also indulged a caller who regularly requests mutilation fantasies. She gave an off-tape description of a 1-hour long call during which she instructed him to use magazine photos of women and a pair of scissors—his arousal came from cutting off one body part at a time. She explained that she took his call because "no one else wanted him." Debbi also said she accepts these calls despite not really wanting to do them. She said:

> I do a lot of little girl calls because I have a certain voice that I can get into. And I have many callers who call and request that from me. Usually I try to steer away from it because I do not want to do the child molestation calls. . . . Usually they start off pretty normal, but then they'll say, "Call me daddy." . . . And they try to justify it by saying, "Oh she's just starting to become a woman and I like that." They do their best to justify it so they don't feel like perverts.

Additionally, several of the operators expressed concern that taking calls involving sexual fantasies with children might influence callers to continue requesting more of these types of call or to actually carry out their fantasies. A few of the operators said there were times when during a phone sex call they could hear children in the background, or the caller puts someone who sounds like a child on the phone. The operators usually respond by hanging up on the caller, or telling the caller that they refuse to do a phone sex call with children nearby.

Phone Sex Operators as Educators and Therapists

There is the belief that women in sex industry are providing some positive, educational service to men, including preventing men from committing violent sexual acts against other women and children.[39] Many of our respondents engage in what could be considered subversive "acts of resistance" against objectionable callers. Chrissy, for example, uses a "good touch–bad touch" response during her "little girl" calls to demonstrate the wrongfulness of adult sexual contact with children. When a caller says to her, "You know I'm going to touch you," she responds with a high-pitched voice, "My mommy taught me about good touch and bad touch. That's bad touch, and I'm going to tell my mommy."

Other workers viewed this aspect of their work as "community service," meaning that they hoped to send a message to callers that certain sexual fantasies and practices were unacceptable or immoral. Olga explained how she responds to these callers:

> I won't go any younger than 15. . . . So anytime anybody wants to fuck a child, I always try to say, "It's just a fantasy and you'd never actually do anything like

that, right?" . . . And I'll make them explain to me why they would never really do something like that.

Another type of community service involves instructing callers that a real phone sex operator does not match the stereotype of a brainless, sex-crazed woman masturbating during the call. Some of the respondents believed they are educating men about women's sexuality. This "education" resembles the "therapy" some sex workers also say they provide to male consumers.[40] Annette wanted men to care about women's bodies and women's pleasure:

> If the guy doesn't care about female orgasm, if the guy says he doesn't like to eat pussy . . . that probably gets me more than anything does. I go on with these guys, "Do you know that the clitoris is like the sexual counterpart of the male blah blah blah?" So many callers could[n't] care less about female orgasms.

Clearly, phone sex workers felt that the callers influenced their lives—not just financially but also in terms of how they viewed their own real-life relationships and how they viewed men in general. Workers tended to report an improvement in their own sexual lives (although they noted obstacles to forming new, or long-lasting romantic relationships due to the stigmatized nature of the job). But they also expressed distaste for the men's regular interest in rape, incest, pedophilia, and bestiality. Operators also viewed as "idiotic" callers who phone when children, a spouse, or an employer is nearby.[41] Finally, workers felt that the men were "putty in [their] hands," and for some this perception bolstered their self-esteem and sense of empowerment. As Pepper said: "I used to get trampled over by men. Now I know they're just stupid."

CONCLUSION

This analysis of the world of phone sex points to several important findings. First, phone sex workers have developed sophisticated methods of impression management. Being in a stigmatized profession, the workers have learned techniques to conceal or misrepresent the nature of their employment to family, friends, and new employers who may disapprove of the nature of the work. These methods include lying, maintaining friendships with others in deviant subcultures (who might aid in corroborating cover stories), and maintaining clear boundaries between home and work.

Second, this study notes the particular ways in which workers are able to maintain self-esteem while working in a deviant job. One way in which phone sex operators reconcile their work with their identity is to view the job in exclusively economic terms. Thus the women may note that though the job may be at times distasteful, the pay is excellent, the hours are flexible, and there are other benefits, such as gifts. Another way self-esteem is maintained is for the worker to distance herself from other types of sex worker, who have physical contact with customers and who risk AIDS, beatings, and arrest. The phone sex operator frequently notes that no "real" sex ever occurs.

Third, this research sheds light on workers' perceptions of the callers and the callers' treatment of the workers. A number of women were disturbed by the violence and degradation in some of the men's calls—fantasies that include rape, dismemberment or mutilation, sex with animals, and child molestation. As in other forms of sex work, even longtime workers report days in which a particular man has said or done something troubling to the worker. The workers report having learned much about the nature of male sexuality, in terms of fantasies and insecurities. These types of call are frequently noted as a negative aspect of the workplace and are often a challenge to the worker's willingness to do the job. Callers are often perceived as "idiotic," "silly," "typically male," or as completely enslaved to their sexual desires. While most callers are viewed negatively, occasionally a worker will experience a caller who has had a positive effect on her. Being called by doctors, lawyers, business executives, and professors can help to reinforce a worker's identity as a skilled, talented employee, as well as a person who is valued by powerful, educated, and wealthy people.

Finally, the fact that at this agency all the workers and the boss are women had a powerful effect on the employees. In an occupation in which employees are frequently subjected to degrading male comments, the opportunity to work in an all-female environment was viewed positively. The workers benefit from the bonding and support they receive from their coworkers at the agency, and they view the company owner as a role model—a strong, intelligent woman who has created a successful business in a male-dominated world. Several workers reported they have learned more about the ways a business works, and that they aspire to run their own business someday. Still others said they are treated with respect by the owner and could never again work for a male boss.

These working conditions, coupled with the financial rewards of the job, present a challenge to theorists who argue that sex work is inherently oppressive and demeaning to the workers.

NOTES

1. The abundance of phone sex advertisements on the Internet indicates that this type of sexual commerce has not decreased in recent years. Commercial phone sex ads in print and on the Internet are primarily of young, white women who are nude or semi-nude, and sometimes shown engaging in sex with men or other women. These photographs are designed to entice callers and to communicate the types of phone sex calls available. These ads also assist the callers in visually constructing their conversational partner. Kira Hall, "Lip Service on the Fantasy Lines," in Kira Hall and Mary Bucholtz, eds., *Gender Articulated: Language and the Socially Constructed Self*, New York: Routledge, 1995, p. 188.

2. "Heavy Breathing," *The Economist* 332 (1994): 64. According to Lane, annual revenues generated by commercial telephone sex can reach up to $1 billion, with up to half of that amount going to long-distance carriers. Frederick S. Lane, *Obscene Profits*, New York: Routledge, 2000, p. 151.

3. Amy Flowers, *The Fantasy Factory: An Insider's View of the Phone Sex Industry*, Philadelphia: University of Pennsylvania Press, 1998; Kathleen Guidroz, "Gender, Labor, and Sexuality in Escort and Telephone Sex Work," Ph.D. dissertation, George Washington University, Washington, DC, 2001; Grant Rich, "Phone Jams: Improvisation and Peak Experience in Phone Sex Workers," *Anthropology of Consciousness* 9 (1998): 82–83; Hall, "Lip Service." Mattley has written about her year-long covert participant observation as a "phone fantasy" operator: Christine Mattley, "Aural Sex: The Politics and Moral Dilemmas of Studying the Social Construction of Fantasy," in Dick Hobbs and Richard Wright, eds., *The Sage Handbook of Fieldwork*, London: Sage, 2006.

4. Erving Goffman, *Stigma: Notes on the Management of Spoiled Identity*, New York: Simon & Schuster, 1963; Edwin M. Schur, *Labeling Women Deviant: Gender, Stigma, and Social Control*, Philadelphia: Temple University Press, 1983.

5. Lana F. Rakow, *Gender on the Line: Women, the Telephone, and Community Life*, Urbana: University of Illinois Press, 1992, pp. 1, 33. Rakow (p. 33) points out that the telephone is not exempt from gendered characteristics. She writes, "Use of the telephone by women is both gendered work—work delegated to women—and gender work—work that confirms the community's belief about what are women's natural tendencies and abilities." For an interesting history of the telephone, see also Claude Fischer, "Gender and the Residential Telephone, 1890–1940: Technologies of Sociability," in Robert Thompson, ed., *The Essential*

Sociology Reader, Boston: Allyn and Bacon, 1998; Michéle Martin, *Hello, Central?: Gender, Technology, and Culture in the Formation of Telephone Systems*, Montreal: McGill-Queen's University Press, 1991; Carolyn Marvin, *When Old Technologies Were New: Thinking about Electric Communication in the Late Nineteenth Century*, New York: Oxford University Press, 1988.

6. Hall, "Lip Service," p. 189.

7. Flowers, *Fantasy Factory*, p. 4. See also Amanda Covington, "Confessions of a Phone Sex Operator," http://lumpen.com; Jack Glascock and Robert LaRose, "Dial-A-Porn Recordings: The Role of the Female Participant in Male Sexual Fantasies," *Journal of Broadcasting and Electronic Media* 37 (1993): 313–324; Hall, "Lip Service"; Lane, *Obscene Profits*.

8. The Economist, "Heavy Breathing"; Cheryl Radeloff, "'He's Got the Whole World in His Hands': The Rise and Development of Phone Sex as an International Industry," unpublished paper, 1997.

9. Flowers, *Fantasy Factory*; Rachel James, "Heart to Heart with a Phone Sex Fantasy Girl," *Gray Areas* 2 (1993): 46–51; Frederick L. Whitam, "Culturally Universal Aspects of Male Homosexual Transvestites and Transsexuals," in Bonnie Bullough, Vern L. Bulloush, and James Elias, eds., *Gender Blending*, Amherst: Prometheus Books, 1997. Hall, for example, examined five fantasy-line companies, all in San Francisco, and of her 12 respondents, one was a man who engages in "cross-expressing," Hall, "Lip Service," p. 202.

10. Guidroz, "Gender, Labor, and Sexuality."

11. Flowers, *Fantasy Factory*; Guidroz, "Gender, Labor, and Sexuality." Mattley, "Aural Sex," for example, describes only male callers.

12. GirlsLovePussyToo.com, accessed September 14, 2008. According to Miller, there is also a growing market for gay and transgender phone sex lines: Edward David Miller, "Inside the Switchboards of Desire: Storytelling on Phone Sex Lines," in William L. Leap, ed., *Beyond the Lavender Lexicon: Authenticity, Imagination, and Appropriation in Lesbian and Gay Language*, New York: Routledge, 1996.

13. Respondents' names are pseudonyms.

14. Guidroz, "Gender, Labor, and Sexuality."

15. Interviews with those working for the agency were done at the work site with the consent of the agency owner, a former phone sex operator.

16. Gary Anthony, Rocky Bennett, and John Money, *Dirty Talk: Diary of a Phone Sex Mistress*, Buffalo, NY: Prometheus, 1998; Miranda Austin, *Phone Sex: Aural Thrills and Oral Skills*, Oakland: Greenery Press, 2002; Flowers, *Fantasy Factory*; Damiana Cate Stone, *My Life in Phone Sex*, Bloomington: iUniverse, 2002.

17. See also Hall, "Lip Service."

18. The agency name is a pseudonym.

19. Flowers, *Fantasy Factory*.

20. Flowers, *Fantasy Factory*, p. 122.

21. Areena, "Aphrodite Electric: A Phone Sex Perspective," *Anything That Moves* 12 (1996): 24–25; Kate Bornstein, *Gender Outlaw: On Men, Women, and the Rest of Us*, New York: Routledge, 1994; Covington, "Confessions"; Flowers, *Fantasy Factory*.

22. Flowers, *Fantasy Factory*, p. 29.

23. See Martin Monto's chapter in this volume.

24. See also Flowers, *Fantasy Factory*.

25. Flowers, *Fantasy Factory*. Although Hall did not mention her respondents' own training, see "Lip Service" for an excerpt from a training manual. One exception is a support group, People Exchanging Power (PEP), which began a professional phone sex service for dominant/submissive callers. PEP's founder, Nancy Eva Miller, asks her operators to read *How to Win Friends and Influence People* and provides annual training via seminars and workshops; see Lane, *Obscene Profits*, p. 166.

26. Flowers, *Fantasy Factory*.

27. It might be tempting to view phone sex work as a route into the world of exotic dancing and prostitution, but our data and the available literature suggest that this is rare; see also Flowers, *Fantasy Factory*. Only one worker in our sample reported being involved in other kinds of sex work.

28. Anne Statham, Eleanor Miller, and Hans Mauksh, eds., *The Worth of Women's Work: A Qualitative Synthesis*, New York: State University of New York Press, 1988.

29. Howard Becker, *Outsiders: Studies in the Sociology of Deviance*, New York: Free Press, 1963.

30. Goffman, *Stigma*.

31. Christena Nippert-Eng, *Home and Work: Negotiating Boundaries through Everyday Life*, Chicago: University of Chicago Press, 1996.

32. See Guidroz, "Gender, Labor, and Sexuality" for a comparison of two groups of sex workers.

33. Contemporary online advertisements for phone sex operators, or PSOs, promise salaries of up to $30 per hour or between $100 and $1500 per week. Several of the ads referred to PSOs as phone actresses and voice artists, and some require trolling, chatroom networking, and IMing. A few were looking for dispatchers and "webcam girls."

34. Flowers, *Fantasy Factory*, p. 122.

35. In *Fantasy Factory*, Flowers reports that phone sex agencies have ways for callers to mail the operators gifts, letters, and photographs. Workers have received flowers, candy, and cash ($100 is common). Spice showed an engagement ring a caller had sent her (his real-life engagement did not work out) along with the appraisal form; the ring was valued at about $4000. Another worker received a new stereo system. The manager documents and photocopies or photographs gifts and letters for security purposes.
36. Pepper noted that prison inmates try to make collect calls all the time.
37. This term was used during an interview with a longtime phone sex operator based in New York City and who works from her home; Guidroz, "Gender, Labor, and Sexuality."
38. Some operators use the legal definition of "consent" when determining which calls they will accept; Lindsay Moore, *"Oh Baby . . . Talk Nasty to Me": The Practical Guide to Succeeding as a Phone Sex Operator*, Sorceress Enterprises, 1995.
39. Skipper and McCaghy identified this notion in their study of strippers: James Skipper and Charles McCaghy, "Stripteasing: A Sex-Oriented Occupation," in James Henslin, ed., *Studies in the Sociology of Sex*, New York: Appleton-Century-Crofts, 1971.
40. See Guidroz, "Gender, Labor, and Sexuality" for claims by escort workers.
41. Or, for example, men who call excessively, such as the basketball coach whose wife divorced him over a $10,000 phone sex habit.

PROSTITUTION

THE ECOLOGY OF STREET PROSTITUTION

Judith Porter and Louis Bonilla

Women who engage in sex work have a wide range of lifestyles and can work in vastly different settings. An understanding of the social context in which prostitution occurs is important in order to promote AIDS prevention and service delivery in this population.[1] Unfortunately, epidemiological models of AIDS risk behavior tend to address prostitution as individual sexual behavior but often ignore its social context. Although patterns of prostitution may differ across cities or regions of the country, much of the research assumes that patterns of street-level sex work are similar.[2] This chapter demonstrates that street prostitution varies considerably by race, drug use, and locale within one city, and on the basis of these differences we suggest targeted strategies to prevent the spread of HIV and to provide needed services to this population. In other words, the social ecology of street prostitution is an important variable in both the manifestation of prostitution and in the kinds of harm-reduction practices that need to be tailored to workers in particular locales.

STREET PROSTITUTION: CHARACTERISTICS AND RISKS

Although it is difficult to provide precise data, some researchers have estimated that about one-fifth of prostitution in the United States is street prostitution and the remainder is spread among massage parlors, bar prostitution, outcall services, and brothels.[3] Street prostitution is the form of prostitution most closely related to HIV/AIDS in the United States because of the connection with drug use, and sex workers have many service needs as well. Injection drug use is most common at the street level, with one-third to one-half of street prostitutes in the United States injecting drugs. Most street prostitutes who are injection drug users used drugs before beginning sex work.[4] They often continue or increase their usage after they start sex work, because they are making more money for drugs and some need to be high to do this work, leading to a cycle of increasing addiction.[5] Some prostitutes work on the street because they have no access to private space for sex work or because there is a reluctance by escort services or massage parlors to employ women with substance dependency.[6] Street workers also are most likely to be poor, are disproportionately members of racial minorities, and are the most likely of any group of sex workers to be arrested.[7] Many are not full-time prostitutes but exchange sex for money or drugs only occasionally and in certain contexts, such as the exchange of sex for crack cocaine.[8]

These women have often worked at low-wage jobs before beginning sex work, but these jobs do not meet their economic needs or they lack employment opportunities. Unstable housing is common, including living in cheap hotels, sharing rooms, and in crack houses or with friends, partners, or intermittently with families. Many have children, living either with family members or in foster care.[9]

Violence is endemic in street prostitution. Street prostitutes experience more incidents of severe violence than other sex workers. In some studies, high percentages of street prostitutes report being raped, assaulted, or robbed.[10] Customers are the most frequent perpetrators of violence, but pimps, police officers, and other sex workers also perpetrate violence.

Women with a history of commercial sex work are at high risk for premature death. Especially pertinent to our Philadelphia study, the Women's Death Review Team, a collaborative effort among the Philadelphia Department of Public Health, the District Attorney's office, and other agencies, tracks the incidence and prevalence of violence-related deaths of women from ages 15–60 in Philadelphia. Ten percent (275) of decedents reviewed between 1997 and 2003 were identified by arrest records and agencies as having a history of commercial sex work. Sixteen per cent (45) of these died by homicide, half of which were unsolved.[11] The characteristics of these women suggest that many of them were street workers.

Prostitutes are popularly viewed as vectors of HIV infection. Of decedents with a history of sex work between 1997 and 2003 in the Philadelphia study, 38% (N = 105) had HIV or AIDS.[12] However, prostitution is not a major vector for the transmission of HIV infection in the United States, in part because street prostitutes are more likely to perform oral sex (a lower risk practice for HIV infection than vaginal sex) with their clients and also because they frequently use condoms with them.[13] Among prostitutes in the U.S. and elsewhere,[14] HIV infection is related to long-term injection drug use or to large numbers of nonpaying sex partners more than to prostitution per se. Studies have found significant differences in HIV seropositivity between sex workers who inject drugs or engage in sex with drug injectors and those who do not.[15] Not only are prostitutes who inject drugs at higher risk generally, but they may not identify their steady, nonpaying partners as being at risk and will thus often share drug injecting equipment or not use condoms with them.[16] In a study of New York street prostitutes, almost half had a history of injection drug use and more than one-third of this sample was HIV positive.[17] Similar findings are reported in a Philadelphia study,[18] where a majority of decedents between 2002 and 2003 with known histories of prostitution (N = 68) also had a history of substance abuse and 49% of the 68 decedents with a known history of prostitution were HIV positive.

Crack cocaine has destabilized the structure of street prostitution in urban areas. The entry of large numbers of crack-addicted women into street prostitution has driven the price of sex down, especially in areas where crack use is prevalent,[19] increasing the level of competition and diminishing prostitutes' bargaining power over price and condom use.[20] Also, before crack, pimps were more likely to house, clothe, feed, and pay for the fixed expenses of their workers, and indeed this was part of the typical arrangement between prostitutes and their pimps.[21] At least on the street level, this is less the case today. Crack-addicted women often do not have pimps or lookouts to protect them because they cannot afford them; they must spend what they earn to maintain their addictions.[22] Also, more prostitutes barter sex for drugs.[23] Because of the presence of frequent and unprotected sex among female crack users, crack use has been viewed as a risk factor for HIV among female sex workers.[24] Inconsistent condom use during oral sex, given the lip damage caused by crack smoking, is associated with HIV seropositivity among crack-addicted sex workers.[25]

Although these issues generally characterize our sample, the type of drug use, race, and location may cause these factors to vary somewhat. Thus, the type of strategy likely to be effective in reducing HIV risk or delivering other type of services may differ among different types of sex worker. While the literature does give some indication of the effect of type of drug used, much of it does not examine sources of variation in the structure of street prostitution by race and locale within one city, neither have the implications of such contextual variations for HIV/AIDS prevention or service delivery among sex workers been widely studied. Our study addresses this very issue.

METHODS

Data were obtained from informal, unstructured interviews conducted with street prostitutes in North Philadelphia and observations from the needle exchange van in the early 1990s. We were trained as outreach workers and trained and certified as AIDS educators by a local Latino community-based organization serving the North Philadelphia area. We volunteered as an outreach team one afternoon a week during a 12-month period. As outreach workers, we distributed condoms, bleach kits, written material on HIV/AIDS, information on HIV testing, and lists of soup kitchens, housing, drug treatment, and other essential services. An important part of our work was to discuss with the women the services they needed and to give them information to connect with these services. The interviews usually lasted several minutes, since the women were often in the process of soliciting clients, but repeated contacts gave us the opportunity to discuss their needs and the context of their work. We taped detailed field notes after each outreach session, which were then transcribed. The quotes presented in the chapter are from these field notes (names have been changed to protect anonymity). Our taped information is reliable because we taped the field notes together, verifying each other's perceptions and noting where we differed.

Our observations validated the information the women gave us, because we saw the type of supply they took and physical signs like needle track marks or blistered lips from crack smoking. Other researchers have similarly used outreach observations to validate self-reports in research on street prostitution.[26] We validated our observations in other ways. We did weekly group AIDS education presentations at two major local welfare offices and a hospital drug detoxification unit in the area we serviced. In addition, we volunteered at a weekly needle exchange program located in one of these areas. In these venues, we were able to confirm our observations by extended personal conversations with the women when they were not at work, with their pimps or male partners, or with staff of these programs.

The study was conducted in North Philadelphia, the poorest area of the city, with a high rate of drug use, poor health, a high rate of sexually transmitted diseases, a large percentage living in poverty, high unemployment, and morbidity and mortality rates far above the city average.[27] Although the area is predominantly African-American, there are also large low-income Latino and white neighborhoods there.

The sample is a nonrandom, convenience sample of street prostitutes who worked in the three major stroll areas in North Philadelphia during our visits on Friday afternoons. In all three areas, the women actively solicited clients by standing on the street or by waving down cars. The areas are several miles apart from each other. One area is the major stroll area for white prostitutes. It is located underneath an elevated railway line in a racially transitional but still largely white, extremely low-income neighborhood on the edge of a commercial district. The area is full of abandoned buildings and factories. Another area is a park in a low-income African-American and Latino neighborhood next to a major expressway. The park is frequented mostly by African-American prostitutes. Neither area has easily accessible hotels or rooms where the women can take their clients; sex is performed mostly in cars. Another area is adjacent to a major urban thoroughfare in a black community. Although the area is primarily a low-income residential area, it is surrounded by commercial establishments, including cheap hotels where the prostitutes can take their clients. Sex is performed in hotels or row houses or in cars, although for privacy the prostitute picked up in a car must leave the area with the john. This area is frequented solely by African-American prostitutes.

We saw an average of six to seven African-American prostitutes every week in the park area (ranging from two to 13 a week over a 12-month period), 10 African-American prostitutes a week in the hotel area (ranging from two to 13), and six white women (ranging from one to eight) underneath the elevated train, although the number of white prostitutes we contacted every week was actually higher because the needle exchange program, heavily frequently by white prostitutes, was in this area. Every week, from one-third to one-half of the women in the park or under the elevated railway were women we had seen at least once before. The women in the hotel area were a more stable population, although some left temporarily and some permanently and were replaced by new sex workers. Over time, the number of prostitutes in the areas varied with the weather, police actions, number of clients on the street, and movement of the women themselves into and out of prostitution. We spoke with at least 150 women over the course of the year.

It is important to note the limitations of this type of research. The research was conducted during street outreach efforts and is not a formal series of highly structured interviews. Many of the data were gathered during the women's working hours, limiting the amount of time they could spend talking to us. This sometimes yielded incomplete interviews when, for example, the women would leave because prospective clients drove by or their pimps or male partners were watching them. It is also important to note the limitations of the sample. The majority of women were full-time street prostitutes who were working in public stroll areas on late Friday afternoons, and hence our sample does not include women in bars, crack houses, or shooting galleries, call girls, part-time prostitutes, or women who work in the areas we covered either late at night or earlier in the week (though the weekend is the busiest time of the week). Our sample is limited to white and African-American street prostitutes and to three areas of North Philadelphia—the target areas of the agency for which we volunteered—and thus these women may not be representative of women who sell sex elsewhere in the city.

Research of this type does, however, have certain benefits. We interviewed women during their working hours and in their work environments, enabling us to observe the *context* in which their activities took place and the social networks among the women. Also, our work as service providers gave us access to these women in a non-threatening situation. Our race and gender did not seem to seriously affect the quality of information we received. We consistently appeared each week, represented a known and respected minority organization, and delivered needed supplies and service information in addition to offering a sympathetic ear. Outreach work also provided an excellent opportunity to compare differences in the context of street prostitution by stroll area.

VARIATIONS IN STREET PROSTITUTION

White Prostitutes

The white street prostitutes usually worked alone or occasionally in groups of two on the edge of a commercial district underneath an elevated railway (the "El"). They were almost all addicted to injectable heroin. We knew this because they frequently told us and also accepted the bleach kits used to sterilize needles that we distributed. They had visible needle track marks and we saw many of them returning used needles at the needle exchange program in this area. An excerpt from our field notes illustrates this:

> We approached a white sex worker and asked if she wanted condoms. She took them, and when we asked if she needed bleach, she said, "I'm a drug addict." She said she'd shared needles with someone who was HIV positive and knew she should get tested, but she was afraid to find out her status.

Most of the white prostitutes' business occurred in cars, although occasionally they worked out of abandoned buildings, where they were more isolated and vulnerable to assaults by their clients. Although there was some variation, the white prostitutes were likely to work for themselves and their boyfriends (who were usually addicted to heroin themselves); prostitution supported the woman and her partner's heroin habit. The white prostitute (usually in her late twenties) was generally older than the African-American prostitutes we met and worked as an isolated individual rather than with a small group of other women. The structure of male control did not involve one man managing several women, but rather consisted of a couple in a steady relationship where the man was the lookout for the woman while she solicited. A similar pattern of male partners as lookouts, with the woman's prostitution supporting both her and her partner's heroin habit, has also been observed in other research.[28] The following field note describing the white male partner of one of these women summarizes the relationship between the white prostitute and her male partner and her working conditions:

> Tony says that the girls out here are usually working for their husbands or boyfriends and they split the profits. The woman has the man looking out for her; they wait in their cars. Tony's wife tells him to which location she will take her johns and how long she will be gone with each. He always takes the license number of the car and if his wife doesn't come back, he'll contact one police officer who is friendly. He says the money is good and it's easy money. He says that 90% of the work the women do here is blow jobs [oral sex], which go for $20. Vaginal sex is $50, but it's rare. Most johns are white businessmen in their fifties who come in for quick blow jobs. A girl can make $200 on a good day. Tony said that the women hate the job. They do it because they have to; they need the money for drugs. The girls work a regular area. He stated that life under the El is very dangerous. He's seen five girls die this year; three were killed by clients and two died from drug overdoses. The cops also entrap and bust the girls regularly.

As crack dealing increased in the area, many of the women became addicted to crack as well as to heroin. The pattern of the woman's working to support her boyfriend's habit as well as her own appeared to be shifting by the end of the research. If a woman broke up with her male partner, she might work on her own without a male lookout in order to use the money to support her addictions:

> Mary said that although many of the girls still had boyfriends, she herself had recently broken up with her longtime boyfriend, who had worked as her lookout. She was using large amounts of heroin and crack, though heroin was still her

primary drug. She made enough money to support both her drug habits and pay for her room and food. She said she would accept only older white men as customers, since she was working without a regular male lookout, and she had to be more safety conscious as far as selection of clients was concerned. She encouraged many of her steady customers to page her at home when they wanted her services, though she still worked on the street by herself if she needed the money.

White prostitutes usually did not have extensive family or supportive friendship networks on whom they could rely. Some of the women came from outside Philadelphia and had no family networks. Others were rejected by their families and had no contact with them. "With us as we are, our families don't want us," one said. The women rarely spoke to us about their children, and it is unclear whether they had children or whether they simply lacked contact with them. In terms of connections between the workers, some told us that they sometimes acted as lookouts for one another if their male partners were not around or they did not have a male partner, and that they would share condoms with other women who did not have them. However, these relationships were typically informal and did not constitute structured friendship networks.

These women appeared to be in bad health with visible signs of dental problems and skin conditions, and they appeared undernourished. They were often dirty or disheveled, and bore signs of being physically assaulted. They were often battered not only by the clients but also by their male partners, as some of the women told us, and they were at risk physically from the health problems associated with drug addiction. In addition, they were generally not connected with social or welfare services. Few of the white prostitutes, for example, had medical cards, welfare, or health insurance. The staff of the local drug detox program at which we gave HIV/AIDS presentations told us that these women tended to enter drug detoxification programs only after a major crisis, like the discovery that their partners are HIV positive, or after they hit bottom, an observation confirmed by our interviews. The effects for addicted women of being so extremely isolated from healthcare are partially revealed in the following field note:

> One white woman was battered, beaten with fresh bruises on her face. She said she was 3 months pregnant and showed us her stomach. She said she didn't have any family in Philadelphia. She came from a southern state 2 years ago. She does not have a medical card, she's homeless, and when I asked her what services she wanted, she implied she needed prenatal care (she pointed to her stomach and

said "for the baby"). She didn't know where to get prenatal services because she didn't have a medical card or relatives to provide any kind of support structure.

These prostitutes were also at very high risk of HIV infection. Although other research has indicated that injection drug use is common among minority prostitutes, in North Philadelphia the white street prostitutes were more likely to be injection drug users than the African-American street prostitutes, thus putting them at risk of HIV infection through injection drug use. Since at least 20% of injection drug users in Philadelphia who were not in treatment tested HIV positive at the time of our study,[29] the chance that these women were already HIV infected was high, a suspicion confirmed by the staff of the local drug detox program. Although they preferred to use clean needles, they sometimes shared needles either because they were "sick" (in withdrawal) and didn't have clean needles available or because their living conditions caused inadvertent sharing. A common problem, for instance, arose from several injection drug users living in the same place: "A white prostitute told us . . . the people in her house all injected drugs and they take her needles when she isn't there. She came back to her room and found the needle obviously used in her absence and the cooker [where drug is melted] full of blood."

These women told us that they often shared needles with regular sex partners or did not use condoms with them, even though they used condoms on a more frequent basis with their johns. Condom use with johns, however, appeared to be inconsistent:

> A white prostitute said a lot of the girls didn't use condoms consistently. She was the only one, she said, who used them regularly. She wouldn't service a date if they didn't use condoms; she didn't care if she lost the money, but she already had endocarditis (inflammation of the heart valve, a common illness among injection drug users) and she was afraid for her health. She said that a lot of the girls were HIV positive or had sexually transmitted diseases and they still didn't consistently use condoms.

These observations on inconsistent condom use were confirmed by other white women we interviewed.

African-American Prostitutes

Our data on African-American street prostitutes were gathered primarily from the two African-American stroll areas: a small area that contained several hotels and row houses, which the women used for their work; and a park area, where business usually occurred inside parked cars. Although there were behavioral differences between the two locales dictated by social context, there were also some similarities in behavior that transcended location and which may stem from race. Although both groups of black prostitutes reported that their clientele came from various racial groups, many of the johns we observed were black men.

Most of the African-American prostitutes we saw in these two stroll areas were addicted to crack and did not inject drugs. They were open about telling us that they were "on the pipe." Many did not know why we were offering them bleach. When we explained that it is used to sterilize needles, we were often told "I don't do that shit." The women frequently displayed blistered or injured lips, visible signs of heavy crack use, but we did not see the needle tracks that we did on the white sex workers. This finding is consistent with a New York City study that similarly found African-American sex workers to be more likely to smoke crack than whites, and white women more apt to use injectable heroin than African-Americans.[30]

Crack seems to have driven down the price of sex for these women, in part because of competition among the women and in part because of informal competition with the women who exchange sex for drugs in crack houses. We were repeatedly told by prostitutes how the influence of crack-addicted women had driven down the price of sex. These field notes reflect a conversation with one African-American prostitute in the park:

> The going rate for a blow job was $20, which is what she charged. Some girls out here give men a blow job for $1.50. They're "real ho's." They drive the price down for the other girls. She could understand it if they were doing it for food or kids, but one girl gave a blow job for $1.50 and bought crack with it and smoked it. She strongly disapproved of this; this was disgusting and she should be driven out. She was giving the girls a bad name because the price was too low. If she knew someone who was giving $1.00 blow jobs, she'd "beat the shit" out of them.

Although women were working for money to purchase drugs, some reported they were also working for money for food or child support:

> The African-American prostitute in the park told us that she was cut off General Assistance which [at the time of the research] only lasted 3 months in Pennsylvania. As a result she has no money to pay her rent. She said she has a drug problem and prostitutes for drugs, but now she also has to prostitute for money for food and rent, which is why she's out early today.

Many of the African-American prostitutes we interviewed, both in the park and in the hotel area, were born in Philadelphia and had networks of relatives in the city with whom they were in contact. Some lived intermittently with different relatives (especially mothers, sisters, and grandmothers). Others lived in abandoned buildings or rented cheap hotel rooms, and still others lived in the row houses out of which they worked. Even in the latter case, however, they often returned to relatives to stay for short periods of time. Many of the African-American prostitutes had regular or semi-regular contact with female family members, usually their mothers.

Rita, for example, saw her mother regularly. Her mother did not approve of Rita's prostitution but accepted it, and Rita lived with her mother and two of her children during the week in another part of North Philadelphia. At the time of the study, 19-year-old Danielle had been working for 2 years in the hotel area and alternated between living with her sister and mother every several weeks. Shakwana said she became pregnant by one of the male hangers-on around the hotel but was still able to return to her mother's to have her baby.

At least some of the women had families of their own in other parts of Philadelphia and worked only on the weekends to supplement their incomes or maintain their addictions:

> Denise lives in West Philadelphia with her two children and her mother. She said she never stayed overnight at the hotel. She goes home when she's done. She said the scene is different in West Philadelphia, a lot slower. In North Philadelphia, it's busier and you make more money. She takes the El every day to work here and takes it home after work.

Most of these women had children. When they discussed their children with us, one common theme was guilt about being "bad mothers," a finding also reported by other researchers.[31] Although the women maintained contact with their families, it was often intermittent, and though some of their children were with female relatives, some were often in foster care:

> LaVerne had a court appointment. The Department of Human Services wanted to put her daughter in a mental hospital because her behavior was bizarre. She was currently in foster care. LaVerne said she didn't feel the child needed to be in a mental hospital; she wanted the child with her mother. LaVerne felt that if she were with her family and got the attention her grandmother would give her, she'd be better. She said the social worker "just wants to take my child away permanently." She lives with her sister and goes home occasionally to see her

JUDITH PORTER AND LOUIS BONILLA

mother. She says her mother will always accept her. She always brings her mother a little money, because she's taking care of two of the children. Her mother deserves to get her welfare, LaVerne said, "because I'm not in any condition to take care of the kids. The family is the most important thing. I feel really sad when I think of my kids."

Many of the African-American prostitutes were on welfare because they had children, and many had medical cards. A number of African-American women told us that they had been in drug treatment programs or received medical examinations for sexually transmitted diseases on a regular basis, and many reported having been HIV tested. Most of these women were also aware of free health services provided at local district health centers, which were available to them even if they did not have medical cards. The majority of African-American prostitutes were aware of access to some healthcare services, however minimal.

African-American Prostitutes in the Park

Although there were similarities in crack use, family networks, and awareness of services among the African-American prostitutes in the two different social settings (the park and the hotel area), there were also differences by locale. The prostitutes who worked primarily in the park and those who worked in the hotel area differed in type of sex practiced, the type of client they saw, their relationship to male pimps or lookouts, the type of violence to which they were exposed, and to some extent, their ability to network with services.

The prostitutes in the park worked primarily out of cars. They tended to perform oral sex, which is quick, and the park provided the privacy for them to do so in a car. The women in the park were more likely to be in a formal relationship with a pimp; in fact, many of the women had pimps watching them as we talked, which made it difficult for us to interact with them and to learn as much about them as we could with the other groups. Although some of the women in the park appeared to be working on their own, more typical was the presence of men who were managing several women in a formal business relationship. For instance, as an example of a behavior frequently encountered, one man came up to us to get condoms for "his girls." When we asked how many he had, he said "three." The men often sat in cars with several women, and the women stood outside the cars and solicited clients. Prostitutes in the park area needed to work out of cars because there were no buildings or wooded areas in the park to conceal their activities. Thus, women were more reliant on working in pimps' cars. Also, because of the transient and unprotected nature of the locale, they told us they needed a pimp for occasional protection from customers, muggers, or other prostitutes. Women also frequently worked in the cars of men who picked them up, and they needed someone to note the license plate numbers of the cars in case they failed to return.

The park prostitutes appeared physically battered, although we were unable to determine who battered them. And because they were controlled by pimps, they were restricted in their ability to informally network with other women about social services. Although our interviews indicated they knew about some social or medical services and used them, they were not aware of as wide a range of service options as were the African-American hotel prostitutes.

African-American Prostitutes in the Hotel Area

The prostitutes who worked in the hotel area occasionally worked out of cars, but since this area is adjacent to a major thoroughfare and is in a heavily traveled residential/commercial area, privacy in a car was extremely difficult unless they left the area. Thus, many brought the clients they solicited on the street to rooms in hotels that rented by the hour or half-hour, or brought the clients to row houses in which some of them lived either regularly or intermittently. We were told by the women that most of the women in the hotel area had regular customers, a practice that was somewhat less frequent in the park, which had a more transient population. Also, they reported more vaginal sex than the park prostitutes, in part because of the privacy granted by the hotel room.

Whereas previous literature indicates that most of the men involved with female street prostitution were pimps or proprietors of business establishments, in the hotel area male roles were more fluid, and many women worked on their own. The presence of so many women working independently had increased because of the widespread use of crack. The women binged on crack, often hitting on the pipe a number of times a day.

Because of this bingeing, many women wanted to spend their money on drugs rather than on male protection. This observation was confirmed both by the women themselves and by men who worked as bouncers in the hotels. As one bouncer told us:

> The girls (in the hotel area) work for themselves. There's no pimps around here. They watch out for each other. They're independent here. They use the money they get for themselves for drugs. They take whatever they can get. The rates

went down around here; whatever they can get, it's enough. If they were using once in a while, they would charge a little higher. But they're using [crack] so much now, they take what [money] they can get.

The bouncer's observations are verified by entries in our field notes:

Tamika looked exhausted and said she had been out continuously from the previous night through the entire following day (we saw her at 4.30 on Friday), yet she did not have enough cash on hand to buy a hoagie for dinner. She implied that she had smoked most of what she had earned.

A group of African-American men in the hotel area fulfilled a variety of roles. Some of the men rented rooms in the hotels and worked there informally as bouncers, were boyfriends whom the women might "help out" with small amounts of cash, were proprietors of small prostitution hotels or sellers of condoms, or were suppliers of drugs. Often, the men fulfilled multiple roles at once, especially at the prostitution hotels. One man, for example, lived at one of the hotels, where he also worked as a bouncer, and had been the boyfriend of at least two prostitutes. Another man who owned the house out of which several of the women work received small, sporadic amounts of cash from the women who slept or worked there as general payment for rent and other services such as drugs. However, the women were not forced to relinquish their earnings to the men without receiving something in exchange; the money clearly belonged to the women who earn it. For instance, some of the women lived in a row house owned by one of the men:

Kim told us that Mike and his brother Tyrone own the house. Tyrone is inside selling drugs. The house is nasty; there's no running water or plumbing. Mike gets the water in a bucket. The girls get paid directly by their dates and don't pay regular rent but pay what they can and give the guys some of their drugs occasionally. "We give Tyrone some drugs or money but that's from our heart." Kim says the johns pay the guys $7.00 a room for 1/2 hour, $10.00 for an hour. . . . Tyrone and Mike make their profits from drug sales, money paid by the johns, and from the sale of condoms to the girls and their dates.

Although the women in the hotel area were also subjected to violence, they stated the violence was not only from clients but often from fights with one another, since they were protected to some degree by bouncers in the hotels and were less likely to be dependent on male managers who could physically abuse them.

The prostitutes in the hotel area were working in a circumscribed area on their own, and they all knew one another. Since they were not dependent on pimps, they were able to both trade information about and access services more easily.

African-American women in the hotel area were at high risk for HIV infection. They frequently performed vaginal sex, a higher risk practice than oral sex. They were usually visibly high on crack when they were soliciting business, which may have discouraged condom use.

Similarities in Street Prostitution

As other studies have demonstrated, most of the women with whom we worked, regardless of race, drug, or location, were at high risk of violence and HIV infection, and they lacked essential services. All of these women were in need of drug rehabilitation and housing services. Although African-American sex workers were more likely than white prostitutes to be living with relatives, their housing conditions were often far from adequate. Many of the relatives subsisted on scarce resources. The white prostitutes generally did not have relatives with whom they were in contact, and thus they and their male partners seemed to have even more acute housing needs. Most of the prostitutes were also in need of financial assistance. African-American prostitutes had generally been on welfare more recently than white prostitutes, but many had had their benefits discontinued. At the time of the research, Pennsylvania's General Assistance program for single low-income individuals lasted only 3 months, after which able-bodied individuals were cut from the program. At least some of the turbulence in these women's lives stemmed from the fact that many who had begun to stabilize their lives with regular housing became homeless when their benefits were discontinued. Without job skills or other resources needed to find and keep a job, and with a drug addiction to satisfy, many of the women resumed prostitution. In addition, difficulties involved with applying for benefits may have deterred women who were eligible from reapplying once their benefits were canceled. Drug dependency, violence, and a shortage of available services, characterized the lives of most of these street sex workers in our sample, findings also observed in other cities.[32]

Differences in Street Prostitution by Race

The white prostitutes worked primarily in cars. Although they appeared to be generally sicker and in worse physical condition than the African-American prostitutes, this probably is a result of their long histories of heroin injection, although it may also have been related to their lesser degree of access to medical services. The white prostitutes were much less connected to or even aware of social and medical services than the African-American street prostitutes in general, including those African-American prostitutes in the park who also worked out of cars. For instance, many African-American sex workers used the local district health centers, but most white prostitutes did not even know where the centers were located. We observed a similar difference with respect to African-American and white sex workers enrolled in the major local drug detoxification program. Both groups of African-American women were more likely than white women to enter the program in this area, even though this particular 1-week residential program was closer to the white stroll area. In part, this may be due to differences in awareness of this service, in part to the white women's reluctance or inability to leave their male partners, and in part to the fact that the white women were less likely to have medical insurance cards. The white sex workers were somewhat less likely to come from Philadelphia, were less likely to have children with whom they were in contact, and even if they came from Philadelphia, were less likely to have family networks on whom to rely for housing needs or links to welfare services. They tended to work to maintain their own drug habits or those of their male partners, and the primary relationship of many of them was with these men, not with other women. However, the relationship with males appeared to be altering somewhat with the growth of crack use among the white women.

African-American prostitutes were more likely to use crack as their primary drug than were white women and were less likely to be injection drug users. They were also more likely to be aware of services, and they networked with kin more than the white prostitutes did. Although some of the racial differences we saw (primarily in health or appearance) were related to the type of drug the women mainly used, the greater networking with kin and social services may be an effect of race, especially since African-American and white prostitutes differed in these aspects irrespective of their geographical location. Several white prostitutes we saw come from the large ethnic Catholic community in Philadelphia. They may have been more ostracized by their families and isolated than the African-American prostitutes because of the hostility of this white community to what is perceived as "deviance." We frequently observed extreme resistance and open hostility toward AIDS educators in predominantly white welfare and job placement offices, which may indicate a denial of drug addiction and HIV infection in white, working-class ethnic communities. These factors discourage contact with family members who are drug addicted or work as prostitutes. African-American sex workers, however, appeared to be less rejected by their families, a finding suggested by other researchers.[33] Although prostitution and drug use are condemned in African-American communities, there is also greater tolerance for deviance in low-income African-American communities. Residents' preferences may be mainstream cultural preferences, but deviance may be more tolerated due to structural barriers faced by these populations in achieving mainstream goals. Someone who deviates may be less likely to be totally excluded from her family. Extensive networks of real and fictive kin in the African-American community have ensured survival in the face of poverty.[34] Thus, compared to white prostitutes, African-American prostitutes may have multiple family roles as mothers, daughters, or sisters rather than more isolated roles as sex workers or addicts. In addition, kinship networks and contact with their children may ensure the women greater access to community services (see Table 7.1).

Differences in Street Prostitution by Location

Street prostitution varied not only by race but also by locale. The African-American women who worked in the hotel area had more services and support

TABLE 7.1 CHARACTERISTICS OF STREET PROSTITUTION BY LOCALE

	WHITE PROSTITUTES	BLACK PARK PROSTITUTES	BLACK HOTEL PROSTITUTES
Primary drug	Heroin (injection)	Crack cocaine	Crack cocaine
Primary work site	Cars	Cars	Hotels
Primary type of sex	Oral	Oral	Vaginal
Typical relation to males	Male partner (1 man, 1 woman)	Male pimps (1 man, several women)	Work by themselves
Family networks	No	Yes	Yes
Connection to social services	No	Yes, somewhat connected	Yes, highly connected
AIDS prevention and service outreach strategy	Needle exchange sites	Mobile vans	Individual outreach teams

networks than the African-American car prostitutes in the park area and the white prostitutes underneath the El. The African-American women in the hotel area all seemed to be connected to services or at least knew where to get them. This may be because the hotel prostitutes had a closer network, protected each other, and were, as one of the male bouncers said, "like a family." Because they were in regular contact with one another (the same prostitutes tended to use the same hotels, even if they did not live in them), information regarding services passed quickly through the street network. Although the African-American women in the park area were less know-ledgeable about services than the African-American women who worked in the hotel area, they were more knowledgeable than the white prostitutes who also worked out of cars and worked for men, perhaps because of the networking with kin in the African-American community.

Violence is commonplace in street prostitution. Although these women were exposed to violence on a daily basis, both white and African-American women who worked out of cars worked in more dangerous and less protected locales and were often exposed to violence not only from their clients but from the men for whom they worked. Women who worked in the hotel area and under the El were not in a formal pimping relationship, though they often informally gave money from prostitution to others. The white women were often in a relationship with a steady male partner who acted as a lookout, and they prostituted for drug money for both themselves and their partner. The African-American women in the hotels were in an informal relationship with male hotel staff and paid them for drugs or sometimes for rent, but they managed their own money. The only formal pimping structure we observed was among the African-American workers in the park, and may have been due to the unprotected and transient nature of the locale. Although we were able to speak with some of the partners or helpers of the white women and African-American hotel prostitutes, it was difficult to access the pimps in the park for information.

There were some similarities in locale across these areas. They were all low- income areas near or easily accessible to heavy traffic, more easily enabling the women to solicit customers. All of these areas also gave them easy access to drugs, since they were in or near locations of extensive drug sales. The women worked in distinct areas by race, however, because of access to drug of choice as well as other factors. The white sex workers, whose primary drug was heroin, prostituted in a location which was in the major area of heroin sales in the city. Also, as one john told us, the presence of fast food establishments allowed the partners of some of these women someplace unobtrusive to take down license numbers of the cars that picked them up.

The African-American prostitutes had easy access to crack sales in areas where they prostituted. The prevalence of very low-income and abandoned housing in the African-American neighborhood in which the hotels were located enabled the women to service their customers without attracting a great deal of attention from the police or neighbors. The African-American park prostitutes were close to the exit of a major highway, but the park provided the ability of workers to work in pimps' cars with a degree of privacy that would not be possible on a city street.

POLICY IMPLICATIONS

It is important to understand the context and structure of street prostitution in order to better access street prostitutes, identify their needs, and link them to AIDS prevention and other services. Our ethnographic data suggest that strategies for AIDS prevention and service delivery for street prostitutes must be differentiated by context including race, type of drug use, and ecological location in North Philadelphia.

Delivery of services must be neighborhood based. Street outreach is an important strategy, because outreach workers know the characteristics of their constituencies, provide personal relationships, and bring information about accessible services directly to the women, as well as bringing them condoms and bleach to prevent HIV infection. Outreach workers are often the primary conduit to essential medical, drug treatment, and legal services for street prostitutes, since these women have a wide variety of needs beyond HIV/AIDS prevention. Poverty, lack of marketable skills, and drug addiction help to push women into prostitution and put them at risk for HIV infection.

The social structure of prostitution in any given area must be identified to specifically design AIDS prevention outreach strategies for the population involved (see last row of Table 7.1). The white prostitutes in our sample were at the greatest risk of HIV infection because of their injection drug use. They were the most isolated from the services and from networks that could help them access services they desperately needed. Also, many were watched by their male partners or lookouts, which made it harder for them to talk with outreach workers, so they were often cut off from information on how to protect themselves or to access the services they needed. Providing services in the stroll area, either through the use of an outreach van or through a program such as needle exchange, is a viable way to reach these women. Even if women do not inject drugs, they can still acquire free condoms from the needle exchange sites. The needle exchange program that started during our research was located outdoors on a street corner in the stroll area. Prostitutes began using the program soon after it started. They received information about AIDS and medical and social services at the site when they came to exchange needles, and over time they began to trust the volunteers. They frequently brought their male partners, who were often willing to talk to us, so it was possible to get information to both the woman and her partner.

Because the African-American prostitutes were more connected to both social service and family and friendship networks, AIDS presentations and distribution of condoms in welfare offices, city-funded health clinics, and drug detoxification units, as well as up to date information on new and existing services of other types, are effective ways of reaching them. In some cases the information might come to them indirectly, through providing information to their families, who often take the information and pass it on. Reaching the African-American car prostitutes in the park directly was difficult because they were watched by pimps. But workers can approach the women through their pimps with the information; unlike the male partners of the white women, the African-American pimps frequently sat in cars in an open park area where the women were soliciting. A mobile van providing condoms, AIDS information, and information on services for crack users may be another way of reaching these women and their pimps. Weiner has described a similar van-based strategy to reach sex workers in New York City.[35]

In the hotel area, a team of outreach workers who walk the streets can be extremely effective. The prostitutes worked on their own, had more freedom to interact, and also were a more consistent population than in the car stroll areas, and so they came to know and trust outreach workers more easily. Using the men in these hotels as gatekeepers was an important strategy in reaching this population. Street networks are particularly important in African-American neighborhoods, where they are strong and effective at disseminating information. We were assisted, for example, by men at the hotels in the distribution of fliers we created which listed various services the women might need. The male gatekeepers were not always cooperative. In one of the hotels the male manager sold the condoms we gave him and tried to keep the women away from us so we could not give them condoms for free.

Because the African-American prostitutes often mentioned their children and expressed concerns for them, addressing the needs of their children or providing drug rehabilitation services that include children may be an important strategy for behavior change in this population.

We do not know whether our findings can be generalized to other locales in Philadelphia or to other cities. However, even if specific contextual patterns differ, our research in Philadelphia suggests that street prostitution is not uniform and that different services must target different groups of prostitutes. Street prostitution is often in flux. Women move into and out of the life or into different types of prostitution and may change the way they work to protect their safety (for instance, using pagers or cell phones to contact regular clients). Neighborhood pressure, in conjunction with police raids on drugs and prostitution, may prompt the women to disperse to other areas. This happened in the African-American hotel area after the research was completed; also, the area of white prostitution moved further away from the commercial area where it was located. Economic redevelopment in an area may cause relocation, and as the type and location of drug sales change, women may move to areas of easy access to their drug of choice. They also may change their style of prostitution, as occurred with the white sex workers in our study; after they started using crack, many began working on their own without male lookouts so they did not have to share to share their drug money

Thus, strategies for reaching these women must be flexible and sensitive to the constraints of the locale in which they are working. A large portion of the epidemiological research on street prostitutes is dependent on a survey research methodology, where questionnaire or interview data are collected from individual sex workers, and does not deal with the social context in which they operate or possible variations in that context. Sensitivity to social context not only adds to our understanding of street prostitution but also can enable the effective delivery of HIV-related education and other services to these women.

NOTES

The authors would like to thank the staff of Congreso de Latinos Unidos for their encouragement and sponsorship, Robert Washington and Arthur Paris for their helpful suggestions, and the sex workers for confiding their concerns.

1. Barbara de Zalduondo, "Prostitution Viewed Cross-Culturally: Toward Recontextualizing Sex Work in AIDS Intervention Research," *Journal of Sex Research* 28 (1991): 233–248.

2. Heather G. Miller, Charles F. Turner, and Lincoln E. Moses, *AIDS: The Second Decade,* Washington, DC: National Academy Press, 1990.

3. Judith Cohen, Priscilla Alexander, and Constance Wofsy, "Prostitutes and AIDS: Public Policy Issues," *AIDS and Public Policy* 3 (1988): 12–22.

4. Priscilla Alexander, *Patterns of Prostitution in North American and Europe.* Oakland, CA: Prostitutes' Education Project, n.d.

5. Juhu Thukral and Melissa Ditmore, *Revolving Door: An Analysis of Street Based Prostitution in New York City*, New York: Sex Workers' Project, Urban Justice Center, 2003.

6. Thukral and Ditmore, *Revolving Door.*

7. Michael Zausner, *The Streets: A Factual Portrait of Six Prostitutes as Told in Their Own Words*, New York: St. Martin's Press, 1986; Arlene Carmen and Howard Moody, *Working Women: The Subterranean World of Street Prostitution*, New York: Harper & Row, 1985; Bernard Cohen, *Deviant Street Networks: and Drugs*, Lexington, MA: D.C. Heath, 1979.

8. Mitchell Ratner, ed., *Crack Pipe as Pimp: An Ethnographic Investigation of Sex for Crack Exchanges*, New York: Lexington Books, 1993; James Inciardi, Dorothy Lockwood, and Ann Pottgieter, *Women and Crack Cocaine*, New York: Macmillan, 1993; Terry Williams, *Crackhouse*, Reading, MA: Addison-Wesley, 1992; Mindy Fullilove, Elizabeth Lown, and Robert Fullilove, "Crack Hos and Skeezers: Traumatic Experiences of Women Crack Users," *Journal of Sex Research* 29 (1992): 257–287; Miller, Turner, and Moses, *AIDS.*

9. Thukral and Ditmore, *Revolving Door.*

10. Thukral and Ditmore, *Revolving Door.*

11. Michelle Henry, Diana Levengood, and Jennifer Keith, *Analysis of Deaths Among Philadelphia Women ages 15 through 60, 2002–2003, Including A Review of Trends 1997–2003*, Philadelphia: Philadelphia Death Review Team, Dept. of Public Health, 2006.

12. Henry, Levengood, and Keith, *Analysis of Deaths.*

13. Miller, Turner, and Moses, *AIDS.*

14. Neil McKeganey and Marina Barnard, *Sex Work on the Streets: Prostitutes and Their Clients*, Philadelphia: Open University Press, 1996.

15. Joyce Wallace, Allen Steinberg, and Adele Weiner, "Patterns of Condom Use, Crack Use, and Fellatio as Risk Behaviors for HIV Infection among Prostitutes," paper presented at annual conference of the American Association of Public Health, Washington, DC, 1992; Carol A. Campbell, "Prostitution, AIDS, and Preventive Health Behavior," *Social Science and Medicine* 32 (1991): 1367–1378.

16. McKeganey and Barnard, *Sex Work*; Miller, Turner, and Moses, *AIDS.*

17. Wallace, Steinberg, and Weiner, "Patterns of Condom Use."

18. Henry, Levengood, and Keith, *Analysis of Deaths.*

19. Ratner, *Crack Pipe as Pimp*; Michelle Shedlin, "An Ethnographic Approach to Understanding HIV High Risk Behaviors: Prostitution and Drug Abuse," in Carl Leukefeld, Robert Battjes, and Zili Amsel, eds., *AIDS and Injection Drug Use: Future Directions for Community-Based*

Prevention Research, Washington, DC: National Institute of Drug Abuse, NIDA Research Monograph 93, 1990.

20. Ratner, *Crack Pipe as Pimp*.
21. John Davidson, *The Stroll: Inner City Subcultures*, Toronto: New Canada Press, 1986; Zausner, *The Streets*.
22. Inciardi, Lockwood, and Pottgieter, *Women and Crack Cocaine*; Shedlin, "An Ethnographic Approach."
23. Ratner, *Crack Pipe as Pimp*; Inciardi, Lockwood, and Pottgieter, *Women and Crack Cocaine*; Fullilove, Lowen, and Fullilove, "Crack 'Hos and Skeezers."
24. Inciardi, Lockwood, and Pottgieter, *Women and Crack Cocaine*; Ratner, *Crack Pipe as Pimp*; Wallace, Steinberg, and Weiner, "Patterns of Condom Use."
25. Joyce Wallace, Judith Porter, Adele Weiner, Allen Steinberg, "Oral Sex, Crack Smoking, and HIV Infection Among Female Sex Workers Who Do Not Inject Drugs," *American Journal of Public Health* 87 (1997): 470.
26. McKeganey and Barnard, *Sex Work*.
27. Department of Public Health, *Vital Statistics Report*, Philadelphia: Department of Public Health, 1992.
28. McKeganey and Barnard, *Sex Work*.
29. Cindy Thomas, Nina Mulia, and Jon Liebman, "HIV Seropositivity among Injection Drug Users Recruited from Street Settings in North Philadelphia," Philadelphia Health Management Company, 1992.
30. Adele Weiner, "Understanding the Social Needs of Streetwalking Prostitutes," Social Work 4 (1996): 97–105.
31. Fullilove, Lowen, and Fullilove, "Crack Hos and Skeezers."
32. Weiner, "Understanding Social Needs."
33. Shedlin, "An Ethnographic Approach."
34. John Gwaltney, *Drylongso*, New York: Random House, 1980; Charles Valentine, *Culture and Poverty*, Chicago: University of Chicago Press, 1980; Carol B. Stack, *All Our Kin*, New York: Harper & Row, 1974.
35. Weiner, "Understanding Social Needs."

CALL GIRLS AND STREET PROSTITUTES: SELLING SEX AND INTIMACY

Janet Lever and Deanne Dolnick

The old fascination with prostitutes as purveyors of "sex without responsi-bility"[1] neglects the reality that some prostitutes are also purveyors of intimacy without responsibility. The most recent explorations of sex work recognize the demand for the latter, which has been marketed as "the girlfriend experience" (GFE). Ads for escorts in print media and online now routinely feature offers of GFE, and it has become a standard feature on the "menus" of brothels worldwide. For example, one Internet ad offers "a true girlfriend experience without the headache," and another reads, "It's less of a business transaction and more like a date with the woman of your dreams!"[2] Recent research highlights the emotional nourishment that is provided in the GFE.[3] A closer look at the actual content of prostitute–client interactions should yield a broader understanding of prostitutes' occupational require-ments, as well as highlight some clients' motives that are rarely recognized.

Arlie Hochschild defined "emotional labor" as "the management of feeling to create a publicly observable facial and bodily display."[4] Although Hochschild doesn't address sex work, we can say that when sex workers display or feign sexual arousal or sexual pleasure for their clients' gratification, they are engaging in emotional labor.

The prostitute, by definition, sells sexual services. Intimacy—a close, affectionate, or loving personal relationship with another person—is not necessarily offered by the prostitute. The hypothesis we test here is that clients expect and receive more emotional services in the form of intimacy from call girls (a term we use to refer to both call girls and escorts) than from street prostitutes.[5] The basis for this hypothesis rests on the higher cost of call girls' services, which restricts their clientele to fairly affluent men. Because the men seeing call girls can pay more, they get more time, as well as settings more conducive to extended displays of intimacy, such as caressing, kissing, conversation, and companionship.

There are, of course, other occupations where opportunities for personal disclosure or intimate touch are part of what the patron pays for, at least implicitly. Scholars refer to the receipt of these services as the commercialization of intimacy, citing the clear-cut cases of the psychotherapist and therapeutic masseuse.[6] More broadly, we can think of feigned or real expressions of caring and interest as part of the "emotional labor" expected of those in the "listening occupations," such as barber, hairstylist, and manicurist, as well as the fabled bartender who lends an ear while he or she pours a drink. A variable among these occupations is the degree to which a client may assume that the service provider is genuinely concerned about the client or the intimate revelations the client has unilaterally offered. Among the occupations mentioned, the psychotherapist is assumed to care the most, the barber, bartender, and nonsexual masseuse are expected to care the least, and the call girl's caring probably lies in the middle ground.

Perhaps what many call girls and escorts are really selling is the *illusion* of intimacy. Hochschild states that, "Once an illusion is clearly defined as an illusion, it becomes a lie."[7] But part of the emotional labor performed by the call girl is to keep the illusion alive; she defines her behavior as a playful "fantasy" rather than an illusion. As the buyer of fantasy, the client is absolved from any responsibility to reciprocate displays of intimacy to the call girl, although some clients do share their feelings and personal aspects of their lives. The client understands that being intimate is part of the call girl's work and that he is not her only client. Both client and call girl *agree to pretend* that her caring and sexual attraction for him are real. Of course, in at least some cases, the caring and attraction are genuine and mutual between the two parties.[8]

Just as there are prostitutes who sell sexual but not emotional services, there are others who sell both sexual *and* emotional services. Here we address the question of how street prostitutes and call girls compare in the sale of sexual services, emotional services, or both. The major contribution of our chapter is the inclusion of call girls, who have rarely been studied by researchers, and the comparative examination of call girls and street prostitutes, as few studies systematically compare two or more types of sex worker.

RESEARCH METHODS

The analysis presented here draws on data and personal contacts from the Los Angeles Women's Health Risk Study, which was conducted by the RAND Corporation in 1990–1991. The authors were staff members on the project. The study had three goals: first, to estimate the size and demographic composition of the female prostitute population in a large metropolis, namely Los Angeles County; second, to collect self-reported data on sex and drug-taking behaviors that put one at risk of AIDS and other sexually transmitted diseases (STDs); and third, to collect blood samples from the prostitutes to test for the presence of antibodies to HIV, syphilis, and hepatitis B. Understanding the emotional labor of female commercial sex workers was not one of the study's goals, but the data can be used to address this issue.

Two subpopulations of female prostitutes interested the researchers. First and foremost, we targeted the numerous and visible prostitutes on the streets. Second, we targeted the various groups that make up the less accessible subpopulation of off-street prostitutes. Unlike other studies of female prostitute populations that are based on convenience samples, the RAND study utilized an "area/day/shift" design to draw a probability sample of 998 street prostitutes. Los Angeles was divided into 79 geographical areas where there was a probability of prostitution taking place, and these areas were randomly sampled; interviews also took place during a random selection of days and times.[9] Women were eligible to participate if they said they had traded sex for money, drugs, or something of value in the last year. The response rate for the street prostitute sample is 61% (assuming all women who refused screening or denied eligibility were simply refusing to participate) or 89% (if all such women were, in fact, ineligible).

Unlike the street prostitution sample, it proved impossible to randomly sample from the hidden and complex off-street prostitute population,[10] but we were able to interview 83 call girls. These women were recruited in three ways: we called their numbers advertised in sex tabloids or phone directories (N = 30); they responded to our ads, fliers, and mass-media campaign (N = 26); or we got their names and numbers through referrals from informants or other women whom we had previously interviewed (N = 27).

Response rates varied by mode of recruitment: the response rate of the women we contacted through their ads ranged from 12%, assuming those who denied eligibility were simply refusing to participate, to 17%, if all such women were in fact ineligible. Although we don't know how many eligible women saw our ads and fliers or became aware of our study via radio and newspaper coverage, we interviewed 26 of the 53 women who called us and claimed eligibility. When personally referred to us by others, women were very cooperative, and we interviewed 27 of the 30 women who came to us via this snowball technique. The authors interviewed nearly half of the call girls and the remainder were interviewed by two other interviewers. A few of the interviews took place over the telephone, but most were conducted in person at a RAND office or were done at a location chosen by the respondent, usually her home.

There were notable demographic differences between the call girl and street samples. Nearly 70% of the street sample was African-American, whereas nearly 80% of the off-street sample was white. The average educational level was 11.6 years in the street sample, a little less than required for a high school diploma, and 13.5 years, or some college, in the off-street sample. Median age, by contrast, was the same, between 29 and 30 years old in both samples.

Women in both the street and off-street samples were paid $25 in cash to participate in a 45-minute interview. One section of the instrument included questions about sexual activities with *all* clients within the previous week, and another section focused exclusively on the sex worker's *last client*, including a sociodemographic description of him, details about the time and place of the interaction as well as what was done, whether there was any prior relationship with him, whether she or he drank alcohol or used drugs during time together, whether a condom was used, and what was given in exchange for the woman's time and services.

None of the items in the lengthy survey was designed to operationalize the concept of emotional labor. In effect, what follows is a secondary analysis of a dataset, much as Marks used items from the General Social Survey to test his idea that Americans find some intimacy—defined as friendship, emotional support, or companionship—with coworkers in the workplace.[11] In the L.A. Women's Health Risk Study, the detailed information that respondents provided about their interaction with the last client lends itself to a univariate comparison of street prostitutes' versus call girls' services that can be taken as proxies for intimacy.

How long and how often the client and prostitute have been seeing each other suggests their levels of familiarity and comfort; what type of setting was used also suggests level of comfort and sharing of personal environment; the amount of time spent together and whether alcohol or drugs were shared are both measures of companionship provided; whether conversation occurred implies at least the opportunity for personal disclosure and detailed knowledge of the other; whether or not nonsexual massage, caressing, kissing, and hugging occurred tells us about affectionate or nongenital touching; and whether the man touched or performed oral sex on the woman's genitals indicates whether there was the type of sexual reciprocity that characterizes most noncommercial sexual relationships.

Although we rely most heavily on the quantitative data described earlier, we also draw on qualitative data in our analysis. First, because we knew so much less about the modus operandi of call girls, we instructed the interviewers to make marginal notations of any commentary offered by the respondents that elaborated on their answers to survey questions; usable marginal notes were available from 75 of the 83 respondents. Second, in the last stages of drafting our results, we found ourselves wanting even more detail and recruited a clique of four call girls to keep a 1-week diary in which they recorded how much time they spent with each client, what was discussed prior to and after any sexual activity, and whether the woman engaged in any "acting" or emotion work to feign intimacy or whether any real intimacy had occurred. We also draw on informal talks about this subject with five male clients and two call girl informants we have known for years.

FINDINGS

The reader should keep in mind that characteristics of the client and details of his transaction with the prostitute are based on her perception and unilateral report. Further, the reliance on data about the "last client" may limit generalization to all clients, although we do not know whether that is so or how much it distorted the data.

Table 8.1 presents a demographic summary of the last client of the street prostitutes and the call girls. Racial differences are striking: Nearly all (more than eight in 10) of the call girls' clients are white, and the second largest racial group is Asian, whereas the streets host a more diverse array of clients. The majority of call girls believed their last client was from the upper income brackets, whereas the majority of street prostitutes believed their client was middle class. These class and race differences were predictable insofar as not all men can afford the higher fees for a call girl's services; the median amount paid by the last client of the call girls was $200, compared to $30 spent on the street (the fees are likely higher today than at the time of the study).

The demographic variable most related to the need for companionship as well as sexual services is marital status. In their pioneering 1948 study of the male sexual behavior, Alfred Kinsey and associates found that single men (especially those who were divorced and in their thirties) were more likely than married men to have had extensive experience with prostitutes. Just as it is

TABLE 8.1 CLIENT CHARACTERISTICS

	STREET CLIENTS (N = 998) (%)	CALL GIRL CLIENTS (N = 83) (%)
PERCEIVED RACE/ETHNICITY		
White	34	82
African-American	40	1
Hispanic or Latino	23	5
Asian	2	7
Other	1	5
ESTIMATED AGE		
Age 20 or less	1	1
Age 21–35	35	32
Age 36–40	26	26
Age 41–50	27	21
Age 51–65	10	16
Over 65	1	4
Could not tell	0	0
ESTIMATED INCOME		
Upper	26	65
Middle	50	27
Lower	12	4
Don't know	12	5
PERCEIVED MARITAL STATUS		
Married	44	36
Not married	32	59
Don't know	25	5

Note: Totals may not equal 100% due to rounding.

presumed that most wives are sexual partners, it is presumed that most also provide companionship.

Of course, some single men are dating or living with someone, and some married men have an equal or greater need for companionship and intimacy, but on average, we can assume that single men's relationship needs are greater than married men's. The fact that a larger percentage of call girls (95%) than street prostitutes (75%) believed they knew their last client's marital status can be taken as another indicator of greater familiarity, although the majority of all sex workers felt they knew their client's marital status. Many married men seek services from call girls and street prostitutes—at least 36% of the call girls' last clients were married, and 43% of street prostitutes' were. But a much higher percentage of call girls' clients were reported to be single—59%, compared with 32% for street prostitutes.

Some men spoke of time with a call girl as superior to the dating scene. They explained that an encounter with a call girl guarantees sex for the equivalent of the price for a nice dinner for two on a regular date in which sex may or may not follow the man's outlay of cash. One attractive, unmarried young chemistry Ph.D. working in industry, when asked why he does not date at all, replied, "I am married to my company." One call girl made the generalization that her single clients like "to party" while her married clients are more awkward and more inhibited by guilt.

Table 8.2 shows the sex worker's relationship to her last client. Some people may be surprised to see that street prostitutes have their share of regular clients (more than one-quarter of last clients), but the call girl is far more likely to set up an ongoing relationship with a man (just under half were men they had "seen" enough to consider "regulars"). Note, however, that call girls had sexual relations for the first time with 40% of their last clients. If indeed emotional services are more expected of the call girl, then she may be under more pressure than her street counterparts to create a comfortable feeling with total strangers a good portion of her working time.

TABLE 8.2 RELATIONSHIP WITH LAST CLIENT

	STREET CLIENTS (N = 998) (%)	CALL GIRL CLIENTS (N = 83) (%)
New client	59	40
Previous client	13	11
Regular client	28	49
First saw previous or regular client		
Last week	4	2
Last month	15	4
Within last year	38	45
Over year ago	43	45
Last saw previous or regular client		
Last week	63	26
Last month	25	36
Within last year	9	34
Over year ago	3	4

In terms of length of relationship with "regulars," there is less difference than expected. Among the men described as previous or regular clients, 49% of the call girls' clients have seen them for longer than a year, compared to 43% of the street prostitutes' clients. In fact, the longest relationship was reported by the street prostitute who claimed she met one "regular" 30 years ago, whereas the longest relationships described by call girls were 10 years in duration. For those relationships that had lasted longer than 1 year, the mean length was 3.8 years for street prostitutes' clients and 4.5 years for clients of call girls. Perhaps because the cost of the interaction is less prohibitive, a majority of regular clients saw street prostitutes as recently as last week, a frequency that only one-quarter of clients of call girls could match.

Table 8.3 shows a dramatic difference in setting where workers and clients meet, or more precisely where workers encountered their last client. While the street prostitutes' initial contact with the customer began on the street, most of their sexual interactions occurred in cars or hotel rooms. Virtually none of the call girls reported "car dates," in contrast to roughly one-third of the street prostitutes. Contrary to the stereotype of a call girl arriving at an out-of-towner's hotel room, only one in six call girls saw her last client in a hotel; by contrast, more than one-third of the street prostitutes saw the last client in the client's hotel room. Nearly two-thirds of call girls' last interactions took place in the privacy and familiarity of either her home or the client's. Surrounded by personal artifacts, the setting is likely to be pleasant and clean, perhaps even luxurious. Equally important as the lack of impersonality in the setting is the fact that sex on regular dates typically occurs in someone's home, so the setting for intimacy with a call girl is often more like that of noncommercial intimate interaction than a commercial one. By contrast, hardly any street prostitutes (2%) saw their last customer in the workers' home.

Table 8.3 also shows a dramatic difference in the amount of time spent with the client. Although close to one-quarter of the call girls spent less than a full hour with their last client, compared to more than half of street prostitutes, only one in 17 call girls spent less than 15 minutes, compared to one in three street prostitutes. One in five call girls had spent 5 or more hours with the last client, much as one might on a regular date. One in 10 street prostitutes spent that much time with her last client.

According to information offered by some of the call girls we interviewed, long "dates" sometimes include having lunch or dinner together, much like a regular date. Our informants say that some women charge for each hour of their time—even for nonsexual activities—whereas others cultivate the fantasy of wanting to be in a man's company by not charging for time spent

TABLE 8.3 CHARACTERISTICS OF LAST TRANSACTION

	STREET CLIENTS (N = 998) (%)	CALL GIRL CLIENTS (N = 83) (%)
Where interaction with client last took place		
Your home	2	30
His home	10	33
His hotel/motel	38	16
Your hotel/motel	9	0
Car or limo	32	2
Other	8	19
How much time spent with last client		
Less than hour	56	23
(less than 15 minutes)	(32)	(6)
One hour	19	38
2–4 hours	16	19
5 or more hours	10	20

Note: Totals may not equal 100% due to rounding.

dining. Some regular clients even get "sleepover" privileges, which accounts for some call girls' reports of long hours for their last interaction.

As stated, the median cost of an encounter with a call girl was $200, nearly seven times the median of $30 spent on a street prostitute. In a society that believes "you get what you pay for," it can be assumed that clients who spend more expect to get more time and services. Answers to our survey item about whether the last client gave the woman anything else besides money or drugs, either as a gift or as part of her payment, 21% of the call girls got something material, but so did 14% of the street prostitutes. The gifts most frequently reported by call girls were jewelry (one let her clients know her preference for antique jewelry), perfume, flowers, and champagne—the type of gifts a man might give to a girlfriend or wife. When street prostitutes reported receipt of something material, it was most often food, cigarettes, or alcohol, but a few reported receiving jewelry or flowers.

Table 8.4 shows that the use of drugs and alcohol often precedes or occurs during the interaction with a client. Sharing the same substance while together is an activity typical of real dates. "Partying together"—at least in terms of sharing alcohol—is more frequent with call girls than street prostitutes, yet it characterizes only a minority of interactions. Also, many more street prostitutes than call girls used drugs or alcohol prior to seeing their last client.

TABLE 8.4 DRUG AND ALCOHOL CONSUMPTION WITH LAST CLIENT

	STREET CLIENTS (N = 998) (%)	CALL GIRL CLIENTS (N = 83) (%)
Woman consumed substance before interaction		
Alcohol	39	21
Drugs	51	6
Alcohol/drugs shared with last client		
Alcohol	7	18
Drugs	8	4
Both	5	4

Table 8.5 highlights responses from a list of 20 possible activities engaged in with the last client. Respondents were shown a card listing sex acts and asked to indicate *all acts* they did during their last encounter. Table 8.5 shows the most common sexual activities performed, whether unusual sexual requests were granted, and the prevalence of sex acts performed on the prostitute's genitals, as well as nonsexual activities that arguably sustain a feeling of intimacy.

The most common sexual activities are also considered among the most intimate sexual activities—vaginal intercourse and fellatio (oral sex performed on the male). These acts were the ones most common for both call girls and street prostitutes. Vaginal intercourse was more common with call girls, but call girls also supplied more manual stimulation of the client's genitals—possibly instead of oral or vaginal sex, but more likely in combination with other acts. About two-thirds of both the call girls (64%) and the street workers (68%) reported that they had used a condom with their last client. Greater differences in this aspect of sexual risk taking emerge when we examine activities with *all* clients in the week prior to our interview; 18% of call girls, compared to 39% of street workers, reported vaginal sex without a condom in the previous week.

The incidence of anal intercourse, domination fantasies (B&D, i.e., "bondage and discipline"), and group sex is very low in both samples, although more frequent with call girls. The low incidence of these acts (see Table 8.5) may dispel one myth about why men use prostitutes. Kinsey suggested that men go to prostitutes to obtain types of sexual activity that they cannot get elsewhere, and his examples included oral sex, sadomasochism, fetishes, and group sex.[12] Letting 732 male clients explain their own motives, Winick found that when men said a prostitute "gives me something different" or "what I want," they were mostly referring to a variation in body type from

TABLE 8.5 ACTS ENGAGED IN WITH LAST CLIENT

	STREET CLIENTS (N = 998) (%)	CALL GIRL CLIENTS (N = 83) (%)
Give him "hand job"	7	26
Give him oral sex	57	45
Vaginal intercourse	51	66
Anal intercourse	0	1
Domination/B&D	0	8
Two or more sex workers together	1	7
Touch woman's genitals	4	26
Give her oral sex	4	17
Nonsexual massage	2	30
Conversation	5	51
Caress, kiss, and hug	3	42

their regular sex partner rather than a variation in sex acts.[13] More recent surveys of clients confirm that most clients seek vaginal and oral sex, rather than unusual variants of sex act.[14] Commenting on what men ask for (not necessarily what they get), some women characterized requests as "normal" or "straight" sex.

Clients who purchase sex acts may or may not engage in acts intended to arouse the female partner. While some men's own arousal is heightened by stimulating a woman's genitals orally or manually, another motive for these acts may be to give pleasure and not just receive it. When we look at sex acts performed on the female partner, the differences between samples are strong. Over one-quarter (26%) of call girls had their genitals touched by the client, compared to only 4% of street workers, while customers performed oral sex on 17% of the call girls but only 4% of the street prostitutes.

The comparison to the frequency of cunnilingus in noncommercial encounters is interesting. In the recent national probability study reported by University of Chicago researchers, 17% of the married women surveyed reported that they had received oral sex during their last sexual event with their husbands.[15] In other words, this sample of call girls was just as likely as to receive oral sex from clients as wives were from their husbands.

When we focus on the intimacies of nonsexual massage, conversation, caressing, kissing, and hugging, the differences are even stronger. Nonsexual massage performed on the client is done to relax and arouse him, and this sensual touch adds to the sense of intimacy of the encounter; 30% of call girls' clients received this personal service compared to only 2% of street workers' clients (the third who were in a car were obviously limited, but two-thirds had the same spatial opportunities of most call girls). A few call girls explained how the massage is as much for their sake as the man's because it fills time so the client thinks he got a lot for the fee. One call girl said: "If we jumped right into sex and he came in 5 minutes, he'd want to come again for his $200."

For most women intimacy includes talk—small talk and deep talk—and research on gender and marital relationships indicates that many men resist this aspect of intimacy.[16] But some men want more talk, too. A poll found that 16% of married men said they were dissatisfied with "the amount of time [they and their] partner spend talking openly about things that are on your mind."[17]

Whether clients get and give verbal intimacy in the form of self-disclosure or listening to the other's disclosures in their noncommercial relationships is not known, but talk *is* included in what most men get in the situation of limited reciprocity with a call girl. Half of the last clients got conversation as part of their interaction with a call girl, compared to only one in 20 on the street. The men's work was the most common topic discussed with the four women who kept post-session diaries, and they claimed it was discussed in great detail. In contrast, a primary complaint of the divorced wives studied by Riessman was that their ex-husbands had refused to relate what goes on in their work world.[18] The diaries revealed that the clients also discussed their children and politics; one talked about his wife and bad marriage. One informant believed she created a "safe space" for her clients, many of whom alleviated their insecurities by asking about the adequacy of their penis size or asking advice about their sexual approach with women, presuming a professional has expertise on these subjects.

Several call girls described having at least one client who wanted only to talk, or to be held. One woman told of holding a client who cried for his entire hour. Another described a new client who cried during his screening interview when he revealed that his wife had left him a year before. Several call girls recognized a parallel between their work and the psychotherapist's; in fact, seeing oneself as a type of therapist is one source of pride for some call girls.

Although most call girls say that they do not like to kiss clients, and that they keep "necking" to a minimum with other diversionary tactics, 42% reported that they did "kiss, caress, and hug" their last client, compared to only 3% of street prostitutes. The literature on street prostitutes consistently shows that they avoid kissing precisely because they perceive it as "too intimate" or as a feature of romance. Kissing is more difficult for call girls to avoid. As one call girl explained: "The street women are just selling sex, they don't have to play the games we do. We make believe we want to be with the guy, and if you want to be with him, then you'd want to kiss him, right? Guys expect a lot for a lot of money." Another call girl stated, "The majority of my clients want to hold you really tight—I don't know if that's a sexual or emotional need—they just want to feel close to someone."

CONCLUSION

We hypothesized that call girls provide greater emotional services to clients than street prostitutes. In particular, clients expect call girls to create at least the illusion of intimacy in the exchange. The data culled from the L.A. Women's Health Study show that call girls are more likely to establish ongoing relationships with regular clients (regardless of their marital status), and some of these relationships last for years. Interactions with call girls are far more likely to take place in settings that are personal, and these settings seem conducive to conversation and affectionate touching as well as sex acts. Call girls are more likely to have their own genitals touched or to receive oral sex, akin to normal intimate relationships, although most clients are more focused on receiving than reciprocating sexual pleasure.

It seems that call girls in effect are selling increments of their time, more typically measured in hours than in minutes, while street prostitutes offer only as much time as needed for the particular sex act agreed on. Call girls' higher prices could be justified by access to cleaner, safer, more comfortable, and more private environments as well as more attractive sex partners, but, in addition to all those advantages, male clients have come to expect more affection and intimacy as well as sex. Moreover, because there is more time, greater familiarity can develop and there is opportunity to do more "ordinary" things together, such as sharing a meal or drinks.

While call girls appear to offer more intimacy than street prostitutes, the data suggest a surprising amount of time and personal service may be offered by the latter to some clients, especially to their regulars or those they see in motels rather than cars. The qualitative data we collected are limited, and we know more about call girls than street prostitutes because we interviewed them in off-street environments that allowed more time and comfort to elaborate answers. Had our interviewers on the street been instructed to collect qualitative data, we might have found fewer differences between the two groups on some of the questions.

Use of diaries was experimental, and we cannot offer detailed analysis from more than a few call girls; however, they yielded enough interesting data to support their use more extensively by future researchers. In particular, diary data and our informal talks with informants are better suited than our survey data to answer this important question: Is the intimacy offered an illusion, or does real intimacy develop over time?

Our limited qualitative data suggest that not all the call girls are being "phony" or acting all the time. Most women we asked said that they really like some of their clients, especially those they have seen for years. As one informant said: "You cannot know someone that long without it being a real relationship." Some claimed to be genuinely interested in being updated on a regular client's life. As in other commercial relationships, the likelihood of intimate exchange typically increases over time and is one reward of customer loyalty.

Call girls should be added to the list of "listening occupations." Several women described what is known as the "stranger on a train" phenomenon where the talker can be more openly revealing because the listener is not part of one's social network. Or perhaps it is the lack of reciprocity and controlled environment that encourage some clients to reveal more to the call girl than they do to friends and family. Encounters with sex workers may offer the "instant intimacy" that some men say they find in bars.

A woman's reaction to sexual stimulation can sometimes be real. Although we know this intimate detail only from one of the women who kept a diary, she noted that she orgasms with some of her clients. But she noted that when busy (it is not uncommon to see three men over a short period of time when business is good), she fakes orgasms, too—a clear-cut example of emotional labor. Another woman's diary entries, also documenting emotional labor, describes how the "affect" during sex may be in large part for show or ego boosting. Her diary included notations like "I did the usual moaning thing" or "I made typical 'into-it' sounds and 'that feels good' remarks."

Our qualitative material includes one example of a call girl's self-conscious preparation for emotional labor. One informant described "psyching herself up" from the moment she takes off her blue jeans to take a shower, put on her makeup, and get into her sexy miniskirt and halter top (if she's going to client's place) or her lingerie (if he's coming to her place)—both costumes for her fantasy performance. Sex workers have to conjure up the "feminine" demeanor of "niceness" and "sexiness" even when they are not in the mood.

The blanket notion that these men owe no reciprocity because a woman's services are paid for is also called into question by one informant—a well-educated, upper-middle-class 29 year old—who continually calls her lawyer, doctor, and accountant clients for help with her personal problems. And some clients desire a real and reciprocal relationship with a call girl. While many enjoy the lack of responsibility in a commercial relationship, other men either have not been able to find intimacy elsewhere and fall in love with a call girl, or they indulge real-life "Pretty Woman" rescue fantasies and try to save a woman from "the life."

Is emotional labor involved when the prostitute is male? Applying Nieva and Gutek's notion of "sex role spillover,"[19] one would expect that the emotional requirements of the job are greater for women than for men doing the same personal service work because "stroking"—supplying socioemotional support—is a gender-based role. West reports minimal expectations for emotion work by male prostitutes in London, who mostly have an aloof attitude, or by their clients, most of whom are seeking nothing more than sexual release.[20] However, some of the young men—especially those who work for higher wages through advertised services—view clients as friends and see conversation as part of what they do with clients. Just as some call girls in our study observed, one male escort noted that "sometimes it's like giving therapy."[21] But in general, emotional requirements are minimal for men. Caukins and Coombs suggest that clients of male prostitutes tend to seek out masculine types who cater to the client's fantasy of having sex with a super-masculine male.[22]

Understanding the personal repercussions of the emotional component of the job of prostitute is beyond the scope of this chapter. Wharton and Erickson describe how women with emotionally demanding jobs suffer negative psychological consequences, including "burnout" and detachment, that can diminish their ability to be emotionally available in their personal relationships.[23] When thinking of "burnout" in doing sex work, researchers are far more likely to focus on physical fatigue, repercussions on self-esteem, or loss of attractiveness. It is possible that more call girls than street workers experience burnout and alienation that involves the toll of coping with the emotional demands of clients. Not only do our data suggest call girls perform more "emotional labor" but that they also perform it less anesthetized by drugs and alcohol, compared to street workers. More research on the emotional dimensions of sex work would heighten the appreciation of the many interpersonal skills required of the women in this occupation, while yielding a more multidimensional portrait of the male client population.

NOTES

This chapter is based on the Los Angeles Women's Health Risk Study, a RAND project supported by Grant R01-HD24897 from the National Institute of Child Health and Human Development. The authors are grateful to David Kanouse and Sandra Berry, the principal investigators, for sharing their data, and to Sally Carson for technical assistance.

1. Alfred C. Kinsey, Wendell B. Pomeroy, and Clyde E. Martin, *Sexual Behavior in the Human Male*. Philadelphia: W.B. Saunders, 1948; Charles Winick, "Prostitutes' Clients' Perceptions of the Prostitutes and of Themselves," *International Journal of Social Psychiatry* 8 (1962): 289–297.

2. Ads quoted in Elizabeth Bernstein, *Temporarily Yours: Intimacy, Authenticity, and the Commerce of Sex*, Chicago: University of Chicago Press, 2007, pp. 128–129. See also Viviana Zelizer, *The Purchase of Intimacy*, Princeton: Princeton University Press, 2005.

3. Teela Sanders, *Paying for Pleasure: Men Who Buy Sex*, Portland: Willan, 2008.

4. Arlie Hochschild, *The Managed Heart: Commercialization of Human Feeling*, Berkeley: University of California Press, 1983, p. 7.

5. An "escort" is anyone who can be reached by calling escort or outcall services that advertise in phone directories, newspapers, magazines, or on the Internet. The "call girl" can only be reached via a referral system, most typically through a madam, another call girl, or a call girl's other clients.

6. Zelizer, *Purchase of Intimacy*; Christine Overall, "What's Wrong with Prostitution? Evaluating Sex Work," *Signs* 17 (1992): 705–724.

7. Hochschild, *The Managed Heart*, p. 46.

8. Bernstein, *Temporarily Yours*.

9. For sampling methodology, see David Kanouse, Sandra Berry, Naihua Duan, Janet Lever, Sally Carson, Judith Perlman, and Barbara Levitan, "Drawing a Probability Sample of Female Street Prostitutes in Los Angeles County," *Journal of Sex Research* 36 (1999): 45–51.

10. Janet Lever and David E. Kanouse, "Using Qualitative Methods to Study the Hidden World of Offstreet Prostitution in Los Angeles County," in James Elias, ed., *Prostitution*, Amherst, NY: Prometheus, 1998.

11. Stephen R. Marks, "Intimacy in the Public Realm: The Case of Coworkers," *Social Forces* 72 (1994): 843–858.

12. Kinsey, et al., *Sexual Behavior*.

13. Winick, "Prostitutes' Clients' Perceptions."

14. See Martin Monto's chapter in this book, and Matthew Freund, Nancy Lee, and Terri Leonard, "Sexual Behavior of Clients with Street Prostitutes in Camden, N.J.," *Journal of Sex Research* 28 (1991): 579–591.

15. Edward Laumann, John Gagnon, Robert Michael, and Stuart Michaels, *The Social Organization of Sexuality: Sexual Practices in the United States*, Chicago: University of Chicago Press, 1994, p. 98.

16. Lillian Rubin, *Intimate Strangers: Men and Women Together*, New York: Harper Perennial Library, 1984; Catherine Riessman, *Divorce Talk: Women and Men Make Sense of Personal Relationships*, New Brunswick, NJ: Rutgers Press, 1990.

17. *Washington Post*/Kaiser Family Foundation/Harvard University, Survey of Americans on Gender. Kaiser Family Foundation, Menlo Park, CA, March 1998.

18. Riessman, *Divorce Talk*.

19. Veronica Nieva and Barbara Gutek, *Women and Work: A Psychological Perspective*, New York: Praeger, 1981.

20. Donald J. West, *Male Prostitution*, New York: Harrington Park Press, 1993.

21. West, *Male Prostitution*, p. 247.

22. S. E. Caukins and M. A. Coombs, "The Psychodynamics of Male Prostitution," *American Journal of Psychotherapy* 30 (1976): 441–451.

23. Amy Wharton and Rebecca Erickson, "Managing Emotions on the Job at Home: The Consequences of Multiple Emotional Roles," *Academy of Management Review* 18 (1993): 457–486.

MALE AND FEMALE ESCORTS: A COMPARATIVE ANALYSIS

Juline Koken, David S. Bimbi, and Jeffrey T. Parsons

Research on sex work has often reflected society's perceptions rather than those of sex workers themselves.[1] Street-based female prostitutes continue to dominate the discourse on sex work,[2] neglecting the diversity of venues and differences among the workers themselves.[3] Moreover, there are very few studies that systematically compare male and female workers who work in the same sector of the sex industry. This chapter explores the experiences of men and women who work as escorts, a form of indoor sex work that is done independently or with the aid of an agency providing client referrals. We draw from the findings of our research on independent male and female escorts, as well as other studies.

Escorts and escort agencies have been described in the literature as far back as the mid-20th century.[4] In an effort to avoid legal prosecution, escorts often frame their services as providing dinner or travel companions or dates for corporate functions. While sex is often implied or assumed to be included in the services on offer, escorts and escort agencies typically avoid any explicit mention of sex for sale. Escort agencies, which serve as referral services connecting escorts with clients, typically operate in large cities (with some exceptions).[5] Escort agencies seek to lend an aura of sophistication and glamour to their services, and escorts are often portrayed as providers of "high-class" companionship.

Many women and men move from escort agencies into freelance independent prostitution, reaching clients directly through advertisements in print media, phone chat lines, or the Internet.[6] Some enter sex work independently, bypassing third parties such as madams, agencies, or pimps.[7] Independent escorts range from those casually involved in sex work on an as-needed basis (for example, placing an ad on a message board when rent is due) to career-oriented escorts who maintain their own websites. Many adult film performers supplement their income through escorting, and may have fan clubs and constitute a niche market within the industry.

The business of escorting requires skill in marketing, building, and maintaining relationships with clients, as well as responding to the needs and variations of the market. While some previous studies have described a period of training and apprenticeship within sex work—typically brothel-based sex work—independent and agency-based escorts often learn the ropes through trial and error. Occasionally, other escorts or friends in the industry offer guidance to newcomers in the business.

The art of screening potential clients appears to vary widely by agencies and individuals. In our own research, we have learned that escort agencies typically collect much less information about clients than independent escorts do. But regardless of whether they are affiliated with an agency or work independently, escorts must possess the skills necessary to recognize clients who are potentially dangerous or law enforcement agents as well as how to negotiate their sexual boundaries in sessions with clients.

The process of acquiring the skills to maintain their safety and well-being is often complicated by escorts' efforts to shield themselves from the stigma of "prostitute." The need to maintain secrecy places a heavy burden on the escort and also limits their ability to network with others in the business who may offer support and guidance.

The advent of the Internet has led to a significant shift in the escorting industry. Prospective escorts may easily learn about advertising and client expectations by reading escorts' online profiles and reviewing sites where clients discuss their experiences. The anonymity of the Internet also provides a forum where escorts may share information about the business through message boards, websites, and private listservs. The increasing popularity of Internet sites where escorts and agencies post profiles has increased the ease of entry; escorts no longer need to depend on third parties to provide introductions to potential clients.

RESEARCH METHODS

The data presented here on Internet based, independent male and female escorts is comprised of two samples.[8] The first study ("The Classified Project") was conducted in the fall of 2000 and aimed to explore the experiences of gay and bisexual male escorts who advertise on the Internet. The topics explored in this project included entry into sex work, sexual negotiation with clients and other partners and recommendations for programming and services aimed at male sex workers.

To identify potential participants for the Classified Project, email addresses of potential participants were identified through advertisements in local gay publications, user profiles on a popular online service, several escort websites and an escort review website. A letter describing the project was sent to these email addresses, and men were invited to call to be screened for the study. All men were assured of anonymity and confidentiality. Snowball sampling also occurred when a description of the project was posted on private escort listservs by men who had completed the study. After subtracting the number of emails that bounced back from invalid addresses, as many as 370 men may have received and read the invitation to participate. Criteria for enrollment in the project were: (1) at least 18 years of age, (2) use the Internet to find clients in the last 3 months, and (3) identification as gay or bisexual. A total of 60 phone calls were received and 46 men completed the study.[9]

Men were not asked to identify themselves and no contact information was collected. After informed consent was verbally reviewed with the participant, an in-depth interview was conducted and tape-recorded in a private setting, followed by a brief survey that the participant completed alone. Each participant received $75 for his participation.

The second study (the "Lady Classified Project") was a partial replication of the Classified Project, and aimed to explore the experiences of independent female escorts who advertise on the Internet.[10] The purpose of this study was to investigate women's coping strategies for managing prostitution-related stigma as well as the emotional demands of the work. Eligibility criteria were: aged 18 and over, currently advertising on the Internet as an escort, and primarily working independently (women who earned most of their income through escort agencies, brothels, or other third-party affiliations were not eligible).

Between September 2007 and February 2008, personalized emails were sent to women using the working names and email addresses they posted on their Internet advertisements. Thirty women agreed to participate in the research. Two interviews were conducted by telephone, seven in a private office at a university, nine at the participant's homes or hotel rooms, and twelve at the research center directed by the third author. After the interview, women completed a short survey assessing demographic characteristics and work-related burnout. All were compensated $100 for participation. No contact or identifying information was collected.

All interviews were audio-taped and transcribed, removing any identifying information from the transcript. The development of a qualitative codebook and subsequent coding of the interview data followed a modified form of team-driven analysis.[11] Team-driven qualitative analysis was ideal for this project, as it expands the potential range of interpretations of data through the addition of others' perspectives, and the inclusion of a sex work community advocate in the coding team enriched the possible range of views on interview themes. The coding team was comprised of the first author and two trained coders, a research assistant and a member of the sex work advocacy community. Following an initial round of structural coding by the team, the first author performed additional rounds of coding, identifying emerging meta-themes and relationships between codes.

Participant Characteristics

The Classified Project

The mean age of the male participants was 39 (SD = 6.27) and ranged from 22 to 47. The sample included 35 white men (70%), seven Latino men (14%), five African-American men (10%), and three Asian/Pacific Islander men (6%). The majority (82%) identified as gay and 18% identified as bisexual. For self-reported HIV status, 80% reported testing HIV negative, 16% reported being HIV positive, and 4% reported never having been tested for HIV. A total of 17 men (34%) reported having a primary male partner or boyfriend. Overall, the men were well educated, with 64% reporting at least a bachelor's degree.

The median income range reported from sources other than sex work was $10,000 to $19,999 with a median income range from sex work of $20,000 to $29,999. The average length of time the men reported working as escorts was 2.7 years (SD = 5.03), with a range from 3 weeks to 25 years. About half the men (N = 23) reported spending at least 12 hours a week escorting or performing escorting-related activities (such as answering phone calls or communicating with potential clients online); 26% spent more than 20 hours a week escorting. The majority of the men (70%) charged $200 an hour, with a range from $75 for "body work" to $250 for "full service."

The Lady Classified Project

The sample roughly reflected the demographic characteristics of women advertising online and working in other indoor sex work venues.[12] The majority of women identified as white (70%), five were African-American or

Caribbean American (17%), three were Asian or South Asian (10%), and one identified as multiracial (white-Asian). Seventy percent of the women were born in the United States. The women ranged in age from 21 to 57, with a mean age of 34. The sample had high educational attainment: 23% were currently enrolled in a college or graduate school, and over one-third had a bachelor's degree or higher. Nearly all (90%) had some college experience.

ESCORT AGENCIES

Escort agencies originated as brothels that sent sex workers out to clients, to call centers that served as the connection between clients and escorts without offering onsite services. The introduction of widespread private telephone use following WWII enabled escort agencies to become viable as venues separate from brothels, and eventually came to dominate the sex-for-sale market.[13] Today, agencies range from a single booker operating with a cellphone to an established office where escorts wait during their shift to be sent to clients. Some agencies even offer temporary housing to escorts and become informal social spaces for escorts to network, discuss clients, and give and receive social support.

Historically, some brothels and agencies have offered workers a period of apprenticeship where men and women new to the sex industry could "learn the ropes." An ethnographic study conducted in the 1970s of the training of "house prostitutes" (novice female brothel workers) describes the importance of transitioning between the "straight" world and "the racket" (the business of prostitution) through a period of intensive training by an experienced madam.[14] This madam taught novice prostitutes sexual techniques, methods of extracting higher fees from clients, and the social norms guiding interaction with other house prostitutes and managing clients. More recently, a study of male and female escorts identified the ways in which becoming a skilled practitioner of safer sex has become an essential component of modern prosti-tutes' professional identity.[15] For men and women who work independently or through escort agencies, learning the normative beliefs and practices of professional prostitutes may be much less formal and acquired on the job through trial and error.[16]

Escort agencies are frequently an entry point for prostitutes who are new to the business. Agencies ease entry into the sex trade by providing a link between the novice escort and an established base of clientele, fielding new clients and screening them, and educating escorts about the "going rate" for time and services offered. In exchange for the services offered the escort by the agency, the escort splits his or her hourly fee with the agency, typically in a 50/50 or 60/40 split. In the Lady Classified Project, many of the women reported entering the sex industry through escort agencies, which they felt would be safer than starting out independently; other women, however, reported being unaware of ways in which escorts might work independently. While some of the men in the Classified Project reported having worked with agencies, more men entered escorting as independents. Our data indicate that many independent escorts are far more intensive in their screening process than agencies (discussed further later).

Agencies typically collect the client's full name (to be verified in person through an ID check) and verify the client's phone number and place of residence or hotel room. A client paying by credit card will have the account verified as well. Agencies frequently also have lists of banned clients, which may be shared between agencies in the interest of keeping escorts safe. Although police most frequently arrest street prostitutes, escorts are also arrested in sting operations where police rent hotel rooms and pose as clients. In addition to the information collected from the client during his initial contact, phone operators at escort agencies must also be skilled in promoting their escorts while subtly screening the client for signs that he may be a police officer, prank caller, or dangerous. Finally, one safety advantage to working with an agency is having someone (typically the phone booker or manager) who knows at all times where the escort is and can potentially intervene if the interaction with the client goes wrong.[17]

In our own research on independent escorts, men and women have described the pros and cons of working for an agency. Some continued to maintain a reduced level of contact with escort agencies in order to supplement the income they gained from seeing clients independently. One woman described it this way:

> I still work for an agency just to supplement, because they have more volume of calls and they're a little more consistent. Of course I get paid less, but it's good to have that fall-back in case I don't have a call for two weeks. I still do that sometimes . . . usually they take a 50/50 split. . . . Sometimes they try to make you work when you don't want to work . . . You don't know who you're going to. They tell you his name, they tell you all the information, but ultimately you don't get to speak to the client before you get to them. So you don't know what they're like. They could be someone who you normally would not have made an appointment with. I've had few bad situations with that. . . . So, I have that on the downside. You have to sort of trust the person on the phone too, so I only work with certain phone girls [booking agents].

Another woman commented on how working with agencies advertising on the Internet led her to independence:

> I went on and off contacting madams or higher-end agencies. I figured maybe she has very high-end clients that are not looking online. But if they're just advertising online, why would I share my money with them? Why not just do it myself?

Some of the men who participated in the Classified Project viewed escort agencies as a useful starting place for entering the business but later transitioned into independent work, often due to dissatisfaction with business and labor practices. One man described his experience:

> I started out . . . at an escort agency. I did that routine for about 2 years, but I found that I was not getting along well with the guys who run the escort agencies. They're mean and you cannot make your own schedule. A lot of times people call at the most inconvenient times. It's always when you can't do it or don't want to do it. . . . But if it's your own ad, you can say no.

Another man objected to how his agency treated clients:

> I had been working with agencies for a year and a half and finally just realized that they were not going to get me as much work as I wanted. . . . I also didn't like certain things about the way they did business. I didn't think they treated the client very nicely. I didn't like the way they clocked it. You call when you get there and they call right when the hour is up. That's not how I want to work with the client. I don't like to clock people. I like it to be fun for them and for me.

Other escorts saw agencies as inherently exploitative and refused to work with them on principle, and described the advantages of being self-employed. One woman stated:

> I've worked with other people, but I've not worked with an agency. . . . I don't want to give somebody half the money I make. And I take much better care of myself than any escort [agency] would, because I've had some really close friends work for escort agencies and they were absolutely miserable.

> *Interviewer* Tell me more about that—how is independent different?

> Everything is in my hands. I pick who I feel I can get along with in person and feel safe with. I screen them myself, and I get to keep all the money. I pick my prices: I lower them when I really need the money or if I like the guy, or I raise

them if I feel like I can get away with it or if the guy has a lot of money . . . and I know he'll pay it. I call the shots all the time.

These narratives reflect the advantages and disadvantages of working with agencies. Agencies may reach a broader client market through advertising than most independents do, and also have a base of repeat clientele who rely on the agency as a resource for a variety of new escorts. Thus many escorts report that agencies are a valuable source of clients, especially when one's own independent business is less busy. At the same time, escorts working with agencies have little control over which clients they are sent to see, potentially leading to uncomfortable situations.

Some agencies provide more than a steady stream of clients. For some escorts, working with an agency may provide access to social support from management and other escorts, as well as mentoring in industry practices. A recent study of a male escort agency in a small American town found that the men employed there utilized the agency for a variety of purposes—as a social space, shelter (some men lived at the agency house), professional training ground, and a place where business was conducted.[18] This agency offered both "incall" (clients could visit the house for sessions with escorts) as well as "outcall" (escorts traveled to meet the clients in their homes or hotels). The manager of this agency not only matched clients and escorts based on client requests but also based on the preferences of individual escorts. Men working for this agency reported that the manager was sensitive to their preferences, a practice that helped keep both escorts and clients happy and maintained a stable business. In fact, the men at this agency frequently viewed the manager and the other escorts as friends in addition to professional colleagues. One man who worked at the agency described it almost as a family environment:

I like the people here. . . . It's like we're all a big brotherhood. It's cool. It's just neat hanging out with them and listening to their experiences.[19]

The physical space provided by the agency became a central location for socializing and accessing social support, a resource many independent escorts report they lack.

The men working at this agency also had the opportunity for some on-the-job training, which resembles in some ways Heyl's description of a female brothel she studied.[20] In the male agency, more experienced escorts mentored novice men, often while out on "double" calls (two escorts for one client).[21] Some of the long-term, regular clients were also utilized as "training clients" by the manager of the escort agency, in that novice male escorts were sent to trusted regulars who would help them learn the ropes—also the practice in Heyl's female brothel.

Many of the men and women who participated in the Classified and Lady Classified projects reported starting out with agencies before transitioning to independent employment. It is possible that as the Internet becomes a more visible and popular venue for advertising, the need for agencies as a link between escorts and clients will decrease.

ADVERTISING

For independent escorts, the art of advertising to attract desirable clients is one of the most essential skills escorts must develop to be successful in their business. Our research on male and female escorts identified a few key strategies used by men and women to maximize their profit in this business. These strategies included the following: presenting one's authentic personality in the advertisement in order to connect with clients they would "click" with on a personal level, marketing specific types of sexual services or fantasy persona, and running a minimal advertisement featuring only basic information. The two ads featured in Figure 9.1 illustrate one type of marketing.

The primary advertising strategy for women and men specializing in more companionate, "girlfriend" or "boyfriend" experiences (GFE or BFE) involves presenting an idealized version of one's actual self. By selling the experience of "bounded authenticity,"[22] an escort works to closely align client expectations with their own personal preferences. These women and men aim to offer sessions that closely resemble a date, one that is pleasurable for both escort and client. One woman described the importance of being "real" this way:

> What I've learned over the years working independently is that the absolute best way to market yourself is to try to find as many like-minded people as you can. You don't try and market yourself to the people that aren't on the same page as you, or have different likes. The more real that you can be, the more you can put of yourself out there as a person, while still maintaining certain boundaries about your personal life. That is going to encourage like-minded people, better chemistry, better repeat clients; then you enjoy your work.

Other escorts endeavored to stand out in their advertisements by stressing their education, intelligence and worldliness. For some escorts, a carefully crafted advertisement not only aims to attract clientele seeking a companionate experience, it also serves to deter clients in search of a more stereotypical "dumb

Figure 9.1 Escort Advertisements. These ads are composites created by the authors.

hooker." One African-American woman related her strategy for subtly correcting clients with racially biased attitudes about women of color:

> I wrote a poem. I wanted to be special. I wanted them to know that they were getting someone intelligent, not a knucklehead. I can't pull off the knucklehead type. I talk too much. And people would know, "listen, you're smart" [laughs]. . . . So I wrote a poem [because] I wanted to be a little bit different than the rest of the ads.

Male escorts who specialized in companionate escorting described similar advertising themes. However, they were far more likely than women to also include information implying their preferred sexual activities and physical assets. These advertisements combined the emphasis on "elite culture" (e.g., describing their education and familiarity with upper-middle-class culture) with a more frankly erotic tone:

> On web pages that I advertise, sometimes they have sections where you can fill in and say like how big is your dick. I also describe myself as a top; I may say

that I am educated, that I lived in Europe for a few years. And my web page is probably one of the most exhaustive web pages for escorts on the Internet today. I advertise my movies. I show pictures from some of the trips that I have been on. What I [am] saying is, "I'm going to spend a great time with you."

These men and women stressed that they were not merely selling sex, they were selling an experience of seemingly genuine affection, mutual attraction, and stimulating companionship.

Other escorts described experimenting with a variety of advertising strategies before settling on one that aimed to maximize their potential client base. Rather than seeking out like-minded clients, these men and women sought to increase their market potential by reaching as many clients as possible. The effort to create an image of "mass appeal" took many forms. One woman described her technique for maintaining client's interest by running multiple advertisements in an effort to keep up with client demand for new faces:

> I buy stock photos online. I look for somebody that looks something like me, and for photos that are not nude or trashy. It might be sensual or show some cleavage, but they're not going to be very explicit. I change ads now and then because they lose popularity once they've been up for a while. Sometimes I have two up at the same time. I have a friend that advertises four or five ads at once, and when she can't go she says that she keeps a commission and I can take the job.

Other escorts attempted to appeal to a variety of client fantasies through careful targeting of photographs and ad text. These men and women assessed market demand for different "types" and then endeavored to embody as many of them as possible. One woman described her ad this way:

> I advertise domination and GFE, so there's both on the website. Just a lot of dildos, strap-ons, and mistress clothes, and then I have sensual bikini ones, lingerie ones, full-clothes on the website . . . . A lot of white men like Asians and I got my boob job so that helps. You use everything as a marketing tool to your best ability.

Men's advertisements also incorporated such fantasy "types" with more explicit references to sexual activity: "[My ad has] been tailored over time. You know what works; what sells; what doesn't. Well, the idea of total top. I'm ex-military. It has a certain cache. Total top. Muscular, masculine sells."

The creativity and entrepreneurial savvy shown in these advertising strategies points to the time, energy, and care that many professional escorts invest in their business.[23] These men and women are seasoned business people, tailoring their approach to reach the maximum number of clients, with less of an emphasis on their own personal preferences.

By contrast, some escorts minimized the effort put into creating an advertisement. For some this strategy appeared to be an effort to distance one's self from escorting, which was viewed as an unpleasant means to an end. These men and women did not create an escort persona, neither did they cater to particular sectors of the client market. One woman described her advertisement this way:

> I guess I'm just a mainstream, general type. I have not created a persona per se. I'm not so into it where I make it—I probably should. I'm a bad business woman as far as that goes because I don't like the business and I kind of do it because I have to. I am kind of trapped. So I don't really take that time to create a persona, to really go all out.

For this woman, feeling "trapped" in sex work left her unmotivated to invest personal resources in her business. A male escort asserted that "men don't read your profile anyway" and kept his advertisement to a more basic format:

> I wrote my profile on AOL, and I just simply state facts about myself, and I have a picture. Tall, blond hair, blue eyes. I just say my rules, which are outcalls only, in Manhattan only. Nothing about my penis size, nothing sexual at all. It's just very plain, to the point. I don't even like to read those long profiles. I don't like to read, you know, three paragraphs on someone. I think you should be simple and to the point.

Escorts who described a more "bare bones" approaches to advertisement were also less likely to display an entrepreneurial or professional orientation to escorting. Instead, escorting was framed as a temporary strategy to earn money.

NICHE MARKETS

Women and men working within the escorting business are a highly diverse group, and many work to expand their network of clientele through offering specialized services that cater to a particular niche market. Some of these escorts are capitalizing on physical attributes that are marginalized in the mainstream sex industry—such as being overweight or a mature age—and they realize that there is a demand for individuals with these characteristics. Others are skilled in offering specialized services to clients, such as role playing or power exchange, fetish activities, or tantra. There is a thriving market for escorts with these special skills and characteristics, and yet in spite of clients' desire for them, their services are often valued less than those of more traditional escorts.[24] This appeared to be especially true for the niche market escorts in the Lady Classified Project, whose rates were significantly lower than the more mainstream women in the sample. Among men in the Classified Project, this difference in hourly rates was not mentioned.

Bondage, Domination, Sadism and Masochism (BDSM)

Several of the male respondents specialized in offering professional domination services, or marketed themselves as "leather daddies." For these men, mature age was a professional asset, and their business was often framed as a legitimate and valued aspect of the BDSM subculture within the larger gay male community:

> I've met so many nice people, and you know, they're very welcoming. So that's [escorting] a good thing in the S&M community. And because I'm in all the magazines, you know [name of fetish magazine], people know me. [They say] "Oh, I've seen your ad."

For the gay men who provided specialized fetish or BDSM services, their rates were not significantly different from those of other male escorts. For the female escorts, however, who were desired for their "exotic" appearance or specialized services on offer, these women's rates fell into the lower range of the spectrum ($180–$300 an hour) where the mode rate was $400–$500 an hour, and ranged up to $1000 an hour. It appears that Echol's observation that there is a price for being different may hold true more for female escorts than for men.[25]

A few of the women offered professional BDSM and role-playing services to their clients. For many, this was a natural extension of their personality and suited them better than "vanilla" escorting. One woman described her transition from regular escorting into being a practitioner of BDSM:

> After being a regular escort and being told to do some things for X amount of dollars, "No I am not gonna do that, I am gonna give you some of the money

back." I realized I am giving a lot of money back and [doing] a lot of arbitration between clients. They are not getting what they want and I am not doing what they want to do. This was happening more than once a week, confrontations. So I met her [an escort skilled in BDSM] and I didn't know more about [BDSM], and she said . . . "I do this, this, and this. This is the deal, this is how much— either go with it or go away." Works much better.

Many of the male and female escorts who specialized in BDSM services expressed that playing a dominant role was more consistent with their natural personae, and they also appreciated the lower risk associated with non-penetrative sexual activities. This lends support to previous research that found that women create "bodily exclusion zones" as a strategy for maintaining emotional boundaries between themselves and their clients as well as for reducing their risk of exposure to sexually transmitted infections.[26]

Tantra

The art of tantric practice was a specialized skill offered by some of the women who participated in the Lady Classified Project. These women offered tantric massage and lessons in tantric breathing practices to their clients. These specialized services appeared to accomplish several goals: maintaining boundaries between themselves and their clients, attracting a certain type of clientele, and capitalizing on their age and years of training and experience as an asset to their business. One woman in her late fifties described her tantric work as preferable to offering "regular sex" to clients, which she experienced as less emotionally satisfying and more physically invasive:

> In my Eros ad I do advocate the tantric massage a lot. . . . When they call you tell them that you have two options. If you want to get intimate it is so-and-so, but you can also have the experience of a tantric massage on the table which is cheaper and which a lot of men go for now because the money is tight! . . . And I don't mind making less money. I prefer doing something that is not so incriminating and does not use my body so much . . . . Yeah, it's safe but psychologically very balancing because a man [will] come out of my place with a smile on his face and so do I, because the tantric massage really relaxes them and they get their release at the end because they need it, because they are so tense.

While there is a niche market within escorting for women of mature age, our mature respondents often offered specialized services such as tantra or BDSM to their clients. It may be that mature women escorts need to supplement their offerings with such specialized services to attract a broader range of clients within an industry that does not value older women.

Big Beautiful Women

In a culture which devalues women of size, the phenomenon of "BBW" (Big Beautiful Women) escorts appears to have flowered into a popular niche market in recent years. Several of our interviewees identified as BBWs, and their narratives reflected the personal impact that escorting had on their body image in a culture where fat women are denigrated:

> It's almost like if you mention the word BBW you're inbox gets full within minutes. I honestly believe that society has put such stigma on women of size, that men are ashamed to admit that they have a thing for women of size or they get a fetish for it because it's something that they're not allowed to have—it becomes taboo. Or they really do just love big girls and when they get a chance to be with one they love it. And it's huge; I mean all my clients, even the clients that had never been with a big girl before love me. And I'm quite big, I weigh almost 300 pounds; I'm tall too, really curvy, and I wear it well. Yeah, it's pretty cool, I like it. . . . Before I was a sex worker, I was completely embarrassed to take my clothes off in front of others, and now it doesn't even phase me. . . . I remember the very first time I had a client who told me to stand up in front of him and take all my clothes off nice and slow, and I'd never done it before like that with anybody because I was so shy. And since then, because of all his praise and because of the way he loved my body, and the way he loved everything about the way I looked [as have] so have many men after that—it's a great ego boost.

For women of size, sex work affirmed their bodies as sexy and desirable; their narratives of escorting as personally affirming were unique within the larger sample of women. The BBWs reported having many clients and little trouble getting work. However, despite their popularity, their rates were in the lowest range of the sample, indicating that while they were desired and valued as part of the niche market, they were still viewed as worth less than escorts who fit a more normative standard of beauty (thin, young, white).

RACE AND RACISM

The subject of race and racism within prostitution has been understudied, although there have been several anecdotal personal accounts of racial discrimination and stereotyping on the job written by sex workers them-selves.[27] Collins argues that, in a society where economic opportunities for African-American men and women are constrained by racial stratification, the black body itself is commodified.[28] In our research on male and female escorts, there was broad agreement that (1) there is an established racial hierarchy within escorting and (2) the white, middle-class men that make up the majority of their clients held racially stereotyped views of and fantasies about escorts of color.

This may explain why women of color, and particularly African-American women, topped the list for women scoring high on burnout. African-American women reported confronting racist attitudes from clients regarding their intelligence and the value of their services. One woman described being marketed in a racially stereotyped way by one agency that she worked with:

> There was this woman that I was working for who was trying to start up her own agency . . . but the way she marketed me was kind of like a knucklehead . . . describing me as someone who likes to be spanked, as this bad girl, and she would put spelling errors, and it was just kind of like low-grade stuff.

Other African-American women in the study described being asked to act out racially stereotyped fantasies requested by a client:

> I had no idea that a lot of white men have this black slave fantasy. And it kind of bothers me, but I just try to separate my emotions from it and say, this is just a role play, this is just entertainment. It's not real life . . . sometimes they want me to call them their master—their white master. Or they want to be my slave. A lot of them have this big black goddess fantasy and they get very turned on despite being subjected to this black woman who's going to boss—a bossy black woman who's just gonna tell 'em where to go and tell 'em what to do and boss 'em around, be aggressive.

There was general agreement among the women that a racial hierarchy stratified the sex industry, placing white women on top and women of color—particularly African-American women—at the bottom. This hierarchy was reflected in the "glass ceiling" reflected in the hourly rates charged by the women in the project. While white women's fees ranged up to $1000 an hour, no woman of color in the sample charged more than $500. The mode rate for white women in the sample was $500; for women of color it was $400. Thus it appears that the value of being white translates into a real business advantage, as acknowledged by one white woman in the sample who charged $1000 an hour:

> Unfortunately, white women are more desirable in certain socioeconomic groups. I know that just from looking through websites, that Brazilian women who come here charge a much lower rate even though they are more attractive and that's apparently the most desirable thing in the business. And I am from far the most physically attractive escort on line; I am fairly attractive and I have certain height, certain body weight and skin type. I am white and that means I can earn more money.

Overall, the rates charges by men of color did not differ from those charged by white men, although men of color did report confronting similar attitudes from some potential clients online:

> I don't get certain clients. I've had a lot of people tell me that I'm like a beautiful body but wrong color. . . . I've had really demeaning comments, like one . . . would basically belittle me to the point to where they don't pay so much for a "nigger," so what is your rate, and I tell them. "Oh that's way too much. I'd never pay that much for a nigger. Twenty-five or thirty bucks, maybe." And that can be really disturbing, emotionally disturbing. . . . What is up with . . . the way that these men think?

Another biracial man talked about negotiating race:

> Sometimes I do advertise that label "biracial." And I get a lot of clients who aren't into strictly black [providers], I guess, but then seeing that I'm biracial, they're curious and they're also more inclined to be interested, instead of you being a black guy. . . . So I get a lot of business that way.

The reports of confronting racism and discrimination in the sex industry were consistent across the samples of male and female escorts. The narratives of African-American escorts were most pronounced in their experiences of racism on the job; Asian, South Asian, and Latino/a escorts in these samples were more likely to report neutral feelings about the impact of their race on their experiences in the industry. These narratives reflect a racial hierarchy in escorting. However, both our male and female samples were majority white, under-representing men and women of color. More research needs to be done on the latter to gain a deeper understanding of the ways in which race and ethnicity shape the dynamics of escort–client interactions.

STIGMA

Female prostitutes have long symbolized sin, immorality, and disease in religious and medical literature.[29] Male prostitutes, who serve primarily male clientele, are doubly stigmatized for their engagement in prostitution as well as breaking the taboo against homosexuality.[30] Unfortunately, social scientific research on sex workers has often reflected and reproduced the stigma against prostitution through work which casts these men and women as victims or deviants.[31] This body of research rarely questions the underlying assumption that prostitution constitutes a social problem.

For persons with concealable stigmas, the decision to conceal or reveal one's membership in a deviant group becomes a crucial strategy for managing the impact of stigma on one's life.[32] Stigma management strategies often take the form of information management techniques such as "passing" (hiding one's stigma in order to pass as a non-stigmatized person) or "covering" (selective disclosure to trusted confidantes or family members). Individuals who possesses multiple concealable stigmas may disclose one while concealing the other. For example, an openly gay man may conceal that he works as a male escort, thus managing two stigmas in different ways.

The marginalized status assigned homosexuals and prostitutes in this society surfaced throughout nearly every one of our interviews with male and female escorts. Awareness of the stigma attached to prostitution shaped men and women's perceptions of their work as well as their choices to disclose or be open about it. One man described his ambivalence about being an escort: "The money's great, and you may have great sex or whatever. You still have the stigma of being, in essence, a prostitute or a houseboy. And that's a hard label to shake mentally sometimes."

Concern about being labeled and judged by one's peers led many escorts to conceal their work:

> I've had difficulty in terms of, not secrecy per se, but it's not the sort of thing that you just share with everyone. "Oh, what do you do?" "I'm a male escort." "What does that mean?" "You know, a male prostitute, I'm a whore." So, inevitably, there tends to be a degree of keeping it quiet and/or lying that's involved, and I don't like that so much.

Female escorts often reported feeling isolated and growing distant from friends and family as a result of the need for secrecy:

> I don't have any really close friends right now. I've been distancing myself from people. . . . A lot of my energy has been focused on my work; I don't want to expose

them to any baggage that I may have. And then, if anyone does find out [about escorting], I don't want—I'm just afraid of getting found out by these folks, because a lot of people know that I'm very open-minded sexually and stuff, but they don't know how open I am. . . . I guess I'm afraid of how they're going to react. . . . I guess I'm kind of ashamed of what I do, and I don't want them to know.

Both male and female escorts who engaged in passing often reported feeling socially isolated as a result. Their efforts to protect themselves from being stigmatized and labeled as prostitutes also may have prevented them from accessing potential social support as they managed stigma and the emotional demands of the work. One woman drew a direct connection between avoiding work-related burnout and disclosure:

I'm out to everyone. All my friends know, my family knows, so I'm completely out with it. . . . And talking about burnout, I think the biggest contributor to burnout is not having a support system. That's where most of your conflict lies, that whole, "Oh am I gonna be judged? How's it gonna be if my mom finds out? How's it gonna be if my boyfriend finds out? Or is my best friend since kindergarten gonna disown me because now all of a sudden I'm doing this?" [*Interviewer* All the consequences.] And all of that stress. I mean of course there's stress involved in the business regardless, but when you couple that on top of everything else, that there's no changing the other factors that are stressors in the business. But when you [have] a support system in place, that really is one of the biggest keys of reducing burnout for me. And that was when I stopped being conflicted about it, really.

This participant, who self-identifies as feminist, explained some of her initial resistance to the stigma associated with prostitution as her rejection of the "virgin/whore" sexual double standard. Her attitude evolved from an initial ambivalence towards her participation in sex work towards one of pride in the services she offered.

Some differences in the perception of prostitution-related stigma emerged between the male and female escorts. Some of the men acknowledged the stigma associated with prostitution among mainstream society, but argued that subcultural norms within the gay community framed being paid for sex as a sign of prestige:

Escorts in the gay community are kind of exalted because anything in the gay community that has to do with physical beauty, whether it's being a bartender or a go-go boy, if you have a higher level of that, you're automatically accepted.

Another man claimed that within the gay community, being offered money for sex is so common as to be nearly unremarkable. This man discovered that disclosing his work as an escort did not result in a loss of social status, as he had feared it would:

> I came out [as an escort] and I had such wonderful support, and people thought it was fun and glamorous, and they wanted to hear all my stories. And I found out that practically every attractive gay man in New York City has done it once, or been offered [money for sex]. . . . Virtually all the people I knew.

For these men, perceiving sex work as being at least somewhat normative within the gay community helped them feel more comfortable being honest about their work with friends and partners. In fact, among the men who reported being in committed relationships (35%), all but two were open with their partners. The women who reported being in committed relationships (33%) were less likely to tell their partners—only half of these women were honest with their partners about their work. In other words, 88% of men in relationships were open, while only 50% of the women were. It is possible that cultural differences in the meaning of non-monogamy and casual sex between the gay community and heterosexual norms may have contributed to the higher levels of disclosure among the men.

Some male and female escorts rejected the stigma attached to prostitution, instead reframing their work in a positive light. These individuals were more likely to be open about their work, and expressed pride in the services they provided to clients. One woman states:

> A lot of people think that we are in the business of selling sex. I don't think we are. I think that the sex is a vehicle to get us into a place where a lot of healing and connection and love can be made. Sex gives us the opportunity to get them in the door or to make the connection. . . . It's just that little glimpse of heaven that everybody wants and it's so nice to know that someone can leave their busy day and take a little vacation for a few hours and go out and not have the road rage that they might have had, and then be nicer to their families, and feel like more of a man, and have more self-confidence, and be more successful in their life. You know, because they are able to take a little bit of time for themselves.

This narrative reflects the framing of escorting as akin to a helping profession such as counseling, where the sex worker contributes to the well-being of the client through the provision of needed services.

The progression from reframing sex work as a positive form of employment into engagement in social activism was a logical step for a small portion of the male and female escorts. This social activism was often linked with a pre-existing political and social identity, such as feminist, gay, or genderqueer. These men and women took pride in their identity as sex workers and engaged in social activism aimed at de-stigmatizing sex work. One man related:

> There's this whole part of me that's sort of, sex workers of the Euro world unite. I do feel that the services that I provide to some very lonely people are very valuable. I find prostitution to be in some ways . . . to be a noble profession. It doesn't hurt anyone, and it helps a lot of people, and I'm always really happy when I visit sites like that, that are for other escorts about people that are very noble and very out there. They are identifying themselves with their name and their picture and everything out in the whole world as escorts, and they're sort of trying to promote escorting as a viable career alternative. It is really hard work, and it takes a certain type of well-rounded personality and some savvy to be successful in it.

Some of these escorts felt that their approach to love and sexuality exemplified a healthy alternative to more mainstream relationship models. For these individuals sex work was part of a broader self-image as sexually liberated, adventurous individuals:

> I'm not one to hide it. Not really any aspect of my life. I mean everyone knows. All my friends know that I have this fantastic, longish relationship with a person that I really love and who really loves me. And for me to be able to do this and for it not to cause any problem, I'm aware, is a kind of hard pill for people to swallow. So, it's kind of nice when I do meet people who are a bit conservative in their monogamy and whatever, that I can actually tell them that. And I make a point of doing that, because I think it might be edifying for them. You know, relationships don't have to be one way. There doesn't have to be jealousy.

These men and women embody what Unger calls "positive marginality," the experience of persons who learn to take pride in their marginalized status while resisting and redefining the social meanings associated with their group identity.[33]

SEXUAL NEGOTIATION

Escorts who engage in sexual contact with their clients are, by nature of their business, at risk for infection with HIV and other sexually transmitted infections. The advent of the HIV pandemic has brought increased attention to the role of sex workers as potential "vectors of disease transmission,"[34] and a focus on HIV has dominated much of the research on sex workers, particularly men.[35] Yet the findings on safer sex practices among male and female sex workers appear to vary based on the venue of the sample.[36] Overall, research on indoor sex workers indicates that the majority of these men and women practice safer sex with their clients.[37]

Research on the practices of escorts has identified a variety of meanings attached to condom use during sex with clients. Moore found that male and female sex workers took pride in their competent use of condoms and other safer sex techniques with clients.[38] For male escorts, condoms are associated with having a professional identity as an escort.[39] Both male and female escorts have been found to value condoms as an emotional barrier between themselves and their clients as well as tools for protecting themselves from HIV.[40] Having managerial and social support from other escorts normalizing condom use with clients increased agency-based male escorts' desire to use condoms with clients,[41] and was associated with nearly universal condom use during anal sex with clients.[42]

Among our male and female independent escorts, there was broad agreement of the risks associated with unprotected anal and vaginal sex, and condom use was considered an "industry standard" for these activities. However, client requests and preferences for unsafe sex were common. One man states:

> It is a big thing. I'm really shocked at how people are taking risks. It's amazing. I do get a lot of requests. . . . Unless I bring it up or get out the condom, they would just sit on my dick and without even asking about it.

Experiences such as those just described led many men to become proactive in their insistence on condom use with their clients:

> I usually take the first step to bring up the issue. If you, the sex worker, make the first thing about safe sex, then they know that you're serious and responsible, and it's not just about money. It's about your will. You, for a sex worker, to make the first comment about "it has to be safe" [are] risking losing business, and they know that. So that impresses them, and that makes them know that you are really going to be safe.

Requests for sex without a condom were less common among women escorts. On the occasions when clients requested unprotected sex, women relied on verbal negotiation to reassert the need for safe sex:

> Yeah, in the rare occasions that that's happened—perfect example, I had a physician. . . . I think he was trying to get me drunk, to see if I would change my boundaries and he was trying to get me to have sex without a condom. And I'm like "no," and he's like "but I'm fixed," and I'm like "that doesn't matter." I said, "We're still using a condom." And he said, "But I don't have any diseases," and I was like, "and I don't either and it's gonna stay that way. This is how I am with everybody—it's consistent."

Condom use for vaginal and anal sex with clients was viewed as expected and normative among the men and women escorts. However, some differences emerged between the samples along lines of HIV status. Among the HIV-positive men who participated in the Classified Project (16%), some occasionally acquiesced to requests for unprotected sex. But even in these situations men would often attempt to reduce the potential for harm:

> I don't really like to do barebacking [anal sex without condoms]. If they insist on it, I will, but I just don't think it's a safe thing to do, not for my own safety. I am selective doing that. I don't bareback on the bottom. I will bareback top, but again, that's their choice. But I let them know up front that I am positive when they want me to do that. So, I'm advising them at the time. . . . I would feel badly not telling them that and doing it.

For this man and some other HIV-positive men in the sample, the risk associated with unprotected sex was seen as being greater for the client than it was for them. This may have contributed to a relaxing of standards for safe sex with clients who were also HIV positive or who were aware of the escort's status and still wanted to proceed without condoms. Ultimately, however, the majority of men and women across both projects agreed that condom use for anal and vaginal sex was not negotiable while on the job.

CONCLUSION

For the most part, female and male escorts share more similarities than differences. Regardless of gender, many independent escorts expressed a dislike for the restricted working conditions and reduced fees associated with working for an agency. These negative experiences were often described as motivating their transition into independent escorting. Women and men described similar advantages to working independently: setting their own rates, creating their own schedule, and having the ability to screen and be selective about their clients. Lastly, escorts of both genders emphasized the importance of condom use for vaginal and anal intercourse with clients, although the use of condoms for oral sex was more variable.

However, female and male escorts did differ in some notable respects. Overall, women charged much more than men, and also varied more in their prices. The average fee for a female escort's time was $400–$500, and as high as $1000 an hour; men charged an average of $200 an hour or session, with far less variability in rates. Unlike other industries, women have a distinct financial advantage in escorting. However, women of color reported hiring discrimination when they sought employment through escort agencies, and as independents commanded lower fees on average compared to white female escorts. Racial differences in earning power were not noted in the male escort sample, although men and women of color were both likely to report being confronted with clients requesting racially stereotyped fantasies about "big black bucks" or "slave girls" and clients who made denigrating comments about their worth.

Both the men and women described offering specialized services such as domination and role play, or catered to niche markets for clients who desired escorts of a specific type (such as "BBW" or "leather daddies"). However, women working in niche markets reported lower wages on average than women in the more mainstream market; this wage difference was not seen among their male counterparts. Thus, while women earn higher wages in escorting than men do on average, they also experience greater wage discrimination associated with their skin color, service niche, age, and body shape. Future research on clients of male and female escorts would benefit from further exploration of client's desires for different types of escort and the reasons why different escorts and their services are perceived as being worth different amounts.

Perhaps the most striking difference between male and female escorts emerged from comparison of their experiences of work-related stigma. Although about one-third of the escorts in each study reported being in romantic relationships, it appeared to be much less of an issue for the men to disclose being a sex worker to their partners. Similarly, sex work appears to be much less stigmatized in general within the gay male community. Where many national gay magazines have published how-to guides or career tips for escorting,[43] it is doubtful that a national women's magazine would publish such articles. Ultimately, escorting appears to be more socially acceptable within the gay community, relieving many men of the stress associated with living a double life, a common strategy for the female escorts. While gay and bisexual men face stigma in the heteronormative mainstream culture, being a member of the gay community appeared to be a "protective factor" reducing male escorts' experience of stigma within their own community.

There is a clear need for more comparative research on sex workers. To identify other differences by gender and venue, future researchers should sample men, women, and transgender workers in sufficient numbers from all venues of sex work—street, brothel, agency, and independents. This will help to clarify the role of both gender and type of work in shaping sex workers' experiences.

NOTES

1. David Bimbi, "Male Prostitution: Pathology, Paradigms, and Progress in Research," *Journal of Homosexuality* 53 (2007): 7–35.
2. Ine Vanwesenbeeck, "Another Decade of Social Scientific Work on Sex Work," *Annual Review of Sex Research* 12 (2001): 242–289.
3. See Chapter 1 in this volume, and Ronald Weitzer, "New Directions in Research on Prostitution," *Crime, Law, and Social Change* 43 (2005): 211–235.
4. Henry Minton, *Departing from Deviance: A History of Homosexual Rights and Emancipatory Science in America*, Chicago: University of Chicago Press, 2002; H. L. Ross, "The 'Hustler' in Chicago," *Journal of Student Research* 1 (1959): 13–19.
5. Michael Smith, Christian Grov, and David Seal, "Agency Based Male Sex Work: A Descriptive Focus on Physical, Personal, and Social Space," *Journal of Men's Studies* 16 (2008): 193–210.
6. Elizabeth Bernstein, "Sex Work for the Middle Classes," *Sexualities* 10 (2007): 473–488.
7. Jude Uy, Jeffrey Parsons, David Bimbi, Juline Koken, and Perry Halkitis, "Gay and Bisexual Male Escorts Who Advertise on the Internet: Understanding Reasons for and Effects of Involvement in Commercial Sex," *International Journal of Men's Health* 3 (2004): 11–26; Juline Koken, *Working in the Business of Pleasure: Stigma Resistance and Coping Strategies Utilized by Independent Female Escorts*, Ph.D. dissertation, Graduate Center, City University of New York, 2008.

8. The Classified Project was funded by New Jersey City University, Jeffrey Parsons, PI, David Bimbi, Co-PI. The Lady Classified Project was funded by a pilot grant awarded to the Center for HIV Educational Studies and Training at Hunter College, Juline Koken, PI.

9. For related studies, see Juline Koken, David Bimbi, Jeffrey Parsons, and Perry Halkitis, "The Experience of Stigma in the Lives of Gay and Bisexual Male Internet Escorts," *Journal of Psychology and Human Sexuality* 16 (2004): 13–32; Jeffrey Parsons, Juline Koken and David Bimbi, "The Use of the Internet by Gay and Bisexual Male Escorts: Sex Workers as Sex Educators," *AIDS Care* 10 (2004): 1021–1035; Jeffrey Parsons, Juline Koken, and David Bimbi, "Looking Beyond HIV: Eliciting Individual and Community Needs of Male Internet Escorts," *Journal of Homosexuality* 53 (2007): 219–240; Uy, et al., "Gay and Bisexual Male Escorts."

10. Koken, "Working in the Business of Pleasure."

11. Kathleen MacQueen, Eleanor McLellan, Kelly Kay, and Bobby Milstein, "Codebook Development for Team-Based Qualitative Analysis," *Cultural Anthropology Methods* 10 (1998): 31–36.

12. Janet Lever, David Kanouse, and Sandra Berry, "Racial and Ethnic Segmentation of Female Prostitution in Los Angeles County," *Journal of Psychology and Human Sexuality* 17 (2005): 107–129.

13. Minton, "Departing from Deviance."

14. Barbara Heyl, "The Madam as Teacher: The Training of House Prostitutes," *Social Problems* 24 (1977): 545–555.

15. Lisa Jean Moore, "I Was Just Learning the Ropes: Becoming a Practitioner of Safer Sex," *Applied Behavioral Science Review* 5 (1997): 43–60.

16. Heyl, "The Madam as Teacher."

17. Smith, et al., "Agency-Based Male Sex Work."

18. Smith, et al., "Agency-Based Male Sex Work."

19. Quoted in Smith, et al., "Agency-Based Male Sex Work."

20. Heyl, "The Madam as Teacher."

21. Smith, et al., "Agency-Based Male Sex Work."

22. Elizabeth Bernstein, *Temporarily Yours: Intimacy, Authenticity, and the Commerce of Sex*, Chicago: University of Chicago Press, 2007.

23. Jan Browne and Victor Minichiello, "The Social and Work Context of Commercial Sex between Men," *Australian and New Zealand Journal of Sociology* 32 (1996): 86–92; Roberta Perkins and Garry Bennett, *Being a Prostitute: Prostitute Women and Prostitute Men*, Sydney: George Allen & Unwin, 1997; Koken, et al., "Experience of Stigma."

24. Kevicha Echols, "The Price of Being Different," *Spread Magazine* 3 (2007): 30–35.

25. Echols, "The Price of Being Different."

26. Teela Sanders, "It's Just Acting: Sex Workers' Strategies for Capitalizing on Sexuality," *Gender, Work, and Organization* 12 (2005): 319–342.

27. Siobhan Brooks, "Exotic Dancing and Unionizing: The Challenges of Feminist and Antiracist Organizing at the Lusty Lady Theater," in F. Winddance and K. Blee, eds., *Feminism and Antiracism*, New York: New York University Press, 2001; Echols, "The Price of Being Different"; Jill Nagle, ed., *Whores and Other Feminists*, New York: Routledge, 1997.

28. Patricia Hill Collins, "New Commodities, New Consumers: Selling Blackness in the Global Marketplace," *Ethnicities* 6 (2006): 297–317.

29. Nickie Roberts, *Whores in History: Prostitution in Western Society*, London: HarperCollins, 1992.

30. Bimbi, "Male Prostitution"; Koken, et al., "The Experience of Stigma."

31. Gail Pheterson, "The Category 'Prostitute' in Social Scientific Inquiry," *Journal of Sex Research* 27 (1990): 397–407; Bimbi, "Male Prostitution."

32. Erving Goffman, *Stigma*, New York: Simon & Schuster, 1963.

33. Rhoda Unger, "Positive Marginality: Antecedents and Consequences," *Journal of Adult Development* 5 (1998): 163–170; Rhoda Unger, "Outsiders Inside: Positive Marginality and Social Change," *Journal of Social Issues* 56 (2000): 163–179.

34. Edward Morse, Patricia Simon, Howard Osofsky, Paul Balson and H. Richard Gaumer, "The Male Street Prostitute: A Vector for Transmission of HIV Infection into the Heterosexual World," *Social Science and Medicine* 32 (1991): 531–539.

35. Bimbi, "Male Prostitution."

36. Parsons, et al., "The Use of the Internet"; Victor Minichiello, "Commercial Sex between Men: A Prospective Diary-Based Study," *Journal of Sex Research* 37 (2000): 151–161.

37. Michael Smith and David Seal, "Sexual Behavior, Mental Health, Substance Use, and HIV Risk among Agency-Based Male Escorts in a Small U.S. City," *International Journal of Sexual Health* 19 (2007): 27–39; Bimbi, "Male Prostitution"; Moore, "I Was Just Learning the Ropes."

38. Moore, "I Was Just Learning the Ropes."

39. Jan Browne and Victor Minichiello, "The Social Meanings behind Male Sex Work," *British Journal of Sociology* 46 (1995): 598–622.

40. Teela Sanders, "The Condom as a Psychological Barrier: Female Sex Workers and Emotional Management," *Feminism and Psychology* 12 (2002): 561–566.

41. Michael Smith and David Seal, "Motivational Influences on the Safer Sex Behavior of Agency-Based Male Sex Workers," *Archives of Sexual Behavior* 37 (2008): 845–853.
42. Smith and Seal, "Sexual Behavior."
43. Bimbi, "Male Prostitution."

CHAPTER

10

PROSTITUTES' CUSTOMERS: MOTIVES AND MISCONCEPTIONS

Martin A. Monto

On February 14, 2008, Temeka Rachelle Lewis, the defendant, received a call from "Kristen." Lewis asked Kristen how she thought the appointment went, and Kristen said that she thought it went very well. Lewis asked Kristen how much she collected, and Kristen said $4300. Kristen said that she liked him, and that she did not think he was difficult. . . . Lewis continued that, from what she had been told, he (believed to be Client 9) "would ask you to do things that you might not think were safe." . . . Kristen responded: "I have a way of dealing with that. . . . I'd be like, 'Listen dude, you really want the sex?'"—Excerpt from a federal complaint filed in New York. Client 9 is former New York Governor Eliot Spitzer.[1]

Until the last decade, efforts to deal with the problems caused by prostitution consisted primarily of arresting prostitutes, sometimes providing them with programs to support their exit from the street. Research on prostitution focused mostly on prostitutes, giving scant attention to the demand side, the customer.[2] Feminist organizations, impassioned by their concern about violence against prostitutes, argued that the lack of attention to male customers was both unfair and ineffective. This led to new policies and research in the 1990s that targeted customers. Feminists and other supporters of these new efforts argued that, while prostitutes were often compelled to participate due to dire economic circumstances, fear of violence at the hands of a partner or pimp, or drug addiction, customers were more clearly choosing to participate.[3] Police began to conduct stings in which female officers posed as decoys to lure and arrest prospective customers. Special diversion programs designed to convince arrested men not to re-offend were started in several cities. And research focusing on customers and their motives led to a wealth of new information about these men.[4]

The recent prostitution scandal involving New York Governor Eliot Spitzer, who had prosecuted prostitution-related crimes while serving as Attorney-General, has drawn renewed attention to customers and their motives. It is undeniably perplexing when public figures like Spitzer, who have so much to lose, risk patronizing prostitutes. Some argue that their power leads to a sense of invulnerability. Others argue that the challenges of public life motivate men to seek a space in which they can drop their public persona and show a different side of themselves.[5] Fortunately, recent research has allowed us to move beyond the commonsense explanations and anecdotal accounts that often follow such an incident, and we now have a significant body of research available to assist us in understanding customers and their motives.

This chapter takes advantage of a range of recent studies in order to identify and correct some misconceptions about customers and explore their motives. There have been a number of insightful qualitative, interview-based studies of customers.[6] At least two nationally representative surveys have included questions about prostitution use, the National Health and Social Life Survey and the General Social Survey.[7] Internet bulletin boards and websites featuring the opinions and experiences of customers provide a potentially important, although as yet underused, source of information about customers.[8] This article also reports original findings based on two samples of arrested customers gathered from men attending "john schools" in 1997–2000 and 2007. Johns schools are intervention programs designed to educate customers in the hopes of discouraging re-offending. Before delving into these findings, a number of misconceptions about customers and prostitution need to be addressed.

MYTHS ABOUT PROSTITUTION

There are several popular myths about prostitution and the men who buy sex from prostitutes. I review these myths now.

Prostitution is a Natural Aspect of Masculine Sexual Behavior

There is a widespread, unexamined assumption among some scholars and the general public that prostitution is the "world's oldest profession" and is essentially inevitable, and that buying sex is something that men naturally do as an expression of their sexuality. Path-breaking research by Alfred Kinsey and his associates in the 1940s contributed to a new cultural awareness that there was a great deal of variety in patterns of sexual expression among men and that a surprisingly high number (69%) of America men had visited prostitutes.[9] Based on Kinsey's work and their own impressions, Benjamin and Masters argued that the number was closer to 80%.[10] Unfortunately, the original Kinsey research was characterized by a flawed sample that probably led to an overrepresentation of more sexually active men, making such generalizations problematic. However, the assumption persisted that prostitution is something men naturally pursue. More recent efforts to legalize prostitution argue that, since prostitution is inevitable, we should avoid marginalizing prostitutes and regulate the practice instead. Even some activists strongly opposed to legalization seem to assume that men, at least those in patriarchal cultures, are naturally motivated to seek out prostitutes.

There is no sound basis for this assumption. Bullough and Bullough argue that prostitution has not existed in all societies,[11] and recent studies using nationally representative samples indicate that most men do not seek out prostitutes. In fact, these studies suggest that the proportion of young men who patronize prostitutes may be declining over time. The 1992 National Health and Social Life Survey (NHSLS) and the more recent General Social Survey both revealed that fewer than one-fifth of men in nationally representative samples had ever had sexual experiences with prostitutes, and fewer than 1% had done so during the previous year. Additionally, the NHSLS data indicated that men coming of age in more recent decades were less likely to have had their first sexual experiences with prostitutes than men from earlier generations.[12]

Prostitution is Monolithic

Contemporary dialogues about prostitution often do not differentiate between its various manifestations. Feminist perspectives, as described by Davis[13] often treat prostitution as either a civil rights issue in which women choose prostitution as a form of sexual expression or economic advancement or as an issue of sexual exploitation in which women are oppressed by men. In any case, there is little emphasis on the dramatic differences in the activities that fall under the heading "prostitution."[14] The term "prostitution" includes the streetside blowjob, the high-priced escort featuring a "girlfriend experience," the teen runaway trying to scrape together enough money for food or drugs, the legal brothels in Nevada featuring a menu of different sexual options, male prostitution, sex tourism, and the crack house exchange of sex for drugs. To treat them all the same analytically or in terms of policy is to miss funda- mental differences in the degree of power and consent of the participants.[15]

Many studies over the past two decades have documented the violence that often accompanies street prostitution.[16] Prostitutes working indoors are also victims of violence, yet their vulnerability varies. For prostitutes in brothels, there is generally less risk, and, depending on screening procedures, escorts may be less vulnerable as well. Weitzer points out that there are many differences between indoor and outdoor prostitution and that policy decisions need to recognize these differences. He advocates a system in which indoor prostitution is decriminalized, while outdoor prostitution, which elicits greater community concern and is characterized by greater violence, continues to be the focus of authorities.[17]

Prostitution is the Private Behavior of Consenting Adults

While not necessarily held by the majority of the population, this mis- conception is particularly problematic. It is used by privacy advocates and participants in the sex industry, both customers and providers, to argue against policies restricting prostitution. To define prostitution as *private, consensual*, and *adult* misses the many different contexts in which prostitution takes place. More importantly, it implies that prostitution is not an issue that warrants public concern or intervention. This notion is misleading on all three counts. First, many participants in prostitution are not adults.[18] Several studies docu- ment the existence of underage prostitution. Second, although it may appear private, violence and exploitation make it a public issue. Additionally, street prostitution is associated with a variety of other problems, including drug use, sexually transmitted diseases, disruptive traffic patterns, and harassment of neighbors by prospective customers, pimps, or prostitutes themselves.[19] Third, the degree of consent in prostitution is best seen as a continuum.[20] It is unreasonable to characterize prostitutes who are minors, addicted to drugs, facing dire economic circumstances, or participating as a result of fear of violence by a pimp as fully consenting. In contrast, other sex workers claim to have made a conscious and deliberate choice to participate. As is true with many other aspects of human behavior, the decision to participate in prosti- tution, and even whether it is really a decision at all, is shaped by a range of factors and contexts.

Prostitution Policy Is Carefully Planned

In general, public policy toward prostitution has emerged haphazardly as police and local officials respond to public concerns.[21] As described earlier, the policy in many cities until about two decades ago was to arrest prostitutes, and this remains the default policy in some communities. Some would argue that this strategy was in line with the traditional perspective on prostitution, in which men were seen as naturally seeking sex and prostitutes were seen as temptresses who led them astray. Feminist concerns about the inequality of this policy led to greater efforts to arrest customers in the 1990s, but this involved little careful planning. Police actions have generally focused on the most visible forms of prostitution, targeting outdoor prostitution or organized operations that have become a public nuisance. More recently, public shaming rituals, such as broadcasting customers' mug shots on television or the Internet, have gained popularity.[22]

Perhaps the most deliberate and planned response to the problem of prostitution has been the emergence of post-arrest diversion programs or "john schools" designed to deter arrested customers from re-offending. Started in 1995 in San Francisco and Portland, there are currently dozens of these programs in cities nationwide. Many of the programs involve the coordinated effort of police, district attorneys, and advocates. Their rationale is that male customers may lack information about the exploitation involved in prostitution, their risk of STDs, the legal consequences of arrest, etc. Once they become aware of these issues, customers may choose not to participate in the future. This deliberate focus on the demand side of the supply–demand equation targets the persons who are viewed as more clearly making a decision to participate in the prostitution exchange and can more easily cease their participation. A recent evaluation of the oldest of these "john schools," San Francisco's First Offender Prostitution Program, indicates the potential of these programs to reduce recidivism among customers.[23] Data gathered from the program in San Francisco and two other cities are the source of the findings presented in this chapter.

RESEARCH METHODS

Anonymous surveys were administered to men attending "john schools" in San Francisco, California, Las Vegas, Nevada, and Portland, Oregon prior to the opening session. More than 80% of men attending completed the surveys. Refusals, late arrivals, and language barriers accounted for the non-completions.

These programs allow unprecedented access to a population that has been long hidden from view. Relying on questionnaires administered to 1342 men attending the schools in San Francisco (N = 1230), Portland (N = 82), and Las Vegas (N = 30) from 1997–2000, I evaluated the attitudes and motives of customers. Additionally, researchers evaluating the San Francisco program provided me with a sample of 178 men who attended that program in 2007. Although these men were given a different questionnaire, two of the items were relevant to the motives of customers (described later). The subjects of the study are not a representative sample of customers. Virtually all were arrested while trying to hire street prostitutes, rather than patronizing escort services or indoor establishments. Additionally, they were arrested in three western cities that may not be representative of the nation. Nevertheless, the data allow us unprecedented access to information collected from a population that had been previously inaccessible.

FINDINGS

Who Are These Men?

Table 10.1 describes the background characteristics of the men arrested for trying to hire prostitutes. The majority (58%) were white, 20% Hispanic, 13% Asian, and 5% African-American. In general, the men were fairly well educated. Thirty-five percent had completed a bachelor's or higher college degree, and 36% reported some college work. Forty-two percent were currently married, 35% never married, 21% divorced or separated, and 2% widowed. Ages ranged from 18 to 84, with a mean of 37. Most (81%) worked full time. One-quarter had served in the military, similar to the proportion of adult men in the United States who have served. During their childhood years, one-third reported that their parents had divorced, 13% had been physically hurt for no reason, and the same percentage said they were touched sexually when a child by an adult.

A number of questions were identical to items on the nationally representative General Social Survey, allowing for comparisons between clients and the general population of American men. Clients were significantly ($p < .05$) less likely to be married and more likely never to have been married than were men in the national sample. Of those who were married, clients reported less marital happiness than the national sample. These differences suggest that prostitution serves as an alternative sexual outlet for some men who do not have a partner or who do not get along well with their partners. In addition, clients were much more likely to report that they had more than one sexual partner over the past year (53%) than the national sample of men (19%).

TABLE 10.1 CUSTOMERS' BACKGROUND CHARACTERISTICS

ETHNICITY	(N = 1313) (%)
White	58
Hispanic, Chicano, or Latino	20
Asian	13
Black	5
Other or combination	4

LEVEL OF EDUCATION	(N = 1329) (%)
Did not graduate from high school	11
High school graduate	18
Some college training	36
Received bachelor's degree	24
Received graduate degree	11

MARITAL STATUS	(N = 1328) (%)
Married	42
Never married	35
Divorced	15
Separated	6
Widowed	2

WORK STATUS	(N = 1302) (%)
Working full time	81
Working part time	7
Student	2
Other	11

AGE	(N = 1248) (%)
18–21	3
22–25	9
26–35	33
36–45	31
46–55	17
56–65	5
66 or older	1

PARENTS DIVORCED AS A CHILD	(N = 1342) (%)
Yes	35

TABLE 10.1 continued

TOUCHED SEXUALLY BY ADULT WHILE A CHILD	(N = 1283) (%)
Yes	13

PHYSICALLY HURT FOR NO REASON AS A CHILD	(N = 1277) (%)
Yes	13

SERVED IN ARMED FORCES	(N = 1342)(%)
Yes	25

Sexual Behavior

Clients' responses to questions about sexuality and the sex industry are provided in Table 10.2. Almost all the men reported having exclusively female sex partners during their lifetime. Asked the number of partners the men had in the previous year, one-tenth said they had had none, 37% had had one, another third had had from two to four, and 19% had had five or more. Although some might expect men who solicit prostitutes to be regular users of pornography, fully 73% of respondents reported viewing pornographic magazines or videos "never" or less than once a month.

Nineteen percent claimed never to have had sexual relations with a prostitute, indicating that their only experience had been propositioning the police decoy. Another 22% claimed not to have visited a prostitute within the past year. Twenty-one percent reported having had sexual relations with a prostitute one time during the past year; 28% reported that they had been with a prostitute more than once over the past year but less than once a month; and 10% responded that they had been with prostitutes more than once a month. The average age of first experience with a prostitute was 24, although some had had their first experience as early as age 9 or as late as age 60. Fellatio was the most common activity with prostitutes (50%), followed by vaginal sex (14%) and "half and half" (fellatio and vaginal sex, 10%). In contrast, a study in Camden, New Jersey, found that vaginal sex was slightly more common than oral sex among its sample of frequent clients. Regarding condom usage, three-quarters reported that they always used a condom when having sexual relations with a prostitute, a figure similar to the New Jersey study.[24]

In terms of their views toward prostitution policy, three-quarters thought that prostitution should be legalized, and 69% thought it should be

TABLE 10.2 CUSTOMERS' SEXUAL BEHAVIOR

SEXUAL ORIENTATION	(N = 1283) (%)
Strictly heterosexual	94
Experience with both	5
Strictly homosexual	1

NUMBERS OF SEXUAL PARTNERS OVER PAST YEAR	(N = 1321) (%)
None	10
1	37
2	17
3 or 4	17
5 to 10	12
11 or more	7

FREQUENCY OF SEX OVER PAST YEAR	(N = 1325) (%)
Not at all	9
Once or twice	9
About once per month	15
2–3 times per month	20
About once per week	18
2–3 times per week	17
More than 3 times per week	7
Do not know	4

HOW OFTEN LOOKS AT PORNOGRAPHIC MAGAZINES	(N = 1342) (%)
Never	34
Less than once a month	39
One to a few times a month	17
One to a few times a week	8
Every day	1
Several times a day	0

HOW OFTEN WATCHES PORNOGRAPHIC VIDEOS	(N = 1311) (%)
Never	37
Less than once a month	34
One to a few times a month	19
One to a few times a week	7
Every day	3
Several times a day	0

TABLE 10.2 continued

AGE AT FIRST SEXUAL ENCOUNTER WITH A PROSTITUTE	(N = 1018) (%)
9–17	18
18–21	33
22–25	21
26–35	20
36–45	6
46 or over	2

CIRCUMSTANCES OF FIRST SEXUAL ENCOUNTER WITH PROSTITUTE	(N = 1047) (%)
Buddies set it up	24
Prostitute approached	32
Approached prostitute without others knowing	29
Family member set him up	5
Visited a brothel	3
Other	7

MOST COMMON SEXUAL ACTIVITY WITH PROSTITUTE	(N = 966) (%)
Oral sex	50
Vaginal sex	14
Half and half (oral and vaginal)	10
Hand job	6
Other	3
Two or more are equally common	17

HOW OFTEN VISIT PROSTITUTES	(N = 1274) (%)
Never have	19
Not within the last year	22
Once during the last year	21
Less than once per month	28
Once or more per month	10

HOW OFTEN USE CONDOM WITH PROSTITUTE	(N = 1024)
Never	4
Seldom	3
Sometimes	8
Often	11
Always	74

TABLE 10.2 continued

PROSTITUTION SHOULD BE LEGALIZED	(N = 1137) (%)
Agree somewhat or strongly	74

PROSTITUTION SHOULD BE DECRIMINALIZED	(N = 1121) (%)
Agree somewhat or strongly	69

decriminalized (the terms "legalized" and "decriminalized" were not defined in the survey). Clients' support for legalization and decriminalization is much higher than that of the general public, probably because they have a personal interest in avoiding arrest.[25]

Are Customers Inclined Toward Violence Against Women?

Research consistently shows that many street prostitutes are victims of violent crime, including assault and rape, much of which is never reported to police. Prostitutes are also overrepresented as murder victims.[26] Some feminists argue that prostitution and violence are inexorably intertwined, used by men as tools to reinforce male privilege. But does it follow that customers are more violent or more likely to hold attitudes consistent with violence than other men?

It is questionable whether customers participating in research such as my own would accurately and honestly report having committed violent acts themselves. Additionally, it is likely that customers might not recognize their own violence as such. The studies of reported victimization of prostitutes shed some light on the issue. If it is true that the prostitutes interviewed in studies on violence actually have hundreds of customers in a given year as reported, then only a small proportion of violent men, perhaps visiting prostitutes multiple times during a given year, could easily account for the levels of violence reported by prostitutes. There is no evidence to suggest that more than a minority of customers assault prostitutes.

My own review of websites, in which customers share consumer information about prostitutes and describe their experiences, indicates that many are aware of violence against prostitutes, and some of those who are aware of it are concerned about it. It is not uncommon for these writers to complain about violence against prostitutes or to encourage others to treat prostitutes with respect. Occasionally, customers reported their own violent acts, such as an unwelcome ejaculation onto a prostitute's face without prior consent. In cases such as this, it is unclear whether the customers or the prostitutes define the experiences as violent, though many clearly are so. O'Connell Davidson's study of so-called "sexpatriates," men who have moved to underdeveloped regions in order to have easy access to prostitutes, also includes a number of enthusiastic descriptions of experiences that involve violence.[27] By contrast, violence is seldom described or reported in the web-based accounts I studied, and these regular users do not view their participation as customers as contributing to violence against prostitutes.

The attitudes of arrested customers of prostitutes do not indicate that this population has a particular inclination toward violence against women. Respondents were asked questions from a widely used Rape Myth Acceptance (RMA) scale. Rape myths are "prejudicial, stereotyped, or false beliefs about rape, rape victims, and rapists" that serve to justify or support sexual violence against women and diminish support for rape victims.[28] The customers in my study were not, in general, more likely to endorse rape myths than other samples of men.[29] Sixteen percent thought that "if a girl engages in necking or petting and she lets things get out of hand, it is her own fault if her partner forces sex on her"; 17% agreed that "in the majority of rapes, the victim is promiscuous or has a bad reputation"; and 9% agreed that "women who get raped while hitchhiking get what they deserve." The findings indicate that most clients do not hold views that justify violence against prostitutes, and it is likely that most of the violence is committed by a minority of customers. Successful prostitution policy should differentiate between customers who perpetrate violence and the remainder of customers.

Why Do Men Go to Prostitutes?

As noted earlier, people tend to assume that the motives of johns are obvious, not worthy of serious exploration. Kinsey's research supported the assumption that seeking prostitution was simply a natural extension of conventional masculine sexual expression.[30] However, more recent research contradicts the notion that buying sexual services is conventional behavior among men.[31] Why, then, do some men seek out prostitutes?

A few researchers have conducted in-depth interviews with the clients of prostitutes. McKeganey and Barnard conducted 66 telephone interviews with men who respond to an advertisement in a tabloid newspaper and nine in-person interviews of men contacted on the street. They also obtained information from 68 men attending a health clinic specializing in sexually transmitted diseases. They argue that men are attracted to paid sex because they desire sexual acts they cannot receive from their partners; they are able to have sex with a larger number of sexual partners; they are attracted to specific physical characteristics; they like the limited emotional involvement; and they are excited by the illicit nature of the act. The authors also suggest that some men seek prostitutes in order to inflict violence on them.[32]

Holzman and Pines interviewed 30 men, contacted through the snowball sampling of acquaintances, in an effort to capture the subjective experience of the prostitution encounter. This sample was one of regular users who had paid for sex an average of more than 50 times. They argue that men's primary motivations for having sexual relations with prostitutes are the desire for sex or for companionship. Men are also motivated by the mystery and excitement associated with the risky encounter, the belief that prostitutes are women of "exceptional sexual powers," and an interest in avoiding emotional involvement or the risk of rejection.[33]

Jordan's in-depth interviews of 13 clients in New Zealand suggest that men's reasons for seeking prostitution vary depending on their personal circumstances and their ability to meet their needs through conventional relationships. Older married men often indicated that their wives were unwilling or unable to satisfy them sexually. Others sought prostitutes because they wanted to avoid committed relationships or felt unable to enter into conventional relationships. Some were motivated by the desire to satisfy intense sexual urges or to have sex with a large number of different women, while others sought prostitutes for companionship, intimacy, or love.[34]

In the present study, customers from the 1997–2000 sample answered 13 questions that assessed their motives for seeking out prostitutes (see Table 10.3). All the items are personalized "I" statements, such as "I have difficulty meeting women who are not nude dancers or prostitutes," and "I like to be in control when I'm having sex." The smaller 2007 sample (Table 10.4), asked customers to identify the "reasons" they had sex with prostitutes. Included in the list are "they will do things sexually that other women won't," "control over the situation," and three other reasons, as well as "other" to allow an exhaustive set of responses.

Table 10.3 reports the percentage of customers who agreed with each "I" statement. I compared the responses of repeat customers (at least two encounters in the past year) to first-time customers; the responses of married men and unmarried men; and the responses of college graduates and non-graduates. Six of the "I" statements were endorsed by over 40% of the respondents. These included "I like to be with a woman who likes to get nasty" (52%); "I am excited by the idea of approaching a prostitute" (43%); "I like to be in control when I am having sex" (42%); "I like to have a variety of sexual partners" (41%); "I want a different kind of sex than my regular

TABLE 10.3 MOTIVES FOR BUYING SEX

STATEMENT	TOTAL (%)	REPEAT USER (%)	FIRST-TIMER (%)	PERCENTAGE AGREEING				
				COLLEGE GRAD (%)	NON-GRAD (%)	MARRIED (%)	NOT MARRIED (%)	
I have difficulty meeting women who are not nude dancers or prostitutes	22.6	26.7*	16.4	18.2*	26.2	20.3	24.4	
I think most women find me unattractive physically	23.8	24.7	22.2	17.0*	27.6	23.2	24.1	
I want a different kind of sex than my regular partner [wants]	40.7	49.2*	28.5	48.2*	36.1	48.5*	34.7	
I am shy and awkward when I am trying to meet a woman	41.4	46.5*	33.5	34.3*	45.1	33.7	46.9	
I would rather have sex with a prostitute than have a conventional relationship with a woman	17.7	22.6*	10.5	18.7	17.3	18.5	17.1	

I am excited by the idea of approaching a prostitute	43.1	53.1*	28.4	55.0*	36.8	45.0	42.0
I don't have the time for a conventional relationship	31.9	36.0*	25.4	33.1	31.2	27.4	35.1
I don't want the responsibilities of a conventional relationship	28.0	32.6*	20.9	27.9	27.9	23.7*	31.1
I like to have a variety of sexual partners	41.2	51.7*	25.8	54.3*	34.0	40.0	42.4
I like to be in control when I'm having sex	41.9	44.9*	37.1	39.2*	43.1	39.0	44.1
I like to be with a woman who likes to get nasty	51.6	57.9*	42.6	53.7	51.0	49.4	53.3
I need to have sex immediately when I am aroused	31.3	36.1*	24.3	30.9	31.8	30.8	31.5
I like rough hard sex	19.1	20.4	17.3	16.7*	20.5	14.7	22.3

* Pearson chi-squared test significant at $p < .05$.

TABLE 10.4 REASONS FOR BUYING SEX, 2007 SAMPLE

REASON	ONE REASON (%)	MAIN REASON (%)
They will do things sexually that other women won't do	17	11
Don't have to worry about a relationship	23	18
Quick easy way to get sex	44	47
Control over the situation	7	3
They need the money, and I help them by paying for sex	5	3
Other	19	18

Note: N = 178 men in the 2007 First Offender Prostitution Program in San Francisco.

partner" (41%); and "I am shy and awkward when trying to meet women" (41%). All the remaining items were endorsed by at least 19% of respondents.

Although the most frequently endorsed item (Table 10.3) would seem to best explain men's reasons for sex with prostitutes, the "woman who likes to get nasty" is not explicitly defined as a prostitute. Still, this item, in conjunction with the second most endorsed item, "I am excited by the idea of approaching a prostitute," supports the idea that one of the attractions of sex with a prostitute is that it is illicit or risky. According to a customer interviewed by Holzman and Pines, part of the attraction was the "element of risk . . . the gambling element."[35] A number of other responses to both sets of questions suggest that prostitution is seen by customers as simply a convenient, quick, easy way for men to get sex, and without the effort of a relationship.

Table 10.4 reports responses to the two "reasons" questions asked of the 2007 sample. The most frequently endorsed reason for seeking prostitutes was that is a "quick and easy" way to get sex (44%). Forty-seven percent identified this as their main reason for having sex with prostitutes. The second most popular reason was "don't have to worry about a relationship" and the third was that "they will do things sexually that other women won't do." Almost 20% selected "other"; however, over half of these responses constituted excuses or denials claiming that the respondent had not had sex with a prostitute or was not seeking sex at the time of arrest.

These responses seem to suggest a "commodified" perspective toward sexuality, in which sex is analogous to a consumer product rather than an aspect of intimate relationships. The desire to "have a variety of sexual partners," the need to "be in control during sex," and the urge to "have sex immediately when I am aroused" also point to this kind of self-focused sexuality. The idea of shopping for a sex partner with particular physical attributes, such as hair color, body type, or ethnicity—which is precisely what some customers seek—also reflects a conception of sex as a commodity rather than as part of an intimate relationship.

Wanting a kind of sex different than what one's regular partner wants (41%) or believing that prostitutes will "do things sexually that other women won't do" supports the idea that some men seek out prostitutes because they can do things with them that other women might find unpleasant or unacceptable. Liking "rough hard sex" (19%) may be not only a sexual preference but also a reflection of a desire to dominate women during sex.

The data also suggest that some men pay for sex because they have difficulty establishing a conventional relationship. Forty-one percent said that they were "shy and awkward" when trying to meet women, 24% felt unattractive physically, and 23% had "difficulty meeting women who were not nude dancers or prostitutes." For some of these men, patronizing prostitutes may be an attempt not only to have sex, but also to establish an intimate relationship with a woman. Jordan describes one very shy client who felt desperately alone and eventually fell in love with a prostitute. When she quit working, he was disappointed. Although he continued to visit prostitutes, he claimed, "It's not sexual relief that I go for—it's to relieve some loneliness that I feel."[36] These responses indicate that, for some clients, frequenting a prostitute may be a way of establishing an intimate connection with a woman.

Further support for all these motives is found in the fact that each item was more likely to be endorsed by repeat users than first-time offenders. (For all but two of these items a chi-squared test of independence indicated significance at the $p < .05$ level.) Repeat users were more than twice as likely as first-timers to report that they had difficulty meeting women who were not prostitutes or nude dancers and were also more likely to say that they were shy and awkward when trying to meet women. A commodified approach to sexuality—that is, an interest in variety, control, and immediate satisfaction— is also more evident among the repeat users.

Motives for buying sex differ according to social class, as indicated here by respondents' education level. College graduates were more likely than non-graduates to indicate an interest in sexual variety and excitement, to want sexual acts different from those their regular partners offered, to want a variety of sexual partners, and to feel excited by the idea of seeking a prostitute. Non-college graduates were more likely to report difficulty meeting women, awkwardness, and feeling physically unattractive. Some of these men may buy sex from prostitutes because of their inability to form conventional relationships with women. Additionally, non-college graduates were more likely than college graduates to say they wanted to be in control during sex. Prostitution may be one way in which they gain some control in their encounters with women. In sum, clients' social class backgrounds make a difference in their reasons for buying sex.

Married clients were more likely than unmarried men to report wanting a different kind of sex than their regular partners. Among unmarried men this may reflect the lack of a regular sexual partner. A married man who has a sense of entitlement to sex may see patronizing a prostitute as justifiable should the wife not meet his perceived sexual needs. Unmarried clients were more likely to report shyness, a liking for rough sex, and a desire to avoid the responsibilities of conventional relationships—all of which could limit their success in forming conventional relationships.

CONCLUSION

The act of approaching a prostitute is a product of many factors. These are likely to include the availability of prostitutes, knowledge of where to find them, access to sufficient money to pay them, risk of being caught or of contracting disease, and ease of securing services. While these practical issues may be important in influencing whether a man *seeks* prostitutes, they tell us little about the needs that the man is trying to fill through prostitution. This chapter sheds light on these motivations.

There is no single or simple reason men patronize prostitutes. Even the conventional notion that "they go for sex" falls short, as some men visit prostitutes in an effort to experience emotional intimacy, and many men who want sex do not patronize prostitutes. Rather, seeking the services of a prostitute appears to reflect a number of motivations, including an attraction to the illicit nature of the encounter, a desire for varieties of sex that may not be provided by regular partners, defining sex as a commodity, and a lack of interest in or access to conventional relationships. All of the influences are more pronounced among repeat users than among first-timers. Motivations appear to differ depending on the class backgrounds of the men, with college graduates more likely to seek the excitement of illicit sex, and non-graduates more likely to report difficulty in forming conventional relationships. Additionally, married men were more likely to be seeking sexual behaviors they could not experience with their wives, and unmarried men were more likely to avoid conventional relationships or report difficulty in securing them. Few men were motivated by the most destructive reasons for patronizing prostitutes—because of a desire for rough sex or because one holds beliefs conducive to rape.

The growing research focusing on customers beginning in the 1990s has shed greater light on this once hidden population. We now have much more insight into their motives and characteristics. Clearly, there are many motives for seeking prostitutes and many variables that predict whether a motivated individual will follow through with behavior. Perhaps most striking is how unsurprising the findings are. If one were to ask a college class to describe the 10 most common reasons why men pursue prostitutes, as I have done many times, the responses would line up pretty well with the findings described here. Although there are many misconceptions regarding prostitution, customers' motives are not among them. While we may never know the distinctive circumstances that led Eliot Spitzer into liaisons with prostitutes, we can be fairly certain that some of his motivations are the same as those described here.

Most of the respondents in my study were arrested on the street. Yet, increasingly, sexual services are advertised and negotiated over the Internet. While this is likely to reduce street prostitution and thus make researchers' contact with street-based prostitutes and customers more difficult, it may make it easier to contact customers who patronize indoor workers and can be accessed online. Future research on patrons of web-based prostitution, organized indoor prostitution establishments, and male prostitutes will be especially helpful. Also in need of future study are the situational predictors that explain why some men but not others choose prostitutes as a means of meeting their sexual or emotional desires. After all, many men sometimes "feel awkward and shy when trying to meet a woman," "want a different kind of sex than their regular partner" provides, or "get excited about the idea of approaching a prostitute." Interviews comparing clients to non-clients are needed to explore how socialization regarding sexuality and masculinity leads some men to consider prostitution as an option.

NOTES

Research for this chapter was supported by a grant from the National Institute of Justice (Grant 97-IJ-CX-0033). I thank Norma Hotaling, co-founder of San Francisco's First Offender Prostitution Program for access to most of the men in my sample. I also thank Steve Garcia and Holly Pierce for their excellent research assistance.

1. Federal Complaint against Mark Brenner, Cecil Suwal, Temeka Rachelle Lewis, Tanya Hollander, 2008. http://www.npr.org/documents/2008/mar/dojfull.pdf.

2. Priscilla Alexander, "Prostitution: A Difficult Issue for Feminists," in Frederique Delacoste and Priscilla Alexander, eds., *Sex Work: Writings by Women in the Sex Industry*, Pittsburgh: Cleis Press, 1987; Martin Monto, "Female Prostitution, Customers, and Violence," *Violence Against Women* 10 (2004): 160–188.

3. Martin Monto, "Holding Men Accountable for Prostitution: The Unique Approach of the Sexual Exploitation Education Project," *Violence Against Women* 4 (1998): 505–517.

4. Martin Monto, *Focusing on the Clients of Street Prostitutes: A Creative Approach to Reducing Violence Against Women*, NIJ Final Report, National Institute of Justice, 1999. http://www.ncjrs.org/pdffiles1/nij/grants/182860.pdf ; Monto, "Female Prostitution."

5. Jeanna Bryner, "Why Power and Prostitution Go Together," *Live Science,* 2008 http://www.livescience.com/health/080311-spitzer-hypocrisy.html; Sam Janus, Barbara Bess, and Carol Saltus, *A Sexual Profile of Men in Power*, Englewood Cliffs, NJ: Prentice-Hall, 1977.

6. Harold Holzman and Sharon Pines, "Buying Sex: The Phenomenology of Being a John," *Deviant Behavior* 4 (1982): 89–116; Jan Jordan, "User Pays: Why Men Buy Sex," *Australian and New Zealand Journal of Criminology* 30 (1997): 55–71; Julia O'Connell Davidson, "The Sex Tourist, The Expatriate, His Ex-Wife, and Her 'Other'," *Sexualities* 4 (2001): 5–24; Julia O'Connell Davidson, *Prostitution, Power, and Freedom*, Ann Arbor, MI: University of Michigan Press, 1998; Elizabeth Plumridge, Jane Chetwynd, Anna Reed, and Sandra Gifford, "Discourses of Emotionality in Commercial Sex: The Missing Client Voice," *Feminism and Psychology* 7 (1997): 165–181.

7. Robert Michael, John Gagnon, Edward Laumann, and Gina Kolata, *Sex in America: A Definitive Survey*, Boston: Little, Brown, 1994; National Opinion Research Center, *General Social Survey, 1972–2000: Cumulative Codebook*, Chicago: NORC, 2001.

8. Roger Kern, *Where's the Action: Criminal Motivations Among Prostitute Clients*, Ph.D. dissertation: Vanderbilt University, 2000; Martin Monto, "Competing Definitions of Prostitution: Insights from Two Studies of Male Customers," presented at the annual meetings of the American Sociological Association, 2001.

9. Alfred Kinsey, Wendell Pomeroy, and Clyde Martin, *Sexual Behavior in the Human Male*, Philadelphia: W.B. Saunders, 1948.

10. Harold Benjamin and R. E. L. Masters, *Prostitution and Morality*, New York: Julian Press, 1964.

11. Bonnie Bullough and Vern Bullough, *Women and Prostitution*, Buffalo, NY: Prometheus Books, 1987.

12. Michael, et al., *Sex in America*.

13. Nannette Davis, "From Victims to Survivors: Working with Recovering Prostitutes," in Ronald Weitzer, ed., *Sex for Sale*, New York: Routledge, 2000.

14. Ronald Weitzer, "New Directions in Research on Prostitution," *Crime, Law, and Social Change* 43 (2005): 211–235.

15. Monto, "Female Prostitution"; O'Connell Davidson, "Prostitution, Power, and Freedom."

16. Mimi Silbert, "Occupational Hazards of Street Prostitutes," *Criminal Justice and Behavior* 8 (1981): 395–399; Nannette Davis, *Prostitution: An International Handbook on Trends, Problems, and Policies*, London: Greenwood Press, 1993.

17. See Chapter 1 in this volume, and Ronald Weitzer, "Prostitution Control in America: Rethinking Public Policy," *Crime, Law, and Social Change* 32 (1999): 83–102.

18. Catherine Benson and Roger Matthews, "Street Prostitution: Ten Facts in Search of a Policy," *International Journal of the Sociology of Law* 23 (1995): 395–415; Mimi Silbert, "Prostitution and Sexual Assault: Summary of Results," *International Journal of Biosocial Research* 3 (1981): 69–71; D. Kelly Weisberg, *Children of the Night: A Study of Adolescent Prostitution*, Lexington, MA: Lexington Books, 1985.

19. Monto "Final Report."

20. Julia O'Connell Davidson, "The Rights and Wrongs of Prostitution," *Hypatia* 17 (2002): 84–98; Monto "Female Prostitution."

21. Weitzer, "Prostitution Control"; Monto "Final Report."

22. Monto, "Female Prostitution."

23. ABT Associates, *Final Report on the Evaluation of the First Offender Prostitution Program*, Washington, DC: National Institute of Justice, 2008. http://www.ncjrs.gov/pdffiles1/nij/grants/222451.pdf.

24. Matthew Freund, Nancy Lee, and Terri Leonard, "Sexual Behavior of Clients with Street Prostitutes in Camden, NJ," *Journal of Sex Research* 28 (1991): 579–591.

25. See Chapter 1 of this book, and Ronald Weitzer, "The Politics of Prostitution in America," in Ronald Weitzer, ed., *Sex for Sale*, New York: Routledge, 2000.

26. John Lowman, "Violence and the Outlaw Status of (Street) Prostitution in Canada," *Violence Against Women* 6 (2000): 987–1011.

27. Julia O'Connell Davidson and Jacqueline Sanchez Taylor, "Child Prostitution and Sex Tourism: Dominican Republic," Research paper, ECPAT International, 1995.

28. Martha Burt, "Cultural Myths and Supports for Rape," *Journal of Personality and Social Psychology* 38 (1980): 217–230.

29. Martin Monto and Norma Hotaling, "Predictors of Rape Myth Acceptance among the Male Clients of Female Street Prostitutes," *Violence Against Women* 7 (2001): 275–293.

30. Kinsey, et al., *Sexual Behavior*.

31. Elroy Sullivan and William Simon, "The Client," in James Elias, Vern Bullough, Veronica Elias, and Gwen Brewer, eds., *Prostitution*, Amherst, NY: Prometheus, 1998; Martin Monto and Nick McRee, "A Comparison of the Male Customers of Female Street Prostitutes with National Samples of Men," *International Journal of Offender Therapy and Comparative Criminology* 49 (2005): 505–529.

32. McKeganey and Barnard, *Sex Work on the Streets*.

33. Holzman and Pines,"Buying Sex."

34. Jordan, "User Buys."

35. Holzman and Pines, "Buying Sex."

36. Jordan, "User Buys."

NEVADA'S LEGAL BROTHELS

Kathryn Hausbeck and Barbara G. Brents

In Nevada's dusty desert, in a small gambling town, visitors might turn off main street and find themselves facing a row of otherwise nondescript wooden buildings with signs saying Mona's Ranch, Inez's D&D, or Sue's Fantasy Club. These rural brothels remind us of a bygone era of itinerant miners, small-town saloons, powerful sheriffs, and women who survived by selling one of the rarest and most sought-after commodities in the Old West: sex.

While this depiction projects a mythic version of the Old, Wild West, the 10 counties in Nevada that license brothels exist within a modern political and economic culture. The Old West culture of ranching and mining is fast becoming a part of the New West's consumer culture built on a service-and-information economy that increasingly sells experiences and adventure tourism, and links the local to the global.[1] Coexisting with frontier towns that grew up around railroad, agricultural, or mining hubs, the New West is marked by fast growing urban centers surrounded by sprawling suburbs. Near the urban centers of Reno and Las Vegas, visitors can find brothels that are generally larger, more upscale, and more modern than those in the frontier towns. Nevada's brothel culture of frontier individualism, libertarian values, mining, agriculture, and ranching exists within the commercial, cosmopolitan, touristic New West.

Nevada is the only place in the United States to have legalized prostitution. Unlike some other countries, where brothels exist in major cities, Nevada's brothels are prohibited in major metropolitan areas. But despite

Nevada's uniqueness and over three decades of legal prostitution, few studies of the industry exist.[2] This chapter examines how legal prostitution in Nevada is evolving from its origins in a rural, Old West culture toward a New West economy and culture situated within modern service and leisure industries. We examine (1) the contemporary structure of the Nevada brothel industry, (2) the relationship between the brothels and the government, (3) brothel owners' relations to one another, and (4) the relation of the brothel industry to the broader tourist economy and culture in Nevada.

RESEARCH METHODS

This study is based on several data sources. We examined newspaper articles and archival data for the historical and sociopolitical context in which brothel prostitution was legalized in Nevada and to identify existing regulations governing the industry; we conducted observations in and collected documents from 13 brothels in Nevada beginning in 1997; we interviewed 40 female brothel workers and 13 owners and managers. In addition, we conducted numerous interviews with a variety of other individuals, including government officials, lobbyists, businesspeople, brothel regulators, former industry employees, and the head of the Nevada Brothel Association. The chapter describes how these individuals view the brothel system, their role and association with this industry, and what they identify as the challenges and benefits of this system of legal prostitution.

HISTORY OF NEVADA'S BROTHELS

The few studies that have addressed the anomalous existence of Nevada's brothels attribute it to some combination of economics and political culture. Most historical studies argue that prostitution arose from the mining economy of the Old West and survived thanks to a libertarian political philosophy that persisted in Nevada more than in other western states.[3] Others have argued that the economic needs of declining rural economies allowed prostitution to outlive its Old West past.[4] We argue that the culture and political economy of the West had several features that help explain the rise of the brothels: an economically unstable, migrant economy; libertarian sexual values; a particular political culture, and the beginnings of a tourist economy.

Nevada's brothels were born of a boom-and-bust mining economy and became a stabilizing force on the frontier. They existed in a sexual culture that saw a legitimate function for prostitution by meeting the biological "needs" of a migrant labor force, while offering a means of survival for some women. As towns developed, prostitution became institutionalized in brothels, which could be regulated in accordance with local sex and gender norms. A libertarian, antigovernment, antiurban political culture also contributed to the eventual legalization of brothels. Over time, the brothels remained in the rural areas despite the growing urban dependence on tourism and a gaming industry that sought to legitimate itself through opposition to legal brothels. These factors remain salient today, and help explain why brothels with origins in the Old West persist today in Nevada's modern New West leisure economy and tourist culture.

The gold rush and silver mining, as well as the railroad industry, drew large numbers of single men to Nevada's harsh desert environment. The instability of this migrant labor force and boom-and-bust economy made it difficult to bring families to settle in Nevada's first isolated mining towns. In these communities of single men and enterprising single women, prostitution thrived. This migrant mining economy was also associated with a particular set of sexual values and politics. Prostitution, if not always individual prostitutes themselves, became an accepted part of the community from the perspective of working men. Women were considered far from equal to their male counterparts. "Good girls" on the frontier needed protection; "bad girls" were sexually available and provided necessary services to frontiersmen. Patriarchal gender roles reflected and reinforced the idea that male sexuality was driven by biological needs that required frequent tending.

Together, the migrant economy and the corresponding libertarian yet paternalistic sexual values kept prostitution alive as mining camps grew into small towns. In the 1920s and 1930s, Nevada created the quick divorce and legal gambling to lure in tourists, and began diversifying its economy. But, during World War I and World War II, the Federal Security Agency pressured county governments throughout the West to pass ordinances banning prostitution in order to prevent "the spread of venereal disease to the detriment of members of the armed forces of the United States sojourning in said city or in the neighborhood."[5] Many counties strongly resisted federal intrusion, but many brothels nevertheless closed.[6]

The rural counties reopened their brothels as soon as World War II ended, although, in 1949, the Nevada Supreme Court ruled that brothels were a public nuisance. Federal military spending and works projects had already begun to transform the Old West culture in urban areas, and these forces slowly chipped away at the brothel businesses in Reno and Las Vegas. In Las Vegas, city managers promised to close down the brothels so that the federal government would build Nellis Air Force Base nearby. In the context of a profitable gaming industry, Reno, Las Vegas, and their county governments had a strong desire to legitimate themselves. They closed the remaining brothels in and near the two cities. Meanwhile, the rural counties, still dependent on their traditional economies and resenting government interference, passed ordinances to avoid the nuisance charges and retain their brothels.[7]

Nowhere is the antigovernment culture more evident than in the popular story of the passage of the statewide legislation in 1971 that allowed the first official brothel licensing. A brash individual, Joe Conforte, opened several brothels beginning in the 1950s and for years battled the local district attorney, claiming the best way to deal with orders to close down was to ignore them.[8] In the 1960s, Conforte took over the famous Mustang Ranch in Storey County, but a district judge ordered him to close the brothel and repay Storey County $5000 to offset costs. Conforte paid but kept the brothel open. Three years later, a county attorney advised Storey commissioners that they needed an ordinance to make the $5000 fee legal. On December 5, 1970, commissioners passed the first brothel-licensing ordinance in the nation.[9]

Meanwhile, rumors spread that Conforte planned to open a brothel in Clark County, the home of Las Vegas. State legislators representing Clark County, still fighting to make gambling look legitimate, scrambled to introduce a statewide bill banning prostitution, which was fought by legislators from rural counties. Finally, in 1971, legislators succeeded by passing a bill making prostitution illegal in counties with populations of more than 200,000, which, at that time, meant only Clark County. The Nevada Supreme Court ruled in 1978 that this prohibition of brothel prostitution in one county tacitly allowed the other 16 counties to license brothels. In the following years, brothel owners in a majority of counties successfully lobbied county commissioners to pass brothel-licensing ordinances.[10] Each county created its own unique ordinance that essentially formalized the existing practices.

THE CULTURAL CONTEXT

A key to the rise and persistence of brothel prostitution is the neoliberal political and sexual culture. The sale of sex in Nevada's brothels became acceptable because there was both a transient labor force and tourist population and a need to generate revenue; because the values of the citizenry were open to a particular definition of gender roles and sexuality; and because there was no powerful external body like the federal government opposing legal prostitution. Legal brothel prostitution is justified by a discourse that maintains that (1) the sale of sex is one of the world's oldest professions and is unlikely to disappear; (2) state and local government-regulated prostitution is superior to illegal prostitution insofar as it is allows for limitations on what is sold, on the terms and conditions of sales, and on brothel ownership and employment practices; (3) such businesses are revenue generating; (4) legal prostitution provides a valuable service to certain individuals who have desires that cannot be easily fulfilled otherwise; and (5) limiting such activities to particular licensed venues curtails related criminal activities (drugs, pimping, violence) and helps control the spread of disease.

Central to these five beliefs is the notion that humans are sexual beings, and that it is inevitable that some women will resist traditional feminine roles and sell sex and that men will want to have sex available on demand. As one local politician explained to us:

> Prostitution isn't going anywhere. There will always be guys passing through town, trucking or working, and guys who can't get a woman themselves. This is a community service to meet natural needs. If we got rid of brothels it would still happen at the truck stops, on streets, and that just isn't good. There will be drugs, violence; it looks bad in the community, bad for families.

The form of legal prostitution that emerged in Nevada places limitations on the kind of sex for sale permitted, the parties involved, and the circumstances under which the exchange may occur. These norms reflect the dominant discourses of gender and sex: in Nevada, only women have ever been recognized as legitimate prostitutes, and the norm of heterosexuality permeates brothel regulations.

Common, too, are discourses of health and safety. It is typical among brothel supporters, community members, and the workers themselves to argue that brothels keep things safe. First, it is perceived as safer for the community—minimizing rape, sexual assault, extramarital affairs, and the spread of disease. Second, it is safer for the workers and the clients. An owner of a small-town brothel told us, "It's safer for the girls here than anywhere else. . . . We take care of them here; the girls need that. It's safer for the men, too, from a health perspective. Guys are afraid of getting something from the street girls; you never know what they have." In our interviews with brothel prostitutes, we found that the regulatory oversight and public scrutiny of the brothels decrease the women's perceived risks to health and safety, and that the workers thus feel empowered. Celeste explained, "We are independent contractors, we have the right to refuse anybody for any reason." Misty concurred, "We can stop them here, we can stop them at the bar." In fact, in addition to mandatory condom usage and constant security, health and safety are important reasons why many women choose to work in Nevada brothels.[11] And despite the restrictions placed on them, the women cited benefits of living and working in a legal brothel. Emili, for example, described the brothel atmosphere this way: "We've got a cook, we've got a sun deck back there, we have a garden, we have a Jacuzzi room—we try to treat each other good."

STRUCTURE OF THE BROTHEL INDUSTRY

Today, Nevada is home to 28 licensed brothels in 10 counties. The legal contexts in which brothels are organized vary significantly by county and proximity to metropolitan areas. Table 11.1 summarizes, by county, the regulations regarding brothel prostitution in Nevada. Clark County is the only county where state law prohibits licensing brothels. A few other counties have ordinances prohibiting prostitution, including Washoe County, which surrounds Reno.

The county is the licensing and regulating body. As shown in Table 11.1, brothels are currently licensed in the unincorporated areas of Churchill, Esmeralda, Lander, Lyon, Mineral, Nye, and Storey counties. Four other counties—Elko, Humboldt, Pershing, White Pine—prohibit brothel prostitution in unincorporated areas but allow it by municipal option; the towns of Elko, Ely, Wells, and Winnemucca license brothels.

The geography of the state has a significant impact on the structure of the industry. Nevada is one of the most rural states in the country, with only two metropolitan areas, Reno and Las Vegas. Most of the state's population resides in these two areas. The average distance between towns is 100 miles, and as much as 200 miles in the more isolated counties. In 2006, 11 of Nevada's counties had fewer than six people per square mile.[12] Of these 11 sparsely populated, frontier counties, 7 have legal brothels. One of the most significant splits within the brothel industry is between brothels in the sparsely populated "frontier" counties and those in the "suburban" counties closest to urban areas.

The largest and most profitable brothels are located in the suburban counties closest to Reno and Las Vegas—Storey, Lyon, and Nye. The brothel industry statewide earned around $45 million in 2008, according to the Nevada Brothel Association, but the eight largest brothels in these suburban counties account for approximately three-quarters of the state's brothel

TABLE 11.1   NEVADA'S BROTHELS

COUNTIES	CURRENTLY LICENSED BROTHELS, 2007	WITHIN 1-HOUR DRIVE FROM MAJOR METRO AREA	POPULATION PER SQUARE MILE, 2006[1]	COUNTY LAW PROHIBITS IN UNINCORPORATED AREAS	TOWNS WITH LICENSING ORDINANCES	TOTAL ANNUAL INCOME FROM LICENSE FEES, ROOM, AND LIQUOR TAXES ($)	TOTAL ANNUAL INCOME FROM WORK CARDS ($)
Carson City	Prohibited by county law	Yes	386.6	Yes			
Clark	Prohibited by state law	Yes	224.7	Yes			
Douglas	Prohibited by county law	Yes	64.7	Yes			
Washoe	Prohibited by county law	Yes	62.5	Yes			
Lincoln	Prohibited by county law	No	0.4	Yes			
Pershing	Prohibited by county law	No	1.1	Yes			
Eureka	No written ordinance	No	0.4				
Churchill	None currently licensed	Yes	5.1			0	
Elko	Two in Carlin	No	2.7	Yes	Carlin	3000	1200
	Four in Elko	No			Elko	12,960	7800
	Two in Wells	No			Wells	10,600[2]	7500[2]
Esmeralda	None open	No	0.2			0	0
Humboldt	Three in Winnemucca	No	1.8	Yes	Winnemucca	25,500	2600[2]
Lander	Two in Battle Mtn[3]	No	1.0			1200	1100[2]

TABLE 11.1 continued

COUNTIES	CURRENTLY LICENSED BROTHELS, 2007	WITHIN 1-HOUR DRIVE FROM MAJOR METRO AREA	POPULATION PER SQUARE MILE, 2006[1]	COUNTY LAW PROHIBITS IN UNINCOR-PORATED AREAS	TOWNS WITH LICENSING ORDINANCES	TOTAL ANNUAL INCOME FROM LICENSE FEES, ROOM, AND LIQUOR TAXES ($)	TOTAL ANNUAL INCOME FROM WORK CARDS ($)
Lyon	Four outside Carson City	Yes	25.7			327,500	26,300
Mineral	Two near Mina	No	1.3			4560	1525[4]
Nye	Four near Pahrump	Yes	2.4			114,375	34,938
	One near Beatty	No					
Storey	Two near Sparks	Yes	15.7			160,000	18,750
White Pine	Two in Ely	No	1.0	Yes	Ely	1490	1275

Notes:
[1] Calculated using data on 2006 Nevada County Demographics, from U.S. Census Bureau, *State and County Quick Facts*, http://quickfacts.census.gov/qfd/states/32000.html. Last updated: Friday, July 25, 2008.
[2] Income from prostitutes' work cards is estimated, as the county issues the same work cards as for other workers.
[3] License fees are paid on two brothels though only one is currently operating.
[4] This total is based on 35 work cards issued, and an estimated 15 renewals at $15 plus 65 new issues.

income.[13] The largest employ up to 80 women at a time. The remaining frontier brothels bring in far less income, and most employ 2 to 10 women at a time.[14]

The economy of both the frontier and suburban brothels remains a migrant economy, just as it was in the Old West. But the nature of that migrant economy is changing. While the small and isolated towns in northern and eastern Nevada have grown since the 1870s to become primarily dependent on service jobs in gambling and tourism, their economies are still far more dependent than those in urban areas on traditional, rural occupations. Seven of Nevada's frontier counties are still primarily dependent on Old West industries of mining, farming, or ranching.[15] But in addition to their economic dependence on the young men who have temporarily left home to earn big paychecks in the mines, frontier counties are increasingly dependent on several new migrant groups—construction workers, the military, truckers, and tourists. Depending on where each brothel is located, it relies heavily on customers from one or more of these groups. These working-class men are considered the core brothel clientele.

But there is also a new type of tourist demanding more "cultured" entertainment in the New West.[16] The National Cowboy Poetry Gathering brings 10,000 people to Elko each winter, and the Burning Man festival in the Blackrock desert north of Reno attracts nearly 35,000 visitors. The rugged amenities that surrounded the migrant miner are being replaced by espresso shops and the Ruby Mountain Brewery in Elko. California's elite have been purchasing ranches near popular areas offering fly fishing, mountain biking, and rock climbing—increasing the cost of living for many locals. The remote, dusty, desert community described at the beginning of this chapter is becoming engulfed in a larger, global tourist culture, complete with its economic shifts toward service-based, leisure businesses.

In some ways, the new breed of tourists who visit the brothels may be no different than the customers in times gone by. However, this new Nevada culture may bring to the brothels customers who are less immersed in the cultural climate of the rugged American West and more accustomed to pop-cultural depictions of commercial sex, or who hold more global and cosmopolitan expectations about the emotional, sexual, and commercial experience of prostitution. As one new owner told us, "I bought this brothel because it reminded me of what an Old West brothel ought to look like." Some brothel customers may desire the experience of Wild West culture as much as their tryst with a prostitute. In the New West, a brothel visit is just another stop on a local tour and an opportunity to collect a good story along the tourist trail, rather than a way to fulfill sexual needs. But other customers

Figure 11.1   Sherri's Ranch Brothel, Pahrump, Nevada. Photo by the authors.

seek to purchase their sexual intimacy in a more upscale, conventionally sexualized market space. As a result, we see that smaller, more remote brothels tend to market the downhome, Wild West, historic experience, while the larger, suburban brothels are re-branding themselves with a more familiar and luxurious, modern sexualized atmosphere (see Figure 11.1).[17]

The workers are migrants as well. Rarely did anyone we interviewed report that local women worked in the brothels. Labor largely comes from outside the town, and often outside Nevada. Many women also report moving between brothels depending on business. When things are slow in one town or region, it is quite common for legal prostitutes to obtain work cards in another county and change brothels; there is a brothel trail along which the working women migrate from region to region, and carry messages and stories from one house to the next. The working women also have the option to leave and work in a different place altogether, or in a different segment of the burgeoning commercial sex industry.

This migrant brothel labor force as well as the many other options for working in the adult sex industry causes frequent labor shortages in the brothels. This is particularly true for the frontier brothels, where locating and retaining women as prostitutes is the single greatest challenge to business survival. It can be difficult to get workers to stay in a small, isolated town when they could be closer to big cities or working in other parts of the sex industry, perhaps selling nude dances and making just as much money. The Nevada Brothel Association sees the availability of jobs as strippers and illegal escorts in Reno and Las Vegas as the greatest challenge to finding and retaining brothel workers. Competition for workers is often intense, and at least one small brothel owner we interviewed accused the larger brothels of unethically enticing the best workers away. One of the most valuable commodities to owners is the "turn outs," girls entering the business for the first time. Dusty is a good example; she entered prostitution for the first time through the brothels. "I just called information. I had worked in a male-dominated type of profession, I was a health supervisor, and always heard the men talk about where they went. I played stupid and I called information and asked how do I get a job, and they said what do I look like? I told them so I came in and I worked six weekends and I got the money I needed."

In an industry where recruiting workers is difficult, attracting new workers is seen as vital to replenishing the work force. This cause was helped in July 2007 when the State Supreme Court overturned two ordinances that prevented brothels from advertising in locations where prostitution is illegal. With this decision, a few brothels are now advertising their services to clients in Reno and Las Vegas, and offering job opportunities to women willing to work in such places.

So, the structure and functioning of the Nevada brothel is changing amid evolving sensibilities regarding the purchase of intimacy and sexual services in the 21st century.[18] On the one hand, the persistence of a migrant economy, economic need, libertarian and neoliberal values, and the isolation of small-town brothels means that in many ways they remain close to the Old West model. On the other, changing metropolitan sensibilities are transforming the businesses and customers, as well as the availability of workers, across the state and especially in the easier to reach, suburban areas outside Nevada's urban areas.

BROTHEL REGULATIONS

The amount of state and local government oversight and regulation in the brothel industry is one of the least surprising elements of Nevada's system. Given the criminalization of prostitution elsewhere in the United States, one would expect that where it is legal, it would be highly regulated. What is interesting, however, is the relative independence that local governments have in regulating brothels. Nevada's state statutes play a relatively small role in regulating brothels. State law restricts prostitution to counties of a certain size, and prohibits brothels from being closer than 400 yards from a school, a religious building, or being on a principal business street. Beyond these regulations, the strictest state intervention comes from the State Health Department.

Since 1985, the health department has strictly controlled sexually transmitted diseases (STDs) in the brothels by imposing stringent health testing on working women. Every prostitute must have a state health card certifying her safe and healthy prior to applying for work in a brothel; this means testing negative for all STDs, including syphilis, gonorrhea, and HIV. Once hired, a prostitute is required to have weekly exams by a registered doctor to certify that she is not carrying any STDs. If she tests positive, she is unable to work until the treatment cures her and the physician reinstates her health card. Additionally, once a month all prostitutes must allow a registered doctor to take a blood sample to determine if she has contracted HIV or syphilis. According to the Southern Nevada Health District, not one case of HIV has been reported by a licensed brothel prostitute since this testing regime was instituted in 1985. Finally, every brothel must post notices at the door and around the brothel informing customers that condom use is mandated by the state. All the prostitutes we interviewed reported that they are supportive of the condom laws as they offer the best protection available to working women. Contracting any STD is detrimental from a financial standpoint because the women lose work time while recuperating.[19]

Local governments are the most important regulators of brothels and regulate both through formal licensing ordinances and through informal norms that govern the "privilege" component of licensing. Formal laws establish license procedures and fees, restrict locations for brothels, require background checks of potential owners, sometimes set their own health guidelines in addition to the state's, and occasionally establish rules for prostitutes' behavior. Local governments vary widely in the licensing and regulation of brothels. As shown in Table 11.1, since brothels are only licensed in the unincorporated areas of Churchill, Esmeralda, Lander, Lyon, Mineral, Nye, and Storey counties, the county is the licensing body. In Elko, Humboldt, Pershing, and White Pine counties, the cities of Elko, Wells, Winnemucca, and Ely license brothels. Counties in the north and eastern parts of the state give licensing rights to the individual cities.

Legal brothels are required to pay various taxes and fees. Counties derive income from annual brothel licenses and new application fees, liquor, and other business license fees, room taxes, personal property taxes, and work cards for workers. License fees and structures vary by county. Some have flat business fees for brothels, and others charge on the basis of the number of rooms or workers. Brothel license fees tend to be higher for counties closer to urban areas than for the frontier counties. New application fees are typically costly, often much more than the yearly license fees. Every county has a liquor tax, which applies to the bars inside each brothel, and these are typically the same as those for hotels. Personal property taxes are usually at the same rate as for any other property. Some counties charge room taxes, and some do not. Sheriffs' departments issue work cards after a check for prior felony convictions. In most counties the cards issued to prostitutes are the same as those that all casino employees must get. Work cards amount to significant income for some counties, yielding up to $100 per year per worker.

Table 11.1 reports revenue to each county from their brothels. Lyon County near Reno and Carson City (the state capital) hosts some of the largest brothels in the state, including the Moonlite Bunny Ranch whose annual business and work card fees yielded the state $353,800 in 2007. In some counties, license fees, and taxes can account for up to 25% of the county budget.[20]

County and city ordinances have essentially institutionalized historical practices. Many of the ordinances simply legalized brothels that already existed and prohibit the creation of new brothels.[21] For example, Lander County limits the number of brothels to two, both in Battle Mountain, at locations where brothels have existed since the turn of the century. Ordinances have therefore severely restrained the growth of the industry. Since 1973 the number of brothels in the state has ranged between 22 and 33, with 28 today. It is unclear whether this was an intentional effort by the counties to restrict growth of a stigmatized but tolerated business, though Pillard argues that county officials indeed intended to limit growth,[22] and it is also unclear how much the owners themselves have lobbied to restrict competition. In any event, competition is greatly controlled by the licensing process, which makes this unlike other service industries and unlike the sex industry elsewhere in the nation. Most counties license only two or three brothels and limit the areas in which they can be located. It is difficult to get a new license. For most potential owners, the only way a new business can open is to buy out an existing license. Existing brothel owners are sometimes the strongest opponents to new licenses because they fear the competition.

Old West sexual norms persist. Not only are brothels located away from the good families of the community, but in some counties (Carlin, Winnemucca, Churchill) men have been explicitly forbidden from working in the brothels.[23] These rules assume that men would either be pimping or getting free sex from the working girls. Only recently have counties changed the rules prohibiting male owners. In addition, informal rules within brothels very clearly reproduce heterosexual norms. Many owners felt that local governments would absolutely not tolerate the sale of homosexual services in the brothels, and that women would never want to purchase sex from straight male prostitutes, especially when, according to one owner, "they can get it free at any bar."

Not only are brothels regulated by a set of formal rules that reinforce Old West sexual norms, there is an informal structure of regulation. Because the brothels are privileged licenses, officials have the power to revoke licenses for any reason and are free to impose all kinds of regulations. In the past these small towns had informal rules as well. For example, rules in one town stipulated that a prostitute's family could not live in the community, the prostitute must be in the brothel by 5 P.M., no men other than customers and repairmen were allowed on premises, and that brothel owners could not seek publicity.[24] Most of these rules have since been abolished.

As independent contractors, brothel workers negotiate and sign individual contracts with the house that spell out the duration and terms of their work. Most women work 3 weeks at a time, but workers, especially established ones, have much flexibility. Women can break the contract at any time, but are not likely to be welcomed back at that brothel. Women usually split half of their earnings with the house, and often must tip housekeeping staff, taxi or limo drivers, bartenders, and other employees. They also pay for their own medical expenses.

Brothels also impose their own house rules, rules that vary greatly. Among the most controversial are those restricting the women's mobility. Large brothels in Nye County and many in the smaller towns require women to live at the brothel for the duration of their contract. Most brothels allow women to leave while off work to run errands; some require an escort from the brothel or limit the amount of time away. But they may not leave the brothel without being health tested again.

A manager of one of the suburban brothels justified these strict rules for health reasons: "Because you never know what she [the prostitute] will do out there." Others justified the rules based on a tradition of unwritten local norms or because "it is just good business practice." As one person associated with a prominent and large suburban brothel explained it:

Nye County has ordinances that differ from other counties; it states that if a working woman is off the brothel property in excess of 24 hours, she must retest for STDs. It takes 48 hours get test results back to the house. It seems useless to allow a woman to come in to work for a day, leave for a day and then come back and have to wait two days for test results in order to go back to work. . . . We don't want to hassle with it, and the girls don't either.

These practices, however, are changing. The largest brothels in Northern Nevada allow women to go home after an 8–12 hour shift. And some women have or share apartments in the nearby towns. Brothel owners find that open shifts allow them to recruit and retain high-quality workers who bring in customers and money. They also use bedrooms more efficiently by having them filled with working (not sleeping) women more of the time.

It is limits on mobility that have led critics of legal brothels to charge that they are "total institutions" that violate the women's human rights. Legal prostitutes, who are restricted in their movement due solely to the nature of their work, are clearly being treated differently than other service workers. However, of the women we spoke to in brothels in frontier counties, none reported feeling constrained. A few who worked in the larger brothels did feel more constrained, but most voiced acceptance of the rules. Most often, we heard such comments as, "It's like living in a dormitory or a sorority." But among women working in brothels where they have more freedom of movement, there was enthusiasm for the more lenient rules. It seems that women may migrate to the type of house and work situation that suits her particular needs and preferences, and the brothel system is diversifying and changing in ways that make these kinds of options more possible.

House rules governing when workers may leave the brothel premises are informal and managed by the owners, and they were also not always strictly enforced. For many of the frontier brothel owners, the exigencies of today's labor market make it difficult to attract workers to a remote brothel, let alone to confine them to their quarters. The rules requiring staying on premises are especially difficult to enforce if the owner wants to maintain good morale. As a result, the best workers sometimes write their own rules. The brothel with the loosest practice was in a frontier town that had only one worker. This prostitute went to a local home each night at the end of her shift. She had worked on and off for about 3 years and the owners justified the relationship by saying she had "never gotten into trouble in town." Notably, however, these owners also had a very good relationship with the community, which made this liberal attitude acceptable locally.

The second point about these informal rules is that they reflect their historic roots in conservative, if libertarian, values. The informal relationship to the community is crucial in brothel culture. The owners walk a fine line between doing their business and pleasing local government and community leaders. As one owner said, if you go outside of proper channels, local politicians can make things tough for you. A former county district attorney told us that "the secret to doing this is good relations with law enforcement." The norms of the Old West seem to prevail, and the law is whatever the community sees fit. In short, the politics of brothels is very local, very delicate, and very informal.

Some communities impose legally questionable regulations out of fear of making waves. Although many of the regulations seem to violate the prostitutes' civil liberties, neither the workers nor the owners want to upset the delicate balance of running a prostitution business in a traditional community. Brothel owners strive to maintain a good image in the community by donating scholarships to high schools, buying jackets for fire departments, participating in local parades, carnivals, and holiday festivities, and planning and running town events. By supplying the Little League with uniforms, organizing the Fourth of July parade, and making regular donations to the local rotary club, some brothel owners have become respectable members of their community who are rewarded with trust and support from local residents.

There are exceptions, and Nye County's Maynard Martin Richards, aka Joe Richards, is one of them. The 74-year-old owner of three Nye County brothels, as well as two massage parlors and a strip club, was indicted by the Federal Grand Jury in March of 2006 on wire fraud charges related to a political bribe in an attempt to change a county ordinance limiting the location of brothels. The case was still pending as of 2009, and while it did not negatively affect other brothel owners, it did cast a pall across an already marginalized and stigmatized industry.

Some political leaders have proposed extending legal brothels to Las Vegas and perhaps Reno, because of the tax revenue that would result and to reduce exploitation of currently illegal workers. Las Vegas Mayor Oscar Goodman has publicly advocated this on several occasions and one state Senator proposed that the legislature should debate the idea.[25] Although controversial, some in the media have supported the idea.[26]

WOMEN IN THE BROTHELS

Despite the legality of the rural brothels, the occupation continues to be stigmatized. This raises several questions about the women who work in the brothels. What are their backgrounds? Do they want to be there? Do they like the work? Do they feel oppressed? We find that the women who work in the brothels are diverse in every way: their ages range from 19 to 55, but most were in their twenties and early thirties. They are predominantly white, but there are women of color. About half of the women we talked to are married or in a long-term relationship. About three-quarters have children. Half had an education beyond high school, a few had done graduate work, and some had graduate or professional degrees.

All the women we interviewed stressed that they made their own choices to enter brothel work. Their stories regarding entry are varied, like those of people in any workplace. Just under half of the women said they entered the brothel because their service industry jobs did not pay enough for them to survive. About one-quarter came to the brothels from some form of illegal prostitution. And about one-quarter came from other legal sex businesses (dancing or film) and see sex work as a career or calling. Workers in the smaller brothels, still governed by older protocols and more paternalistic values, likely experience their workplace differently than those in larger brothels near Reno and Las Vegas, but in all brothels we found that the women were strong, open, and often had close bonds with others in the house. They are in the business to make money, and some do quite well. For example, Ricki told us, "I ended up really successful; I made a lot of money. I had a real regular who paid for my boob job and helped me buy a house, furnished my house." Alice, from a Northern Nevada brothel, did not plan to stay in the business her entire life, but saw great benefits to working in a legal brothel: "I'd like to go back to school. If you utilize your time and you use your money wisely, this is a wonderful business to do it in. It's quick money, its good money, it's all taxed, it's legal."

But many workers say they do it not just for the money but also because they like the work and the people they work with. Ricki found that the brothel helped her get her life together and after about 2 months she felt that it was home:

> Whether you got along with everyone or not, it was your family. People are glad to see you when you come in. I've got tons of Christmas cards. I have people that really care, and I think that was something that was missing all my life. So for me, it was just like an extended family, it was a home. . . . So there was that camaraderie.

Misty, from a small rural brothel, also felt that it was a pleasant place to work: "You are actually given respect [by] the customer, [and] the girls respect you because they know how you feel. The customer has to respect you. They can't be calling you a whore or nothing or they have to leave."

All the women told us it was their choice to work in the brothels. None said that they were forced to work there or unable to leave if they wanted. We did not find anyone who was trafficked into a brothel, neither did anyone know of anyone else who had been trafficked. The regulations, work cards, contracts, and visibility of legal prostitution all reduce the chances of trafficking in the legal brothel sector. While we have no data on how many women had pimps, few women mentioned them. Some talked about using their time in the legal brothels to get away from an abusive pimp. The owners talked quite derisively about pimps and made clear that they were not allowed near the brothels. As one owner pointed out, if an abusive pimp shows up at a legal brothel, he goes to jail.

Safety was one of the most important advantages that women stressed in their choice to work in the brothels. They felt, and our research backs this up, that Nevada's legal brothels offer the safest environment available for women to sell consensual sex.[27] There are a number of mechanisms in the brothels to guarantee the women's safety. To protect women from unruly customers, there are panic buttons in the rooms. Brothel staff listen to all negotiations between the prostitute and client, and they say they can usually tell at that point if there are going to be problems. Women can and do turn away any client who worries her. There is generally increased scrutiny of clients—from the moment they walk into a brothel they are in a public space, and even when they are in the privacy of the woman's room, others are not far away. Finally, because these are legal businesses, managers can and do call police if a customer gets out of hand. It is in the brothel owner's business interest to operate a safe house, both to attract customers and to retain workers.

Women's health is protected as well. Women are tested regularly, but more importantly, customers are required by law to wear condoms. All the women we interviewed indicated that they used condoms; very few customers resisted, and those who did were quite easily convinced. Women also wash a customer before each sexual encounter, and at that point can look for external signs of diseases. Several of the women we talked to had turned customers away because of what they found in these checks. Importantly, the women told us they were free to turn customers away for any reason. There is a strong financial incentive not to do so, but the fact that they *could* contributed to the women's sense of safety.

THE NEVADA BROTHEL ASSOCIATION

One way to analyze the present state of the Nevada brothel industry and its likely future is to consider the ways in which individual brothel businesses and their owners interact with one another. This relatively small and unique industry has formed a lobbying coalition to protect its collective interests from conservatives, gaming interests, and others who oppose legal prostitution.

The Nevada Brothel Association (NBA) was formed in 1984, largely on the initiative of Joe Conforte, in order to lobby for owners' collective interests and to educate policymakers. The association's lobbyist is George Flint, undeniably the most visible advocate of brothel prostitution in Nevada despite the fact that he is not a brothel owner or manager; he is a full-time justice of the peace at his own wedding chapel in Reno. For the last several years, and until recently, brothel owner Geoff Arnold was a close partner with Flint in his role as President of the NBA. Generally, the association brings together most of the largest, powerful brothels in the state, as well as some of the smaller rural brothels. The NBA reflects and reproduces the relative power among brothels. The executive committee consists of the owners of the largest brothels, and several smaller brothels report that they feel that their unique interests are overlooked by the NBA. In terms of internal organizational dynamics, most of the money for the Nevada Brothel Association's operations has historically come from the eight largest brothels.

There are few NBA meetings, and most of the brothel owners participate only sporadically in organizational planning and decision making. Most of the brothel owners are geographically isolated from one another and in infrequent contact. The NBA offers a service to the brothel industry despite the tensions over specific issues and occasional regional and personality clashes. One rural brothel owner put it this way: "We don't participate much. George works for the big brothels most of the time, but we know it's out there and looking out for our interests. If something comes up, we'll participate then."

As the man at the helm, Flint is skilled at public relations and brokers media interest in the brothels by strategically participating in documentaries and news reports as an informed advocate of the brothels. According to most of the legislators and lobbyists we spoke with, Flint is a seasoned and respected lobbyist in the Nevada legislature. His passionate, experienced, and politically skilled voice gives legitimacy to the organization and the Nevada Brothel Association has been successful in maintaining the brothel industry's legal status. While a state ban on brothel prostitution is a remote possibility, it remains a concern of the industry.

The NBA has not attempted to push for legislation to expand the rights of brothels. The laws regulating the location and number of licenses could conceivably be overturned as unfair restraint of trade, for example. These and similar policies remain largely unchallenged. Why this reluctance to fight for more favorable legislations? For one thing, owners recognize that the state poses little threat to the general legal status of brothels, so most politics is still local. Most of the individual brothel owners can influence politicians and civic leaders individually, without the help of the NBA. As long as they remain good corporate citizens vis-à-vis local governments, and continue to bring revenue into the local economy, most owners feel little threat to their livelihood. They would prefer to accept traditional restrictions than raise controversy in their communities or across the state. And little economic incentive to change the system exists because licensing restrictions limit competition. As a result, a good profit often can be made even at a small brothel with only two or three women. In large brothels, the profit margin can be even bigger. All of this could change, however, if the brothels are drawn into national regulatory discussions about the relationship between prostitution (legal or otherwise) and sex trafficking. Should all forms of prostitution become conflated with sexual slavery, the brothels would face a much larger challenge than they have ever faced in their home communities or in Nevada.

In its attempt to simply preserve the existing brothel system rather than initiating changes more favorable to owners, workers, and the industry, the association believes that keeping quiet is strategically best. Customers can have their sexual needs met safely and efficiently, as long as it remains a largely hidden exchange. Geoff Arnold, President of the NBA, sums it up nicely on the NBA's homepage (http://www.nvlb.com/president.htm):

> We have a wild, wonderful, and very dynamic industry. . . . The industry is life itself, and it is a living remnant of the Old West. . . . Of course there were always the working ladies helping to make the world a better, brighter, warmer, and more human place. They deserve more thanks and recognition than they ever receive, for they were and are an important part of our communities and lives. The fundamental law of the Old West was a "Live and Let Live Attitude." It still exists and it is a large part of what makes Nevada a unique and special place. If what your neighbor does or thinks doesn't hurt you, then you leave him be. As the uniqueness of cultures of our Americas fade into sameness and political correctness such that even Southern accents fade away, I am so thankful that Nevada retains some lasting character of the Old West. It is an endearing and fragile virtue.

Before legalization, many of the owners were women, as it was considered inappropriate for anyone other than a woman to run the business. Since legalization, brothels are more likely to be run by men and the biggest brothels are more likely run by partnerships or corporations. For years, many owners were descendants of or trained by Joe Conforte and Sally Burgess. While many of these owners have now left the business, much of the traditional brothel culture remains; among the remnants is an old-timer mentality that sees the industry as endangered by outsiders coming into the business just to "make a buck." They maintain brothels need to fly low, under the radar. These corporate businesses bring in a more corporate and bureaucratic model of selling sex. They see the brothels as a natural continuation of the wide and growing array of legal, adult sexually oriented businesses, and increasingly manage the women, the informal house rules, their business practices, and customer relations in ways that make their brothels much more like other service and leisure industry businesses. To paraphrase Dennis Hof discussing his dreams for the Moonlite Bunny Ranch, "We want to be the McDonald's of sex" and although he said that McDonald's is too low class a comparison, he embraced the analogy.

Some in the industry—including George Flint—have a wary acceptance of corporate presence in the industry. Flint referred to one newcomer who had previously been a condominium developer:

> He scared me to death because he wanted to operate it like a regular business. Conforte says these new people don't know the business. . . . In some ways, when you see a business run by a square, it puts us on edge. The delicateness, the sensitiveness, the tenuousness of it. Aggressive marketing frightens us all. . . . They jeopardize their ability to survive and make legislators very nervous.[28]

Increasingly, newer owners talk of the business as if it is similar to any other small business, except for being more delicate and perhaps more precarious in its legal standing. These owners are pushing for a more bureaucratized workplace. One owner of a very small brothel reported that his biggest labor complaint is that the women "don't take a business approach to their work. They get absorbed in the party and don't work the bar as well as they could. There is a tendency for them to make only the dates they are comfortable making and not really hustle." By the same token, owners and managers of larger, more modern brothels see the opposite trend: the women working for their brothel are increasingly business savvy, and some even market themselves as a brand.

The NBA's charismatic leadership by George Flint, its inability to mobilize all brothels, its deference to local needs rather than long-term collective needs or federal trends, and a prevailing attitude of quiet compliance to conserve the status quo all attest to an ongoing Old West attitude. At the same time, the organization faces challenges from newer, modern brothel owners whose business model is less an old-time saloon than a more global, touristic commodity to be marketed and sold to a broad and diverse clientele.

CONCLUSION

We draw four major conclusions. First, it is clear that the legal brothels of Nevada are in the midst of transition from an Old West small business model, to a business enterprise that looks and operates ever more like other mainstream leisure and service industry. That many regulations differ among counties attests to the power of local tradition and the influence of charismatic community leaders. The persistence of restrictions on brothel owners and workers that would be rejected as unfair and unconstitutional for other legal businesses exemplifies the Old West pattern of local norms governing business enterprises. In sum, the structure of the brothel industry is still partially characterized by the culture of the Old West.

This is the anachronism: brothels still exist in Nevada because they have a rich history that has been ensconced in the rural economies and culture of the Old West. This tradition has normalized brothel prostitution, allowing it to persist even in the changing context of the postindustrial economy, the growing metropolitan sensibility and tourist market, and the modernizing culture of the New West. In some of these smaller towns, brothels seem to fit more comfortably in the Old West than the global late capitalist marketplace. And yet changes such as the emergence of the Nevada Brothel Association, the influx of outside business interests into the brothel industry, the new business practices introduced by corporate owners, the changing tourist market and the increase in state oversight through the State Health Department regulations have all contributed to the apparent adaptation of brothels to the contemporary economic and cultural climate in Nevada. Further, we argue that the brothel industry in Nevada is beginning to use similar marketing strategies and business forms to other tourist service industries. The brothels are increasingly selling individualized, interactive touristic experiences: workers sell their services in a regulated context, but they are encouraged to do so in ways that are unique, fill market niches, and make customers feel absolutely individual, special and emotionally connected.[29] Increasingly exporting the images and messages of the brothels to distant markets, via advertising, TV shows, more sophisticated marketing efforts, and cross-industry pollination by expanding into other legal sex industry businesses are all new practices that move the brothels out of the dusty mirage of the Nevada desert and closer to the mainstream of modern touristic economies and commodity cultures. The irony is that this same heightened visibility that is now helping to sustain many of the large brothels by becoming more like other service industry sectors also makes Nevada brothel prostitution a potential target for antiprostitution activists.

Second, the brothel industry had not previously been integrated into the larger service economy or with other components of the legal sex industry, but that is changing. While smaller, rural brothels remain largely invisible and localized enterprises, the larger and more urban brothels are increasingly visible, verbal, and strategic in their external marketing and internal business practices, helping to mainstream them into the leisure industry. Although the brothel industry is quite separate from other types of sexually oriented businesses for several reasons, connections are developing. Other adult businesses, such as gentlemen's clubs, adult book/video stores, adult toy stores, and phone/cybersex operations, often defend their status as legal businesses on the basis that they do not sell actual sexual contact. This means that building alliances with brothels, even though they are legal in Nevada, may tarnish the image of adult businesses operating in regions where prostitution is illegal and stigmatized. Adult businesses also compete with brothels, and the competition would increase were brothel prostitution legalized in Reno and Las Vegas. Despite this, some brothel owners are cross-fertilizing their brothel business with other legal adult businesses (for example strip clubs, Internet sex sites, and adult film production).

Third, it is clear that the historical marginalization of legal prostitution has been a response to the conventional sexual norms and values that permeate American society writ large. The brothel industry recognizes the tensions and risks inherent in selling sex. To survive, in the past brothels thought that they must remain quiet and invisible, be as innocuous as possible, and do business in highly traditional ways. Given recent changes in the larger economy and culture of Nevada, the U.S. and the global commercial marketplace, a new reality has emerged for brothel owners and supporters. Quiet, quaint, and remote is no longer the recipe for the brothels' survival. Now, the strategy for larger brothels seems to be to adopt a business model that embraces the ways of touristic cultures and leisure economies: to package and sell unique experiences (with memorabilia and souvenirs to boot), sexual encounters laden with emotional labor, and individualized service—or the appearance thereof—all in a safely sexualized space, for workers and customers alike.

That said, there remains widespread resistance to establishing brothels that cater to nontraditional clients or sexual services. For example, a few years ago an entrepreneur interested in opening an all-male gay brothel in Pahrump was discouraged as it was seen as too politically controversial. Likewise, nearly every brothel owner scoffed at the idea of staffing male prostitutes to service heterosexual women. While a few county ordinances explicitly prohibit hiring male prostitutes in brothels, in many parts of Nevada the absence of male brothel prostitutes is more a product of tradition and gender role stereotypes (men cannot perform on demand; women do not have the money or desire for sex, or they can get it for free).

Finally, based on all of this, we argue that the Nevada brothel industry is in the midst of an historical transition. Rooted in the Old West but facing the challenges of a highly sexualized commercial culture throughout the United States and, indeed, much of the world, the traditional Nevada brothel system has been at a crossroads. Finding the status quo increasingly untenable for workers, owners and clients, there has been notable change in the industry. From owners defending their right to advertise in order to remain economically viable, to generating links between the brothels and other sexualized entertainment and leisure industries (the Moonlite Bunny Ranch's ongoing series, *Cathouse*, on the HBO television channel; the owners of Sherri's Ranch running a strip club and a racy ultralounge in Las Vegas, etc.), the brothel industry is beginning to use strategies and business practices that are much more like those in other service and leisure industries. Although Nevada gaming interests remain generally opposed to legal prostitution, there is little argument that American culture generally, and Las Vegas' tourist culture specifically, has become highly sexualized and sex is used to sell an endless array of goods, services and experiences. The gap between the brothel industry and other legitimate business enterprises narrows. But, as the composition of the state legislature changes over time—with fewer and fewer of the old guard who helped legalize prostitution involved in Nevada politics—and the Nevada Brothel Association continues to experience tension and divisiveness, the brothel industry does not have the luxury of overconfidence.

The integration of brothels into their communities, a state tradition that permits the sale of sexual services, the profitability of the brothels for savvy owners and the cities or counties in which they operate, clients' demand for safe, legal, and personalized commercial sexual encounters, and the promise of potentially lucrative employment options for women who choose to prostitute, are all powerful forces supporting the continued existence of legal prostitution. But to survive, brothels will need to continually adapt to the imperatives of the global tourist economy and sexualized consumer landscape, and behave as if they are legitimate businesses deserving the same opportunities and regulations as any other businesses. This is likely to improve work conditions and employment options for working women, as well as close the gap between Nevada's unique brothel industry and other mainstream leisure businesses and service industries. As such, it is not useful to examine the sex industry as generalized "other" to mainstream businesses; as a simple, anachronistic, Old West patriarchal institution; or as a local oddity or exotic site. To capture the complexities and shifting realities of the Nevada brothel industry requires nothing less than a rethinking of these legal businesses in a larger framework: one in which federal politics matters as much as state, and in which legal brothels are embedded in the global market of adult commercial services. The terms of this analysis must consider how the transition away from an Old West model may simultaneously solve some problems for working women and for the brothels, while generating others.

NOTES

The authors thank Crystal Jackson and Jennifer Heineman for their invaluable assistance.

1. William Reibsame, ed., *Atlas of the New West: Portrait of a Changing Region*, New York: Norton, 1997. See also Hal Rothman, *Devil's Bargains: Tourism in the Twentieth Century West*, Lawrence: University Press of Kansas, 1998.
2. Exceptions include John Galliher and John Cross, *Morals Legislation Without Morals: The Case of Nevada*, New Brunswick, NJ: Rutgers University Press, 1983; Ellen Pillard, "Legal Prostitution: Is It Just?" *Nevada Public Affairs Review* 2 (1983): 43–47; Helen Reynolds, *The Economics of Prostitution*, Springfield, IL: Charles Thomas, 1986; Guy Rocha, *Brothel Prostitution in Nevada: A Unique American Cultural Phenomenon*, Master's thesis, San Diego State University, 1975.
3. Rocha, *Brothel Prostitution*; Richard Symanski, "Prostitution in Nevada," *Annals of the Association of American Geographers* 65 (1974): 357–377; Reynolds, *Economics of Prostitution*.
4. Galliher and Cross, *Morals Legislation*.
5. Wells Emergency Ordinance No. 24, cited in Symanski, "Prostitution in Nevada."
6. Symanski, "Prostitution in Nevada," pp. 363, 355.
7. Gabriel Vogliotti, *The Girls of Nevada*, Secaucus, NJ: Citadel Press, 1975; Rocha, *Brothel Prostitution*; Symanski, "Prostitution in Nevada"; Doug McMillan, "Nevada's Sex-for-Sale Dilemma," *Reno Gazette-Journal,* November 9, 1986.
8. Mike Sion, "Conforte Changed the Face of Nevada Bordellos," *Reno Gazette-Journal,* January 20, 1995.

9. Sion, "Conforte"; Authors interview with George Flint, Nevada Brothel Association, December 12, 1997; Vogliotti, *Girls of Nevada*.

10. Sion, "Conforte"; Pillard, "Legal Prostitution: Is It Just?"; Ellen Pillard, "Rethinking Prostitution: A Case for Uniform Regulation," *Nevada Public Affairs Review* (1991): 1: 45–49.

11. Barbara G. Brents and Kathryn Hausbeck, "Violence and Legalized Brothel Prostitution in Nevada: Examining Safety, Risk, and Prostitution Policy," *Journal of Interpersonal Violence* 20 (2005): 270–295.

12. *U.S. Census Bureau: State and County Quick Facts*. http://quickfacts.census. gov/qfd/states/32000.html, last revised Friday, July 25, 2008.

13. The Nevada Brothel Association estimated that this figure was down at least 20% from the previous year due to the 2008 economic recession.

14. Authors interview with George Flint, Nevada Brothel Association, January 14, 2009.

15. Rural Policy Research Institute, "Nevada Demographic and Economic Profile," Truman School of Public Affairs, University of Missouri-Columbia, May 2006. http://www.rupri.org.

16. Reibsame, *Atlas of the New West*, p. 112.

17. Barbara G. Brents and Kathryn Hausbeck, "Marketing Sex: U.S. Legal Brothels and Late Capitalist Consumption," *Sexualities* 10 (2007): 425–439.

18. Viviana Zelizer, *The Purchase of Intimacy*, Princeton, NJ: Princeton University Press, 2005.

19. Brents and Hausbeck, "Violence and Legalized Brothel Prostitution."

20. Kathleen Hennessey, "Nevada Brothels Want to Be Good Neighbors, Pay Tax," *Associated Press*, May 10, 2005; Larry Henry, "Brothel Tour Off," *Las Vegas Sun,* April 17, 1997.

21. For further detail on brothel regulations, see Barbara G. Brents and Kathryn Hausbeck, "State Sanctioned Sex: Negotiating Formal and Informal Regulatory Practices in Nevada's Legal Brothels," *Sociological Perspectives* 44 (2001): 307–332.

22. Pillard, "Legal Prostitution," p. 45.

23. Male prostitution does not exist in any of Nevada's legal brothels. Outside these three counties, however, men are sometimes employed as managers or bartenders within brothels.

24. Pillard, "Legal Prostitution," p. 45.

25. Erin Neff, "Legalized Prostitution: Vegas Brothels Suggested," *Las Vegas Review-Journal*, October 24, 2003; Sam Skolnick, "Mayor Keeps Prostitution Legalization Debate Going," *Las Vegas Sun*, January 23, 2009.

26. Geoff Schumacher, "Goodman's Brothel Views Aren't Irresponsible," *Las Vegas Review-Journal*, September 9, 2007.
27. Brents and Hausbeck, "Violence and Legalized Brothel Prostitution."
28. Authors interview with George Flint, December 12, 1997.
29. Brents and Hausbeck, "Marketing Sex."

TRENDS

REMAKING THE SEX INDUSTRY: THE ADULT EXPO AS A MICROCOSM

Lynn Comella

Every January the Adult Video News (AVN) Adult Entertainment Expo (AEE) rolls into town and sets up shop at the Sands Expo and Convention Center in Las Vegas, transforming it into one of the world's largest adult playgrounds. An intoxicating mix of big business, public relations, flesh on parade, and celebrity gawking, the AEE is a crowded, bustling scene peppered with images of brightly colored dildos and vibrators, scantily clad porn starlets striking suggestive poses for star struck fans, and elaborate "mega-booths" designed to increase the visibility and brand identity of industry heavy hitters like Hustler, Wicked, and Vivid Video. The 4-day event attracts roughly 300 exhibitors and 30,000 attendees—adult retailers, manufacturers, porn producers, industry talent, fans, public relations experts, and members of the media—all of whom descend on Las Vegas to experience the colorful panorama of an industry that continues to grow, diversify its offerings, and strives to garner mainstream acceptance.

The size and popularity of the adult entertainment industry in the United States is hard to ignore. Although exact figures are difficult, if not impossible, to pinpoint, it is estimated that the sex industry—which includes everything from print, DVD, and Internet pornography to pay-per-view channels, video on demand, strip clubs, and adult novelties—generates between $10 to $14 billion dollars annually, making it an extremely lucrative segment of U.S. consumer culture.[1] From television shows like *Sex and the City* and the Canadian import *Talk Sex* with Sue Johanson, to films such as *Inside Deep Throat* and *Zack*

285

and Miri make a Porno, the American cultural landscape is increasingly rife with references to sex toys, strippers, call girls, porn stars and porn producers—lending further support to the claim that what was once considered risqué and culturally taboo is increasingly commonplace and mainstream.

The rise of the Internet and the success of e-commerce businesses have also extended the reach and cultural visibility of an industry that for many decades existed almost entirely on the margins of society. Technological advances, combined with the growth of the women's market and the mainstreaming of adult novelties, have created new opportunities for entrepreneurs hoping to capitalize on consumers' seemingly endless fascination with sex and the desire for bigger and better orgasms.

The AVN Adult Entertainment Expo, which is one of many such trade shows that take place each year, both within and outside the U.S., is a microcosm of the sex industry and thus offers a sociologically rich window into the marketing and mainstreaming of sex in American society, even as such mainstreaming is resisted by some sectors of society. It also provides an opportunity to assess the challenges confronting the industry as it struggles to address issues of piracy, declining DVD sales, and the availability of free Internet porn—all of which are taking a bite of out its profits. Indeed, the myth that the sex industry is recession proof, and able to make money hand over fist without trying, was effectively put to rest with the global economic downturn of 2008–2009. Many adult businesses are now working harder than ever to keep their competitive edge and, in some instances, stay afloat in tough economic times.

Today, the figure of the male consumer, which continues to drive much of the output of the adult industry, exists alongside a newly idealized version of the female shopper who is willing to spend $175 on a vibrator at an upscale sexual boutique. Longstanding industry bigwigs like Larry Flynt and his Hustler Empire share the stage with feminist sex toy businesses and upstart sex toy manufacturers interested in bringing the concept of "lifestyle branding" to the adult industry. It is an interesting mix of old guard and new, convention and innovation, as the adult industry seeks to be both responsive to change and profitable.

This chapter examines how the adult industry is transforming, indeed *re-branding*, itself in response to an evolving and rapidly changing marketplace, one that is no longer defined exclusively by images of "sleazy" men in trench coats surreptitiously slinking into dimly lit and dank porno shops. How is a new age of sexual entrepreneurs attempting to "makeover" the adult industry—turning "crass" into "class"—through their orchestrated appeals to new kinds of sexual consumers and their creation of new sexual tastes and experiences?

STUDYING THE SEX INDUSTRY

I have spent the past decade studying what is commonly referred to as the "women's market" for sex toys and pornography, with an explicit focus on the history and retail culture of women-owned and -operated sex toy businesses.[2] In the course of researching this market—a highly gendered subset of the sex industry—I have learned a great deal about the mainstream adult industry. The reason for this is simple: the women's market exists in constant dialogue, and occasional friction, with the broader adult industry. Indeed, it is impossible to understand the cultural specificity of women-oriented sex toy stores, and the women's market for sex toys and pornography, without understanding how these cultural forms have been purposefully *re-gendered* and recoded by sex-positive feminist entrepreneurs in ways that distinguish them from their more traditional, male-oriented, and stereotypically "lowbrow" counterparts.

My research on the women's market can be situated within the broader tradition of ethnographic studies of cultural production. According to communication scholar Lisa Henderson, research on cultural production has historically "sought to make concrete the universe in which designated 'cultural producers' (TV writers, broadcast journalists, filmmakers, etc.) do what they do."[3] Scholars working in this tradition have analyzed the making of television talk shows,[4] consumer markets,[5] and feminist organizations.[6] These studies map "the particular power relations, the context, within which both the identity and the effects of any particular practices are determined."[7] In the field of sexuality studies, there is a growing body of research that draws on these traditions in order to better understand how sexual consumer culture is *made*—by whom and under what conditions.

A great deal of research and social commentary about sexual consumer culture continues to suffer from three major shortcomings: essentialism, moral revulsion, and the "fallacy of misplaced scale," Gayle Rubin's term for the tendency to imbue sexuality with an overstated sense of cultural significance.[8] These deficiencies have significantly limited the kinds of cultural knowledge we have about a very popular, and extremely diverse, sector of American consumer culture. In recent years, there has been an uptick in research on sexual consumer culture that seeks to replace moral outrage with empirical analysis; overgeneralizations with nuance; and universal narratives with multiplicity.[9] This growing body of empirical research demonstrates that there is no "one size fits all" analysis of the sexual marketplace—despite repeated assertions to the contrary, a point I will return to later in the chapter.

I employ multiple methods of data collection, including in-depth interviews, participant observation fieldwork, and archival research. I have conducted over 70 in-depth interviews with sex-positive retailers, sales staff, marketers, sex toy manufacturers, and pornographers from across the country. I also spent 6 months in 2001 working on the sales floor at Babeland, a feminist-owned, women-oriented sex toy business in New York City. During this time, I assisted customers, rang up sales, attended staff, marketing, and management meetings, and had the opportunity to both observe and participate in interviews for the hiring of new staff. I also visited a number of women-run sex toy businesses across the country, from Chicago and Madison to Boston and Albuquerque. In addition, I attended three adult industry trade shows, the 2008 and 2009 AEE and the 2008 International Lingerie Show, all which took place in Las Vegas.[10] There, I talked to numerous industry professionals and attended various trade events and seminars, the latter of which were tape recorded and subsequently transcribed. I also reviewed popular press coverage of adult industry trade shows in order to see how these events were represented by both the mainstream and alternative media, including bloggers.

ADULT EXPO CULTURE

The year 2009 marked the 11th anniversary of the AVN Adult Entertainment Expo, an event described by one industry professional as the "Super Bowl of the adult industry."[11] According to a blogger writing for *Adult Entertainment Today*: "In the past, AEE was the one event you could not miss. If you wanted to be a major player in the business, you had to bite the bullet. Attending AEE was merely part of the cost of doing business."[12] For many years, a version of the Expo existed as an offshoot of the Consumer Electronic Show (CES), an annual electronics trade show that also takes place in Vegas. According to Paul Fishbein, President of AVN Media Network, the adult industry felt marginalized by CES.[13] "They took the money but didn't promote the adult event and the adult vendors were all over at the Sahara [instead of the Sands, where the CES was located]. Some companies came to us and asked us to do a stand-alone event. So it was definitely time [for our own show]."[14]

Home Entertainment Events, the company that organizes the Expo and oversees its vast logistics, estimates that of the roughly 30,000 attendees that visit the show each year, approximately 12,000 are industry professionals, 17,000 are fans, and 1000 are members of the press. The Expo strives therefore to be different things to different groups of people, all of whom have a role to play in ensuring the show's success.

The Expo, first and foremost, is a trade show where industry professionals from all over the world gather to network, unveil new products, make business deals, and market their brands. It is a place where new business relationships are cultivated and old ones solidified. The Expo also functions as an important promotional showcase and public relations event, both for AVN and the larger adult industry; it is an opportunity for members of the mainstream and alternative press to see, and by extension write about, new products, breakout performers, upstart companies, and the latest technological innovations to hit the industry. Public relations consultants are on hand to pitch stories to the press and point them in the direction of what is new and notable. Daily press releases are issued and a number of companies prepare press packets and provide sample products and DVDs to journalists covering the show. Finally, the Expo offers fans the opportunity to meet and interact with their favorite porn stars and performers. Most companies recognize the value of fans and use the Expo as an opportunity to thank them for their support. "It's the fans that make talent into stars," stated Expo spokesperson Shawn Devlin.[15]

There is an important synergy, then, that exists between these different elements of Expo culture. As Jason Maskell, a spokesman for Harmony Films explains: "We want the buyers, the press and ultimately the consumers to see [our company] as the global producer of fine X-rated entertainment that it is."[16] In order to accomplish this, companies spend a great deal of money trying to outdo one another with elaborate booths, gimmicks, and giveaways as they jockey for the attention of distributors, retailers, fans, and, importantly, the press.

For many attendees, *sexual spectacle* is an undeniable part of the Expo's allure.[17] This is especially true for fans, a group that comprises more than half the show's total audience. Most, although certainly not all fans, are men who travel to Las Vegas from all over the U.S. and other parts of the world, forking over $80 for a day pass ($200 for 3 days) and the chance to rub shoulders with industry favorites such as Tera Patrick, Jessica Drake, Joanna Angel, and Belladonna. A considerable part of the Expo's visual spectacle is designed with fans in mind: the costly mega-booths, the presence of performers who patiently pose for pictures and sign autographs, the attention-grabbing gimmicks, such as girl-on-girl "make-out" sessions, the abundance of T&A, and free porn DVDs that are handed out at many booths (see Figure 12.1). These strategies are all geared toward building and sustaining a loyal fan base and, if marketing experts are correct, boosting future sales and profits.

There is evidence to suggest that fans are playing an increasingly important role in Expo culture. The 2009 AEE, which I attended, offered a full slate of "fan seminars"—including "how-to" sex education workshops with sexpert author Jamye Waxman, who led a workshop on the female orgasm, and adult film star Nina Hartley, who talked to fans about how to

**Figure 12.1
Hustler Booth,
2008 Adult
Entertainment
Expo. Photo by
the author.**

achieve a fulfilling sex life. "Don't try to have sex like a porn star," she advised the crowd of about 50 people, as she emphasized the importance of fostering sexual intimacy, openness, and generosity. Not far from the seminar stage, FyreTV, a company specializing in home porn delivery that utilizes Internet Protocol TV (IPTV) technology, held fan contests that drew consistently large crowds to its main stage. Throughout the weekend, willing fans competed in pole dancing contests, wet t-shirt contests, and vied for the title of "Hottest Ass" and "Hottest Fan." The size of the crowd, combined with its enthusiasm, suggested that FyreTV's marketing efforts were a hit.

While fans flock to the main exhibition hall upstairs, a quieter, less frenzied, and altogether different expo is taking place downstairs in an exhibition hall reserved solely for members of the trade. Downstairs in the B2B (business-to-business) Marketplace, manufacturers and distributors display, for the benefit of thousands of retailers who attend the Expo, the latest in technologically innovative sexual gadgetry and products. Retailers have the opportunity to meet with vendors face to face, scout new vendors, make deals, network, and promote their businesses without having to elbow eager fans out of the way. Introduced in 2004, the B2B Marketplace has been an extremely successful addition to the business culture of the Expo, providing an opportunity for business-to-business networking that many attendees see as invaluable.

For Greg DeLong and Chris Clement of NJoy, a small company that produces a line of sleek, stainless steel sex toys, industry trade shows like AEE are an indispensible part of growing their business, both in terms of sales and brand recognition. DeLong and Clement are mechanical engineers who, several years ago, decided to try their hand at making sex toys. "Our advantage is that we know how to make things . . . and the market is begging for new products," DeLong told me. The business partners realized that consumers—especially women—were looking for well-designed, well-crafted sex toys—a need that was not being filled by the mainstream adult novelty industry. "People have been waiting for this," DeLong continued. "They have been waiting for designers to come into the market."[18] NJoy—along with companies like Tantus, Fun Factory, Lelo, and OhMiBod—is the vanguard of what some see as a "new age" in the adult industry, where high-end products, lifestyle branding, and a new kind of business savvy is redefining the marketplace.

OhMiBod is an interesting example of a company riding the wave of this new age of quality and brand consciousness. OhMiBod is a vibrator that plugs into an iPod and vibrates to the rhythm of whatever music is playing. The concept behind OhMiBod is a relatively simple one: let's bring music and pleasure together to create the ultimate "acsexsory"—a term trademarked by OhMiBod—for the iPod generation. (At the 2008 Lingerie Show, I listened to Justin Timberlake's "Sexy Back" as OhMiBod, which I was holding in my hand, pulsated in sync with the song.) "Many of the vibrators that are on the market today are intimidating," says Suki, OhMiBod's creator. "This is why when it came to designing OhMiBod the direction was to make it extremely approachable by keeping the design elegant and making it intuitive to use. I want OhMiBod to be the first socially acceptable vibrator."[19] The idea of producing a vibrator that would be socially acceptable to women who might otherwise be intimated by the idea of purchasing a sex toy guided the development and design of OhMiBod. In only a few short years, OhMiBod has cultivated a brand identity as a hip, fun, and sophisticated vibrator—the kind of product, the company hopes, women will not be afraid to leave on their bedside table. As Brain Vatter of OhMiBod told me: "We are still doing warm-up laps in this industry when it comes to quality and branding." Despite this, the trend within the adult industry is in the direction of producing quality products that are well designed, durable, and pretty.

The Expo's organizers work hard to ensure that the show evolves apace with an ever changing and expanding industry. This is perhaps nowhere more evident than in the trade seminars offered to industry professionals. Seminar topics run the gamut, from discussions of piracy and obscenity law to staying competitive in a changing marketplace and reaching female consumers. The seminars feature industry "gurus"—successful business owners, CEOs, distributors, and content providers from different sectors of the industry—mainstream, fetish, the women's market—who are invited to discuss various issues considered relevant and pressing to the adult industry.

One of the most popular forums is the legal seminar. Here, lawyers with connections to the adult industry provide business owners with updates on federal obscenity cases, discuss zoning ordinances, and outline changes to the 2257 Law, the record keeping requirement for producers of adult content, which is intended to keep minors from working in pornography. The laws that govern adult businesses are constantly changing, and the ability to keep up with these changes, even minor ones, can mean the difference between jail and freedom. As lawyer Jennifer Kinsley succinctly remarked: "Obscenity prosecutions are statistically the least likely, but statistically the scariest." Having a good lawyer, then, especially one with adult industry experience, is key for many businesses.

The Expo's seminar series attracts fledgling entrepreneurs hoping to start their own businesses and seasoned retailers with 30 years experience who are looking for ways to maintain their profit margins in a rapidly changing marketplace. The workshops are a form of "professional development"; they offer attendees practical advice and tips about how to tailor their product mix, design their retail spaces and websites, and train their sales staff in order to run the best, and most profitable, business possible. The seminar series also provides an opportunity for industry professionals to stay abreast of the latest industry trends.

INDUSTRY TRENDS

Several trends have gained traction in the adult industry in recent years. Among them are the growth of the women's market for pornography and sex toys; consumer demand for quality products and designer sex toys; the greening of the adult industry; and the mainstreaming of adult novelties.

These trends have contributed to the re-branding of the adult industry, a point I return to later in the chapter.

Women's Market

By early 2008, the women's market for sex toys and pornography had become what many industry insiders considered to be the hottest growth market in the adult industry. "Women have dollars, believe me," *Penthouse* executive director Kelly Holland told a standing room only crowd at the 2008 AEE, "and they love to spend [them] on things they feel enhance their self-esteem, their intelligence, [and] their sexual lives." Ken Dorfman, the National Sales Manager for Doc Johnson's, one of the largest sex toy manufacturers in the world, used dollars and cents to make a similar point: "One guy shopping alone—average sale $8. Two guys, $12. But one female shopping alone—average sale $83. Two females shopping together, $170."[20]

What was until very recently a relatively small segment of the mainstream adult industry—the women's market for sex toys and pornography—has acquired newfound economic and cultural cache, a development that has been noted by industry analysts, journalists and academics alike.[21] Many adult-oriented businesses, from sex toy manufacturers and porn companies to adult retailers, are responding to this trend by recalibrating their business practices with an eye toward wooing women. Traditional "brick and mortar" adult retailers, for example, are removing their video arcades, painting their stores to make them lighter and brighter, hiring female staff, and placing a greater emphasis on quality products and customer service. They are softening the edges of their businesses and taming the often harsh and in-your-face representations of sexuality long associated with the adult industry, all in the hope of appealing to women and, ultimately, increasing their profits.

What the mainstream adult industry is only now discovering—that women watch porn, use sex toys, and are willing to spend money on both—is not news for the dozen or so women-owned and -oriented adult businesses across the country. Retail businesses like Eve's Garden, Good Vibrations, and Babeland, feminist pornographers like Candida Royalle and Tristan Taormino, and sex-positive sex toy manufacturers like Tantus and Vixen, among others, were cultivating the women's market for sex toys and pornography long before women were identified as the consumer niche *du jour*. These companies brought a feminist voice and an alternative vision to the sexual marketplace. They advocated for quality products, accurate sexual information, and for women to be taken seriously as both sexual agents and consumers, challenging the very idea of "business as usual" within the larger adult industry.

Today, women's increasing power—as entrepreneurs, cultural producers, and consumers—in an industry long associated with men, is nothing short of revolutionary. Turn the clock back 10 or 20 years and this was far from the case. It wasn't just that female entrepreneurs often found themselves marginalized by the industry's "old boys' network," but their perspectives and contributions were very often disregarded. When Candida Royalle first starting making pornography for women and couples in the early 1980s, she encountered difficulty finding distributors who were willing to place her videos in retail stores, because they didn't understand what she was making: "Erotica for women? What's that?" According to Royalle, her films were virtually unrecognizable to mainstream adult distributors who were used to something that looked completely different. "It wasn't the typical box cover with the blonde, big-boobed babe. Instead, it was always a loving couple . . . the whole presentation was different."[22] Royalle worked hard to convince, indeed *educate*, mainstream adult distributors and retailers that there was a market for the kind of sex-positive, women-oriented porn she was making, films where women were shown enjoying themselves—and having real orgasms.

The process of convincing the mainstream adult industry that there was a women's market for pornography and sex toys was not something that happened overnight. When author and sex columnist Tristan Taormino decided to turn her best selling book, *The Ultimate Guide to Anal Sex for Women*, into an instructional sex video in the late 1990s, she faced many of the same challenges that Royalle had faced 15 years earlier. As Taormino explained:

> I pitched [the project] to maybe ten different producers, including John [Stagliano] and they all shot me down. . . . I was basically talking about making a "how to" video for women. These are two things that the porn industry does not acknowledge or understand. When I say "how to" they think "boring instructional" and when I say "for women," they are like, "We have no idea what you mean." We are still at the beginning of pornographers acknowledging women as consumers of porn.[23]

The type of marginalization, and outright sexism, that many female entrepreneurs experienced navigating the often hostile terrain of the male-dominated adult industry meant that for many years, women-oriented retailers, manufacturers, and porn producers existed on a parallel plane, only occasionally overlapping with the mainstream industry. For example, Rachel Venning, co-founder of Babeland, a leader in the women's market, did not attend the AEE until 2007—14 years after Babeland opened its doors for business. "I didn't think [the AEE] was relevant to what we were about," she explained. "I thought it seemed like porn, porn stars, and the objectification of women. For years, I really didn't see Babeland as part of the adult industry. I've always thought of us as significantly different, more akin to a bookstore or a community center or something in health and wellness. . . . So even though the AVN show had been going on for years, I just didn't really notice or care."[24] Today, the mainstream industry is actively courting sex-positive female entrepreneurs, such as Venning and Taormino, and mining their expertise about the women's market.

Quality

As the women's market grew, female entrepreneurs and consumers began placing new demands on the adult industry. One of the most important of these was for quality products that would not break the first time they were used, that were ergonomically designed with women's bodies in mind, and that were aesthetically pleasing to look at. According to Metis Black, the President of Tantus, Inc., the mainstream sex toy industry for decades revolved around the idea of "planned obsolescence":

> [Retailers] would stock the same items over and over because the model [of retailing] was based on a guy buying a product, taking it to his hotel room, using it while he was one the road with whomever, and then throwing it away; so the fact that it wasn't going to last very long wasn't important. What was important was that it cost $20 and it was going to be there for the here and now. And the next time, that person is going to buy the same item for $20 because it worked for them before.[25]

Throughout the 1990s, women-oriented sex toy businesses like Good Vibrations, Babeland, and Grand Opening led the call for quality sex toys, forcing the hand of the industry to make products that met higher standards and to accept the return of items that proved defective. According to Cathy Winks, former manager at Good Vibrations, the adult novelty business for a long time "didn't put any more care into the products that they were making than crackerjack toys . . . because they figured that people were too ashamed and embarrassed about what they were buying and would be more inclined to just blame themselves if the toys didn't work than to blame the manufacturer." As the women's market developed, this began to change. Manufacturers had to "to try a little harder to make something that will last a little longer, have a better motor, look prettier, [and] have more appealing packaging."[26]

In time, both manufacturers and retailers realized that they were dealing with a new and more sexually sophisticated consumer—what Greg DeLong characterizes as "intelligent perverts with disposable income." This group is comprised of people who are willing to pay more for products that are well made and look good, a shift that has helped create an opening for savvy designers and engineers to think seriously about the adult industry as a potentially ripe market for their creative talents.

What we are seeing today, is what some describe as a sex toy revolution, one aimed at a new class of sexual consumers—what we might think of as a new "sexual taste public"—that is willing to spend anywhere between $100–$400 on a sex toy. "Luxury vibes are the big, big change that I have seen in the last year," Babeland Director of Purchasing Alicia Relles told a standing room only crowd at the 2008 AEE:

> In our last month of sales [at Babeland], we had the Form 6 [which retails for $175] outsell any other vibrator in our store and that is a record for us. That's never happened. The Rabbit has been the top seller in our stores for 10 years. Now, we have beautiful, ergonomic luxury toys . . . people are looking for these savvy, gorgeous well-made toys. . . . Women are willing to spend a little more money for something that is beautiful and works well and has versatility, and is well made and going to last a long time.[27]

In response, a number of adult manufacturers and retailers are riding the luxury sex toy wave, helping to bring sex toys from the "shady back streets to shiny high streets."[28]

Green Products

The recent emphasis on quality products has not only generated a market for "couture" sex toys, but it has also helped draw attention to the manufacturing materials frequently used to make the majority of sex toys on the market today. Much of this attention has focused on phthalates (pronounced *tha-lates*), a group of industrial chemicals known as "plasticizers" that are used to make hard plastics soft and pliable. Phthalates are found in a variety of products, from children's toys and shower curtains to medical devices and sex toys. The problem with phthalates is that they break down over time and release harmful gasses, which cause toys to discolor, get sticky, and have an unpleasant taste and odor. Although research findings are inconclusive about the potential health risks caused by exposure to phthalates, studies have shown that some are carcinogenic, a finding that caused the European Union to ban them from children's toys.

Over the past several years, the "greening" of the adult industry and the topic of "toxic toys"—including products containing phthalates—have garnered media attention.[29] A growing number of manufacturers and retail businesses are sounding the call for safer sex toys and greater industry regulation. Among the businesses leading the charge for healthy toys is the sex-positive feminist retail business Smitten Kitten, located in Minneapolis. Smitten Kitten's owners, Jennifer Pritchett and Jessica Giordani, founded the Coalition Against Toxic Toys (CATT), a not-for-profit organization intended to educate consumers and increase awareness about the kinds of manufacturing ingredients commonly found in sex toys. "Our philosophy," according to Pritchett, "is if we know how dangerous these chemicals are for children and dogs, we don't want any contact with them, either."[30] Smitten Kitten's efforts have been redoubled by other socially progressive feminist retailers like Self Serve in Albuquerque, which launched "Phthalate Awareness Month" in March 2008 to raise public awareness about the dangers posed by the plastic softeners. Self Serve is one of a number of retailers opting to sell only phthalate-free and nontoxic sex toys made from platinum-grade silicone, glass, and stainless steel, making eco-friendly options an important part of their brand identity. These efforts are beginning to "trickle up" to larger manufacturers and retailers, and new, decidedly "green" sex toy companies, such as Earth Erotics—with the tagline, "Doing it green"—are finding a home in the adult industry.

The greening of the adult industry has also drawn attention to issues of responsible manufacturing and the problem of packaging and waste. ("Make Love, Not Waste," proclaimed a recent news item about bringing environmental concerns into the bedroom.) Ellen Barnard, co-owner of A Woman's Touch in Madison Wisconsin, tries to buy products from smaller manufacturers whenever possible, preferably ones she can actually visit. She is stocking more items made from wood and glass that are produced by smaller manufacturers and artisans who are responsibly sourcing their materials. This can be challenging, however, in an industry where most products are mass produced overseas in China. A growing "cottage industry" in sex toys is making the task of finding healthy and green toys a bit easier for progressive retailers. Leading the way are two women-run, California-based manufacturers, Vixen Creations and Tantus. Both businesses are known for making high-grade, 100% silicone sex toys. (Silicone has long been considered an ideal material for sex toys, because it is nontoxic, nonporous, and warms to the touch.) Vixen employees hand pour and "pull" all of its dildos and butt plugs in a workplace that looks more like an artist's studio than a factory. Tantus, similarly, prides itself on the fact that it makes all of their products in the

United States, uses "eco-friendly" and nontoxic materials such as platinum-grade silicone and aluminum, and recycles its scrap materials. Increasingly, companies are selling rechargeable batteries and looking for ways to reduce packaging and recycle waste. Many of these efforts have been spearheaded by smaller, progressive manufacturers and retailers who hope these changes will catch on within the larger adult industry.

Mainstreaming

Another industry trend is the "mainstreaming" of adult novelties. Sexually oriented products that at one time could only be purchased at adult stores and boutiques are now making their way onto the shelves of Wal-Mart. Online retailers like Amazon.com are also cashing in on the sex toy boom. By late 2007, Trojan's Vibrating Touch fingertip massager could be found on the shelves of Rite Aid and Walgreens, and Jimmyjane's Form 6 vibrator could be purchased at Sharper Image stores.[31] Many in the adult industry see the mainstreaming of adult products as a good thing, as something that will ultimately help normalize ideas about sex and extend the reach of the adult industry into new and previously untapped markets.

In many ways, it is not surprising that the mainstreaming of sex toys and the newfound emphasis on "quality" is dovetailing with the growth of the women's market. These trends, I suggest, are the result of concerted efforts to make sexually oriented products more "respectable"—and therefore more acceptable—to segments of middle America that previously would never have dreamed of going into an adult store. It is a movement that, importantly, has been led by sex-positive retailers, manufacturers, and porn producers who have been at the vanguard of transforming the adult industry. Sex toy packaging with sultry images of porn starlets has been supplemented with softer and more sanitized iconography; discourses of sexual health and education, as opposed to titillation, are increasingly used as marketing platforms; and a new breed of sex toy manufactures are bringing issues of sleek design, quality manufacturing, and lifestyle branding to an industry historically not known for these things. "What we are seeing is a confluence of cultural shifts," explained Greg DeLong of Njoy. "What started 30 years ago with Joani Blank and Good Vibrations—that it is okay for women to use sex toys—has continued to evolve." For industry detractors, however, the growth and mainstreaming of the adult industry is not a source of celebration, but further evidence of society's acceptance of, and desensitization to, the sexual exploitation of women—a discussion to which I now turn.

SEXUAL POLITICS

Industry trade shows like the AEE are microcosms of the sex industry at large, and as such they become battlegrounds for competing perspectives about the extent to which the adult industry victimizes or empowers the workers. While many journalists choose to report on the more salacious and titillating aspects of the Expo, such as blowup dolls, bondage exhibits, and scantily clad porn stars, others duly note industry trends, breakout performers, and companies making a splash and leaving their mark.[32] Invariably, however, the media also become vehicles for industry detractors and antipornography proponents who use the Expo as an occasion to remind the American public that the adult industry's *raison d'être*, at least as far as they are concerned, is to debase women and perpetuate misogyny, all in the hope of making a quick capitalist buck.[33] In these accounts, pornography is frequently equated with torture, cruelty, and "woman hating." It is blamed for perverting human intimacy and maintaining men's domination over women. And that sense of empowerment that some women working in the adult industry describe? Well, you can chalk that up to false consciousness and a misplaced sense of sexual agency. It is claimed that all women, and men for that matter, are harmed by the sex industry—whether they realize it or not.[34]

There is certainly nothing new about this kind of totalizing, anti-sex industry rhetoric and the kind of moral outcry that typically accompanies it.[35] It is a continuation of themes that have defined the antipornography feminist position since the heyday of the feminist sex wars in the 1980s: sexual danger, victimization, injury, and harm. Although the commercial context is different—indeed the industry has grown, not waned—the concerns, and the overarching analytic framework, remain essentially unchanged. It is a world in which shades of gray do not exist: there is "good" sex and "bad" sex; positive sexual representations and dangerous ones; and very real differences between male and female sexuality.

One of the major problems with the antipornography feminist movement is the very definition of pornography its supporters invoke. In an article published shortly after the 2008 AEE, antiporn activist–academics Gail Dines and Robert Jensen claim that, "pornography, at its core, is a market transaction in which women's bodies and sexualities are offered to male consumers in the interest of maximizing profit."[36] Definitions matter, precisely because they establish the parameters and terms of debate. For Dines and Jensen, pornography is a one-dimensional, monolithic entity. While they acknowledge in the same article that there are degrees of difference in the "overtly woman-hating sex" depicted in pornography—female-friendly films depicting ordinary women kissing are, in fact, different from films where a woman is being penetrated by three men at once—these differences, in the end, do little to alter their conclusion that all pornography, regardless of its content, objectifies, and subordinates women. In their schema, pornography is a closed circuit of representation that constructs only *one* truth about sexuality: men's domination over women. It is a specious, over-simplistic argument at best, but one that continues to hold sway.

As many cultural and media studies scholars will attest, systems of representation and discourse are far more complicated than this. Cultural meanings are polysemic and open to multiple readings and interpretations; representations and discourses are actively created, recreated, negotiated, and resisted. Foucault, for example, argues that we are "dealing less with a discourse on sex than with a multiplicity of discourses, produced by a whole series of mechanisms operating in different institutions."[37] Stuart Hall maintains that representation "implies the active work of selecting and presenting, or structuring and shaping: not merely the transmission of an already existing meaning, but the more active labor of making things mean."[38] Surprisingly, these poststructuralist insights, including social constructionist theory, seem to have had very little, if any, impact on the perspectives advanced by antipornography activists, many of whom are driven by moral outrage and use heavy-handed rhetoric as substitutes for empirical evidence and well-substantiated arguments. As Lisa Henderson notes, if "sexual alarm drives engagement [with sex], if you only come to the discussion of sex when you don't like what you see, that is all you can find."[39] Thus, antipornography feminists continue to be trapped by an essentialist framework that reduces pornography to a singular cultural narrative about sex, gender, and power, altogether sidestepping any engagement with gay, lesbian, transgender, and feminist pornography—systems of representation that would invariably complicate their arguments about the intractability of "woman-hating sex" in pornography.[40]

The claims advanced by antipornography activists certainly do no go unchecked.[41] Nina Hartley, a porn performer who has worked in the adult industry since the 1980s, responded in print to one report of the 2005 AEE convention, arguing that the writer's account focused "at length on the most distasteful aspects of what she saw and heard, but makes no mention of any attempts to establish direct communication with any of the women who work in the adult video industry."[42] Indeed, a disregard for the voices and experiences of women working in the industry is perhaps one of the most consistently conspicuous absences in antipornography writing. "It is that much easier to characterize all female sex workers as degraded, humiliated, and unhappy if you've never talked to any of us," Hartley contends. She continues:

> None of the diversity of our vibrant, raucous, and contentious creative culture
> seems to have attracted [the writer's] notice. By focusing on one or two examples
> she finds particularly heinous, she obscures the broader truth, which is that the
> marketplace of sexual entertainment contains products for almost every taste and
> orientation, including material made by and for heterosexual women and
> couples, lesbians and gay men. . . . By no means does all of it, or even most of it,
> conform to the author's notions of porn-as-expression-of-misogyny.[43]

Adult industry trade shows such as the AEE are powerful reminders of just how diverse and dynamic the adult industry is. There is no single, uniform market represented at these events, but numerous markets and various sexual taste cultures and publics, including male, female, and transgender, straight and queer, mainstream and alternative, vanilla and kinky. This reality is very often overlooked or intentionally downplayed by industry detractors, such as Dines and Jensen, who are unable or perhaps unwilling to see the adult industry as anything other than a bastion of male-oriented consumption that perpetuates the exploitation of women. Yet the Expo's visible intersection of market sectors, retailers, manufacturers, consumers, and fans reveals a far more layered and nuanced picture of an industry that—like other segments of the culture industry—is neither homogenous nor fixed and unchanging.

REBRANDING THE SEX INDUSTRY

Recent changes in the adult industry—a turn toward women, toward quality products, toward nontoxic and high-end sex toys that can now be found on the shelves of Sharper Image—are the result of decades' old efforts to normalize sex and make sexually oriented products more respectable. These marketplace transformations are emblematic of what some see as a "re-branding" of the adult industry. They are also the result of conversations that are happening among some industry professionals about how to redefine themselves, their businesses, and the products they sell in the hope of gaining greater cultural legitimacy and a larger share of middle-class consumers who prefer shopping at "stylish" sexuality boutiques instead of "dirty" bookstores.

Some manufacturers and retailers contend that the adult industry is at a crossroads. The time has come, they suggest, for a public relations makeover, one where "porno shops" are recast as "sexual health boutiques" and "dildos" are sold as "sexual health products." More than just a gimmick or a silly game of semantics, a growing number of companies see these changes as an important business strategy aimed at "broadening sales potential [and] marketplace options."[44]

This emphasis on re-branding—what one writer described as "taking the sleaze out of sex toys"—is about reducing stigma and growing the market. Some companies are making concerted efforts to do this by removing all references to "adult" and "novelty" from their marketing materials in order to garner mainstream media exposure and gain access to new sales channels that might otherwise be predisposed to avoid "adult" products. According to Metis Black of Tantus: "The more that we distance ourselves from porn and the adult industry, the more apt we are to get mentions in *Marie Claire, Women's Health, Men's Health*, or *O Magazine*. This is central to our business plan and we are not alone."[45] Ian Denchasy, co-owner and founder of Freddy and Eddy, suggests that one way to facilitate this transformation is by highlighting issues of sexual health and education, while simultaneously downplaying the language of "pornography": the latter, he thinks, keeps the adult industry on the cultural fringes. "From a practical standpoint, relying less on pornography as a profit center means more opportunities to focus on education and customer comfort. . . . We view the re-branding of our sexual health, education and entertainment industry not as some gimmick . . . but as a serious attempt to accurately define what we do and who we are."[46]

Not everyone, however, is comfortable with what they see as a "linguistic sleight of hand" promoted by a few "self-anointed arbiters of sexual legitimacy." Tony Lovett, editor of *Adult Novelty News*, recently commented on what he called an "extreme industry makeover":

> Sadly, there will always be those who use *porn, dildo*, and similar expressions with contempt. Even sex remains a dirty word to many in this country, and already carries enough shameful baggage without our industry's implicit demonization of toys and porn that don't pass some arbitrary muster. If we choose to look down on those who prefer a blowup doll to a pricey vibrator, then we have truly lost our way.[47]

It is unlikely that a time will come when the adult industry will have to make an either–or decision between promoting "porno shops" or "sexuality resource centers," selling blowup dolls or pricey vibrators. If industry observers and professionals have learned anything over the course of the past decade, it is that consumer demand for adult entertainment is diverse enough to support an increasingly segmented marketplace. Sexual titillation *and* education, Larry Flynt *and* Tristan Taormino, sexual "lowbrow" *and* "middlebrow" can and do coexist. Indeed, the success of sex-positive, women-oriented retail businesses like Good Vibrations, Babeland, and Early to Bed have not put traditional porno shops out of business; feminist pornographers have not supplanted mainstream adult companies like Hustler or Wicked. Rather, these businesses have brought new voices, new products, and, importantly, new consumers into the sexual marketplace, expanding adult industry offerings and, in the process, leaving an indelible imprint.

Today, the boundaries between "mainstream" and "alternative" segments of the adult industry are increasingly porous. Feminist "sexperts" like Tristan Taormino and Jamye Waxman are now collaborating with mainstream adult companies, such as Vivid Entertainment and Adam and Eve, respectively, to produce their own video series. And, in October 2007, Good Vibrations, the venerable women-oriented sex toy emporium based in San Francisco, was purchased by GVA-TWN, an Ohio-based adult wholesaler and distributor. For GVA-TWN chief operating officer Joel Kaminsky, combining forces with Good Vibrations made a great deal of business sense: "Our strengths are infrastructure, inventory, and financial strength. And [Good Vibrations] have a lot to bring to the table in helping us reach out to women and couples of all genders, and in training our staff."[48] For both companies, the sale was viewed as a win–win situation: Good Vibrations received a much needed infusion of cash and GVA-TWN gained a leg-up on competitors also hoping to tap into the growing women's market.

These kinds of business associations, what some might see as "unlikely bedfellows," are, I argue, the wave of the future for the adult industry. After all, market *segmentation*, which is the overall trend, is not the same thing as market *segregation*. The changes currently underway in the adult industry are forcing longtime industry players to think outside the box, and to cross-pollinate in interesting and novel ways. The result is a proliferation of new, hybrid business models that are blending and borrowing from different segments of the adult industry. What the sex industry might look like in 5 or 10 years remains to be seen. But one thing is certain: we will undoubtedly get our first glimpse at how the adult industry is continuing to evolve and adapt to a rapidly changing commercial environment at industry trade shows, which will remain the best way to gauge what is new, what is notable, and, importantly, what direction the industry is headed.

NOTES

1. Frank Rich, "Naked Capitalists," *New York Times Magazine*, May 20, 2001; David Cay Johnston, "Indications of a Slowdown in Sex Entertainment Trade," *New York Times*, January 4, 2007.

2. See Lynn Comella, "It's Sexy. It's Big Business. And It's Not Just For Men," *Contexts* 7 (Summer 2008): 61–63; Lynn Comella, *Selling Sexual Liberation: Women-Owned Sex Toy Stores and the Business of Social Change*, Ph.D. dissertation, University of Massachusetts, 2004.

3. Lisa Henderson, "Sexuality, Cultural Production, and Foucault," paper presented at Sexuality after Foucault Conference, University of Manchester, Manchester, UK, November 2003.

4. See Joshua Gamson, *Freaks Talk Back: Tabloid Talk Shows and Sexual Nonconformity*, Chicago: University of Chicago Press, 1998; Laura Grindstaff, *The Money Shot: Trash, Class, and the Making of TV Talk Shows*, Chicago: University of Chicago Press, 2002.

5. See Katherine Sender, *Business, Not Politics: The Making of the Gay Market*, New York: Columbia University Press, 2004; Arlene Davilla, *Latinos, Inc.: The Marketing and Making of a People*, Berkeley: University of California Press, 2001.

6. See Kathy Davis, *The Making of Our Bodies, Ourselves: How Feminism Travels Across Borders*, Durham, NC: Duke University Press, 2007; Amy Farrell, *Yours in Sisterhood: Ms. Magazine and the Promise of Popular Feminism*, Chapel Hill: University of North Carolina Press, 1998.

7. Larry Grossberg, "Can Cultural Studies Find True Happiness in Communication?" *Journal of Communication* 43 (1993): 89–97, at p. 90.

8. Gayle Rubin, "Thinking Sex: Notes for a Radical Theory of the Politics of Sexuality," in Henry Abelove, Michelle Barale and David Halperin, eds., *The Lesbian and Gay Studies Reader*, New York: Routledge, 1993.

9. For examples see: Elizabeth Bernstein, *Temporarily Yours: Intimacy, Authenticity, and the Commerce of Sex*, Chicago: University of Chicago Press, 2007; Barbara G. Brents and Kate Hausbeck, "Marketing Sex: U.S. Legal Brothels and Late Capitalist Consumption," *Sexualities* 10 (2007): 425–439; Katherine Frank, *G-Strings and Sympathy*, Durham, NC: Duke University Press, 2002.

10. I received press credentials for the AEE in 2008 and 2009. These credentials gave me access to all facets of the Expo, including the main exhibition hall where the fans congregate, the B2B Marketplace, and the various trade seminars.

11. Ian Denchasy, "Retail Review: Redefining the Adult Industry," www.avn.com, June 26, 2008.

12. "Why has AEE Gotten Smaller?" www.aetoday.com, January, 2008.

13. Adult Video News began in 1982 as a newsletter to educate video store buyers and viewers about the emerging adult video market. Since then, AVN Network has grown into a media conglomerate that includes

several publications and a popular online presence. AVN also sponsors several adult industry trade shows, including the Adult Entertainment Expo and the Adult Novelty Expo.

14. Paul Fishbein, email correspondence with the author, February 11, 2008.

15. "Buy a Fan Ticket to the 2008 AVN Adult Entertainment Expo and Video Chat with the Hottest Adult Stars," AEE Press Release, October 31, 2007.

16. "Harmony Films Builds Brand at AVN Adult Entertainment Expo, Company Press Release, January 18, 2008.

17. The AEE is not the sexual free-for-all that people might imagine. There are rules and codes of conduct that must be followed on the convention hall floor by both attendees and participants. For example, there can be no alcohol on the conventional floor, and absolutely no sexual solicitation of any kind. A few otherwise topless women cover their nipples with tape.

18. Greg DeLong, Interview with the author, April 8, 2008.

19. Suki, OhMiBod Press Release, January, 2008.

20. As quoted in "B2B Means Business," *The AVN Adult Entertainment Expo Show Guide*, 2008, p. 50.

21. See Feona Atwood, "Fashion and Passion: Marketing Sex to Women," *Sexualities* 8 (2005): 392–406.

22. Candida Royalle, telephone interview with the author, November 7, 2001.

23. Tristan Taormino, telephone interview with the author, November 2, 1999.

24. Rachel Venning, email correspondence with the author, January 24, 2008.

25. Metis Black, telephone interview with the author, April 1, 2008.

26. Cathy Winks, telephone interview with the author, June 27, 2002.

27. Alicia Relles, "What Women Want," Adult Entertainment Expo, January, 2008.

28. This description comes from Lelo.com, "About Us," accessed November 1, 2008.

29. See Jenn Ramsey, "ANB Examines Sex Toy Materials, avn.com, January 26, 2007; Tristan Taormino, "Dangerous Dildos, Part 1," *Village Voice*, January 30, 2007; Tristan Taormino, "Dangerous Dildos, Part 2," *Village Voice*, February 13, 2007.

30. As quoted in Ali Tweten, "The Smitten Kitten Talks Toxic Sex Toys," *University Chronicle*, April 3, 2008.

31. K. Brewer, "How the Mainstream Market is Cashing in on Sex Toys— and What it Means for Novelty Retailers," *AVN Novelty News* (January–February 2008): 44–48; Jessica Rae Patton, "Make Love, Not Waste: Bringing Environmentalism into the Bedroom," *E Magazine* (September–October 2008): 40–41.

32. See Benjamin Spillman, "Whatever (Sex) Turns (Sex) You (Sex) On," *Las Vegas Review-Journal*, January 12, 2008.

33. See "Packaging Abuse of Women as Entertainment for Adults," *Toronto Star*, January 26, 2008.

34. For an interesting discussion of men's relationship to pornography, see Chris Boulton, "Porn and Me(n): Sexual Morality, Objectification, and Religion at the Wheelock Anti-Pornography Conference," *Communication Review* 11 (2008): 247–273.

35. See Lynn Comella, "Looking Backward: Barnard and Its Legacies," *The Communication Review* 11 (2008): 202–211.

36. Gail Dines and Robert Jensen, "The Anti-Feminist Politics behind the Pornography that 'Empowers' Women," www.opednews.com, January 24, 2008.

37. Michel Foucault, *The History of Sexuality, Volume 1*, New York: Vintage Books, 1978, p. 33.

38. Stuart Hall, "The Rediscovery of 'Ideology': Return of the Repressed in Media Studies," in Michael Gurevitch, et al., eds., *Culture, Society, and the Media Studies*, London and New York: Routledge, 1992, p. 64.

39. Lisa Henderson, "Slow Love," *Communication Review* 11 (2008): 219–224, at p. 222.

40. On October 1, 2008, I was an invited respondent to a lecture given by Robert Jensen at the College of Southern Nevada. Not once during Mr. Jensen's hour-long talk about the pornography industry did he mention that there are women who produce and consume pornography. For a response to his talk see Marisa Christensen, "Pornography Discussion Relies on Generalizations," *The Rebel Yell*, October 6, 2008.

41. Lynn Comella, "Porn Show Coverage Too Cliched," Letter to the Editor, *The Las Vegas Review-Journal*, January 17, 2008.

42. Nina Hartley, "Thus I Refute Chyng Sun: Feminists for Porn," Counterpunch.org, February 2, 2005.

43. Hartley, "Thus I Refute."

44. Metis Black, "Playing the Name Game," *Xbiz*, March 2008.

45. Black, "Playing the Name Game."

46. Ian Denchasy, "What's Wrong with Sexual Health?" avn.com, August 5, 2008.

47. Tony Lovett, "Extreme Industry Makeover," avn.com, March 26, 2008.

48. As quoted in Ilana DeBare, "Good News for Good Vibrations—it's Being Sold," *San Francisco Chronicle*, September 28, 2007.

13

SEX TOURISM AND SEX WORKERS' ASPIRATIONS

Denise Brennan

I write this chapter during the waning months of the Bush administration. In recent years, the administration's Trafficking in Persons Office at the Department of State, has crafted policies around the assumption that prostitution always involves coercion and sex trafficking.[1] Yet my ethnographic research in the Dominican Republic with adult women who voluntarily choose to engage in the commercial sex industry has become an example of a place the Bush administration claims does not exist: a sex-tourist destination involving women who choose to sell sex, and, who keep all of their earnings.

This chapter explores the development of a political economy of sex in a globalized world and how sex-tourist destinations' economic and social relations become caught up in this sexual economy.[2] By examining women's paid sexual labor in the Dominican Republic, where women workers have a fair degree of control over their working conditions, we will see poor women take advantage of opportunities in a global economy. Sosúa's sex workers try to use the sex trade with foreign men not just as a survival strategy but as an advancement strategy. The chapter also considers why sex tourists travel to buy sexual services that they could buy at home. Neocolonial race-based fantasies and stereotypes inform sex tourists' (and foreign residents') expectations and experiences in Sosúa.

POOR WOMEN'S WORK AND GLOBALIZATION

The proliferation of sex-tourist destinations throughout the developing world reflect global capital's destabilizing effects on less industrialized countries' economies. This economic globalization not only shapes women's work options in the developing world but also forces them into insecure, and possibly dangerous, work. In sex-tourist destinations we find the tremendous effects of global capital: its redirection of development and local employment into the tourist industry, especially women's work and migration choices; its creation of powerful images, fantasies, and desires that are linked to race and gender; and its generation of new transnational practices from which foreigners extract more benefit than locals. By examining hierarchies within transnational spaces, we meet individuals, particularly women, who are typically left out of conventional accounts of economic globalization—those who keep houses and hotel rooms clean, food prepared, and tourists sexually satisfied. The growth of the sex-tourist trade in the developing world and poor women of color's participation in it not only are consequences of the restructuring of the global economy but also of women's central role in the service sector of tourism. Women perform the majority of this kind of service-oriented labor, and since they often are paid less than men, their relatively cheap labor has assured that destinations are affordable for even the most budget-conscious travelers. Yet much of the scholarship and discussion in the media about globalization do not consider the starring role women play in opening up more and cheaper vacation possibilities for those traveling to the developing world.

In sex-tourist destinations we see up close what has been called the "global feminization of labor." Much of the feminist scholarship on globalization attends to questions of women's agency—not just women's "responses" to globalization but also their attempts to make globalization work for them. The daily struggles of women in sex-tourist sites document women's attempts to overturn the inequities of globalization. Despite the idiosyncrasies of sex-tourist business in different parts of the world, they all allow for examination of key themes in feminist scholarship. What kinds of obstacle prevent sex workers from achieving their financial goals? What does it mean for women's power and agency in the global sex trade when they work without pimps, but, rather, directly with sex tourists? And what are the challenges to traditional gender relations and ideologies when women out-earn local men? The particular characteristics of sex-tourist destinations allow us to see whether poor women in local places can "leave the worst excesses of patriarchal oppression behind" and find new and beneficial opportunities within globalization.[3]

And what of those who travel to these sites to buy sex? European men get on a plane to buy sex that they could purchase in their home towns and cities. European consumers of paid sex have an array of choices in Europe and the prices are sometimes just as low as they are in sex-tourist destinations in the developing world. Yet sex has become a currency of transnational negotiations and migratory desires. Every sex-tourist destination has specific selling points and attracts particular kinds of consumer for particular experiences with paid sex. The contributors to Manderson and Jolly's book on sex for sale throughout Asia, for example, present a variety of desires among sex tourists.[4] But, what precisely is being transacted in sex-tourist exchanges—beyond the act of sex—is elusive and depends on the individual and the setting.

Sex-tourist destinations do share some basic characteristics: women's poverty leads them to migrate internally or internationally to participate in the sex industry, and inexpensive travel opportunities have permitted more (and less moneyed) tourists to circulate the globe. Part of sex tourists' experiences is not just that the sex is cheap, but that *everything* is cheaper than at home. As sex tourists can afford nearly everything they desire, they can enjoy "feeling rich." Even though they might find sex workers in their home country who charge cheap prices for sex, there will be other sex workers whose services they could not afford. Sex tourists in the developing world can play at being "big men." Their money goes much farther, they have much more of it compared to most locals, and they are sexually and romantically pursued by many young, beautiful women. As one analyst noted, "The increase in male demand for paid sex is logical in the sense that privileges which were formerly restricted by class, race, and gender are now available to everybody; there is no need to be rich to exploit women in very poor countries."[5]

SEX TOURISM IN THE CARIBBEAN

Sex tourism not only provides economic opportunities for those selling sexual services, but it also can have tremendous effects on the local economy in which it develops. In the case of Sosúa, the town in the Dominican Republic where I did my research between 1993 and 2003, sex tourism quickly and flamboyantly changed daily life—especially for Dominican women—in different ways than has tourism more generally. Over the span of a few years, beginning in the early 1990s, a range of individuals—Dominican, Canadian, European—flocked to the town. Poor Dominican women were drawn into Sosúa's sex trade, establishing new internal migration patterns. They continue to migrate from throughout the Dominican Republic to work in Sosúa's sex trade, where many hope to meet and to marry European or Canadian men who can sponsor their migration off the island. In this sense not just sex—but also love—are commodified in Sosúa.

Whether these encounters between foreign tourists and Dominicans emphasize the "exotic" (First World tourists seeking to observe, interact with, and take photographs of the "authentic" Other) or the "erotic" (First World tourists seeking to have sexual relations with the dark-skinned, "authentic" Other), international tourists often "seek in the margins of the Third World a figment of their imagination."[6] But in Sosúa, Dominicans themselves have "imaginings" about Sosúa's opportunities, the tourists, their money, and the tourists' lifestyles back home. Consequently, the fantasies are often bilateral. In this economy of desire based on difference, Dominican sex workers and foreign sex tourists forge new practices and meanings of "love" that grow out of the tourist and sex-tourist trades. Sosúans and, increasingly, foreign sex tourists, understand that many relationships that begin in Sosúa are strategic performances by Dominican citizens for visas.

Poor Dominican women (and men) also migrate to Sosúa to work in its tourist restaurants, hotels, bars, and shops. Like prospectors searching for gold, Dominican migrants imagine that once in Sosúa "anything could happen," and it has the reputation of being a town in which Dominicans can get rich quick. It is this fantasy of what *might be* that keeps so many new people arriving everyday. Meanwhile, some foreign tourists fall in love with living in a Caribbean "paradise" and move to Sosúa permanently. Although Dominican sex workers and other Dominican migrants usually end up disappointed and no better off economically than when they first migrated to Sosúa, foreign tourists and residents often find what they are seeking. This chapter examines how Dominican migrants to Sosúa's tourist and sex-tourist industries strategize for the future regardless of the outcomes. These migrants attempt to circumvent asymmetries of power to turn Sosúa into a space of opportunity, rather than a space of exploitation and domination and are engaged in an ongoing struggle to wrest some of the profits and control away from the foreign owners who have taken over Sosúa.

SOSÚA AS A TRANSNATIONAL PLACE

With its constant influx of Dominican and Haitian migrants seeking work in the sex and tourist trades and of European tourists seeking to play, as well as a large foreign-resident community living there year-round, Sosúa became a transnational sexual meeting ground. So many foreigners visitors live in Sosúa that Dominicans often see it as a town outside the Dominican Republic. With no place to buy a plate of Dominican rice, beans, and chicken in downtown Sosúa at Dominican prices, the town indeed looks and feels "un-Dominican." Instead, Sosúa's streets, lined by German beer gardens and kiosks selling European newspapers, remind its passersby that many non-Dominicans now live, own businesses, work, and vacation there. As a banana plantation for the United Fruit Company in the early part of the 20th century, and a sanctuary for European Jews at the beginning of World War II, Sosúa has long been an economic, social, and cultural crossroads between the local and the foreign. Known now both for its beaches and for its sex bars, Sosúa's development into an inexpensive tourist and sex-tourist destination is the latest phase of its encounters with the outside world. Tourism and sex tourism have only sped up and intensified Sosúa's engagement in the global economy.

Since Sosúa both offers sex for sale and houses an economically powerful foreign expatriate community, foreigners are more likely than Dominicans to find what they are seeking there. Sex tourists, for example, can pay to fulfill their sexual fantasies, while expatriates can buy a life of comfort at a cheaper cost than in Europe or North America. Sosúa emerges as a kind of trans-national space in which many imagine that their dreams for better lives will be attained. Yet globalized hierarchies of race, class, gender, citizenship, and mobility dictate whether these dreams are realized. Possibilities for economic mobility do exist in such transnational spaces but they are available only for a few. Many foreign residents reinvent their daily lives, installing pools and hiring domestic help, while Dominicans only rarely make significant improvements to their economic status in tourist economy, even though they imagine their prospects otherwise. Although most foreigners are from the working to middle classes, they have sufficient resources to travel inter-nationally or even to move permanently overseas if they so desire. Meanwhile, Sosúa's sex workers have limited resources and face numerous legal constraints to migration off the island.

SEXSCAPES

Sosúa's sex trade stands apart from many other sex-tourist destinations in the developing world because it does not involve pimps or the coercion of women into selling sex, and therefore it allows sex workers a good deal of control over their working conditions. I do not suggest that these women do not risk rape, beatings, arrest, and HIV infection; the sex trade can be dangerous, and Sosúa's trade is no exception. However, Dominican women are not trafficked into

Sosúa's trade but usually are drawn to it through social networks of family and female friends who work or have worked in it. The absence of pimps in Sosúa is critical to sex workers' lives. Without them, Sosúan sex workers keep all their earnings, essentially working freelance. They decide how many hours they will work, with whom, and for what price. Sosúa's sex trade is also notable for its two tiers: one with Dominican clients and the other with foreign clients. The meager earnings with Dominican clients make this sale of sex a survival strategy, whereas the benefits of working with foreign clients make women's use of sex tourism an advancement strategy. Without the transnational connections that can grow out of relationships with foreigners —faxes, money wires, clients' return visits, and the possibility of traveling to or moving to clients' home countries—Sosúa's sex trade would be no different from sex work in any other Dominican town.

As Sosúa became known as a place where tourists can buy sex, Sosúa and Sosúans experienced monumental changes. Because sex tourism has played a critical role in the town's transformation, I see it as a space inextricably tied up with transactional sex. I use the term *sexscape* to refer to both a new kind of global sexual landscape and the sites within it. Sexscapes link the practices of sex work to the forces of a globalized economy. Defining characteristics are international travel from the developed to the developing world, consumption of paid sex, and inequality. In a sexscape, there are differences in power between the buyers (sex tourists) and the sellers (sex workers) that can be based on race, gender, class, and nationality. These differences become eroticized and commodified inequalities. The exotic is transformed into the erotic—both privately in consumers' imaginations and quite publicly by entire industries that make money off this desire for difference. These differences, between sex workers in the developing world and sex tourists traveling from the developed world, are essential to distinguish sexscapes in the developing world from red-light districts (or other sites where paid sex is available) in the developed world. Within sexscapes, the sex trade becomes the focal point of a place, and the social and economic relations of that place are filtered through the continual selling of sex to foreigners. In contrast, the sex trade in red-light districts in the developed world—such as in Frankfurt, Rome, Brussels—by no means defines social and economic life outside of these districts. Neither do the female citizens of these places necessarily become associated with sexual availability. As Altman notes, although sex is "a central part of the political economy of all large cities," few cities base their economies on sex.[7]

When sexscapes emerge within a globalized economy, hierarchies of race, class, gender,[8] citizenship, and mobility create undeniable power differentials between the actors in these geographic spaces, which, in turn, give them unequal opportunities. There are very different and often uneven opportunities for foreigners and locals, and men and women, while race and age also play a role. The asymmetries and inequalities that result from the mix of differences in Sosúa reveal an unevenness. In this sexscape, the buyers eroticize these differences—particularly gender and racial differences—as part of their paid sex experiences. Meanwhile, the sellers often struggle to capitalize on these differences. One way is through their "performance of love."

PERFORMING LOVE

Beyond the assumed transaction of sex for money, complex politics of relationships are at work in the encounters between sex workers and sex tourists. As they present themselves as sexually desirable and available to both attract and to anchor sex tourists to their own lives and futures, they also deploy love strategically. This role playing is not without costs, however, as sex workers find themselves both exploited and exploiters in a cascade of customers, suitors, boyfriends, and partners. Dominican sex workers' strategies to get ahead (*progresar*) through sexual commerce with foreign tourists—successful or not—often hinge on their performance of love. Of course, the sex trade in any locale relies on the charade that sex workers desire their clients and enjoy the sex. Yet in Sosúa's sexscape, some workers also pretend to be *in love*. This is highly strategic. With so many financial demands on them as single mothers (nearly every sex worker I met was a mother), and so few well-paying jobs available to them, Dominican sex workers in Sosúa who perform well at being "in love" have much at stake. Keeping transnational ties open is a daily task for some workers. Many send faxes to several foreign clients at the same time with whom they have simultaneous ongoing relationships (it costs under $1 to send or receive a fax at the telecommunication offices in town). For some, dropping by these services to see if they have received any faxes is a daily ritual. Those considered lucky receive faxes instructing them to pick up money at the Western Union office in downtown Sosúa—something that also occurs in other sex-tourist sites.[9] Others receive word that their foreign clients or boyfriends are planning a return visit. The most envied women receive "letters of invitation," essential to obtaining a tourist visa to visit the men in their home countries.

Sex workers' active emotional labor is clear in their performance of "love" in their faxes. Workers less experienced at building transnational relationships come to colleagues, such as Elena, who has a proven track record of receiving money wires and return visits from clients. Elena has helped compose letters and faxes for women who were uncertain about what to do with the addresses, fax numbers, and telephone numbers clients gave them. She helped a sex worker, Carmen, for example, write a letter to a Belgian client who had sent her a money wire and then abruptly stopped corresponding with her. Carmen came to Elena because, at the time, Elena was living with Jürgen and was experienced, indeed successful, at transnational courting. Elena's advice was simple and centered on Carmen's performance of love: "You have to write that you *love* him and that you miss him. Write that you cannot wait to see him again. Tell him you think about him every day." Following Elena's guidelines, Carmen composed the following letter that I helped her translate into English:

> Dear ____, I have been thinking of you every day and have been waiting for a fax to hear how you are. I got your money wire, thanks. But I still want to see you. Please send me a fax at the following number—, and if possible, a fax number where I can reach you. I miss you very much and think of you all the time. I love you very much. I wait to hear from you. I hope you come to visit again very soon.

> Many kisses, Carmen

Carmen never heard from this client again.

Sensing which men are not already married, and are likely to continue corresponding and to return for future vacations or to extend an invitation to visit Europe or Canada, often proves an elusive skill. While sorting through all the pictures and letters of her European clients, Nanci, for example, commented on which ones seemed the most serious about keeping in touch. She deemed several too young and thus not likely to follow through on the relationships. Nanci had honed her ability to detect which transnational suitors were worth pursuing during her 4 years in Sosúa. She had been receiving money wires on and off from five or six European men at the same time. Her many and varied transnational ties were envied and difficult to replicate, yet many tried. Stashed away in a spare pocketbook, Nanci kept a bundle of letters and faxes. She also had photos of the men back home and photos of her with the men during their vacations in Sosúa. Taped to her wall were photos of at least 15 different foreign men. Several of them had returned to Sosúa to see Nanci and expressed interest in bringing her to Europe and marrying her. Expressing her love for them, and how much she missed them, were central themes in Nanci's performance of love with her suitors.

SEX TRADE AS MIGRATION STRATEGY

Poor women use the sex trade as a first step to marriage and greater financial security in other sex-tourist destinations. Kamala Kempadoo, for example, writes about migrant Colombian and Dominican women who work in the sex trade in Curaçao, whose work with clients might develop into relationships that lead to marriage. Women also might pay to acquire Dutch citizenship by marrying, which means that migrant women could stay and work legally as sex workers in Curaçao or travel to Europe without restriction.[10] A similar dynamic is found in some other Caribbean nations, such as Jamaica, as well as in some Asian countries such as the Philippines and Thailand. In each case, women see the sex trade as a possible route to marriage to western men and migration to their countries.[11] Much like the perceptions Dominican sex workers maintain of life in Europe, Filipina and Thai sex workers also hope for a better life for themselves and their children in the West. Like their Dominican counterparts, these Asian women lack other opportunities for legal migration.

With much of any tourist experience relying on fantasy, tourists on vacation often engage in behavior and activities they would never engage in at home, such as paying for sex or having interracial relationships. Male tourists in Sosúa often told me that they never had paid for sex at "home," but since they were on vacation they thought, "why not?" Chant and McIlwaine also found that some foreign men—who had not intended at the outset to pay for sex—did so in Cebu's bars in the Philippines, they claim because of "peer pressure." One man boasted to his friends, for example, that he had bought five women in one night.[12] In encounters between locals and foreign tourists, locals often have more practical goals—such as laying the groundwork to receive money wires from tourists once they return to Europe—and might need to "perform" for tourists to achieve them, whereas foreign tourists primarily seek fun and pleasure.

Relationships also can be a kind of stage to resist racial hierarchies and inequalities based on gender, class, and citizenship. For example, the strategizing of Dominican women can have long-term economic results. Some clients have paid for the education of their "girlfriend's" children or have helped sex workers get a fledgling business off the ground (such as a clothing store or hair salon). In addition, sex work can be used as a means to achieve privileged schooling, well-paying jobs in the civil service, or access to certain residential quarters.[13]

Sex workers' transactional use of marriage is an age-old story. What is new is how marriage-as-transaction operates in a globalized world where legal crossing of national borders requires passports and visas. In Sosúa's sexscape, marriage between Dominicans and western men emerges as an economic strategy as well as a legal route to securing the papers necessary to migrate off the island. Research on so-called mail-order brides vividly underscores how marriage to foreigners is often the only viable option for legal migration for citizens of certain countries. For example, young Chinese women are able to gain the exit visas and passports that most Chinese spend years waiting for— or never get—by marrying foreign men through marriage introduction agencies.[14] Research on marriage-as-transaction, illustrated by these practices, demonstrates that the western feminist critique of marriages based on the traditional division of labor does not consider the calculus of women who have "worked in fields or a factory for subsistence since childhood."[15] For them, marriage, even those that take the most traditional forms—and are not based on "love"—can be a vacation from backbreaking work and chronic financial crises. With their own workloads lightened, their material comfort improved, and the possibilities to remit money back to their families expanded, marriage for economic security can be good enough.[16] Indeed, although some sex workers ideally might hope for love and greater gender equity in a marriage to a foreign man (compared to traditional inequality with local men), most regard these marriages strictly as business transactions.

THE CLIENTS

What about the sex tourists? Most of the clients I interviewed initially traveled there based on recommendations of friends, and most had visited other sex-tourist destinations. These seasoned sex tourists told me that they were "bored" with other destinations and decided to "try" Dominican women. Over the years, the returning tourists get to know the owner–operators of the small hotels, lunch shacks, restaurants, bars, and nightclubs they frequent. These places might not be grand, but what they offer is warm hospitality by owners who know their customers and go out of their way to make them feel at home. Since German tourists often frequent German-owned establishments that serve German food and beer, and British, Canadian, and Dutch tourists also tend to go to bars or restaurants owned by fellow countrymen, these tourists know they can have conversations in their native language with the owners and other customers. And, of course, returning sex tourists can look for their favorite sex workers, with whom they may have been corresponding.

Just as they enjoy the familiar vibe in the unpretentious bars, hotels, and restaurants that they frequent, sex tourists also see sex workers' lives up close.

Once the clients accompany women to their rooms in barebones boarding houses, they see the daily demands of poverty. The unfinished walls and ceilings and lack of plumbing and lighting clash with idealized fantasies of having uncomplicated sexual relationships with these relatively "undemanding" women. As soon as tourists step out of the tourist zone and into the private world of the women, they confront—even if only for an hour—the reality of how the poor live in their tourist destination. Since women usually have photographs of their children on their walls, their clients get a glimpse into these women's many obligations. Women report that when clients return the next day to take women out to lunch, or the next evening, they bring gifts with them for the women's children. Thus, clients learn early on in encounters with Sosúa's sex workers that getting involved with these women could take many forms.

Race plays a central role in how white western sex tourists imagine Afro-Dominican sex workers. Women's skin color was mentioned again and again in my interviews (and is a recurring theme in tourists' postings on sex-tourist Internet sites). A group of German men told me, for example, "Dominican women are beautiful, there is a range of skin color." Others made explicit the connections they saw between skin color and sexual proficiency. German sex tourists and a bar owner laughed about German women, with whom "it's over quickly." In contrast, they ribbed one another about how much Dominican women enjoyed sex, and attributed their "natural" sexual skills to the climate: "When the sun is shining, it gives you more hormones."

As sites in the developing world become known as sites for sex tourists, sex for sale can come to define these countries—and the women who live there—in the North American and European imaginations. In her description of Thailand, Annette Hamilton, for example, points to the popular image of the "alluring, very young woman" as the "central icon for the quintessential Thai experience," which cements the "Western identification of Thailand with sex for sale, or 'play-for-pay'."[17] Associations between nationality, race, and sexual prowess draw sex tourists to sexscapes in the developing world, where they not only buy sex more cheaply than in their home countries but can live out their racialized sexual fantasies. Sex-tourist destinations often depend on racial differences between the buyers and the sellers as well as the men's fantasies about the local women, rooted in colonial racist discourses and, more recently, influence by media depictions and Internet discussions and photos.

Sex tourists' girlfriends or wives or ex-girlfriends and ex-wives are imagined points of contrast. Sex tourists in Sosúa, for example, constantly compare Dominican women to European women, and imagine the latter as more sexual, compliant, and as making fewer demands. Misogyny among these foreign men directed toward western women "back home" can play a role in the men's racialized sexualization of women as "Other" in the sexscapes to which they travel. Hamilton describes a "profound misogyny" expressed by western sex tourists toward western women in her research in the sex trade in Bangkok.[18] In Jeremy Seabrook's interviews with male sex tourists, they told him they traveled to Thailand because western women were not as compliant or as feminine as Thai women. They came to Bangkok to "escape into the fantasy of men-as-men and women-as-women, an uncomplicated distribution of roles which provide a refuge from life."[19] In the Dominican Republic it is also common for European men to seek long-term relationships with Dominican women as a break from the "demands" of "liberated" European women. They have fantasies not only of "hot and fiery" sex but also of relationships that reflect more "traditional" gender roles than they might have in their relationships with European women. Sosúa's sex workers embrace their foreign clients' misogynist comments about European women as a way to distinguish themselves as better and more exciting lovers, so they too take part in perpetuating racialized and sexualized stereotypes.

These associations between nationality, race, and sexual prowess have been fueled not only by sex tourists and sex workers but also by various commercial enterprises that cater to and perpetuate these associations. In Thailand, for example, brothel owners or sex-tour operators might include fees for foot massages in their bill for sexual services because western men perceive Thai women as being "tender," "a quality conspicuously absent from the sex industry in the west."[20] Seabrook observes: "Men feel particularly cherished by what they experience as the compliance, eagerness to please, and considerateness of Thai women." Indeed, during their initial contacts with Thai women, the men describe themselves "as being over the moon, being on cloud nine, walking on air, and wondered what they have been doing, wasting their life until now." Although these sex tourists' racism and stereotypes about Asians inform their expectations and even their experiences, they "rarely see [that] this idealization of 'Oriental' women is racist."[21] Similarly, many sex tourists hold strong racialized notions about Afro-Caribbean women.[22]

OUTCOMES

Despite sex workers' strategizing, a recurring story seems to unfold: most workers end up just getting by, rather than improving their socioeconomic status or their children's futures. Women's migration strategies cannot work, for example, unless the foreign clients follow through on their promises of visa sponsorships and marriage. At any time these men could stop sending money wires or decide to withhold help in the visa process. Since the late 1980s, when Europeans began vacationing in Sosúa in significant numbers, only a modest number of them have married Dominican women, let alone sponsored their migration to Europe. And, while stories circulate in sex workers' circles about women living in Europe with former clients-turned-husbands, nearly every sex worker also recounts stories in which foreign men break their promises to Dominican women. Particularly striking is the impermanence of the women's "successes" and "failures." As unpredictably as foreign men begin sending money wires, they stop sending them. Promises to sponsor a woman's visa can go unfulfilled. And, of course, marriages can come to an end.

Moreover, the women themselves move in and out of sex work. Sex work is not always a steady activity but might occur in conjunction with other income-generating activities. It can be an activity that some women (and men) take up for short periods or as part of an annual work cycle. Unlike some other places, however, most women in Sosúa's sex-tourist trade do not simultaneously work in other income-generating activities. However, former sex workers may combine paid work (outside the sex trade) with "love work:" A transactional approach to romantic and sexual relationships with foreign men as boyfriends. And, of course, since sex work and the relationships that grow out of it—both long-term relationships and marriage—are business transactions, sex workers and former sex workers do not see these relationships with clients as restricting their sexual or romantic lives. Rather, they maintain sexual—and possibly romantic—relationships with Dominican men while they simultaneously build and maintain a roster of transnational suitors.

Only a few women I met during my first trip to Sosúa in 1993 were still working in the sex trade in 2003. Most have long since returned to their families in towns and cities throughout the island. Those who have stayed in Sosúa have moved on from sex work. Some have married Dominican men— usually men who were their boyfriends while they sold sex. These marriages, the workers explain, are for "love." Others continue to look to foreign men for resources and visas. I never could have predicted back in 1993 that some of them—who had no ties to men overseas and who were not actively seeking to establish them—would eventually marry foreign men and move to Europe. And of course the reverse has happened: women whose relationships with foreign men seemed fairly secure have experienced the dissolution of these relationships, resulting in the women's return from Europe to the Dominican Republic and their associated downward economic mobility.

DENISE BRENNAN

VARIATION IN SEX WORK

There are a wide range of workers' experiences within the sex trade, some beneficial and some tragic. Women enter sex work for diverse reasons and have greatly varying experiences within it. Even within Sosúa, conditions in the sex trade are highly divergent: there are Dominican and Haitian workers; women who work with either foreign or Dominican clients; women who receive money wires from foreign clients; women who receive financial help from local, regular Dominican clients; women who live with or are separated from their children; and women who have AIDS, or have been raped or battered, and those who have not. These differences are crucial to shaping a woman's capacity for choice and control.

The debate about how scholars, activists, and sex workers understand women's sexual labor centers on issues of agency and victimization, as well as economic empowerment and powerlessness. Some assert that women are forced to choose sex work because of their race, class, nationality, colonial status, and gender and do not have a "choice." To them, all forms of sex work are exploitative and oppressive. Yet, Dominican women have room for maneuvering within the sex trade. It is not simply a story of women who use sex work as a survival strategy but also of women who try to use sex work as an *advancement* strategy. Marriage and migration off the island are the key goals. These women see Sosúa's sex trade and marriage to foreign tourists as an avenue to economic success—a way not just to solve short-term economic problems but to change their lives (and their families' lives) through migration overseas.

Like feminist ethnographers who explore larger structural forces that contribute to poor women's oppression while also highlighting how these women try to improve their lives, I consider both the structures of inequality in workers' lives and their creative responses to them, and conclude that there is a great deal of *intentionality* in these women's use of the sex trade. Their creative strategizing, the ways they attempt to use the sex trade to move beyond daily survival, presents an important counterexample to claims that *all* sex workers in *all* contexts are powerless victims of violence and exploitation. These women, local agents caught in a web of global economic relations, try to take advantage (to the extent that they can) of the men—and their citizenship—who are in Sosúa to take advantage of them. In Sosúa's bar scene, foreign sex tourists might see Dominican sex workers as exotic and erotic and pick out one woman over another in the crowd, as a commodity for their pleasure and control, but Dominican sex workers often see the men, too, as readily exploitable. The men are potential dupes, essentially walking visas, who can help the women leave the island—and poverty.

Despite this distinction between sex work as an advancement strategy and sex work as a survival strategy, there nonetheless remains a tension between the efforts of marginalized women to get ahead and the role of local and global forces that constrain them. My research catalogs many stories of sex workers' disappointment with Sosúa, its tourism, and foreign men. Sex workers' relationships with foreign men inevitably fall short of mutual exploitation since white foreign male tourists are better positioned than Afro-Dominican female sex workers to leave Sosúa satisfied with their experiences there. Sex workers in Sosúa are at once independent and dependent, exploitative and exploited. There are women who are content with what they have achieved through sex work as well as those who have suffered humiliation and abuse.

CONCLUSION

Tourism and sex tourism have dramatically transformed this Caribbean beach town, with unequal opportunities for its Dominican residents, on the one hand, and foreign residents and tourists, on the other. With few secure, income-earning possibilities, poor Dominicans migrate to Sosúa to cash in on the tourist boom. They bank on the myth of endless opportunity in tourist spaces where vacationers spend their money, and they imagine that in this "non-Dominican" town they will make much more money than they could in other Dominican towns. They arrive in search of a better life, as do the foreigners who take up residence in Sosúa. Yet even though the imagination allows individuals throughout the world to fantasize about a better life, the attainability of this fantasy depends on who is doing the imagining and where. Unlike western men who realize in Sosúa their dreams of an early retirement and lives of comfort that otherwise would not have been affordable in their home countries, Dominicans who migrate there are less likely to fulfill their aspirations. Their gains are on a much smaller scale than the significant socioeconomic leap foreign residents can make in Sosúa.

Transnational spaces not only are sites of new economic, cultural, and sexual possibilities but also are locations that can reproduce existing inequalities. Sex workers in the Third World might exercise more control over their working conditions than they would in factories, as domestics, or in other sites, and they might try to use the sex trade as a strategy of advancement, but their decisions and actions constantly collide with those of sex tourists. As one savvy sex worker, Ani, put it, sex workers who come to Sosúa often end up disillusioned: "They hear they can make money, and meet a gringo, so they come to Sosúa. Some women enter sex work because they want it all so fast. They come with their big dreams. But then they find out it is all a lie."

The failure of the majority of Dominican workers to leave with foreign husbands, visas, or fattened bank accounts underscores the inequalities between male and female, rich and poor, black and white, sex worker and sex tourist. The male clients' vacations come to an end, and most of them, on returning home, do not continue to communicate with or send money or gifts to the workers they met during their holiday. Meanwhile, sex workers remain in Sosúa hoping that their "ticket" is on the next plane full of foreign tourists, ready not only to have sex—but also to feign love—for a shot at leaving the island.

NOTES

1. See Denise Brennan, "Competing Claims of Victimhood? Foreign and Domestic Victims of Trafficking in the United States," *Sexuality Research and Social Policy* 5 (2008): 45–61. See also Chapter 14 of this volume and Ronald Weitzer, "Moral Crusade against Prostitution," *Society* 43 (2006): 33–38.

2. See also Denise Brennan, *What's Love Got to Do with It? Transnational Desires and Sex Tourism in the Dominican Republic*, Durham, NC: Duke University Press, 2004.

3. Amitra Basu, "Editorial," *Signs* 26 (2001): 943–948, at p. 943.

4. Lenore Manderson and Margaret Jolly, eds., *Sites of Desire, Economies of Pleasure: Sexualities in Asia and the Pacific*, Chicago: University of Chicago Press, 1997.

5. Susanne Thorbek, "Introduction," in Susanne Thorbek and Bandana Pattanaik, eds., *Transnational Prostitution: Changing Global Patterns*, New York: Zed, 2002, p. 2.

6. Edward Bruner, "Tourism in the Balinese Borderzone," in Smadar Lavie and Ted Swedenburg, eds., *Displacement, Diaspora, and Geographies of Identity*, Durham, NC: Duke University Press, 1996, p. 157.

7. Dennis Altman, *Global Sex*, Chicago: University of Chicago Press, 2001, p. 11.

8. Although this chapter focuses on women sex workers, racialized male bodies are also sought by white tourists in sexscapes. For a study of gay sex tourism in the Dominican Republic, see Mark Padilla, "'Western Union Daddies' and Their Quest for Authenticity: An Ethnographic Study of the Dominican Gay Sex Tourism Industry," *Journal of Homosexuality* 53 (2007): 241–275.

9. On Cuba, see Amalia Cabezas, "Between Love and Money: Sex, Tourism, and Citizenship in Cuba and the Dominican Republic," *Signs* 29 (2004): 987–1015.

10. Kamala Kempadoo, *Sexing the Caribbean: Gender, Race, and Sexual Labor*, New York: Routledge, 2004.

11. Cabezas, "Between Love and Money"; Deborah Pruitt and Suzanne LaFont, "For Love and Money: Romance Tourism in Jamaica," *Annals of Tourism Research* 21 (1995): 422–440; Kamala Kempadoo, ed., *Sun, Sex, and Gold: Tourism and Sex Work in the Caribbean*, Lanham, MD: Rowman & Littlefield, 1999; Sylvia Chant and Cathy McIlwaine, *Women of a Lesser Cost: Female Labor, Foreign Exchange, and Philippine Development*, London: Pluto Press, 1995.

12. Chant and McIlwaine, *Women of a Lesser Cost*, p. 225.

13. Ann Stoler, "Educating Desire in Colonial Southeast Asia," in Lenore Manderson and Margaret Jolly, eds., *Sites of Desire, Economies of Pleasure*, Chicago: University of Chicago Press, 1997, p. 44.

14. These Chinese women's transnational use of marriage has earned them a reputation as "gold diggers" searching for foreign "airplane tickets." Constance Clark, "Foreign Marriage, 'Tradition,' and the Politics of Border Crossings," in Nancy Chen, Constance Clark, Suzanne Gottschang, and Lyn Jeffry, eds., *China Urban: Ethnographies of Contemporary Culture*, Durham, NC: Duke University Press, 2001, p. 105.

15. Nicole Constable, *Romance on a Global Stage: Pen Pals, Virtual Ethnography, and "Mail-Order" Marriages*, Berkeley: University of California Press, 2003, p. 65.

16. Brennan, *What's Love Got to Do with It?*

17. Annette Hamilton, "Primal Dream: Masculinism, Sin, and Salvation in Thailand's Sex Trade," in Lenore Manderson and Margaret Jolly, eds., *Sites of Desire, Economies of Pleasure*, Chicago: University of Chicago Press, 1997, p. 145.

18. Hamilton, "Primal Dream," p. 151.

19. Jeremy Seabrook, *Travels in the Skin Trade: Tourism and the Sex Industry*, London: Pluto, 1996, p. 36.

20. Seabrook, *Travels in the Skin Trade*, p. 3.

21. Seabrook, *Travels in the Skin Trade*, p. 3.

22. Kempadoo, *Sexing the Caribbean*; Coco Fusco, "Hustling for Dollars: *Jineterismo* in Cuba," in Kamala Kempadoo and Jo Doezema, eds., *Global Sex Workers*, New York: Routledge, 1998.

SEX TRAFFICKING: FACTS AND FICTIONS

Ronald Weitzer and Melissa Ditmore

Sex trafficking has become a hot issue over the past decade. The media have increasingly covered the issue, often in a sensationalized manner; an influential moral crusade has been in the vanguard in influencing popular perceptions of the problem; and governments and international bodies have devoted substantial resources to fighting trafficking. This chapter examines (1) facts and popular fictions regarding sex trafficking and (2) the main social forces shaping U.S. government policy in this area.[1] The chapter is based on an analysis of activists' pronouncements, interest group documents, publications of government agencies, and relevant legislation. We show that many of the popular claims regarding both trafficking and prostitution are dubious if not entirely fictional, yet activists have met with remarkable success in getting their views incorporated in government policy and law enforcement practices. These activists are part of a larger moral crusade fighting the entire sex industry.

A MORAL CRUSADE PERSPECTIVE

A *moral crusade* is a type of social movement that defines a particular condition or activity as an unqualified evil and sees its mission as a righteous enterprise with both symbolic goals (attempting to redraw or bolster normative boundaries and moral standards) and instrumental ones (providing relief to victims, punishing evildoers).[2] Some moral crusades are motivated by genuine humanitarian concerns and desires to help victims while others are mainly interested in imposing a set of moral standards on others. In either case, these campaigns typically propound inflated claims about the magnitude of the problem (e.g., the number of victims), assertions that exceed the available evidence.[3] At the same time, crusades usually present horror stories about a problem, in which the most shocking cases are described and presented as typical. Casting the problem in highly dramatic terms by recounting the plight of highly traumatized victims is intended to alarm the public and justify draconian solutions. Finally, crusade leaders consider the problem unambiguous: they are not inclined to acknowledge gray areas and are adamant that a particular evil exists precisely as they depict it.[4]

Crusade Organizations

The antitrafficking movement is dominated by groups who have a larger agenda. A coalition of the religious right and antiprostitution feminists have become the dominant force in the antitrafficking debate. Faith-based members include Focus on the Family, National Association of Evangelicals, Catholic Bishops Conference, the Traditional Values Coalition, Concerned Women for America, Salvation Army, International Justice Mission, Shared Hope International, Religious Freedom Coalition, and numerous others. The premier antiprostitution feminist organization in the United States is the Coalition Against Trafficking in Women (CATW). Others include Equality Now, the Protection Project, and Standing Against Global Exploitation (SAGE).

Members of these conservative religious and feminist groups hold opposing views on other social issues, such as abortion and same-sex marriage, but they largely agree on prostitution and pornography. The single-issue focus of most of these feminist groups—targeting the sex industry exclusively—trumps all other issues and facilitates their willingness to work with rightwing groups. The partners in this alliance clearly recognize the strategic advantages of coalition work in enhancing the legitimacy of their campaign, as a bipartisan enterprise. Two prominent activists wrote an op-ed: "Feminists should stop demonizing the conservative and faith-based groups that could be better allies on some issues than the liberal left has been."[5] Another leader, Laura Lederer, describes the benefits of this alliance: "Having faith-based groups come in with a fresh perspective and a biblical mandate has made a big difference" in that abolitionist feminists "would not be getting attention internationally otherwise."[6]

"Abolitionist feminist" refers to those who argue that the sex industry should be entirely eliminated because of its objectification and oppressive treatment of women, considered to be inherent in sex for sale. It is important to note that mainstream feminist organizations have been far less active in this debate and have been overshadowed by the abolitionists. The premier national women's rights organization, the National Organization for Women, makes no mention on its website of sex trafficking and has entered the debate only sporadically.[7] Another major mainstream association, the National Council of Women's Organizations, is silent on these issues, though its website does provide a link on trafficking. Because the debate over prostitution and pornography has been so divisive among feminists in the past and members continue to disagree, it is not surprising that organizations not directly involved with this issue would avoid it altogether.

The crusade's claims have not gone unchallenged. Among the groups that stand opposed to the current antiprostitution campaign are the Sex Workers Outreach Project, Network of Sex Work Projects, the Global Alliance Against Trafficking in Women, and the Sex Workers Project in New York.[8] These organizations conduct research on trafficking and/or provide assistance to individuals involved in sex work, but they do not condemn sex work per se.[9] Their primary concern is the empowerment of workers and harm reduction via provision of condoms, counseling, and other support services. Because they reject the goal of abolishing sex work, they have been increasingly marginalized and dismissed as the "pro-prostitution lobby" in the discourse of the preeminent antitrafficking forces.[10] They had virtually no access to U.S. government officials during the Bush administration (2001–2008), when antiprostitution forces gained tremendous influence over policymaking. Abolitionist forces helped to transform the campaign against sex trafficking into an official government campaign against prostitution.

FACTS

What are the facts regarding sex trafficking? This question is easy to pose but more difficult to answer. We do know that relocation from one place to another for the purpose of selling sex has long existed, although it has only recently become a public issue. We also know that there are victims of coercive or deceptive enticement into the sex trade: people are transported, without their consent or fully informed consent, to locations where they are forced to engage in prostitution. Reports from around the world indicate that coercive sex trafficking is by no means fictional.[11] It is a serious violation of human rights, and the growing international awareness of the problem and efforts to assist victims and punish perpetrators are welcome developments.

We also know that sex trafficking can be quite lucrative for the third parties involved. In fact, there are "few other criminal activities in which the profit-to-cost ratio is so high."[12] The most exploitative procurers, traffickers, and managers make huge profits off the labor of workers who accumulate little if any money of their own, while other workers spend years working off the debt they owe for their travel expenses and other costs related to migration. In addition, an unknown number of third parties are involved in sexual exploitation and violence, demanding sex from their workers, sometimes over a long period of time.

We do not know *how many* persons are trafficked across borders every year; neither do we know how many of these persons are trafficked for work in the sex industry versus other types of work. Likewise, we do not know the proportion of such people who have been trafficked by force or deceit versus the number who have migrated with full information and consent regarding the type of work and the nature of the working conditions. We do know that a proportion of migrants are indeed acting with awareness and volition. An investigation of Korean women working in massage parlors in New York, for instance, concluded: "Invariably, the Korean women said they knew the kind of work they were expected to perform. . . . The women had relative freedom of movement and had joined the sex business of their own free will. . . . [They] had a lifestyle as prostitutes that did not fit the stereotype of the trafficked woman."[13]

Even when no force or fraud is used, it would be mistaken to assume that facilitators are necessarily benign agents. Some trafficked individuals do not understand the terms of the contract or fully appreciate the impact of debt bondage or how difficult it can be to pay off the debt. Some facilitators alter the terms of the agreement after transit or renege on specific promises. In this scenario, the woman's initial consent is compromised by subsequent, unexpected job requirements. Other workers have little prior awareness of the specific working conditions or risks involved in sex work in the new locale. For those who sold sex in their home country, working conditions in the destination country may be far worse in terms of health, safety, accommodation, and the sexual services required of them.[14] Others enter the sex industry reluctantly, out of an obligation to support their families or because of tacit pressure from relatives—not uncommon in the Third World. A study funded by USAID found that many of the Vietnamese women working in Cambodian brothels had been recruited and transported by their mothers and aunts, not by professional traffickers.[15]

The diversity of experience is illustrated in a recent report on individuals arrested during police raids in the United States.[16] Lilly, who came from Asia, was categorized by the U.S. government as a victim of trafficking but does not self-identify as trafficked. She was not forced into sex work, but had to work off a debt for travel expenses. She was arrested during a raid: "At the time, I didn't have any debt and I told them this. . . . I then continued to work in prostitution for my own reasons, to pay bills. . . . Then the law enforcement perceived me as a victim. I was identified as having been trafficked."[17] Some sex workers do not admit that they have been trafficked when pressed by government officials. Another woman self-identified as trafficked, and it was her husband who trafficked her into prostitution. She said: "I really loved my husband. But any money I earned I had to give to him, so I didn't benefit and it didn't make any sense for me to continue working like that and it made more sense for me to find other work and keep the money."[18]

Marta traveled to the U.S. from Latin America. Her husband had also pushed her into prostitution, controlled her money, and was sometimes violent, but Marta did not want to leave him or prostitution. Marta described her situation as follows:

> I wasn't hoping someone would come take me out of prostitution. . . . I would say listen to the women, because some people do it out of necessity, some people are forced to work in prostitution, but there are others who are not. When I say for "necessity," I mean that there are those of us who have nothing in our country, and we do it to get a little house or buy a piece of land, and it can be the easiest way to achieve that.[19]

In other words, some migrant women who have entered prostitution have complex experiences and relationships with intermediaries and a variety of goals and desires, including dreams of a better life for their families.

In her summary of research on the motives of migrant sex workers, Laura Agustín writes, "Many people are fleeing from small-town prejudices, dead-end jobs, dangerous streets, and suffocating families. And some poorer people *like* the idea of being found beautiful or exotic abroad, exciting desire in others."[20] This is not to romanticize the sex trade, but it serves as a useful counterpoint to the ways in which actors are depicted by antiprostitution crusaders. A study of Vietnamese migrants who had relocated in Cambodia found that almost all of them knew that they would work in a brothel in Cambodia and their motivations consisted of "economic incentives, desire for an independent lifestyle, and dissatisfaction with rural life and agricultural labor." After raids on the brothels by "rescue" organizations, the women "usually returned to their brothel as quickly as possible."[21] The researchers argue that criminalizing the sex industry "forces [the workers] underground, making them more difficult to reach with appropriate services and increasing the likelihood of exploitation." Similar findings have been reported in Europe, where the women are "often aware of the sexual nature of the work. . . . Many migrants do know what is ahead of them, do earn a large amount of money in a short time selling sex, and do have control over their working condition."[22] One investigation of trafficking from eastern Europe to Holland, based on interviews with 72 women, found that few of the women were coercively trafficked and that a "large number" had previously worked as prostitutes:

> For most of the women, economic motives were decisive. The opportunity to earn a considerable amount of money in a short period of time was found to be irresistible. . . . In most cases recruiting was done by friends, acquaintances, or even family members.[23]

The facilitators made travel arrangements, obtained necessary documents, and provided money to the women. In Australia "the majority of women know they will be working in the sex industry and often decide to come to Australia in the belief that they will be able to make a substantial amount of money. . . . Few of the women would ever consider themselves sex slaves."[24]

These are not isolated reports; others have shown that a proportion of migrants sold sex prior to relocating or were well aware that they would be working in the sex industry in their new home. One analyst concludes that, "The majority of 'trafficking victims' are aware that the jobs offered them are in the sex industry."[25] Whether this is indeed true for the majority of those who have relocated to another locale and end up selling sex, it is clear that traffickers do not necessarily fit the "folk devil" stereotype popularized by the antitrafficking movement. Some facilitators are relatives, friends, or associates who recruit workers and assist with migration, and these individuals have a qualitatively different relationship with workers than do predators who use force or deception to lure victims into the trade.

Another fact is that agencies often have difficulty both identifying and gaining the cooperation of individuals that they believe have been trafficked. An assessment of local U.S. law enforcement responses to trafficking found: "Law enforcement may also be reluctant to intervene in sex and labor trafficking situations due to a belief that victims were complicit with their own victimization."[26] Another problem involves the methods commonly used to "rescue" people, typically taking the form of aggressive police raids on brothels. Law enforcement officers typically rely on a person's appearance, particularly fear and lack of cooperation with police, as a strong indicator of whether a person has been trafficked.[27] However, this fear and unco-operativeness is also the single greatest obstacle to identifying a person as trafficked.[28] Raids sometimes help to free individuals from coercive situations, but in the U.S. and other countries such raids are often counterproductive, resulting in the detention and further victimization of sex workers or their deportation from the country, rather than freedom or support services.[29] In the U.S., some law enforcement agents interviewed by the Sex Workers Project insisted that raids are an ineffective antitrafficking tool: these officials believed that "the nature of the crime and the nature of the victims make raids not effective. . . . You need a victim to be willing to open up and tell you. . . . I don't see raids being a consistently effective tool," and another stated, "I question the effectiveness of raids. If the point of the raid is to uncover a trafficking operation, then the crux of the thing is the mental situation, people living in a situation of terror. The blitz approach of interviews that have to take place in raids are not that helpful." The raids are "such an overwhelming situation, and why would they trust us?"[30] One official revealed, "We lose lots of potential victims after the raids." In other words, antitrafficking raids, which are the prevailing tactic, are viewed as ineffective if not counterproductive even by some of the agents involved, who are in the best position to assess them.

Antitrafficking raids are more likely to result in deportations than in assisting victims. A Department of Homeland Security press release revealed that in 2008, 483 people were placed in immigration proceedings after antitrafficking raids.[31] One enforcement official revealed that the government had a larger objective than that of rescuing victims: "The goal is not to rescue victims, but to harm the network; women get deported . . . and you don't rescue a victim, but do take out the network."[32] This approach was faulted by the Women's Commission for Refugee Women and Children: "There is a need for immigration and labor reform that would yield dramatic results in protections for trafficked and exploited persons in the informal economy."[33]

In short, the evidence indicates that (1) identifying and assisting trafficking victims is extremely difficult and (2) migration for sex work is a complex and varied process. There are *multiple migration trajectories and worker experiences*, ranging from highly coercive and exploitative to informed consent and conscious intentionality on the part of the migrant. Such complexities, nuances, and variations in the forms and processes of trafficking have been ignored by abolitionist forces and by governments influenced by these forces. In what follows, we have distilled the core claims made by crusade organizations and their allies in the Bush administration, claims that have largely converged over the past decade.

FICTIONS

Claim 1: Sex trafficking is inseparable from prostitution, and prostitution is evil by definition

Prostitution is defined by the crusade as an institution of male domination and exploitation of women. CATW's website proclaims: "All prostitution exploits women, regardless of women's consent. Prostitution affects all women, justifies the sale of any woman, and reduces all women to sex." It can never qualify as a conventional commercial exchange like other service work nor can it ever be organized in a way that advances workers' interests. As activist and State Department official, Laura Lederer, insists: "This is not a legitimate form of labor. . . . It can never be a legitimate way to make a living because it's inherently harmful for men, women, and children. . . . This whole commercial sex industry is a human-rights abuse."[34]

Morality is central, of course, for religious conservatives, who view prostitution as sexual deviance, as a cause of moral decay, and as a threat to marriage because it breaks the link between sex, love, and reproduction. As the founder of Evangelicals for Social Action stated, the campaign against prostitution and sex trafficking "certainly fits with an evangelical concern for sexual integrity. Sex is to be reserved for a marriage relationship where there is a lifelong covenant between a man and a woman."[35] And an article in *Christianity Today*, titled "Sex Isn't Work," stated, "When sex becomes commerce, the moral fabric of our culture is deeply damaged."[36] A government crackdown on prostitution (as well as pornography) thus ratifies the religious right's views on sex and the family.

The claim that prostitution is intrinsically evil is a tenet that does not lend itself to evaluation with empirical evidence, unlike most of the other claims outlined later. We do not, therefore, consider this claim a "fiction" because it cannot be proved or disproved. But it is crucial to the abolitionist paradigm because it is the very keystone on which all other claims rest.

Activists argue that prostitution is the root cause of trafficking and inseparable from it. The conflation of trafficking and prostitution is motivated by the crusade's ultimate goal of eliminating the entire sex trade.[37] Activist Donna Hughes, for example, calls for "re-linking trafficking and prostitution, and combating the commercial sex trade as a whole."[38] Not only does she equate the two ("sex trafficking of women and children—what's commonly called prostitution"),[39] but also claims that "most 'sex workers' are—or originally started out as—trafficked women and girls."[40]

This claim is fictional: studies have not demonstrated that "most" or even the majority of prostitutes have been trafficked. Moreover, prostitution and trafficking differ substantively; prostitution is a type of work, migration and trafficking involve relocation to access a market. Both empirically and conceptually, it is inappropriate to fuse prostitution and trafficking.[41] Furthermore, to do so obscures other types of trafficking, such as for work in agriculture, construction, and domestic service.

Claim 2: Violence is omnipresent in prostitution and trafficking

Prostitution is defined as a form of violence against women, categorically and universally, and the same claim is made for sex trafficking. Antiprostitution activists have consistently tried to erase the distinction between coercive trafficking and voluntary migration to work in the sex industry, and insist that victimization is the hallmark of all sex work.

The claim that violence is pervasive in prostitution and trafficking cannot be confirmed. Since no study uses a random sample because the population of sex workers is unknown, and all rely instead on convenience samples of persons researchers manage to access, all figures on the incidence of violence are questionable.[42] Thus, the frequent assertion that victimization is pervasive violates a fundamental scientific canon—namely, that generalizations cannot be based on unrepresentative samples. The well-known danger of generalizing from small convenience samples and anecdotal stories is routinely ignored by abolitionist writers.[43]

It is important to treat coercion as a *variable* rather than a constant. Some traffickers believe that they can win compliance from the individuals they relocate by the use of persuasion rather than overt violence. In fact, one study of traffickers found considerable variation in their methods, and suggested that there has been a recent trend toward the reduction of coercion, precisely because traffickers see it as being in their interest to do so—in reducing the chances of escape, maximizing profits, or avoiding law enforcement attention.[44] The use of coercion is even less salient for intermediaries who assist workers with the latter's full knowledge and consent.

Claim 3: Sex workers lack agency

The denial of agency is evident in the crusade's very framing of the problem as one involving "prostituted women," "trafficking," and "sexual slavery"—terms that are frequently used by abolitionists. The central claim is that workers do not actively make choices to enter or remain in prostitution. The notion of consent is deemed irrelevant, and activists have pressed governments to criminalize all sex work, whether consensual or not: "Legislation must not allow traffickers to use the consent of the victim as a defense against trafficking," argue Raymond and Hughes.[45] This crusade rejects the very concept of benign migration for the purpose of sex work, since prostitution is defined as inherently exploitative and oppressive. Instead, the more nefarious term "sex trafficking" is applied to every instance of relocation to a destination where the individual sells sex.

Research on the sex industry highlights variation, rather than uniformity, in the degree to which workers feel exploited vs. empowered and in control of their working conditions.[46] Workers do not necessarily see themselves as "prostituted" victims lacking agency and instead have made conscious decisions to enter the trade. These workers are invisible in the discourse of the anti-prostitution crusade precisely because their accounts clash with abolitionist goals.

Regarding sex trafficking, it is impossible to measure the ratio of agency to victimization—i.e., voluntarily vs. involuntary migration. Although a significant number of migrants have made conscious and informed decisions to relocate, as discussed earlier in the chapter, the crusade presents only the worst cases and universalizes them. Traffickers are vilified as predators, rapists, and kidnappers involved in organized crime and sexual slavery. And clients are equated with traffickers. A leading coalition member, Michael Horowitz of the conservative Hudson Institute, says of traffickers and clients, "We want to drive a stake through the heart of these venal criminals. This is pure evil."[47] Donna Hughes wrote, "Men who purchase sex acts do not respect women, nor do they want to respect women."[48] These depictions have influenced programming: Shared Hope International started a "Predator Project" to focus on "profiling and punishing those who prey on and profit from exploiting vulnerable women and children."[49] Again, these characterizations are apt for some actors involved in sex trafficking but the crusade's sweeping claims are caricatures.

Moral crusades typically report anecdotal horror stories in order to demonstrate the gravity of a targeted evil. This strategy is abundantly evident in the discourse of antitrafficking forces and of the U.S. government. Typically, the testimonials of a few "rescued" victims are presented as evidence. Horror stories and photos of young victims are prominently displayed in government publications and websites. Such depictions dramatize human suffering and are designed to cause alarm and outrage, and this strategy can be quite effective. For example, several members of Congress—including the sponsors of trafficking legislation—have stated that they became interested in trafficking only after hearing a particular victim's testimony.[50] And the official discourse repeatedly invokes "women and children" victims. Claims about threatened children are a staple of many moral crusades.

Claim 4: Sex trafficking is prevalent and increasing, now at epidemic levels

The size of a social problem matters in attracting media coverage, donor funding, and attention from policymakers. Moral crusades therefore have an interest in inflating the magnitude of a problem, and their figures are typically unverifiable and/or very elastic. The antitrafficking crusade claims that there are "hundreds of thousands" of victims,[51] and that trafficking has reached "epidemic" proportions worldwide. Shared Hope International, for example, claims that trafficking is "a huge problem, and it's continuing to grow."[52] SAGE director Norma Hotaling recently claimed that "there are thousands of trafficked women in San Francisco"—a vague figure presented with no documentation.[53]

When concrete numbers are presented, they vary and fluctuate dramatically. Although a report by a CIA analyst acknowledged in 2000 that "no one U.S. or international agency is compiling accurate statistics," the report then claimed that "700,000 to 2 million women and children are trafficked globally each year."[54] In 2003, State's maximum figure had grown to 4 million, but 2 years later it inexplicably fell to 600,000–800,000 victims of all types of trafficking, of which "hundreds of thousands" were said to be trafficked into prostitution.[55] No explanation has been given for the huge fluctuations from year to year in the official figures. Similarly, it is frequently asserted by several agencies that 80% of all trafficking victims are women and 50% children—figures that are, again, unverifiable given the clandestine nature of the trade.

Like the global numbers, domestic figures have changed drastically and inexplicably in a short period of time. In 2000, the CIA report mentioned earlier claimed that 45,000–50,000 persons were trafficked into the United States annually. This figure was totally unreliable, based largely on extrapolations from foreign newspaper clippings by one CIA analyst.[56] Yet the figure was cited in the 2000 *Victims of Trafficking and Violence Protection Act* (TVPA) as justification for the new law, which states unequivocally that "Congress finds that . . . approximately 50,000 women and children are trafficked into the United States each year" (TVPA, §102[b1]). The State Department's *Trafficking in Persons* report repeated the figure in 2002, but just 1 year later, State's figure fell to 18,000–20,000 (a 60% drop) and the 2004 and 2005 *Trafficking in Persons* reports reduced the number to 14,500–17,500 a year. By then, the legislation and enforcement machinery were firmly in place.

Severe sex trafficking is defined in the TVPA as the use of "force, fraud, or coercion" to induce an adult to perform a commercial sex act, or inducing a person under age 18 to perform a commercial sex act, regardless of whether force or fraud is used. This definition does not apply to adults who willingly travel, with some kind of assistance, in search of employment in the sex industry. However, the figures presented by advocates and officials often lump the latter kind of migration into the trafficking category, which inflates the number of victims, and some agencies treat all sex workers as trafficked.[57]

Leading members of Congress and the Bush administration accepted these numbers uncritically, but some have recently questioned even of the lower figures. The Justice Department appears skeptical:

> Most importantly, the government must address the incongruity between the estimated number of victims trafficked into the United States—between 14,500 and 17,500 [annually]—and the number of victims found—only 611 in the last four years [2001–2004]. . . . The stark difference between the two figures means that U.S. government efforts are still not enough. In addition, the estimate should be evaluated to assure that it is accurate and reflects the number of actual victims.[58]

A recent General Accountability Office (GAO) evaluation was very critical of the prevailing figures, which it found to be based on "methodological weaknesses, gaps in data, and numerical discrepancies." The GAO concluded that (1) "country data are generally not available, reliable, or comparable," (2) the "U.S. government has not yet established an effective mechanism for estimating the number of victims," and (3) the same is true for international NGOs working in the trafficking area.[59]

The 2008 *Trafficking in Persons* report states that 1379 trafficking victims were identified between 2001 and mid-2008, but this figure remains but a fraction of the number of persons allegedly trafficked into the U.S. during this time period (using the official conservative figure: 14,500 x 7.5 years = 108,750).[60] This report, for the first time, provided no number of persons trafficked into the United States but instead used the vague term "thousands":

> The United States is a destination country for thousands of men, women, and children trafficked largely from East Asia, Mexico, and Central America for the purposes of sexual and labor exploitation. A majority [63%] of foreign victims identified during the year [FY 2007] were victims of trafficking for forced labor.[61]

Notably, almost two-thirds of identified victims were trafficked for labor rather than the sex trade.

Some scholars uncritically accept these crusade claims. Kathryn Farr, for example, boldly asserts, "The sex trafficking industry is voluminous, and it is expanding at an ever-accelerating rate. . . . Over 1 million are trafficked into the sex industry, and the volume just keeps increasing."[62] Her sources are activists and American government agencies—precisely the sources that critics find highly dubious.

In fact, *there are no reliable statistics on the magnitude of the problem*, and the figures can only be described as guesswork. Even ballpark estimates are dubious, given the clandestine and stigmatized nature of the sex trade. The high numbers have not gone unchallenged. The United Nations Educational, Scientific, and Cultural Organization's (UNESCO) Bangkok office suggests that most of the statistics being circulated are probably "false" or "spurious:" "When it comes to statistics, trafficking of girls and women is one of several highly emotive issues which seem to overwhelm critical faculties."[63] Researchers have criticized the national, regional, and international statistics proffered by activists, organizations, and governments for their "lack of methodological transparency" and source documentation,[64] for being extrapolated from a few cases of identified victims (who are unrepresentative of the victim population),[65] and for the lack of a standard definition of "victims" as a basis for estimates of the magnitude of the problem.[66]

It is also claimed that the sex industry is *expanding* at an unprecedented rate, increasing the market for trafficked workers, and that the number of victims is steadily increasing. The director of the evangelical International Justice Mission, for example, refers to "the growing trafficking nightmare," and CATW proclaims that "local and global sex industries are systematically violating women's rights on an ever-increasing scale."[67]

Internationally, it is clear that sex trafficking has increased in *some* parts of the world, especially from the former Soviet Union and eastern Europe. The breakup of the Soviet empire and declining living standards for many of its inhabitants has made such migration both much easier and more compelling than in the past.[68] But an increase in trafficking since the demise of the Soviet Union does not mean that trafficking is growing now. Instead, it may have leveled off. A report by the International Organization for Migration points to this very possibility: the number of trafficked persons in southeastern Europe that were identified and assisted remained virtually the same (declining slightly) between 2003 and 2004.[69]

In short, given the underground nature of this trade, estimates of both its current magnitude and changes over time are highly dubious, which means that claims regarding a growing worldwide epidemic cannot be confirmed.

Claim 5: Legalization would make the situation far worse than it is at present

The crusade considers legal prostitution detrimental in two respects: practically (by magnifying all the problems associated with prostitution, and by increasing the amount of trafficking) and symbolically (by giving the state's blessing to a despicable institution and condoning men's exploitation of women). Antiprostitution forces often express concern about what they perceive as the "normalization" of prostitution in various parts of the world. Normalization is seen in the very premise behind state-regulated, legal prostitution. CATW's mission is broad: to "challenge acceptance of the sex industry, normalization of prostitution as work, and to de-romanticize legalization initiatives in various countries."[70]

A second assertion is that legalization causes or serves as a magnet for increased sex trafficking. The claim is based on the notion of least resistance: legalization removes the constraints on a formerly illegal and circumscribed enterprise and thus leads to its proliferation. CATW's co-director declares that "legalized or decriminalized prostitution industries are one of the root causes of sex trafficking."[71] And Linda Smith, director of Shared Hope International, testified in Congress that the government should "consider countries with legalized or tolerated prostitution as having laws that are insufficient efforts to eliminate trafficking. . . . Where there is a strong adult sex industry, the commercial sexual exploitation of children and sex slavery increases."[72] Concerned Women for America claims that "legalizing prostitution does not remedy the problem of sex trafficking but rather increases it."[73]

The causal link between legal prostitution and trafficking has not been empirically established. In fact, the State Department's own assessments appear to undercut this claim: in its 2005 *Trafficking in Persons Report*, several nations where prostitution is legal (Australia, Germany, Holland, New Zealand) were found to "fully comply with minimum standards for the elimination of trafficking."[74] Moreover, the *Report* reveals that the Dutch authorities report a "decrease in trafficking in the legal sector," a finding confirmed by other analysts.[75] Rather than being a magnet attracting migrants into a country, it appears that legal prostitution may help *reduce* trafficking due to enhanced government regulation and oversight of the legal sector. And the obverse may also be true: "Traffickers take advantage of the illegality of commercial sex work and migration, and are able to exert an undue amount of power and control over [migrants]. . . . In such cases, it is the laws that prevent legal commercial sex work and immigration that form the major obstacles."[76] As Murray writes, "It is the prohibition of prostitution and restrictions on travel which attract organized crime and create the possibilities for large profits, as well as creating the prostitutes' need for protection and assistance."[77]

Research indicates that, under the right conditions, legal prostitution can be organized in a way that enhances workers' safety, health, and job satisfaction. This includes studies of legal prostitution systems in Australia, Holland, Nevada, and New Zealand.[78] None of this is to suggest that these systems are problem free, but the evidence from these sites contrasts strikingly with the image of proffered by the antiprostitution crusade.

In short, the core claims of this moral crusade are either exaggerated, unverifiable, or demonstrably false—depending on the claim in question. Common to all of these claims are sweeping declarations that ignore counterevidence and give prominence to anecdotal stories describing worst cases. Crusade claims are contradicted by a large body of social science research. This research shows that prostitution and trafficking take multiple forms and exists under varying conditions, which translates into diverse experiences for workers—a complexity that undermines sweeping generalizations.[79]

INSTITUTIONALIZATION OF CRUSADE CLAIMS

Some moral crusades fail to achieve any of their goals, while others succeed in influencing public opinion, legislation, or organizational practices. If the social problem identified by activists is accepted by the authorities as a bona fide problem, the crusade may gradually become institutionalized in state policy. *Institutionalization* may be limited or extensive—ranging from consultation with activists, inclusion of leaders in the policy process, material support for crusade organizations, official endorsement of crusade ideology, resource mobilization, and new legislation and agencies to address the problem. The institutionalization of the antiprostitution crusade follows this trajectory.

During the final years of the Clinton administration, there was some limited accommodation of crusade demands. The TVPA was passed in late 2000, which created the State Department's Office to Monitor and Combat Trafficking in Persons. Antitrafficking activists were pleased with the new agency but dissatisfied with the statute's definitions and provisions regarding trafficking. TVPA distinguished "sex trafficking" (which may be voluntarily entered into) from "severe trafficking" (which involves "force, fraud, or coercion" or persons under age 18); TVPA protections and sanctions apply only to severe trafficking.[80] The Clinton administration distinguished forced and voluntary prostitution, did not link prostitution to trafficking, did not claim that legal prostitution increases trafficking into a country, and resisted mandatory sanctions against nations with poor records in combating trafficking. Abolitionists unsuccessfully lobbied the Clinton administration to reconsider each of these positions.[81]

After George Bush took office in January 2001, the movement's access to policymakers steadily increased. The director of the State Department's trafficking office, John R. Miller, revealed in 2005 that the federal government has been "working closely with faith-based, community, and feminist organizations" to combat all forms of prostitution.[82] Miller credits these groups with keeping trafficking on the front burner: "They're consumed by this issue. I think it's great. It helped get the legislation passed, it helped spur me. I think it keeps the whole government focused."[83] Antiprostitution forces frequently network with government officials during private meetings, at conferences, and at hearings—giving them unique opportunities to shape the terms of the debate and subsequent policy changes. Groups that do not share the crusade's views have been denied such access.[84]

Consultation evolved into a more formal, ongoing collaboration. Many antiprostitution and antitrafficking groups are now official "partners" with government agencies. The Department of Health and Human Services (HHS), for example, created a Rescue and Restore Coalition, which formally aligns HHS with many of this crusade's organizations.[85] An even stronger indicator of inclusion is the circulation of actors between a social movement and government agencies, with the resulting amalgamation of their ideological positions. Some former antiprostitution activists are now working in key government agencies. For example, a prominent antipornography activist in the 1980s, Laura Lederer founded the antitrafficking Protection Project in the 1990s, and was later hired as a senior advisor in the State Department's trafficking office. Lederer's inclusion within the government is part of the reason the State Department has adopted a discourse and policies identical to those advocated by the Protection Project.

Government funding of movement organizations is a third type of institutionalization. Groups that shared the Bush administration's perspective on the sex industry benefited materially in several ways. First, the government has spent considerable funds sponsoring antitrafficking conferences throughout the world, which occur frequently; one in Washington, DC, in February 2005 had a $1.8 million price tag.[86] Organizations critical of U.S. government trafficking policy have not been invited to these events. Second, under the Bush administration's Faith-Based Initiative, a huge amount of federal grant money has been awarded to religious organizations in the U.S. and abroad that are involved in promoting a conservative social agenda, including antiabortion programs, abstinence education, and church-run social services.[87] Among the organizations receiving government funding are prominent abolitionist feminist organizations (CATW, Protection Project, SAGE), faith-based organizations (Catholic Conference of Bishops, Salvation Army, International Justice Mission, World Vision, Shared Hope International) and their allies around the world.[88] These groups receive funding to conduct research and/or to identify and rescue victims. For example, Raymond and Hughes received $189,000 from the National Institute of Justice to write a report on trafficking, a report that drew sweeping conclusions based on interviews with just 40 persons.[89] In fact, the quality of much of this funded research has been questioned by the GAO, which cited the State Department's own inspector general's concern with "the credentials of the organizations and findings of the research that the Trafficking Office funded"; the inspector general called for rigorous peer review and greater oversight of the funding process.[90] And the former director of HHS's antitrafficking program, Steven Wagner, went even further in criticizing the distribution of millions of dollars to antitrafficking groups and the lack of accountability involved: "Those funds were wasted. Many of the organizations that received grants didn't really have to do anything."[91]

The ultimate type of institutionalization involves changes in government discourse, policy, and law consistent with crusade interests and demands. In other words, the movement's central goals become a project of the government. This has occurred under the Bush administration. In a remarkably short time span, the crusade's ideology was accepted, incorporated into official policy, and implemented in agency practices. This institutionalization is apparent in (1) the public pronouncements of government officials,[92] (2) the official positions of government agencies, including State, Justice, USAID, and HHS, (3) the State Department's annual *Trafficking in Persons Report*, (4) the State Department's seminal document, *The Link between Prostitution and Sex Trafficking*, (5) and the laws reauthorizing the TVPA in 2003, 2005, and 2008—hereafter, TVPRA. Leading antiprostitution activists played a key role in shaping this legislation.[93]

The publications and websites of HHS, State, and Justice cite or provide links to the writings of prominent crusade members (e.g., Donna Hughes, Janice Raymond, Melissa Farley), which effectively privileges their opinions. Such references can be found on the State Department's website, which also proclaims that prostitution "is inherently harmful"; that it "leaves women and children physically, mentally, emotionally, and spiritually devastated"; that legal prostitution "creates a safe haven for criminals who traffic people into prostitution"; and that prostitution is "the oldest form of oppression."

Activists successfully pressed the U.S. government to adopt a policy denying funding to organizations that were not sufficiently committed to abolishing prostitution or that dispensed condoms and other assistance to workers without trying to rescue them. Today, to be eligible for U.S. funding, any foreign NGO working on the trafficking front must declare its opposition to legal prostitution. The State Department's website is unequivocal: "No U.S. grant funds should be awarded to foreign non-governmental organizations that support legal state-regulated prostitution." Similarly, the AIDS funding law of 2003 (known as the Global AIDS Act) requires that any international organization working to curb AIDS must "have a policy explicitly opposing prostitution and sex trafficking" if it wishes to receive such funding. This applies to American groups insofar as they work with or subcontract work to international organizations. Organizations that do not take a position on prostitution, as well as those that favor decriminalization or legalization, are thus ineligible for AIDS funding from USAID or HHS. Similarly, the Justice Department now requires anyone applying for funding to conduct research on trafficking to certify that they do "not promote, support, or advocate the legalization or practice of prostitution."[94] Failure to do so results in summary denial of funding.

These funding restrictions eliminate consideration of competing points of view or research findings and further institutionalize the perspective of antiprostitution forces. Because of the restriction, several NGOs have rejected government funding. In May 2005, 171 American and foreign organizations signed a letter to President Bush opposing the antiprostitution pledge because they believe the policy interferes with promising interventions that require building trust with sex workers and only heightens the stigma associated with sex work.

Activists have pressed the government to criminalize not only trafficking but also "the commercial sex trade as a whole,"[95] and they have met with some success thus far. The key legislation on sex trafficking refers to "commercial sexual activities," defined as "any sex act on account of which anything of value is given to, or received by, any person."[96] The 2005 TVPRA contains a section on combating domestic trafficking in persons that repeatedly refers to the need to investigate and combat not only trafficking but also the "demand for commercial sex acts in the United States" (§201[a]). A recent assessment indicated that some antitrafficking agents equate trafficking and prostitution in their enforcement activities: "Some local task forces have focused exclusively on prostitution, making no distinction between prostitution and sex trafficking."[97] (Since 2006, the Justice Department has funded 42 multi-agency law enforcement task forces to identify and assist trafficked persons.)[98] The 2005

TVPRA authorizes $25 million a year for increased prosecution of those who "purchase commercial sex acts" (§204[1b]) as well as other local efforts to crack down on customers (§204[1c]).

The TVPRA was reauthorized in December 2008 for another 3-year period.[99] The 2008 law enhances enforcement capabilities—with the creation of an integrated database, expanded surveillance of the sex trade, and funding "to examine the use of Internet-based businesses and services by criminal actors in the sex industry" (§237[c]). Funding is significantly increased for foreign and domestic antitrafficking programs run by the State Department, Labor Department, and HHS (§301). The antiprostitution pledge remains in the 2008 TVPRA.

CONCLUSION

The antiprostitution/trafficking campaign has made considerable progress in transforming itself from crusade into a project of the U.S. government, becoming almost fully institutionalized in official discourse, legislation, and enforcement practices under the Bush administration. During this period, there has been a remarkable osmosis between crusade and government ideology and policy preferences.

All the hallmarks of a moral crusade are evident—framing a condition as an unqualified evil; creation of folk devils; zealotry among leaders who see their mission as a righteous enterprise; presentation of claims as universalistic truths; use of horror stories as representative of actors' experiences; promulgation of huge and unverified numbers of victims; and attempts to redraw normative boundaries by increased criminalization. Prostitution is depicted as immoral or intrinsically harmful, and systems of legal prostitution as dens of iniquity and oppression. Activists (and now government officials) have presented questionable statistics and anecdotal horror stories as evidence of a worldwide epidemic of coerced prostitution.

What is particularly striking is the degree to which current claims recapitulate arguments made a century ago regarding "white slavery," a problem that was largely mythical.[100] It has been argued that "today's stereotypical 'trafficking victim' bears as little resemblance to women migrating for work in the sex industry as did her historical counterpart, the 'white slave'."[101]

Coercive sex trafficking is by no means fictional. Force and deception are realities in the sex trade, and there are indeed victims in the U.S. and abroad. But instead of focusing on unfree labor, the campaign has broadly targeted all sex work. What is largely missing from crusade discourse is attention to the root causes of migration and trafficking, including barriers to women's employment and economic advancement throughout the world. Crusade leaders occasionally mention structural factors, but this has been overshadowed by the dominant moral discourse and by a focus on individual victims and customers (the "demand"). A leader of Concerned Women for America seemed to dismiss the role of socioeconomic conditions when she stated: "While the U.N. blames social and economic disparities for fostering trafficking, the demand for prostitutes is the driving force behind sex trafficking."[102]

An alternative model would (1) pay more attention to the socioeconomic conditions that promote sex work, (2) focus on unfree labor rather than prostitution per se, (3) faithfully represent workers' varied experiences in prostitution, and (4) identify concrete ways of enhancing workers' health, safety, and control over working conditions.[103] A full discussion of policy implications is beyond the scope of this chapter, but any such discussion must take into account differences between types of prostitution. In other words, policies should be sector specific. Some workers, concentrated in the upscale echelon (call girls, escorts), are not interested in leaving the trade,[104] and their biggest concern is being arrested. Other workers, both internationally and domestically, whether trafficked or not, want to leave the sex industry, yet other employment options offering livable wages are woefully lacking. In the United States, most cities provide virtually no government-funded support services for sex workers. Desperately needed are resources for temporary housing, counseling, healthcare, and job training. Regarding sex trafficking, as noted earlier, interventions focused on persons who are unequivocally victims and perpetrators of coercive trafficking would be a superior strategy to the undifferentiated and often counterproductive practices of many faith-based rescue organizations, whose practices are driven by this moral crusade's broad goal of abolishing the entire sex industry worldwide.

NOTES

1. This chapter is a revised and updated version of an article by Ronald Weitzer, "The Social Construction of Sex Trafficking: Ideology and Institutionalization of a Moral Crusade," in *Politics and Society* 35 (September 2007): 446–475. Sage Publications.
2. Stanley Cohen, *Folk Devils and Moral Panics*, New York: St. Martin's, 1972; Erich Goode and Nachman Ben-Yehuda, *Moral Panics: The Social Construction of Deviance*, Cambridge, MA: Blackwell, 1994.
3. Cohen, *Folk Devils*; Goode and Ben-Yehuda, *Moral Panics*.

4. Joel Best, *Random Violence: How We Talk about New Crimes and New Victims*, Berkeley: University of California Press, 1999, pp. 103–118.

5. Phyllis Chesler and Donna Hughes, "Feminism in the 21st Century," *Washington Post*, February 22, 2004.

6. Laura Lederer, quoted in Mindy Belz, "No Sale," *World Magazine*, March 25, 2000.

7. Mainstream feminists have been involved in the debate at certain junctures. During international negotiations over a U.N. treaty on sex trafficking in January 2000, Gloria Steinem and the presidents of NOW and Planned Parenthood sent a letter to President Clinton protesting the administration's refusal to define all types of prostitution as "sexual exploitation" and insistence that only forced prostitution be so designated. (See Barbara Stolz, "Educating Policymakers and Setting the Criminal Justice Policymaking Agenda: Interest Groups and the 'Victims of Trafficking and Violence Act of 2000'," *Criminal Justice* 5 [2005]: 407–430, at p. 418.) Later, the New York State chapter of NOW pushed for provisions in the New York antitrafficking law that equated sex work with trafficking and for provisions that increase penalties for clients of sex workers, a bill that was passed. NOW's New York City chapter led a campaign to encourage print media to eliminate advertising for sex work businesses. And National NOW signed on to a joint letter with CATW and Equality Now (dated January 24, 2008) to Senator Biden (chair of the Judiciary Committee) during the negotiations leading up to the 2008 TVPRA, encouraging him to expand the Mann Act to combat all prostitution.

8. Melissa Ditmore, "Trafficking in Lives: How Ideology Shapes Policy," in Kemala Kempadoo, ed., *Trafficking and Prostitution Reconsidered: New Perspectives on Migration, Sex Work, and Human Rights*, Boulder: Paradigm, 2005.

9. Gretchen Soderlund, "Running from the Rescuers: New U.S. Crusades Against Sex Trafficking and the Rhetoric of Abolition," *NWSA Journal* 17 (2005): 64–87.

10. Elisabeth Bumiller, "Evangelicals Sway White House on Human Rights Issues Abroad," *New York Times*, October 26, 2003; Nina Shapiro, "The New Abolitionists," *Seattle Weekly*, August 25, 2004; Laura Blumenfeld, "In a Shift, Anti-Prostitution Effort Targets Pimps and Johns," *Washington Post*, December 15, 2005.

11. On trafficking into the United States, see, for instance, Anthony DeStefano, *The War on Human Trafficking: U.S. Policy Assessed*, New Brunswick, NJ: Rutgers University Press, 2007.

12. Phil Williams, "Trafficking in Women and Children: A Market Perspective," in Phil Williams, ed., *Illegal Immigration and Commercial Sex*, London: Frank Cass, 1999, p. 153.

13. DeStefano, *War on Human Trafficking*, p. 88.

14. Joanna Busza, Sarah Castle, and Aisse Diarra, "Trafficking and Health," *British Medical Journal* 328 (June 5, 2004): 1369–1371.

15. Thomas Steinfatt, *Measuring the Number of Trafficked Women and Children in Cambodia: A Direct Observation Field Study*, Washington, DC: USAID, 2003, p. 24.

16. Melissa Ditmore, *Kicking Down the Door: The Use of Raids to Fight Trafficking in Persons*, New York: Sex Workers Project, 2009. The names of women quoted here are pseudonyms.

17. Ditmore, *Kicking Down the Door*, pp. 32–33.

18. Ditmore, *Kicking Down the Door*, p. 52.

19. Ditmore, *Kicking Down the Door*, p. 26.

20. Laura Agustín, *Sex At the Margins*, London: Zed, 2007, pp. 45–46.

21. Busza, Castle, and Diarra, "Trafficking and Health"; see also the identical findings in Steinfatt, *Measuring the Number*, pp. 23–24.

22. Laura Agustín, "Migrants in the Mistress's House: Other Voices in the Trafficking Debate," *Social Politics* 12 (2005): 96–117, at pp. 98, 101.

23. Judith Vocks and Jan Nijboer, "The Promised Land: A Study of Trafficking in Women from Central and Eastern Europe to the Netherlands," *European Journal on Criminal Policy and Research* 8 (2000): 379–388, at pp. 383, 384.

24. Linda Meaker, "A Social Response to Transnational Prostitution in Queensland, Australia," in S. Thorbek and B. Pattanaik, eds., *Transnational Prostitution*, London: Zed, 2002, pp. 61, 63.

25. Jo Doezema, "Loose Women or Lost Women? The Re-emergence of the Myth of 'White Slavery' in Contemporary Discourses of 'Trafficking in Women'," *Gender Issues* 18 (2000): 23–50, at p. 24.

26. Amy Farrell, Jack McDevitt, and Stephanie Fahy, *Understanding and Improving Law Enforcement Responses to Human Trafficking*, Boston: Institute on Race and Justice, Northeastern University, 2008, p. 111.

27. Farrell, et al., *Understanding and Improving*, p. 76.

28. Farrell, et al., *Understanding and Improving*, pp. 82–83.

29. Ditmore, *Kicking Down the Door*, p. 20.

30. Officers quoted in Ditmore, *Kicking Down the Door*, pp. 9, 38.

31. Department of Homeland Security, Press Release, December 18, 2008.

32. Official quoted in Ditmore, *Kicking Down the Door*, p. 36.

33. Women's Commission for Refugee Women and Children, *The U.S. Response to Human Trafficking: An Unbalanced Approach*, New York: WCRWC, 2007, p. 6.

34. Lederer, quoted in Bob Jones, "Trafficking Cops," *World Magazine*, June 15, 2002.

35. Ron Sider, quoted in Shapiro, "New Abolitionists."

36. Timothy Morgan, "Sex Isn't Work," *Christianity Today*, December 29, 2006.

37. Dorchen Leidholdt, "Prostitution and Trafficking in Women: An Intimate Relationship," *Journal of Trauma Practice* 2 (2004): 167–183.

38. Donna Hughes, "Wolves in Sheep's Clothing: No Way to End Sex Trafficking," *National Review Online*, October 9, 2002, p. 2.

39. Donna Hughes, quoted in University of Rhode Island Press Release, "Expert on Sex Trafficking Contributes to Passage of Historic New Law," January 11, 2006.

40. Donna Hughes, "Accommodation or Abolition?" *National Review Online*, May 1, 2003, p. 1.

41. Kamala Kempadoo, ed., *Trafficking and Prostitution Reconsidered: New Perspectives on Migration, Sex Work, and Human Rights*, Boulder: Paradigm, 2005.

42. Ronald Weitzer, "Flawed Theory and Method in Studies of Prostitution," *Violence Against Women* 11 (2005): 934–949.

43. One example of this tendency is the report on sex trafficking authored by Janice Raymond and Donna Hughes. Their report, funded by the Justice Department, is based on interviews with only 40 women who were involved with organizations committed to getting women out of prostitution. From this small and skewed sample the authors draw numerous, sweeping conclusions about victimization. (Raymond and Hughes, *Sex Trafficking of Women in the United States*, Washington, DC: Department of Justice, 2001.)

44. Rebecca Surtees, "Traffickers and Trafficking in Southern and Eastern Europe," *European Journal of Criminology* 5 (2008): 39–68, at p. 60

45. Raymond and Hughes, *Sex Trafficking*, p. 25.

46. Weitzer, "Flawed Theory"; Ronald Weitzer, "New Directions in Research on Prostitution," *Crime, Law, and Social Change* 43 (2005): 211–235; Ine Vanwesenbeeck, "Another Decade of Social Scientific Work on Prostitution," *Annual Review of Sex Research* 12 (2001): 242–289.

47. Horowitz, quoted in Blumenfeld, "In a Shift," p. A16.

48. Donna Hughes, *The Demand for Victims of Sex Trafficking*, University of Rhode Island, 2005, p. 7, report funded by the U.S. State Department.

49. http://www.sharedhope.org/what/predatorproject.asp.

50. Blumenfeld, "In a Shift."

51. Goode and Ben-Yehuda, *Moral Panics*, pp. 36–44.

52. Quoted in Jerry Markon, "Human Trafficking Evokes Outrage, Little Evidence," *Washington Post*, September 23, 2007, pp. A1, A8–A9, at p. A9.

53. Hotaling, quoted in Meredith May, "Sex Trafficking: San Francisco is a Major Center for International Crime Networks that Smuggle and Enslave," *San Francisco Chronicle*, October 6, 2006.

54. Amy O'Neill Richard, *International Trafficking of Women to the United States*, Washington, DC: Central Intelligence Agency, 2000, p. 3.

55. U.S. Department of State, "The Link between Prostitution and Sex Trafficking," Washington, DC: Department of State, 2004.

56. Markon, "Human Trafficking Evokes Outrage, Little Evidence."

57. Steinfatt, *Measuring the Number*, p. 11.

58. U.S. Department of Justice, *Efforts to Combat Trafficking in Persons in Fiscal Year 2004* (Washington, DC: Department of Justice, 2005), p. 4. Between FY 2001 and FY 2004, the Justice Department prosecuted 131 persons for sex trafficking offenses, and obtained 99 convictions. Though relatively low for a 4-year period, the figures were almost five times higher than during the previous 4 years, a period prior to the TVPA. See Attorney General, *Report, 2004*, p. 20.

59. General Accountability Office, *Human Trafficking: Better Data, Strategy, and Reporting Needed to Enhance U.S. Anti-trafficking Efforts Abroad*, Washington, DC: GAO, 2006, pp. 2, 10, 3, 14.

60. U.S. Department of State, *Trafficking in Persons Report, 2008*, accessed December 21, 2008. http://www.state.gov/g/tip/rls/tiprpt/2008/. As of December 2008, 787 T-visas – a 4-year temporary visa, created for trafficked persons under the 2003 TVPRA – have been given to trafficked persons in the U.S. An additional 682 T-visas have been given to family members of trafficked persons. Reported in the *Federal Register* v. 73, no. 240 (December 12, 2008), pp. 75, 552.

61. U.S. Department of State, *Trafficking in Persons Report, 2008*; see also "U.S. Government Domestic Anti-Trafficking in Persons Efforts." http://www.state.gov/g/tip/rls/tiprpt/2008/105385.htm.

62. Kathryn Farr, *Sex Trafficking*, New York: Worth, 2005, p. 3.

63. See www.unescobkk.org/culture/trafficking. UNESCO's Trafficking Statistics Project is an ongoing project attempting to assess the scale of the problem.

64. Liz Kelly, "You Can Find Anything You Want: A Critical Reflection on Research on Trafficking in Persons within and into Europe," *International Migration* 43 (2005): 235–265, at p. 237.

65. Guri Tyldum and Anette Brunovskis, "Describing the Unobserved: Methodological Challenges in Empirical Studies on Human Trafficking," *International Migration* 43 (2005): 17–34.

66. Elzbieta Gozdziak and Elizabeth Collett, "Research on Human Trafficking in North America: A Review of the Literature," *International Migration* 43 (2005): 99–128.

67. Gary Haugen, International Justice Mission, Testimony before Congressional Human Rights Caucus, U.S. House of Representatives (June 6, 2002); CATW: www.catwinternational.org.

68. Louise Shelley, "The Trade in People in and from the Former Soviet Union," *Crime, Law, and Social Change* 40 (2003): 231–249.

69. International Organization for Migration, *Second Annual Report on Victims of Trafficking in South-Eastern Europe*, Geneva: IOM, 2005, p. 12. The numbers were 1329 in 2003 and 1227 in 2004.

70. www.catwinternational.org.

71. Janice Raymond, "Ten Reasons for Not Legalizing Prostitution," *Journal of Trauma Practice* 2 (2003): 317.

72. Linda Smith, Testimony before Committee on International Relations, House of Representatives, Hearing on the State Department's 2002 *Trafficking in Persons Report*, June 19, 2002, p. 66.

73. www.cwfa.org.

74. U.S. Department of State, *Trafficking in Persons Report, 2005*, Washington, DC: Department of State, 2005.

75. Transcrime, *Study on National Legislation on Prostitution and the Trafficking in Women and Children*, Report to the European Parliament, 2005, p. 121. There has also been an overall decrease in prostitution establishments (brothels, window units) since legalization in 2000, arguably because of stricter regulation.

76. Kamala Kempadoo, "Introduction: Globalizing Sex Workers' Rights," in Kemala Kempadoo and Jo Doezema, eds., *Global Sex Workers: Rights, Resistance, and Redefinition*, New York: Routledge, 1998, p. 17.

77. Alison Murray, "Debt Bondage and Trafficking," in K. Kempadoo and J. Doezema, eds., *Global Sex Workers: Rights, Resistance, and Redefinition*, New York: Routledge, 1998, p. 60.

78. Barbara Brents and Kathryn Hausbeck, "Violence and Legalized Brothel Prostitution in Nevada," *Journal of Interpersonal Violence* 20 (2005): 270–295; A.L. Dalder, *Lifting the Ban on Brothels*, The Hague,

Netherlands: Ministry of Justice, 2004; Crime and Misconduct Commission, *Regulating Prostitution: An Evaluation of the Prostitution Act 1999, Queensland*, Brisbane, Australia: CMC, 2004; Prostitution Law Review Committee, *Report of the Prostitution Law Review Committee on the Operation of the Prostitution Reform Act 2003*, Wellington, New Zealand: Ministry of Justice, 2008.

79. Vanwesenbeeck, "Another Decade"; Weitzer, "Flawed Theory"; Weitzer, "New Directions."

80. The TVPA created a new federal crime of "severe trafficking" in persons, which could result in a prison term of 20 years.

81. Dorothy Stetson, "The Invisible Issue: Prostitution and Trafficking of Women and Girls in the United States," in Joyce Outshoorn, ed., *The Politics of Prostitution*, New York: Cambridge University Press, 2004.

82. John Miller, "A Modern Slave Trade," *New York Post*, May 22, 2005.

83. Miller, quoted in Bumiller, "Evangelicals Sway White House."

84. Ditmore, "Trafficking in Lives"; Shapiro, "New Abolitionists"; Penelope Saunders, "Traffic Violations," *Journal of Interpersonal Violence* 20 (2005): 343–360.

85. The following are some of the formal "coalition members" in the Rescue and Restore Coalition: CATW, Protection Project, Evangelicals for Social Action, Family Research Council, SAGE, Sex Industry Survivors, Break the Chain Campaign, Religious Freedom Coalition, Focus on the Family, American Conservative Union, Culture of Life Foundation, Christian Medical Association, Concerned Women for America, Restoration Ministries International, and many other Christian organizations. See Attorney General, *Report to Congress on U.S. Government Efforts to Combat Trafficking in Persons in Fiscal Year 2004*, Washington, DC: Department of Justice, 2005, Appendix 2.

86. Shapiro, "New Abolitionists."

87. Thomas Edsall, "Grants Flow to Bush Allies on Social Issues," *Washington Post*, March 22, 2006; Esther Kaplan, *With God on Their Side: George W. Bush and the Christian Right*, New York: New Press, 2005, pp. 214–218.

88. To cite just a few examples, in FY 2003 and FY 2004, CATW received $482,000, SAGE $200,000, the Protection Project $492,000, Donna Hughes $158,000, the Catholic Bishops Conference $600,000, Shared Hope International $500,000, World Vision $500,000, and the International Rescue Committee $2,666,000. See Attorney General, *Report to Congress on U.S. Government Efforts to Combat Trafficking in Persons*

in Fiscal Year 2003, Washington, DC: Department of Justice, 2004; Attorney General, *Report, 2004*.

89. Raymond and Hughes, *Sex Trafficking*; Coalition Against Trafficking in Women, *Coalition Report*, Amherst: CATW, 2001, p. 7.

90. GAO, *Human Trafficking*, 25.

91. Wagner, quoted in Markon, "Human Trafficking," p. A8.

92. Richard Land, quoted in Bumiller, "Evangelicals Sway White House."

93. Stolz, "Educating Policymakers"; Testimony at Congressional Hearing on Trafficking in Women and Children in East Asia and Beyond, Subcommittee on East Asian and Pacific Affairs, Committee on Foreign Relations, U.S. Senate, April 9, 2003.

94. National Institute of Justice, *Solicitation: Trafficking in Human Beings Research and Comprehensive Literature Review*, Washington, DC: Department of Justice, 2007, p. 4.

95. Hughes, "Wolves in Sheep's Clothing," p. 2.

96. TVPA 2000, §103[3]; TVPRA 2005, §207[3].

97. Women's Commission for Refugee Women and Children, *The U.S. Response to Human Trafficking*, p. 14.

98. Farrell, et al., *Understanding and Improving*, pp. 90–91.

99. William Wilberforce Trafficking Victims Protection Reauthorization Act of 2008.

100. Doezema, "Loose Women or Lost Women."

101. Doezema, "Loose Women or Lost Women," p. 24.

102. Janet Crouse, quoted in "Human Trafficking Now Tied for World's #2 Crime," Concerned Women for America website, December 6, 2005.

103. Barbara Sullivan, "Trafficking in Women: Feminism and New International Law," *International Feminist Journal of Politics* 5 (2003): 67–91.

104. See Chapters 8 and 9 in this volume.

CONTRIBUTORS

Sharon A. Abbott received her Ph.D. in Sociology from Indiana University in Bloomington, and now works for the Population Council.

Jill A. Bakehorn is a Ph.D. candidate in Sociology at the University of California, Davis. Her chapter in this volume draws on her dissertation research exploring women-made pornography. Research interests include the social construction of gender and sexuality and their representations in popular culture.

David S. Bimbi is Assistant Professor of Health Sciences at LaGuardia Community College, City University of New York, and a Faculty Affiliate at the Center for HIV/AIDS Educational Studies and Training in New York City. He is a social psychologist specializing in behavioral health. David has published numerous articles with his co-authors on male sex workers. He recently began working on developing evidence-based programs for trans-gender women and hopes to begin research on sex work with this population.

Louis Bonilla received his M.P.A. degree from Princeton University. He is the Executive Director of the Gay and Lesbian Latino AIDS Education Initiative (www.galaei.org), a nonprofit organization that focuses on issues affecting Philadelphia's Latino and lesbian, gay, bisexual, and transgender communities.

Denise Brennan is Associate Professor of Anthropology at Georgetown University in Washington, DC. She is the author of *What's Love Got to Do with It? Transnational Desires and Sex Tourism in Sosúa, the Dominican Republic* (2004). Currently, she is writing a book on the resettlement of formerly trafficked persons in the United States, *Life after Trafficking: Resettlement after Forced Labor in the United States*.

Barbara G. Brents is an Associate Professor of Sociology and affiliate of the Women's Studies department at the University of Nevada, Las Vegas. With

Kathryn Hausbeck she has been conducting research on the Nevada brothel industry and sexual commerce in and around Las Vegas for the last 15 years, and they have a forthcoming book on the topic, *The State of Sex.*

Michelle Carnes is a Ph.D. candidate in Anthropology at American University in Washington, DC. Her publications include a chapter on women's sex videos as liberatory teaching tools in the anthology *Pornification* (2007), and a chapter in the anthology *Shifting Positionalities* (2009) about heterosexist media coverage of black same-sex desiring women's parties in New York City. Her dissertation, entitled *Do it for Your Sistas*, is a 3-year ethnography of black same-sex desiring women involved in erotic performance events.

Lynn Comella is Assistant Professor of Women's Studies at the University of Nevada, Las Vegas. Her research and teaching interests include media and popular culture, gender, sexuality, and ethnographic research. She is the author of several articles and is completing a book on the history of feminist sex toy stores and the growth of the women's sex toy market in the United States.

Melissa Ditmore, Ph.D., is currently on the board of the Global Network of Sex Work Projects, and has been an author on all the reports released by the Sex Workers Project in New York City. She is editor of the *Encyclopedia of Prostitution and Sex Work* (2006), and edits the annual journal *Research for Sex Work*. Melissa has written extensively about sex work, migration, and trafficking.

Deanne Dolnick received her M.A. degree from California State University in Northridge. She has worked for the Rand Corporation, and was an interviewer and researcher on the Los Angeles Women's Health Risk Study on Prostitution.

Katherine Frank is a cultural anthropologist and a faculty associate at the College of the Atlantic in Maine. She is also a fiction writer and former exotic dancer. Her writings include *G-Strings and Sympathy: Strip Club Regulars and Male Desire* (2002) and the co-edited *Flesh for Fantasy: Producing and Consuming Exotic Dance* (2006). Katherine has also written on pornography, feminism, monogamy, swinging, and reality television.

Kathleen Guidroz is Assistant Professor of Sociology at Mount St. Mary's University in Maryland. Her research interests include gender, labor, and sexuality. In addition to her work on commercial telephone sex, she has written on escort work and sadomasochism. She is currently researching U.S. organizations that provide services to sex workers, and is coediting a book on race–class–gender intersections.

Kathryn Hausbeck is Associate Professor of Sociology at University of Nevada, Las Vegas, and Senior Associate Dean of the Graduate College. She studies commercial sexuality, late capitalist culture, and urban issues. Kathryn has a forthcoming book co-authored with Barbara Brents on Nevada's legal brothels, *The State of Sex*.

Juline Koken, Ph.D., is a social psychologist and Project Director at the Center for HIV/AIDS Educational Studies and Training in New York. She is also a postdoctoral fellow in Behavioral Science Training at the National Development and Research Institute. Her research interests center around the ways in which emotion management and stigma coping strategies shape the experiences and well-being of sex workers of all genders. Forthcoming work includes an article on feminist theory and prostitution. For a future project, Juline plans to research the clients of sex workers.

Janet Lever is Professor of Sociology at California State University in Los Angeles, has spent over 35 years examining sexuality as part of her broader interests in gender studies. Current research interests include office romance as well as predictors of sex satisfaction and infidelity. From 1991 through 1998, she coauthored the "Sex and Health" column for *Glamour* magazine. In addition to numerous articles in professional journals, Janet has also written dozens of popular articles for magazines like *Playboy, Ms., New Woman*, and *Sexual Health*. Since 2002, she has conducted annual online sex surveys sponsored by *Elle* magazine and posted on msnbc.com.

Martin A. Monto is a Professor of Sociology at the University of Portland in Portland, OR. His research explores the intersections between gender, deviance, and social psychology. Specific interests include customers of prostitutes, homophobia, sexual assault, and equality of opportunity. He has published numerous articles on the customers of prostitutes.

Jeffrey T. Parsons is Professor and Chair of the Psychology Department at Hunter College, City University of New York, and also on the doctoral faculties for Social-Personality Psychology and Public Health at the Graduate Center of the City University of New York. His research focuses on the intersections of sexuality, sexual risk behaviors, substance use, and identity. He is the Co-Director of the Center for HIV Educational Studies and Training, and has published extensively on the sexual practices of male sex workers.

Judith Porter is Professor Emerita of Sociology at Bryn Mawr College. Her major research interest is AIDS and injection drug use. She has studied crack addiction and HIV transmission, barriers to drug user treatment among Puerto Rican heroin users, and factors related to lack of drug user treatment among drug injectors, as well as needle exchange programs as a bridge to services, funded by a National Institute for Drug Abuse grant. She assists Congreso de Latinos Unidos as an AIDS educator and is the Vice-Chairperson of the Mayors Executive Commission on Drugs and Alcohol in Philadelphia.

Grant J. Rich is Assistant Professor of Psychology at the University of Alaska in Juneau. He received his Ph.D. from the University of Chicago. Current research includes positive psychology, cultural psychology, health psychology, and workplace ethnography. He has written for such publications as *American Anthropologist*, *Ethos*, *Family Relations*, *Massage Magazine*, *Massage Therapy Journal*, *Journal of Sex Research*, *Journal of Youth and Adolescence*, and *Psychology Today*, and is editor of the book *Massage Therapy: The Evidence for Practice*. A licensed social worker, he has served on the boards of several social service agencies.

Joe A. Thomas is Professor of Art History and Chair of the Department of Visual Arts at Kennesaw State University, GA. His focus is sexuality and representation, particularly in modern and contemporary art and in Renaissance Europe. He has written entries on gay pornography for glbtq.com and contributed essays to *1000 Erotic Works of Genius* (2008). He is currently working on an essay about the cultural meanings of gay porn produced outside the U.S., as well as curatorial projects.

Ronald Weitzer is Professor of Sociology at George Washington University in Washington, DC. He has written extensively on the sex industry in the United States and abroad, and is currently writing a book on political conflicts over prostitution policies in selected nations. He is frequently contacted by the media for information and comment on issues regarding the sex industry. A second major area of expertise centers on police relations with racial and ethnic minorities, and he has two books on this topic.

INDEX